THE POLITICS OF MIRTH

THE POLITICS OF

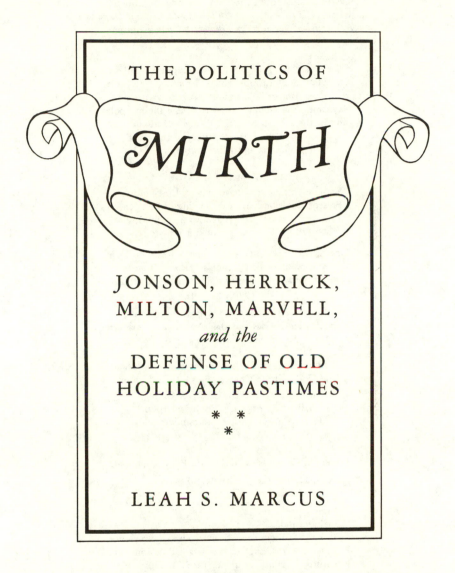

MIRTH

JONSON, HERRICK,
MILTON, MARVELL,
and the
DEFENSE OF OLD
HOLIDAY PASTIMES

* *
*

LEAH S. MARCUS

THE UNIVERSITY OF CHICAGO PRESS
Chicago and London

LEAH S. MARCUS, professor of English at the University of Wisconsin, Madison, has written numerous articles and is the author of *Childhood and Cultural Despair: A Theme and Variations in Seventeenth-Century Literature.*

FRONTISPIECE: Tollet's window, designed for Betley Old Hall, Staffordshire, 1621, depicting a maypole, morris dancers, and figures associated with the Maygames: the Hobbyhorse (just below the maypole), and in the bottom row, the Fool, the Lady of May, and the Friar. Courtesy of the Victoria and Albert Museum.

Sections of chapter 3 have appeared previously in " 'Present Occasions' and the Shaping of Ben Jonson's Masques," *English Literary History* 45 (1978), 201–25. © 1978 by The Johns Hopkins University Press.

One section of chapter 4 has appeared previously in "The Occasion of Ben Jonson's *Pleasure Reconciled to Virtue,*" *Studies in English Literature, 1500–1900* 19 (1979), 271–93.

Brief segments of chapter 5 appeared previously in "Herrick's Hesperides and the 'Proclamation made for May,'" *Studies in Philology* 76 (1979), 49–74.

The University of Chicago Press, Chicago 60637
The University of Chicago Press, Ltd., London
© 1986 by The University of Chicago
All rights reserved. Published 1986
Printed in the United States of America
95 94 93 92 91 90 89 88 87 86   5 4 3 2 1

Library of Congress Cataloging-in-Publication Data

Marcus, Leah S. (Leah Sinanoglou)
  The politics of mirth.

  Bibliography: p.
  Includes index.
    1. English literature—Early modern, 1500–1700—History and criticism. 2. Manners and customs in literature. 3. Holidays in literature. 4. Literature and society—England—History—17th century.
5. Festivals—England. 6. England—Social life and customs—17th century. 7. Great Britain—Politics and government—1603–1649. I. Title.
PR429.M36M37   1986   820'.9'355   86–7133
ISBN 0-266-50451-4

For Emily

Contents

Acknowledgments

The interactions among literature, political ideology, and social and economic change are often far less straightforward, less unidirectional, than we take them to be. If this book manages to demonstrate that, I will consider it a success. Much the same needs to be said for the writing of the book itself. It has been a vital process of give and take with friends, students, and colleagues. I owe particular thanks to Stephen Orgel, Annabel Patterson, and John M. Wallace for their encouragement during the early stages and to Patricia Fumerton, Stephen Greenblatt, Richard Strier, and Andrew D. Weiner for perceptive criticism of the manuscript as a whole. Mark Eccles's generous and timely reading has saved me from numerous errors. But perhaps my largest debt is to those who have followed the book's progress all along with patient advice and support: Judith Kegan Gardiner, Michael Lieb, Claude J. Summers, and above all, Leonard Tennenhouse. My many debts to friends who have shared their work in manuscript are recorded in the notes, but special thanks go to Peter Stallybrass, whose zest for our common enterprise is an inspiration to us all. Research support for the project was provided by the National Endowment for the Humanities, the Huntington Library, the Research Board of the University of Illinois, its Institute for the Humanities (ably directed by Robert V. Remini and Jonathan Arac), and the Graduate School of the University of Wisconsin. I owe warm thanks to all of these and to the staffs of the Newberry Library, the Huntington Library, the British Library, and the British Public Record Office. Kent Reames put several chapters on disk and Robert Grotjohn checked footnotes. My thanks to them, and to my husband David and daughter Emily, who reminded me time and again that there is more to life than *Mirth*.

Introduction:
The Politics of Mirth

John Selden, a shrewd observer of his times, claimed that "Ceremony keeps up all things; 'tis like a penny glass to a rich spirit, or some excellent water; without it the water will be spilt, the spirits lost."[1] "Like a penny glass": he found ceremony trifling in itself, yet essential to things of much greater value, "keeping" them "up" both in the sense that it preserved them and that it elevated and separated them from lesser things. Selden's remark captures a paradoxical truth about ceremony, whether in the form of Anglican ritual or the elaborate state ritual of the Stuart court as it was perceived by its seventeenth-century advocates. It was simultaneously disparaged and found necessary—inconsequential, a "thing indifferent," yet vital for the continuing well-being of the institutions it "kept up."

The present study will focus on a marginal group of ceremonies related to the rites of church and state but practiced only sporadically in the seventeenth century—the traditional popular pastimes associated with seasonal holidays like Christmas, May Day, Whitsuntide, St. Bartholomew's Day and Michaelmas. Each holiday had its own customs: dancing about maypoles, mumming, feasts of misrule or periods of sanctioned lawlessness; each was likely to include some overturning of the normal order of things, a festival inversion of the social and ecclesiastical hierarchy. By comparison with courtly and ecclesiastical ceremonial, the old calendar customs were highly volatile. Before the seventeenth century, they had sometimes been countenanced or even promoted by the official hierarchy; but just as often, they had been suppressed as an immoral threat to the social order. Their equivocal status has survived into the present. We might consider, for example, the contradictions that surrounded May Day and still surround the holiday's twentieth-century vestiges. Traditionally, May Day had been an official feast day of the Catholic and Anglican churches. It carried associations of fertility, renewal, frolicks in the greenwood, and restored community. But it was also a favorite occasion for riots by apprentices and other youths. On "Evil May Day" in 1517 there were large and bloody battles between London apprentices and aliens. Even in Stuart England, the holiday frequently erupted into anarchy. Today, in socialist and communist countries, May Day is a workers' holiday, a festival of class solidarity. On the other hand, in areas which are strongly influenced by Catholicism or conservative Anglicanism, many of its old religious associations are preserved in dilute form and it is celebrated by activities like the making of maybaskets or the weaving of daisy chains for the Virgin. A former graduate student has kindly supplied me with an account of a minor skirmish she witnessed between conflicting ideologies of May Day:

> In May 1978 when I was at Sussex University, a group of British women held an anti-morris dance on one of the lawns between classroom buildings. Instead of clacking wooden poles together, the women wielded long, half-cooked spears of rhubarb. Pieces of the limp stuff kept flying off, and each time that happened, the dancers shouted with dignity, "Rhubarb! Rhubarb!" A crowd of onlookers gathered, and I overheard an elderly gentleman murmur to his friend, in a genuinely offended tone, that this travesty of a time-honored custom was an affront to British decorum. I refrained from asking him whether he thought that the seventeenth-century morris dancers had been bastions of the social order.[2]

According to my informant, the anti-morris dance of the women was a political protest directed against male domination of the morris dance (from which women are traditionally excluded) and by implication against more significant forms of antifeminism. It was a travesty of old custom designed to recapture some of the radical energy that had surrounded the original. But for the elderly gentleman who watched in horror, the ancient ceremony of the morris was associated with a conservative vision of national order; he read the protest correctly as a challenge to that vision. Even today, in Britain at least, the old customs remain a touchstone for wider ideological conflict, and their political implications alter along with the social context.

Had seventeenth-century morris dancers been bastions of the social order? Not necessarily, but the elderly gentleman's veneration of the old customs is an attitude that can be traced to seventeenth-century policy. The Stuart kings undertook an interesting experiment: they actively promoted the old holiday pastimes as essential "penny glasses" for the preservation of their authority and that of the Anglican Church they headed, the welfare of which they considered intimately bound to their own. By placing their official stamp of approval on the old pastimes, James and Charles I attempted to extend royal power into an area of ambivalence and instability, to channel the equivocal status of popular festival into what we can perhaps call an official "paradox of state"—a condition of happy ambiguity in which the license and lawlessness associated with the customs could be interpreted as submission to authority. In his *Basilikon Doron*, even before he was anointed King of England, James had published his views as to the utility of the traditional customs in governing the lower orders. Commoners were prone to "iudge and speake rashly of their Prince"; the best remedy against this fractiousness was good rule, which meant severity tempered with mildness. One aspect of "courteous" mildness, James advised his son and heir apparent Prince Henry, was the support of old pastimes:

> In respect whereof, and therewith also the more to allure them to a common amitie among themselues, certaine dayes in the yeere would be appointed, for delighting the people with publicke spectacles of all honest games, and exercise of armes: as also for conueening of neighbours, for entertaining friendship and heartlinesse, by honest feasting and merrinesse: For I cannot see what greater superstition can be in making playes and lawfull games in Maie, and good cheere at Christmas, then in eating fish in Lent, and vpon Fridayes, . . . so that alwayes the Sabboths be kept holy, and no vnlawfull pastime be vsed: And as this forme of contenting the peoples mindes, hath beene vsed in all well gouerned Republicks: so will it make you to performe in your gouernment that olde good sentence,
>
> *Omne tulit punctum, qui miscuit vtile dulci.*
>
> (*James*, 27)[3]

James saw to it that his views on the encouragement of old pastimes were well known in England. *Basilikon Doron* was reprinted in 1603 and 1616; in 1618 he amplified and clarified his policy in a famous and controversial declaration that became known as the *Book of Sports*. That document did not *require* the practice of Sunday and holiday pastimes, but it did require, in the face of virulent Puritan opposition, that such pastimes be allowed: "And as for Our good peoples lawfull Recreation, Our pleasure likewise is, That after the end of Diuine Seruice, Our good people be not disturbed, letted, or discouraged from any lawfull Recreation; Such as dauncing, either men or women, Archery for men, leaping, vaulting, or any other such harmelesse Recreation, nor from hauing of May-Games, Whitson Ales, and Morrisdances, and the setting vp of Maypoles and other sports therewith vsed, so as the same be

3

had in due and conuenient time, without impediment or neglect of diuine Seruice."[4]

Some of James's politic zeal for the encouragement of old customs had, of course, been anticipated by his predecessor on the throne. Queen Elizabeth I had reportedly liked to see her people "merry" and had been keenly aware of the potential link between public ceremony and the maintenance of order. She had even created her own annual holiday, her Accession Day, as the occasion of elaborate state tilts and other sports and rituals but also for divine worship, the ringing of parish church bells, and the reading of a special festival liturgy written by the queen herself which reminded her subjects, according to Romans 13, "Let every soul be subject unto the higher powers: for there is no power but of God; and the powers that be, are ordained by God." Despite the directness of such appeals for public order, when it came to the promotion and regulation of traditional pastimes, Queen Elizabeth allowed her policy to remain ambiguous and kept her personal taste in the background. The adamant Sabbatarians who unleashed the Marprelate pamphlets against plays, old pastimes, and the ecclesiastical hierarchy were able to convince themselves that the queen was on their side. Such measures as Queen Elizabeth did take for the regulation of pastimes were issued much less publicly than James I's declaration.[5]

Under James and Charles I, however, the Elizabethan ambiguity was dispelled. James I in particular tended to regard traditional English customs as an integral branch of his power. He viewed any attempt to suppress them as an affront to his prerogative. James's sensitivity on the subject long predated his coronation as King of England in 1603. Indeed, his early experiences in Scotland had predisposed him to associate his personal and royal autonomy with the maintenance of festival. Even after the Reformation and despite the opposition of the Kirk, the Scottish court had kept up a tradition of holiday mirth which intermingled the sacred and the secular. There was a flourishing of "Godlie" reformation ballads and carols that parodied secular dance tunes very much in the manner of medieval sacred parody. Even at a very young age, as long as he was at liberty to do so, James consciously cultivated the arts and traditional pastimes, surrounding himself with poetry and state rituals to enhance the prestige of his court. When he was "kidnapped" by the Kirk faction, his "Castalian band" of poets was dispersed and his court pastimes abolished.[6] He was forced to endure several years of factional tug-of-war and a corresponding waning and waxing in his valued "public mirth."

Given his early education in the interpenetration of the ceremonial and the political, it is not surprising that James was prone to identify the exercise of his royal autonomy with the promotion of traditional pastimes. His attitudes did not change markedly after he left Scotland for England. For King James, the traditional sports, although "indifferent" in themselves, were essential insofar as they "kept up" his sacred authority and served as a visible link between himself and his people, an affirmation of power and community. The king himself stood behind efforts for the promotion of public festivals like Robert Dover's famous annual Cotswold Games, inaugurated in 1612. Dover's spring games revived and expanded an old holiday tradition—games and contests at Whitsuntide. They were intended to encourage interest in public pastimes among the local gentry and the many visitors who flocked to see them. Dover presided over the games himself, resplendent in a "Hat and Feather and Ruff" that had belonged to King James. The royal clothing was, according to contemporaries, given to Dover "purposely to grace him and consequently the Solemnity."[7] So the king was symbolically present in the jovial person of Robert Dover, who was clad in his garments and encouraging "public mirth" in the Cotswolds. Not all contemporary interest in such revivals can be attributed to the intervention of James. He was able to tap a vein of sentiment that predated his accession in England, but his zealous patronage altered the terms in which holiday customs could be perceived. Increasingly with the passing of the years, they became part of the symbolic language of Stuart power.

By reissuing the *Book of Sports* in 1633, Charles I made it clear that he intended to continue his father's policies. Although he took considerably less personal interest in the old customs than James had, Charles was much more rigorous about enforcing the *Book of Sports*. Under Charles and Archbishop Laud, the old pastimes were distanced from the court but at the same time sacramentalized. The fostering of old festival practices became very closely tied to the vexed matter of enforcing religious conformity, and the pastimes were increasingly perceived as extensions of liturgical worship. The English Church, as Laud and King Charles envisioned it, was a sacred space apart, a ceremonial enclosure walling off the world outside. The old pastimes were a way of taking the Church out into the world and molding the countryside into an image of ecclesiastical order; they become an extension of sacred space. The advocacy of traditional pastimes allowed King Charles to maintain a sense of connectedness with the lower orders while simultaneously setting himself apart. Neither James nor Charles I countenanced the riotous side of festival, at least not in principle. They insisted that pastimes had to be contained, practiced freely only within lawful limits. But their consistent position was that the customs, well managed, would serve to buttress authority by dissolving seditious impulses that might otherwise threaten church and state. They anticipated the "escape valve" theory of festival still current among one school of modern anthropologists—the view that holiday inversions of hierarchy are essentially normative and help to perpetuate a preexisting system by easing, at regular, predictable intervals, tensions that might otherwise build to a full-scale challenge of the system.[8]

The Stuart program for encouraging old calendar customs met with strong opposition. Indeed, the *Book of Sports* assumed an importance out of all proportion to the humble pursuits it sanctioned. It quickly became a focal point for political and religious controversy, polarizing public opinion, intensifying or even helping to create disaffection with the court and the established church. There is considerable evidence that the *Book of Sports* exacerbated contemporary opposition to the central government rather than defusing it as the Stuart kings had hoped. And yet, the opponents of the *Book of Sports* tended to agree with the Stuarts about the normative functioning of the pastimes. The capacity of old customs to "keep up" a corrupt system was a major reason why they had to be suppressed. In her well-known critique of the Stuarts, Lucy Hutchinson noted that under their rule, "state interest" had been "mixing and working itselfe into the interest of religion." The court itself under James she termed a "nursery of lust and intemperance" which insinuated its own nature into the countryside through James's sponsorship of public games: "To keepe the people in their deplorable security till vengeance overtooke them, they were entertain'd with masks, stage playes, and sorts of ruder sports. Then began Murther, incest, Adultery, drunkennesse, swearing, fornication and all sort of ribaldry to be no conceal'd but countenanced vices, favour'd wherever they were privately practis'd because they held such conformity with the Court example." Mrs. Hutchinson recognized the "King-craft" underlying royal support for old pastimes and seems to have agreed with James I that the sports "contented the peoples mindes," or at least the minds of the ignorant and easily influenced. But for her and for many others who shared her views, the "King-craft" behind the *Book of Sports* clouded and enervated the nation, eroding its highest goals and stifling the potential for reform.[9]

We have abundant evidence as to the opinions of articulate contemporaries on the value of Stuart "public mirth"—both from the policy's advocates and from its bitterest enemies. But we do not have a very clear sense of the actual impact of the pastimes on those groups of people, especially the semiliterate and illiterate peasantry, who continued to keep them up. One very useful term that will surface from time to time in our discussion is *survivalism*. It is used here to describe a type of agrarian consciousness that fuses cyclical, communal economic activities, like sowing and harvesting, with the maintenance of old collective customs and collective village order. Seventeenth-century commentators describe this pattern with enough frequency that we can assume something approximating it did exist among some rural people: contemporary controversialists on both sides discussed the mentality of survivalism as something that could still be encountered in the countryside.[10] But the relationship between survivalism and dominant social and political structures of the Stuart era is not always easy to determine. The fact that the old festival customs were regarded as normative by many literate contemporaries did not necessarily make them so.

Today there is strong divergence among anthropologists and social historians on the thorny question of how festival "liberty" functions. The dominant "escape-valve" theory has been challenged from a number of quarters. Following Marx, Mikhail Bakhtin has emphasized the subversiveness of popular festival, but where Marx argued that its radical critique of existing authority has served historically to precipitate class conflict, Bakhtin has taken the more problematic position that festival forms are completely separate from the official culture, "outside of and contrary to all existing forms of the coercive socioeconomic and political organization, which is suspended for the time of the festivity."[11] Although Bakhtin has been criticized for his inattention to the motives that might incline an official elite to countenance the suspension of its authority, he may be right about how holiday "liberty" is perceived by those in the midst of it. For its wholehearted participants, it may indeed be experienced as a joyous breaking free of all boundaries and limits, but that leaves open the question of its actual relationship with the hierarchy it seems to overthrow. Some of the most interesting recent theorists have argued for festival's inclusion of both normative and revisionary impulses. Its seemingly lawless topsy-turvydom can both undermine and reinforce—it can constitute a process of adjustment within a perpetuation of order; the precise balancing of the two functions depends on local and particular factors and creates different effects at different places and times.[12]

My own bias is toward this last and supplest model, but I cannot hope, and would not attempt, to determine the social functioning of the old calendar customs in Stuart England. Nor will I attempt to reach general conclusions about the politics of marginality, though my discussion of particular cases may prove useful to researchers who are undertaking such an inquiry. Instead, I will seek to establish connections between royal theory and specific literary practice. The Stuart kings were committed to the maintenance of a "paradox of state" by which festival freedom was seen as a sign of submission to royal power. They were interested in fostering a form of social control that erased its own actions and its links to a central authority, a form of control that looked and felt like liberty. Just as they "kept up" the old pastimes, James and Charles I made it their business to encourage poets and playwrights who were willing to write in defense of "public mirth." And yet, as in the practice of the pastimes, the literature defending them was often cast in a language of "liberty" that effaced the most obvious signs of the authority it was meant to support. More often than we have recognized, the appeal to "public mirth" in the Stuart period was an appeal to royal authority.

That does not mean that either the writers or the texts they produced were totally subservient to the court. Those who wrote in defense of Stuart policy had—or at least took—considerable liberty with it, adapting festival's traditional upheaval of hierarchy to their own artistic ends. Many seventeenth-century poets and virtually all seventeenth-century playwrights had at least a tangential interest in the Stuart policy toward traditional pastimes in that it impinged upon their own vocation. We have already noticed how the young King James attempted to make the Scottish court a haven for arts and pastimes. In England he had the wealth and resources to further his vision of royal magnificence on a much vaster scale. In addition to direct patronage, there was also a significant strategic alliance between the defenders of plays and poetry and the defenders of popular festival. Opponents of the old holiday customs often condemned poetry and drama as well, pointing out that they shared the same pagan or popish origins and branding them as more cultivated variants of the same essential corruption. By failing to differentiate among disparate cultural forms and condemning them all with the same vehemence, Puritan extremists helped to create a climate in which all were defended in the same essential terms. There was a coalescence of proartistic sentiment around the figure and policies of the king, but the obvious commonality of interest between artists and ruler did not guarantee the subjection of the artists. If anything, it seems to have made at least some of them more wary, more defensively protective of their own autonomy. Even as they wrote in praise of "public mirth," many of them developed strategies for preserving their own "liberty," for saving their art from engulfment in the ethos of the court. The festival art in defense of festival had its own potential for subversion.

For several of the poets we shall be discussing, if not for the Stuart monarchs as they expressed themselves publicly, festival "liberty" was revisionary as well as normative. Art at court was often profoundly conservative in that it tended to uphold the existing framework of church and state. It was also capable of subjecting that hierarchy to searching criticism of its easy assumptions—a criticism that might issue in a return to a revitalized order in proper "escape-valve" style or might instead generate new forms and syntheses that would validate change and make such a return inconceivable. It is difficult to accept the notion that Stuart kings might have tolerated overt criticism. They have generally been portrayed as cultural autocrats, interested only in an art that reflected their own grandiose notions of royal power and pre-rogative.[13] This study will question that model, suggesting a subtler and more dynamic set of interactions among the king, his public policy, and the art intended to praise it. In theory, the Stuarts were indeed inflexible as to the political functioning of art. In practice, I would suggest, they allowed considerably more latitude and not merely by default or out of some sleepy incapacity to perceive what their supposed panegyrists were up to. The Stuart kings accepted or at least tolerated, perhaps even on occasion encouraged, an art as much revisionary as normative—or at least they were willing to do so if the loyalty of the poet behind the stimulus for reform was unquestioned. As in the practice of the old pastimes themselves, so in the literature surrounding them, consider-able freedom was tolerated so long as it could be contained—or at least could *seem* to be contained—within a framework upholding authority.

These generalizations about the relative independence of seventeenth-century poets apply with particular force to Ben Jonson, the "Father" of the poetic tradition in defense of Stuart public mirth as of so many other important seventeenth-century forms. Rather than attempting some vast overview of his work from that perspective, however, we will look closely at only the works he produced during the early years of his close association with King James I, years during which both he and the king, each in his own sphere, were in the process of creating a set of paradigms for the proper management of festivity. Between 1611 and 1617, most of the poetic themes in defense of Stuart "public mirth," the themes that were to reverberate through the work of Jonson's sons and stepsons, were launched in Jonsonian productions at court. Our focal point for the discussion of Ben Jonson will be the masque, a festival form performed in connection with Christmas, Epiphany, or Shrovetide celebrations at court, which contains its own generic mechanisms for the airing and overthrow of holiday misrule.

The Jacobean masque can be regarded as a symbolic enactment of Stuart policy toward holiday topsy-turvydom. In the antimasque, all sorts of monstrous and subversive impulses are allowed their time of "liberty" to vent themselves and challenge the very government author-ities that sit observing the entertainment. Invariably, these potentially ruinous forces are quelled by the intervention of some reforming energy associated with the policy and person of the king. Royal power enters the world of the antimasque in the form of some symbolic personage who imposes order on the subversive energies of festival at court much as James I actually intervened to regulate pastimes in the country and place the stamp of his authority upon them. Very frequently, the king himself or at least his close associates at court are implicated in Jonson's antimasques: the "misrule" to which the antimasques grant temporary liberty is a subversion of order and virtue linked directly to the king and royal misrule.[14]

James I was a curious and contradictory figure, combining a theoretical devotion to Stoic balance and moderation, a "mean" in all things, with a seemingly ungovernable appetite for excess. Unlike most monarchs, he created a considerable body of writing about the principles of government—a windfall for budding authors who wished to write in his defense, since his treatises and proclamations gave them a set of texts to imitate in their own rhetoric of praise. But James's actual practice of the art of government—both in the nation at large and within himself— was often so massively at odds with his theory that simple panegyric became quite difficult for artists who wished to retain a sense of their own independence and probity. Specific instances of this radical disjunction are notoriously easy to come by. In *Basilikon Doron* James had praised moderation in diet, yet his court was marred by prodigious bouts of eating and drunkenness of the sort described by Sir John Harington in 1606, when a masque planned for the visiting King of Denmark was destroyed by the obvious inebriation of its masquers. The Queen of Sheba, missing the stairs, fell into the Danish monarch's lap; he himself, attempting to dance with her, collapsed and had to be carried off to bed. The entertainment went forward without him, but with a strange jarring between the intended elevation of its allegory and the infirmity of its execution:

> Most of the presenters went backward, or fell down; wine did so occupy their upper chambers. Now did appear, in rich dress, Hope, Faith, and Charity: Hope did assay to speak, but wine renderd her endeavours so feeble that she withdrew, and hope[d] the King would excuse her brevity: Faith was then all alone, for I am certain she was not joyned with good works, and left the court in a staggering condition: Charity came to the King's feet, and seemed to cover the multitude of sins her sisters had committed; in some sorte she made obeysance and brought giftes, but said she would return home again, as there was no gift which heaven had not already given his Majesty. She then returned to Hope and Faith, who were both sick and spewing in the lower hall.[15]

And so the royal entertainment staggered to its conclusion.

In other court pastimes, James I was equally associated with excess. He would hunt for days at a time, ignoring the pleas of his officials that essential business be attended to. He took a real delight in watching earthy sports and buffoonery, even as performed by his own courtiers. According to Sir Anthony Weldon's account, "after the King supped, he would come forth to see pastimes and fooleries; in which Sir Edward Zouch, Sir George Goring, and Sir John Finit, were the cheife and Master Fools, (and surely the fooling got them more than any other's wisdom) sometimes presenting David Droman and Archer Armstrong, the King's fools, on the back of other fools, to tilt one another, till they fell together by the ears: sometimes they performed antick-dances." One sure way of attracting James's attention was to call out the old May Day sports, as Francis Beaumont did in the second antimasque to his *Masque of the Inner Temple and Gray's Inn* (1612–13): the king was so pleased by its rude, sprightly "country jollity" that he called for it again at the end. The unruly antimasque got the last word.[16] Clearly for a monarch so embroiled in old pastimes himself, the matter of their regulation was no empty issue. In masques at court, which all too often had to hold their own against considerably less refined forms of entertainment, it is not only the nation but also the court that is symbolically reconstituted through the intervention of the royal will. Jonson's strategy in the masque and in plays closely linked to royal policy is often to pit King James against himself, to muster his laudable ideals in defeat of his less exalted practice—enacting the monarch's victory over his own misrule, a hard won triumph that demonstrates his capacity to work a similar transformation upon the nation.

During the years that we will study, the connections between Jacobean policy and Jonsonian political rhetoric are so many and complex that it is tempting to assume direct collaboration between the king and the poet. We know that James actually participated in the writing of court entertainments in Scotland, a matter which will be taken up in the next chapter; but we have no comparable information for England beyond the circumstantial evidence provided by Jonson's texts. It is likely that at least on some occasions, the king did play an active part in determining the subject and message of entertainments at court. Given the monarch's strong sense of the political functioning of art and his own literary pretensions, it is hard to imagine that he would have been able to resist the temptation to intervene. But such intervention as may have existed is not likely to have provided the poet with anything approximating a clear artistic mandate. The court artist possessed considerable freedom, but he was also sometimes an actor in an ongoing political drama for which he had not been provided all the cues. At times James may deliberately have withheld information or encouraged a rhetorical direction he intended to repudiate later, allowing Jonson a "license" which would mire the poet in difficulties from which the king could retire into serene aloofness, his political purpose gained and subsequently disavowed. The profession of court poet was a dangerous one: Jonson not infrequently risked imprisonment or at least royal disfavor as a result of the political message his art seemed to convey. Time and again, we find contemporaries reporting that his masques had failed to arouse the king's interest. Yet the very elements that made Jonson's profession dangerous also made it attractive for a man of strong mettle and combative instincts. And for Jonson at least, the rewards were usually greater than the risks. James I made his support for the poet quite clear: by continuing to engage Jonson to fashion court productions despite the poet's occasional transgression of acceptable artistic license, by granting him his pension, and by allowing him to assume the honorable style of Laureate. When Jonson devised Jacobean court entertainments he was almost certain to offend at least a part of his audience. But when he was absent he was missed.[17] Despite the obvious unbridgeable differences between the king and the poet, there appears, at least during the years that we will study closely, to have been a genuine and significant bond between them.

Jonson's own personality mirrored some of his royal master's most obvious strengths and foibles. He does not appear to have shared the king's delight in the carnival grotesquerie of traditional pastimes: when he wrote in defense of James's "public mirth," he tended to hedge his praise with ambivalence, searching for ways to elevate festival even as he depicted its earthy delights. And yet, like James, he was a man divided against himself, a proponent of classical restraint and moderation who was given to unusual excess in practice, a "tun of a man" whose monster belly and vinous habits coexisted uneasily with his artistic principles. Some of the power of Jonson's art derives from the dynamism of its containment of excess—a classicism compelling in part because it is so hard won. Jonson was also like the king in his view of his own authority. As James was jealous of his power and prerogative, so Jonson was touchy about challenges to his "rule" of the realm of English poetry. Both "absolutists" liked to model themselves upon dogmatic principle. Even Jonson's strong advocacy of the plain style may owe something to James's marked preference for plainness over aureate diction. At least in James the poet found a strong supporter for his own stylistic experimentation. Moreover, Jonson frequently modeled his own activities upon significant achievements of the king, publishing his *Works* in 1616 to coincide with the publication of the *Works* of James I, going himself to Scotland in 1618 in imitation of the royal progress of 1617.

Despite all the petty irritations and discord that must have marred the relationship, Jonson saw himself in James and found the king's favor profoundly gratifying. At least at times, he expressed an unfeigned desire to gratify the king in return. When William Drummond showed Jonson his utterly un-Jonsonian panegyric "Forth Feasting," composed to celebrate James's visit to Edinburgh in 1617, Jonson wished he had written it himself because it had pleased the king (*Jonson*, 1:135). Perceptive recent studies have noted Jonson's tendency to organize his personal allegiances as a system of fathers and sons like "father" William Camden and the "Sons of Ben": if so, James was obviously a father.[18] But it is in the nature of fathers to inspire rebellion along with love. Against Jonson's unquestionably genuine desire to please so supportive a monarch we must counterpoise the poet's equally strong need to feel autonomous. Jonson also told Drummond that he wished he had taken Holy Orders so that he could preach before the king, and "would not flatter though he saw Death" (*Jonson*, 1:141). The remark perhaps conveys an element of ruefulness over the ethical compromises he was forced to make in his profession of court poet. But it is aimed much more squarely against those who preached at court more openly than the poet was able to do, and who, despite their mantle of divinity, were generally less courageous than the poet in their castigation of royal "misrule." Jonson owed his success with James in part to his careful balancing of praise and blame, his knack, born perhaps of a genuine feeling of kinship, for creating an art that mirrored James's most treasured ideals without losing touch with that significant element of the royal being that was mired in earthy excess. In his masques at court and in at least a few of his plays, Jonson confronted the king with himself, but in a way that challenged the monarch to become his own best self.

There was no such kinship between Jonson and Charles I. Jonson's eclipse as court poet under Charles has been considered from a number of significant perspectives and I do not propose to cover the same ground. But it is perhaps worth noting that Charles's markedly different temperament and his utter repudiation of the grosser, more carnivalesque elements of his father's tastes and comportment made some of Jonson's most daring and interesting strategies for the containment of Jacobean misrule inappropriate under Charles. We might suppose that Jonson the moralizer would have welcomed the new monarch's greater civility, his mastery over the excess that had marred his father's rule. But the old bonding, the feeling of common enterprise between king and poet in the conquest of vast personal frailty, was gone. Charles had preempted one of the most interesting and challenging aspects of the poet's task in the defense and containment of festival. Even hostile witnesses acknowledged that King Charles was "temperate and chaste and serious."[19] He had banished misrule from his own comportment, even from the *mores* of the court, at least by Jacobean standards, and this deprived Jonson of one of his most telling artistic strategies—the creation of a dynamic interplay between personal and public levels of holiday disorder to generate moral renewal around the figure of the monarch. Moreover, the new king's distaste for vulgarity left Jonson without recourse to the comic realism that had supported his vision of public mirth in the works for James I.

Officially, of course, Charles countenanced public mirth. He republished the *Book of Sports* in 1633 after an imbroglio over Church Ales in Somerset convinced him and Archbishop Laud that it was time to reassert the Church's tolerance for such "harmelesse" customs. With the renewal of the *Book of Sports* there were court revivals of Elizabethan and Jacobean plays that portrayed the old sports sympathetically. The aging Jonson was even brought out of semiretirement to devise court entertainments in support of the renewed declaration as he had for its initial publication under James. I shall argue later that his quasi-Elizabethan *Tale of a Tub* dates from this period, its anachronism devised by the poet to contribute to the wave of antiquarian nostalgia for a vanishing "Merry England" that surrounded the republication of the *Book of Sports* in 1633–34. But these efforts did not restore Jonson to his earlier influence. Jonson's art of festival, with its grotesquerie, its strenuous mastery of the felt energies of carnival disorder, had gone out of style at court.

That is not to say that Caroline art at Whitehall had no potential for regenerative revision. Although Charles's advisors worried about his intolerance for criticism, the king was quite capable of criticizing himself. Kevin Sharpe has recently advanced the interesting suggestion that for Charles, the court masque was as much a confessional as an affirmation of power—a forum for acknowledging his "sins of state" along with proposed correctives.[20] Charles was not the figure of massive personal contradiction that his father had been, but his reign was marked by considerably more ambivalence about the management of festival license. Instead of embodying the turbulent energies of festival within his own person, he banished it to the margins, simultaneously asserting the privilege of holiday license and separating it from himself. He encouraged, or at least tolerated, a burgeoning literature in support of traditional pastimes but more at the fringes of court culture than at its center, while in masques at Whitehall, he "confessed" and repudiated the liberties that his own policy seemed to tolerate.

By the Caroline period, the advocacy of public mirth was clearly linked to the monarchy in most literate people's minds. Political offshoots of the *Book of Sports* controversy could be encountered almost anywhere: in small communities where there were sporadic conflicts between justices of the peace who tried to dampen the sports and holiday celebrants who claimed the "liberty" of pursuing them; in parish churches where ministers were ordered to read out the *Book of Sports* to their congregations (though some refused) and the legality of old pastimes was debated from the pulpit; even in Parliament where the matter surfaced during every session until the beginning of Charles's Personal Rule and where Thomas Shepherd, an advocate of old pastimes, had been expelled in 1621 for the "scorne and Malepeirt gesture" with which he derided opponents of the king's *Book of Sports*.[21] Because of this cultural saturation, there was no particular need to broadcast royal policy through the medium of the masque during the Caroline period, at least not until almost the outbreak of the Civil War. What we often find instead is the assertion of distance. In court entertainments, unworthy elements of Stuart policy are cast off as forms of misrule and the old customs themselves refined, abstracted, and assimilated into more elevated ritual structures associated with the liturgy of the Church.

Thomas Carew's *Coelum Britannicum*, performed during Shrovetide, 1634, offers perhaps the most clear-cut example of this official disavowal. The masque was danced less than a year after the republication of the *Book of Sports*. At least implicitly, Carew's work defends the traditional pastimes in that it incorporates Shrovetide customs into its own structure. Momus, its critic figure, talks about his appropriateness to the season and the masque enacts a Lenten ritual of humiliation and regeneration.[22] But while Carew's masque mirrors the holiday occasion through its adaptation of Shrovetide traditions, it casts a critical light on the management of public pastimes. Carew's antimasque of Plutus is clearly meant to recall Charles's promulgation of the *Book of Sports* less than a year before. Plutus, or Wealth, summons a group of country folk and bids them enjoy their pastimes as a manifestation of his own authority very much in the manner of the Stuart kings. However, the morality of his call for "public mirth" is compromised by his very nature: the "naked root" of his gold has inspired the "golden fruit" of country jollity. Plutus invites the rural rout, in a spirit of festive merriment,

> Cease from your labours when Wealth bids you play,
> Sing, dance, and keep a cheerful holiday.

Then *"they dance the fourth anti-masque consisting of country people, music and measures"*—precisely the picture of rural solidarity that the *Book of Sports* had encouraged, except that the wellspring of it all is gold, not benevolence (*Inigo*, 2:575). What the antimasque of Plutus actually demonstrates is how easily simple folk can be controlled by superior power: an "official" promotion of traditional customs is turned to base purposes that display the ease with which it can be corrupted. In that sense Carew's antimasque is a public "confession" of a weakness in royal policy. But there is also a corrective adjustment. Plutus and his country merrymakers are banished and he is admonished to seek better companions: the manipulation of public mirth for the uses of wealth and power is allowed no place in the reformed court of King Charles I. The antimasque of Plutus may have been aimed specifically against the *Realpolitik* of Charles's father, James I, who had advocated "playes and lawfull games" for frankly political reasons. The rejection of Plutus dissociates King Charles from such unabashed "King-craft," or at least announces his displeasure with contemporaries who were continuing to argue for the social utility of the old customs without considering the inherent worth of the authority they kept up. In *Coelum Britannicum* the defense of public mirth, along with nearly every other important Caroline policy, is refined and transformed by the "purer fire" of Religion, Truth, and Wisdom; the pastimes themselves are banished in favor of more elevated ritual. When the old calendar customs do appear in the art of the Caroline court, they are often either rarefied to the point that they lose their popular character and can be merged into larger quasi-liturgical structures like the penitential purgation of *Coelum Britannicum*, or they are miniaturized and distanced in the form of decorative emblems, attributes of the king but encapsulated and set carefully apart.[23]

Accordingly, it is not in the official art of the Caroline court that we can expect to find a wholehearted espousal of the old calendar customs. While royal policy was weighed and shriven at court, it was promoted from other quarters during the 1620s and 1630s, especially by a wing of the Anglican Church. A remarkable number of treatises and poems in defense of old holiday customs were composed by pro-Laudian churchmen. William Laud, like the king, took measures to distance himself from the *Book of Sports*. At the same time, he encouraged his subordinates to come to the aid of the embattled pastimes. The Laudian party disseminated an image of the Anglican priest as a wellspring of *jouissance*—a village master of ceremonies rather like Robert Dover who keeps up old parish customs and spreads good fellowship, renewing the ties between the official hierarchy and alienated elements of the local community through his irresistible merriment, his own comportment disarming any suspicion that the "liberty" of old pastimes was incompatible with innocence. At least some parish priests strove to match the paradigm. An account of the activities of Thomas Laurence, George Herbert's successor at Bemerton, shows how one proponent of the *Book of Sports* worked to promote the old customs. When Laurence was sequestered in 1646 as part of Parliament's eradication of Laudian elements in the church, it was alleged by local Puritans that he had "bin a great Inovator in his church at Bem[er]ton." He "caused A May Pole to bee sett upp at his dore and also in the same place a bowleinge Green: & kitleinge Alley. It beinge Adioyninge to the church yard, wherein euery Saboth day here was dauncinge bowlinge & kitleinge and himselfe to Countenance itt. Hee vsually gaue the fidlers six pence & his dynner, on y[e] Saboth date." There was also Sunday dancing "vsed in his own howse, wch hee Countenanced, w[it]h the presence of him selfe and famyly & maynteined it to bee very fitt for Recreation." And Laurence was not unusually zealous by Laudian standards: there are accounts of similar parish campaigns on the part of other priests, some of whom actually prefaced their invitation to public merriment with quotations from the *Book of Sports*.[24]

Such open social engineering on behalf of royal and ecclesiastical authority may appear to us to merit the reproof of Carew's antimasque of Plutus. But most of the Laudian proponents of the *Book of Sports* would not have seen themselves as operating on a purely political level. For the churchmen, as for King Charles I, James I's frankly political reasons for encouraging old pastimes had become an embarrassment. Increasingly as Laud's influence waxed within the Church, we find the traditional customs justified not on grounds of social utility, but as vehicles of divine grace. This sacramentalizing strain is discernible already in the festival art of Jonson—we shall find inklings of it in his *Bartholomew Fair*, though Father Ben was clearly wary of the trend even as he half espoused it. But in his followers, especially those associated with the church, it emerges with greater strength. Jonson's friend Bishop Richard Corbett projects the Laudian image of ecclesiastical geniality in his verses: when he penned his rolicking ballads in defense of fairies, maypoles, and other such symbols of vanishing country "Mirth" he certainly did not regard himself as stepping outside the bounds of his clerical vocation; rather, he was lamenting the passing of a time when divine beneficence had been communicated through the agency of popular customs. Nor did Jonson's "Son" Robert Herrick set aside his priestly function when he vowed in the "Argument" of *Hesperides* to "Sing" of *"May-poles, Hock-carts, Wassails, Wakes, / Of Bride-grooms, Brides,* and of their *Bridall-cakes."*[25] Composed by a man who was both a Cavalier poet and an Anglican priest, Herrick's *Hesperides* offers by far the most interesting and sustained defense of the Laudian "politics of mirth" by an actual churchman. As I shall contend when we discuss *Hesperides* later on, Herrick frequently enacts the Laudian role of jolly parson in his verses, stage-managing festival observances very much in the fashion of contemporary Laudians like Thomas Laurence in order to call down divine blessings upon the earth and restore village community.

For the Laudian party, the old pastimes were still theoretically "things indifferent" like many of the elements of church ritual promoted by Laudians, but they were elevated in importance along with ecclesiastical ritual itself. Conservative Anglicans envisioned the parish church and churchyard as a sacred enclosure set off by its ritual order from the everyday world outside. The wall that sometimes enclosed the parish church and its environs gave "due distinction, state, and reuerence to the Temple of Almighty God" and separated it from "profane wayes and base places." Against an "opinion in too many men" among Laud's contemporaries that "because Rome had thrust some unnecessary and many superstitious ceremonies upon the Church, therefore the Reformation must have none at all," Laud himself argued that "ceremonies are the hedge that fence the substance of religion from all the indignities which profaneness and sacrilege too commonly put upon it." Hence his revival of the ancient ritual for the consecration of churches and his zeal for the elevation and railing of the altar.[26] But Laud's privileging of ecclesiastical space was perceived by many of his contemporaries as setting the church at too great a distance from the village communities that were its sustaining lifeblood. One important reason why the old pastimes were promoted so strongly by Laudians, we can speculate, was that the customs appeared to offer a remedy for the social alienation created by the reverencing of things ecclesiastical. As the church, the altar, and Anglican ceremonial were elevated and set off from the people, pastimes were invoked as a bridge back to them, diminishing the distance imposed by the Laudian concept of the church as a sacred space apart. For traditionalists, holiday pastimes were extensions of sacramental worship with the mercurial capacity of enfolding disorder within their own sacred order. They could therefore serve as a trustworthy link with elements of the national life from which the king and the church had seemed to withdraw.

The growing separation between the top and bottom strata of the social hierarchy, made visible through the Laudian "enclosure" of the church, had its secular counterparts. As Mark Girouard and others have noted, the English upper classes took an increasing interest in privacy during the early Stuart period. Aristocrats were withdrawing from the rural communities that surrounded their estates and fashioning a more intimate life apart. According to the old semimythic pattern, the great hall of a country house served as a place of interaction for all of the rural community—the Lord and Lady would dine and keep holidays with their yeomen and other laborers. By the seventeenth century, that was quite rare, if indeed the practice had ever existed with anything approaching the universality lamented by nostalgic contemporaries.[27] A companion theme to the decline of traditional hospitality was the movement toward enclosure—not ecclesiastical enclosure, but the related phenomenon of hedging off common fields and forests for private use, excluding villagers who claimed customary rights to the land.

Official policy toward enclosure was ambivalent: on the one hand, the Stuart kings countenanced or at least tolerated the lawful enclosure of common land; on the other hand, they sought to erase the emerging commercialization of court and countryside by urging a return to older forms of aristocratic life. Both James and Charles I issued regular proclamations ordering the gentry and aristocracy who had collected about London and Whitehall to return to their country estates and maintain hospitality and holiday pastimes in the "good old fashion" of England. Again, as in ecclesiastical policy, Stuart "public mirth" was envisioned as a cure for social alienation. In official pronouncements, in court masques and poetry, the old calendar customs are invoked to erase the mark of otherness and bring the aristocrat and the villager into a healing festival interaction that would dissolve the animosities created by new social and economic modes. James I even wrote a Horatian elegy in order to further the program, a poem titled in one manuscript version "An Elegie written by the King concerning his counsell for Ladies & gentlemen to departe the City of London according to his Majesties Proclamation."[28] Paradoxically, in this policy area the court was against the court. By its wealth, its brilliance, its promise of immense financial gain for those who achieved high place, the court attracted provincial gentry and aristocrats to London; but at the same time, the Stuart kings sought to cancel out the court's cultural magnetism by ordering the upper classes to "Get thee to the country."

As a literary mode pastoral is always associated with urbanity and sophistication. Also, seventeenth-century writers had numerous classical and Renaissance precedents for their own ventures into the form. But as with King James in the composition of his "Elegy," the particular timing of their work, the classical model they chose, and the specific shaping they gave it, were often dialectically engaged with the royal project to repastoralize England. To recognize the insistence with which the early Stuarts promoted what they liked to call "Affection for the Country" is to look on seventeenth-century pastoralism from a completely altered perspective. What the Stuart kings were advocating, however implausible the project may appear to us in hindsight, was a reification of pastoral vision—the export of a courtly mode to the countryside in a way that imprinted royal power on the rural landscape.

In the masques, poems, and plays of Ben Jonson, in the poetry of Herrick and other sons of Ben, we frequently find strong "anticourt" sentiment combined with a movement back toward the simple patterns and pastimes of English rural life. That literary current is uneasily bound up with the policy of James and Charles I.

That is not to say that every seventeenth-century masque or poem expressing anticourt sentiment was actually *of* the court—only that we need to pay particularly close attention to a given work's immediate cultural context and handling of pastoral and festival devices in order to gauge its meaning and intended impact. Particularly during the Caroline period, the royal preempting of so many motifs of country life made the question of artistic autonomy interesting and problematic. As a counter example to Herrick's *Hesperides* we shall consider Milton's *Comus*, a masque written and performed only a year after King Charles's republication of the *Book of Sports* in 1633. *Comus* is as thoroughly immersed as any Whitehall entertainment in the festival traditions for its own occasion of Michaelmas, but designed, as I shall argue in detail, to win arts and pastimes back from the domination of the court and the Laudian wing of the church. The Earl of Bridgewater, for whom the masque was written, was a trusted ally and servant of King Charles I. Yet he had a sympathy for Puritan causes which his royal master did not share; he tried to function as autonomously in office as conditions would allow. Milton's masque celebrates the Earl of Bridgewater and his administrative seat at Ludlow Castle as an independent locus for political and religious reform, echoing festival motifs made commonplace by court and conservative Anglican practice, but turning the "official" forms against their very source to expose contradictions in the Stuart politics of mirth. Milton was of course no son of Ben; it might be more accurate to call him a stepson. Milton's Ludlow masque replicates the stringent Jonsonian tactic of offering trenchant criticism under the protective veil of holiday "license." But the young Milton's art of festival pushes toward a much more radical social and political transformation.

In 1634 when *Comus* was performed, Milton had still not broken with Anglicanism; Laud had only recently been named Archbishop and the policy of "Thorough" had not yet permeated the church. Opposition to the *Book of Sports* was stronger and shriller than ever, but many moderates hoped for a reformation of Stuart policy from within existing governmental and ecclesiastical structures. By the end of the same decade, with the outbreak of civil war, that optimism, or what was left of it, was shattered. The fact that Maying, morris dancing, and other kindred idolatries had been so closely associated with royal power in most people's minds made the old customs as vulnerable as the royalist cause.

Maypoles, church festivals, and all forms of Anglican "public mirth" were abolished through a series of Parliamentary ordinances, and the Laudian priests who had promoted them were systematically replaced. But that does not mean that the old customs vanished altogether. They simply went underground. The third and final phase of our investigation will consider how the Stuart politics of mirth was transmuted when there were no longer Stuarts at Whitehall to sustain it. During and after the Civil War, royalists hermeticized the interdicted pastimes, gave them cryptic forms and sank them into the rural landscape where they could be read as vestiges of the vanished culture, a language of covert opposition. We shall examine this interesting development by looking at a pair of contrasting poets who offered radically different readings of the sub-merged politics of mirth: Richard Lovelace, Cavalier poet *par excellence,* whose verses construct a paradigm for the Interregnum transformation of holiday motifs; and Andrew Marvell, who read Lovelace's poems, admired him, imitated him, but also wrote himself out of the Caroline ethos and created a new point of literary departure for the regenerative energies of festival.

During and after the English Civil War, there was a resurgence of the threatening side of May Day and its age-old association with the "mis-rule" of public mayhem. Among some radical groups, holiday mirth shook loose from the Stuart mechanisms that had contained it and reasserted itself as class violence. Indeed, the Civil War itself was commonly depicted as a "world upside down"—a series of carnival inversions which were stampeding out of control. Marvell's poetry wittily portrays the unleashing of festival disorder and tries out some of the traditional Stuart devices for keeping it within bounds, then moves beyond them and creates new ways of turning the liberating energy of festival to national moral renewal. Our study could easily continue beyond Marvell: as the introductory anecdote from the University of Sussex suggests, some of the antinomies surrounding the *Book of Sports* controversy in the seventeenth century are still alive today. We could easily consider eighteenth-century writers like Oliver Goldsmith, the literature associated with Chartism, then Wordsworth and the later nineteenth century—in which motifs derived from the Stuart politics of mirth became particularly pervasive—then perhaps Thomas Hardy, whose *Tess of the d'Urbervilles* is among other things an eloquent commentary upon the demise of survivalism. But lacking world enough and time for forays into later periods, we will stop with Andrew Marvell.

Thus outlined, our project may appear fatally mired in topicality—in local paricularities so ephemeral that they are scarcely worth recovering. As Angus Fletcher has complained, "There is a pathos in the occasional;

by commemorating the moment, the poet insists on its loss. Every occasional poem is a tomb."[29] But a peculiar mark of the Renaissance art in defense of festival is that it both acknowledges and transcends the pathos of the occasional. It is almost always bittersweet, accepting its own frailty along with the ephemeral existence of the holiday it celebrates. Yet it is also strong and demanding, requiring a continual revision and balancing of perception on the part of audience and readers in order to achieve its complex effects. Ben Jonson saw his masques as a fusing of the topical and the timeless: "Though their voice be taught to sound to present occasions, their sense or doth or should always lay hold on more removed mysteries."[30] For Jonson, topicality—engagement with "present occasions"—was a generic requirement of the masque, a given whose "voice" had to be interpreted if the "sense" of its "more removed mysteries" was to be grasped. Without some immersion in the immediate milieu of Jonson's masques, we cannot hope to understand their structure and rhetorical complexity. Accordingly, we shall find ourselves moving constantly into areas seemingly distant from the matter of public mirth: into Stuart policy toward the theater; into the vexed question of law and its power over festival; even into demonology. Like the historical and anthropological study of popular festival undertaken by Natalie Davis, Clifford Geertz, and others, any inquiry into the literature of festival as a subtle artistic instrument for mirroring and transforming accepted social realities requires a careful eye to what those realities were, or were perceived to be by contemporaries. We will experience such art as entombing its occasion (and perhaps us hapless readers as well) only if we fail to dig ourselves out of its mire of topicality, to move beyond the "voice" to the "sense" of the masque, its articulation of "more removed mysteries."

The same generalization applies with diminished force to the poetry of "public mirth" that developed out of the Jonsonian masque tradition. The poetry tends to be less particularized, less anchored in the specifics of a given communal event, but it is still powerfully bound to the social milieu it reflects and refashions. In a discussion of seventeenth-century drama, Stendhal remarked that "Toute idée politique dans un ouvrage de littérature . . . est comme un coup de pistolet au milieu d'un concert."[31] A pistol shot in the middle of a concert, shattering the privileged separateness of the concert hall, forcibly reminding the audience of the continuing presence of the world outside, however carefully shut out. Such, perhaps, was the galvanic effect of identifiable "idées politiques" in the literature we are about to examine: not so unnerving as a pistol shot in that they were an accepted element of the form, but nevertheless melding art back into life and destroying its separateness, precipitating the audience into a different level of alertness, an active process of questioning that, ideally at least, would alter them and through them the collectivity to which they belonged. Like the old pastimes themselves, the literature of festival was both disparaged and found necessary by those who valued it most highly. They called its poems and masques trifling, "mere" sport, the follies of a night. Yet in practice, they treated such productions as essential instruments for finding and expanding the boundaries of social order. For all the language of disparagement, there was nothing fundamentally frivolous about the Stuart politics of mirth.

Pastimes and the Purging of Theater:
Ben Jonson's *Love Restored* and *Bartholomew Fair*

"And never rebel was to arts a friend," John Dryden observed in *Absalom and Achitophel*. That notion is, of course, untenable: one wonders what John Milton would have made of it. But it was a common perception in seventeenth-century England, at least in certain circles. Traditional pastimes and the theater were parallel cultural forms in that they held the same ambivalent status, outside the rules of ordinary life, yet integrally bound up with it. They tended to happen together, masques, plays, and traditional games all being particularly rife at holiday times and enjoyed in the same places—at court and, in the London area, in the no-man's-land of the liberties, outside the City's legal jurisdiction and under the protection of the crown. Queen Elizabeth I had been an avid, if frugal, supporter of the drama and the "precise people" who had ventured to condemn plays and players during her reign had sometimes acknowledged warily that they were opposing a group "privileged by a Prince."[1] Under the Stuarts, however, defense of the drama came to be much more closely tied to defense of the monarchy. As in the case of the *Book of Sports*, James I deliberately forced the issue. He made the theater a royal monopoly—a branch of his prerogative—so that anyone attacking the drama was assailing an aspect of his power.

During his reign in Scotland, as part of his campaign for "delighting the people with publicke spectacles of all honest games," James had made active efforts to lure traveling English players to his court; but when they came, he had to contend with the opposition of the Scottish Kirk. We have a full record of some 1599 skirmishes in Edinburgh. A group of English players who "had acted sindrie comedies in presence of the King" purchased his warrant to "gett them an hous within the toun" so they could perform before the public. They then advertised their "comedeis" with trumpet and drums through the streets of Edinburgh. The local ministers took alarm at the "profanatioun" likely to follow and called a session of the Kirk to enact an ordinance against the plays. James took this move "in evill part, as made purposelie to crosse his warrant," and after much back and forth with the ministers, ordered the ordinance rescinded. They claimed they had fulfilled the king's warrant " 'for your warrant craved no more but an hous to them [the actors], which they have gottin.' 'To what end, I pray you, sought I an hous,' said the King, 'but onlie that the people might resort to their comedeis?' 'Your warrant beareth not that end,' said Mr. Robert [spokesman for the Kirk], 'and we have good reasoun to stay them from their playes, even by your owne acts of parliament.' The king answered, 'Yee are not the interpreters of my lawes.'" For James, power, not public morality, was the issue: eventually he succeeded in asserting his prerogative and the ministers backed down.[2]

When he became King of England in 1603, James took steps to protect himself against any repetition of the humiliating battles of Edinburgh. Only ten days after arriving in London, he issued a patent reconstituting the Lord Chamberlain's Men as the King's Men and authorizing them "freely to use and exercise the Arte and facultie of playing Comedies, Tragedies, Histories, Enterludes, Moralls, Pastoralls, Stage plaies, & such other like . . . as well for the recreation of our loving subjects as for our solace and pleasure." Then he systematically annexed all the major theatrical companies to the royal household. A statute of 1604 gave James's action the force of law; the power to license and keep players was taken away from the nobility and limited to the crown. He also claimed sole authority to license London plays and playhouses. With the passage of time the Master of the Revels' jurisdiction gradually expanded through the provinces, threatening and in some cases quashing local efforts to outlaw plays and pastimes.[3] Contemporaries noted that James seemed not to relish plays in performance as Queen Elizabeth had. Nevertheless, he called for many more at court: twenty-three during the winter season of 1609–10 and never fewer than eleven, except in the year of Prince Henry's death.[4] James seems genuinely to have believed that his sponsorship of the theater would "keep up" royal authority, harnessing the potential subversiveness of the form to the goal of public quiet.[5] That is not to say that the royal monopoly successfully curbed the license of the theater or even that James was strongly interested in censorship. A more accurate formulation might be that by laying claim to drama as an institution, he enclosed theatrical license within the structure of royal power, defusing what might be perceived as attacks on himself and the official hierarchy by giving them a fixed status within the structure. Those who ventured to condemn the drama *as a form* during Jacobean times had to reckon with the fact that they were taking on an institution that "belonged" to the king; those who wished to defend it could rest their arguments on the foundation of royal authority.

Thus Thomas Heywood's *An Apology for Actors,* designed in part to uphold the honor of the royal monopoly against the "railing liberty" of slanderers, points out that the profession "hath beene esteemed by the best and greatest" and claims to need no proof of this proposition beyond the fact of James's sponsorship: "the Royall and Princely seruices, in which we now liue." Heywood grounds his lofty view of actors and their privileges in the theory of divine right: "Kings & Monarches are by God placed and inthroaned *supra nos,* aboue vs, & we are to regard them as the Sun from whom we receiue the light." To attempt to suppress the privileges granted players by the king's own authority is therefore to "meddle" with the sovereign's "beauty and brightness." Of course Heywood did not mean that every Stuart play is *about* the glory of the king, only that the drama as an institution was an aspect of royal magnificence, particularly the drama that flourished at court.[6] The same arguments applied to the Stuart court masque, in which the "beauty and brightness" of the king were actually displayed. The masque was much more costly than the drama—a single performance at court might run to several thousand pounds—and there were numerous complaints that such extravagance would eventually ruin England. But for the king and his apologists, the masque's elaborateness was justified as a manifestation of the glory of the monarch and therefore of the power and splendor of the nation. Masques were a "liturgy of state" that kindled foreign respect much as the Anglican liturgy was meant to inspire reverence toward the Church.

In his biography of James I, William Sanderson defended all courtly festivities and theatrical arts as schools of virtue and correctors of vice. The king's *"Feasts, Masks,* [and] *Comedies"* are "necessary *Mirrors, wherein mens Actions are reflected to their own view.* Indeed some men privy to the uglyness of their own guilt have been violent, not onely to crack but to break in pieces all those *Looking-glasses, least their own deformities recoyle, and become eye-sores to themselves.'"* The less worthy the viewer, the less value he will find reflected in the royal "mirror"; the more "envious" he is of the power of the king, the more likely he will be to see the drama and other courtly arts as an abuse of power. Sanderson applies to the political sphere a theory of holiday "folly" familiar from Erasmus and Shakespeare[8] and echoed by Jonson himself, who claimed that "all representations, especially those of this nature in court, public spectacles, either have been or ought to be the mirrors of man's life" (Preface to *Love's Triumph Through Callipolis, Masques,* 454). Jonson asked of these mirrors, "If I see any thing that toucheth mee, shall I come forth a betraier of my selfe, presently? No; if I be wise, I'le dissemble it; if honest, I'le avoid it: lest I publish that on my owne forehead, which I saw there noted without a title. A man, that is on the mending hand, will either ingeniously confesse, or wisely dissemble his disease. And, the wise, and vertuous, will never thinke any thing belongs to themselves that is written, but rejoyce that the good are warn'd not to bee such; and the ill to leave to be such" (from *Discoveries, Jonson,* 8:634). For James I and for Ben Jonson, condemnation of the essential nature of the masque and the drama was always self-reflexive. To attack these forms in the name of whatever exalted ideal was to unmask one's own incapacity for the virtue they can teach.

Enemies of the stage regularly charged that plays rested on lies and hypocrisy, reminding their readers that the Greek word *hypocrite* had meant both actor and pretender. But defenders of the drama were quick to return the charge. Those who muttered against plays and masques were "open Saints and secret varlets" who concealed their true natures for nefarious ends.[9] In *Love Restored,* when Robin Goodfellow is accused of hypocrisy he answers, "We are all masquers sometimes." The joke operates on a number of levels. Robin is in fact a member of the theatrical company The King's Men, playing the part of Robin Goodfellow, a spirit of country jollity, who, in turn, has attempted to pass himself off as a hypocritical Puritan feather-maker—disguise upon disguise upon disguise. But his challenger is also an actor and therefore also a "hypocrite," a player of roles. The need to act, mime, and take pleasure in such functions, Robin implies, is a natural human trait. It can either uplift or debase, depending on the degree to which it is acknowledged and therefore made open to regulation and refinement. This is a standard Jacobean argument for the drama, as for other traditional customs. By extension, it is an argument for the royal monopoly. By claiming the power to "license" and regulate it, James was ensuring that the human needs it met would be channeled to the betterment of the nation. Otherwise, the argument went, those needs were likely to be driven underground, twisted toward evil and seditious ends.

Ben Jonson's *Love Restored* and *Bartholomew Fair* both hinge upon the unmasking of hypocrites. The enemies of the masque and the drama are revealed as role players themselves and subverters of the national order in whose interest they claim to act. As I shall demonstrate, both works were explicitly designed to support royal prerogative in the management of "public mirth." Indeed, we have some reason to believe that Jonson wrote both at the specific request of the king. During the years between 1612 and 1614 there was a fierce concentration of anti-Puritan rhetoric in performances at court, including the revival of works like Ben Jonson's *Alchemist* (*Jonson*, 9:225). According to John Aubrey, it was King James who "made" Jonson "write against the Puritans, who began to be troublesome in his time" (*Jonson*, 1:180). Certainly Jonson himself felt sufficient antipathy for certain elements among that group to have attacked them without royal prodding. And yet "writing against the Puritans" is unusually prominent in *Love Restored* and *Bartholomew Fair*, even by Jonsonian standards, and we have circumstantial evidence linking both works to James.

Love Restored, produced on Twelfth Night, 1612, is the first Jonsonian masque to center on James's difficulties with Puritans and other "rebels" against authority and also the first, except for the wedding masques, which Jonson did not write explicitly for someone other than the king. Queen Anne had danced her last masque in 1611, and Prince Henry had died during 1612. *Love Restored* resembles the masque written by James himself in Scotland and makes a similar point about the relationship between court and country pastimes. *Bartholomew Fair* was performed at the Hope Theater on 31 October 1614, then dedicated to James and performed before him the very next day, All Saints' Day, the traditional opening date for winter festivities at court. William Blissett has pointed out that such a "double premiere" was most unusual; ordinarily more time elapsed between a play's public debut and its performance at court.[10] It would have been nearly impossible to make all the arrangements and revise the text as Jonson did, with a new prologue and epilogue to James I, in the small space of twenty-four hours. The court premiere was almost certainly arranged in advance, which suggests that the play was expected to have special significance for the king. *Love Restored* and *Bartholomew Fair* are deeply immersed in the same set of policies and problems. During much of the time between the masque and the play Jonson was absent in France, so that the two works are nearly contiguous in terms of Jonson's artistic production despite the gap in time between them. Both works castigate London vice and defend James's sponsorship of the theater but are no mere panegyric for all that. What they offer instead is a tart dialectic that praises the king to the extent that he had managed to extricate himself from abuses he had helped to create. One of the things that makes both works so vital is their refusal of easy antitheses. The king is never altogether insulated from the "misrule" he is praised for correcting.

* i *

Love Restored is not one of Jonson's major productions, but it is worth discussing because it inaugurates the important Jonsonian theme of asserting a tie between humble devotion to the king and a love of traditional pastimes. In it Robin Goodfellow is denied entrance to a masque at court but manages to sneak in anyhow, and the masque is transformed as a result. *Love Restored* has received relatively little critical attention and much of that has been negative. Jonas Barish has objected to the "erosion of decorum" by which Robin Goodfellow is elevated from his country clownishness and to Jonson's handling of Plutus, the God of Money, an "equivocal symbol for Jonson's purposes, since in fact the masque cannot proceed without him, without the expenditure, that is, and hence prior accumulation of large sums of money."[11] Stephen Orgel has found *Love Restored* structurally flawed, the first Jonson masque to begin "by acknowledging itself" a theatrical production, but completely dominated by the "tiny comic drama" of the antimasque.[12] The main masque of *Love Restored* is indeed lame and pallid by the usual Jonsonian standards. It lacks all the transforming spectacles for which Inigo Jones had already become famous, and in fact, Jones was not involved in the production. But Jonson uses the absence of Jones and his "machines" to challenge our preconceptions about what a court masque must be. Here, as in Jonson's more fully realized productions, the masque's seeming inadequacies and irregularities are built into its rhetorical scheme.

Love Restored is a masque about the inabililty to make a masque. It begins in apparent paradox. Masquerado appears and confesses disarmingly, "I would I could make 'em a show myself" (*Masques*, 186). But if he, a masquer, does not make the masque, who does? The rest of Jonson's work answers that implicit question.

To anyone acquainted with James I's financial difficulties during the years before *Love Restored,* one obvious answer might be that money makes a masque. In 1608 James was said to be sighing over his debts, which by Christmas 1609 were expected to total £ 341,383.[13] This alarming sum was not reached, in part because the king and his advisors found new sources of revenue. Among other things, they revived a feudal custom allowing the king to collect a levy toward making Crown Prince Henry a knight. In 1610–11, however, James was still deeply in debt. He spent much of that period struggling with the House of Commons over subsidies and is reported to have found their intransigence in money matters close to treasonous.[14] At the same time, the City of London was also balking over the king's requests for loans. Parliament would grant subsidies only to the extent that the king would cede areas over which he claimed prerogative. James did yield some of his rights, but refused to give way on the issue of church government and ceremonies. In disgusted defiance of the House and their parsimoniousness, James dissolved Parliament in early 1611 and granted six of his favorites the enormous sum of £ 34,000.[15] By the end of the year, quite understandably in view of James's profligacy toward his favorites, money was very scarce at court. A major reason for the relative spareness of *Love Restored,* by comparison with splendid earlier productions like *Oberon* and *The Masque of Queens,* was undoubtedly a shortage of funds. But in the view of some royal advisors, the basic problem was not money but loyalty. They were convinced that the money did exist—wealthy Englishmen were joining the ranks of the gentry at a rapid pace—but such climbers were interested only in their own enrichment and held back financial support out of envy of the power of the king.[16]

Toward the end of 1611, in yet another creative effort to raise revenue, the royal government had sent out a number of letters under the Privy Seal "requesting" loans in specific amounts from prominent individuals across the country. By the time *Love Restored* was performed on Twelfth Night, funds had started to come in, but too slowly. Some of those called upon could not pay: a Sir Gamaliel Capell begged to be excused until Lady Day and added plaintively that the £ 40 lent to Queen Elizabeth still had not been returned; a William Style asked that his father be relieved of a loan of £ 20 on the grounds that he was £ 1000 in debt and his Christmas hospitality had been "heavy upon him"—an explanation which is likely to have found some sympathy at court.[17] But a significant number of his majesty's subjects simply refused to pay. In some areas of the country there seemed to be an inverse relationship between wealth and willingness to support the king: a memorandum of 25 December notes that Somerset, an area of significant opposition to the crown, had sent in £ 700 less than Wiltshire, although Somerset was bigger and more powerful.[18] Only two months before, the City of London had celebrated its own wealth in a Lord Mayor's Show called *Chruso-thriambos: The Triumphes of GOLDE* for the Honorable Company of Goldsmiths. That entertainment was at best ill-timed, given the dearth of money at court.[19] The king's advocates could point to the "cheerfulness and liberality" of rural folk like the people of the poor county of Huntingdonshire, who had responded to the levy for Prince Henry by vowing that "the young Prince shall command all they have in the world," and contast this warmth and loyalty with the recalcitrance of a great many wealthier subjects in Parliament, London, and elsewhere, who refused to sacrifice their own means to meet the needs of the king.[20]

This is close to the analysis offered in *Love Restored*. But Jonson was by no means blind to the excessive spending at court. His masque reestablishes a lost middle ground between dearth and wild extravagance by applying some of the lessons of the king's recent experience to the life of the court itself. Robin Goodfellow, the embodiment of traditional country mirth, unmasks rebellion but also initiates a reform of the masque.

At the beginning of *Love Restored,* Masquerado complains that the masque cannot go forward because harmony has been lost at court, as in fact it had as a result of the king's difficulties over money. There is only "wild music"; Cupid has grown so hoarse that he cannot play his part. When this impostor Cupid comes in, however, we immediately realize there has been some mistake. He sounds more like Rancor than Love. In imitation of the arguments and even the rhetorical cadences of the king's Puritan and parliamentary opponents, he claims to withhold his support from the "tyranny" of the masque and other court revelry on grounds of morality and social utility. The masque and similar "feathered vanities" are a seedbed of vice and the "ruin of states" (*Masques,* 192). He sets himself up as a reformer of unprofitable "custom," even that custom which is "authorized in this place to all license of surquidry" by the king himself. Such "superfluous excesses," he claims, are what has ruined the reputation of Love "both in town and country." The fact that all these pompous Latinisms are uttered by a mere boy Cupid makes the arguments more ludicrous than credible (and to anyone acquainted with James's fiscal extravagance, they would have been credible enough), but Masquerado fails to recognize the imposture. Plutus is unmasked by Robin Goodfellow, the humble representative of traditional country loyalty, just as the stubbornness of England's subsidy-evading citizens and gentry had been "unmasked" by the free generosity of the rural people in places like Huntingdonshire.

Plutus is not exactly the God of Money; it would be more precise, if impossibly awkward, to call him "The Making of Money a God." As he fulminates, it becomes clear that what he really wants is the social levelling of everyone but himself. All privilege of rank is to be abolished and the social hierarchy reordered on the basis of money alone. He dismisses Robin as too rude for his company. Then he proceeds to dismantle the court. The king and courtiers are to dwindle down to a household no more splendid than that of a moderately prosperous Londoner and content themselves with middle-class pastimes: "Masquing, and revelling? Were not these ladies and their gentlewomen more housewifely employed, a dozen of 'em to a light, or twenty—the more the merrier—to save charges, i' their chambers at home, and their old nightgowns, at draw-gloves, riddles, dreams, and other pretty purposes, rather than to wake here, in their flaunting wires and tires, laced gowns, embroidered petticoats and other taken-up braveries?" (*Masques,* 192). He pleads for economy, a perfectly acceptable virtue, but in its name he urges the eradication of all public mirth—the "necessary *Mirrors*" of outward splendor which make the king self-evidently a king. After Plutus's true identity is exposed, he reverts to the solipsism which has underlain his arguments all along. His noble and high-sounding motives collapse into an ooze of self-love: "Alas! how bitterly the spirit of poverty spouts itself against my weal, and felicity! But I feel it not. I cherish and make much of myself, flow forth in ease and delicacy, while that murmurs and starves" (*Masques,* 194). It becomes all too clear that he opposes the "vanities" in "high places" only because he wishes to hoard all the "ease and delicacy" for himself—precisely the king's view of those who were able to help support him but nevertheless refused. Jonson clearly meant to caricature London wealth in particular. Plutus satirizes civic self-boosterism of the sort that had erupted in the 1611 pageant *Chruso-thriambos,* which had displayed London goldsmiths luxuriating in the stuff of their trade at a time of severe dearth for the king. But London was not the poet's only target.

Once Plutus is revealed in all his miserly sordidness, the way is cleared for the revival of Love—the main masque can now go forward. But it will be a masque freed from "The Making of Money a God" and freed of the assumption that stupendous expense is a necessary part of the form. Robin's timely intervention reinfuses the court with rustic English values which they have lost on this hoarse and inharmonious Twelfth Night. It is significant that Masquerado, the masquer, has failed to recognize Plutus, although he has managed to catch the "reformed" cadences of his Puritan rhetoric. The court has been unable to diagnose what ails it and has required help from outside. Jonson suggests that the weakness which allows the confusion of money and love is a weakness which exists in the court as in the nation at large, even among those who might be masquers or viewers of the masque. Plutus mistakes love for money—he sees only that masques are expensive, not that they are inspired by loyalty to James. But the courtiers are in danger of mistaking money for love—they suppose that masques must be endlessly expensive and elaborate in order to manifest their devotion. Robin Goodfellow sets them straight by reestablishing the separateness of love and money; the masque can then be revived, rebuilt without impossible expense on its first principle of loyalty to the king.

By recognizing Plutus beneath his disguise, humble Robin demonstrates that he has more insight than Masquerado or the rest of the disordered company. At precisely that point of recognition, Robin's speech patterns change; he gives up his folksy garrulousness for a more elevated tone and language. This may be an erosion of decorum, as Barish has complained, but it has Christian sanction and important meaning for the masque. It is an enactment of the traditional holiday motif of *deposuit potentes*. Plutus, who claims to rule all, is pushed to the bottom of the hierarchy and even outside it, where he has placed himself by his contempt for Robin and the king; humble Robin is exalted for his fidelity and insight; and all those witnessing the masque, that most elaborate of forms, are taught the value of simplicity.

For someone who spent much of his creative energy on the theater, Jonson was singularly distrustful of elaborate spectacle and illusionary effects.[21] This distrust can be documented long before Jonson's celebrated quarrel with Inigo Jones in the 1620s and 1630s. In the epistle "To Sir Robert Wroth," for example, which was written before 1614 and possibly about the same time as *Love Restored,* Jonson congratulates Wroth on his life in the country, where he is spared the courtly excess symbolized by the masque:

> Nor throng'st (when masquing is) to haue a sight
>   Of the short brauerie of the night;
> To view the iewells, stuffes, the paines, the wit
>   There wasted, some not paid for yet!
>
> (*Jonson,* 8:96–97)

Here the masque is portrayed as a costly jumble of externals by contrast with more wholesome forms of holiday revelry in the country, where art is woven into the fabric of communal life. At Christmas, Comus, the traditional god of masquing and banqueting, "puts in" to help celebrate Wroth's feast. The hall is "open," ringing with "mirth, and cheere"; the gentry and "rurall folke" mingle comfortably "with losse of state, or reuerence"; competition, "lawyer fees," and urban preoccupations are forgotten (*Jonson,* 8:98).

In Jonson's work, art invariably becomes suspect if it strays too far from communal feeling and reciprocity. That is what has happened to the court masque. For Robin Goodfellow, the masque is a nobler relative of holiday "gambols o' the country" like "selling of fish, short service, shoeing the wild mare, or roasting of robin redbreast" (*Masques,* 188); he hopes to contribute some of his own "feats" to the Twelfth Night celebration for the king. In theory the masque was open to all comers, like Wroth's "open hall" in the country. But in fact, Robin is denied entry while citizens' wives, who are richer than he but in no way his social betters, are admitted. At court this Christmas, traditional hospitality has been lost. Although the court needs Robin desperately, it is so hedged about by machines and complexities and restrictions that he is almost shut out.

All of the "thousand hazards" Robin runs to enter are in fact related to visual aspects of the masque, to the production of the elaborate "motions" and special effects for which Inigo Jones was renowned. Robin is dropped as from a stage "ladder," nearly "mazarded" by a trap door, laughed out of the assumed role of "engineer" who "belonged to the motions," out of the roles of tire woman, musician, feather-maker, and out of his fine "device" of "bombard man," as well as forty others, "of wiremen, and the chandry, and I know not what else; but all succeeded alike" (*Masques*, 191). He even tries assuming a foreign tongue (which may also remind us of Inigo), but that fails, too. He succeeds only by abandoning all efforts to become part of such proliferated artifice and being simply himself. Jonson's meaning is clear: it is the court's worship of externals like the elaborate "machines" of the revels which has kept Robin out and therefore kept them in bondage to Plutus. Inigo Jones was not involved in the staging of *Love Restored* because he was working on another entertainment, Thomas Campion's *Lord's Masque* in honor of the marriage of Princess Elizabeth. Jonson slyly uses Jones's preoccupation with that elaborate project as an occasion for demonstrating that the master artificer's work is unnecessary, or even damaging, insofar as it makes the masque inaccessible to loyal country souls like Robin. Jonson's analysis thus supports the position of some otherwise loyal opponents of the court masque who objected not to the form in itself, but to the oversumptuousness with which it was generally staged.[22]

When the spirit of country devotion does manage to enter, however, he easily breaks the vicious circle which has kept the court in bondage. Plutus's power collapses; Love is brought back from its icy exile in remote areas of the kingdom and restored to vigor by the presence of the king. With the revival of Love, community and reciprocity are rekindled at court. Poetry and music enter the masque for the first time and the "sports of Love" return. Thanks to Robin's overturning of the viewers' perceptions, those in attendance will be able to see a masque and experience the splendor of court pastimes without being enslaved to "mighty shows" and the enormous debts which such productions often entailed. *Love Restored* cost very little: a mere £ 280 as opposed to £ 1087 for *Oberon*, and several times that for some earlier productions (*Jonson*, 10:522, 533). But it nevertheless carries out all the mimetic and hortatory functions necessary to the court masque. In the main masque of *Love Restored*, Jonson deliberately transfers the vocabulary associated with Jones's stagecraft to the masquers themselves. There are no "motions" with changing lights and scenery. The masquers themselves are the only ornaments required in this courtly presence. The pattern and variety of their dances will form the "motions" which display their transformation from subservience to Plutus to restored integrity and insight.

Jonson's minimalist masque is designed not to destroy the form, but to save it from its own tendency to excess. Its essence of Love is separated from its accidents so that Love can be recognized and strengthened. Many contemporary critics of the masque were, like Plutus, inclined to see it as mere sham and disguise. But *Love Restored* establishes true identities. When Robin Goodfellow hears that the performance is in doubt, he exclaims, "Does anybody know themselves here, think you? I would fain know if there be a masque or no" (*Masques,* 188). People about court seem not to know themselves, and Robin suggests a connection between this deficiency and the inability to make a masque. At the outset, Jonson posits *Love Restored* as a theatrical production: Masquerado makes numerous references to the company acting the professional parts; he perceives his own role as separate from his actual identity and feels called upon to assure the audience that he can "speak truth" although "under a vizard." Plutus, on the other hand, protests that he is "neither player, nor masquer"; he sees in the mirror of the masque only his own unacknowledged purposes and turns out to be a most insidious actor against the power of the king. Robin is an occasional player of parts, but nevertheless always recognizably himself and able to recognize others. Through his uncovering of the hypocrite Plutus, Robin dissolves the negative potential of role playing and its "vizards" become a means toward self-knowledge and self-betterment.

The main masque of *Love Restored* celebrates the power of the masque as a form to transform roles into identity. The masquing courtiers are at first introduced in their "disguise" of allegorical personages. But they are inspired by Love, who is inwardly and outwardly the same; his external attribute is a lighted torch and he is lighted from within by the "bright beams" of the king. Under Love's tutelage, through the form and measure of the dances, the courtiers will become those attributes which at first they only symbolize:

> Till all become one harmony
> Of honor and of courtesy,
> True valor and urbanity,
> Of confidence, alacrity,
> Of promptness and of industry,
> Hability, reality.

35

Nor shall those graces ever quit your court,
Or I be wanting to supply their sport.

(*Masques,* 196)

Jonson's clear and graceful latinisms seem designed to dispel the last echoes of Plutus's tortured latinate diction. The poet offers the dancers a model through language for the simplicity in identity they seek. And indeed, by the end of the first dance Love's inspiration has had the desired effect. It is impossible to tell whether "love's in them, or they're in love." The masquers, like Love himself, have become inwardly and outwardly the same. The first dance therefore confers identity. The second ennobles: through their ordered interaction with the ladies, the courtiers are linked symbolically with the higher harmonies of the universe.

We may find all this a bit lame by Jonsonian standards, as perceptive readers have. But we are at a disadvantage in that our only record of the performance is the printed page. The success of the main masque is entirely dependent on the "motions" of the dancers and on the audience's recognition, through their perception of the unity of dancers and dance, that harmony has returned to court. Some viewers of *Love Restored* may well have considered the work flawed because it lacks the marvelous transformation scenes provided on other occasions by the artificer Inigo Jones. But if they did, they demonstrated their failure to understand the "motions" of the dancers and to internalize Jonson's difficult message that money does not make a masque. Jonson did not, of course, mean to banish spectacular staging from all masques to come, although a part of him may have covertly wished to. The final song promises that in the future, there will again be "shows" at court under the auspices of Love. Rather, Jonson was using this 1612 "occasion" of financial dearth to cleanse the court of its addiction to externals and thus make dearth less likely to recur. If *Love Restored* has had its intended impact and Plutus has indeed been exorcized from Whitehall, when "shows" return to the masque (and Inigo himself with them), they will be kept within bounds, close to their origin in love and communal feeling. The masque will be vindicated against its detractors and become self-evidently what in essence it is: a mirror of virtue, a discoverer of vice and sedition.

We might suppose that James would have been less than pleased with *Love Restored*'s critique of the extravagance of the usual court masque, particularly in view of James's own extravagance during the previous year of 1611. But Jonson appeals, as he so frequently does, to the king's nobler side against his weaker. If James was too often incapable of resisting the importunities of his favorites, he nevertheless made the virtue of moderation one of his guiding ideals: "I am euer for the *Medium* in euery thing. Between a foolish rashnesse and extreame length, there is a middle way."[23] In his *Book of Bounty* (1610), he had acknowledged his overliberality and attempted to curb it by forbidding his servants and subjects to sue for monetary favors that would strain his own or public finances. He had also attempted to find a "middle way" in household expenses by curbing the lavishness of the court, but then he encountered complaints about the decline of his hospitality. The king was, in effect, caught between two manifestations of Plutus: the parsimoniousness of those outside the court who resented all public mirth, and the irresponsibility of those at court who resented any limitation on it. *Love Restored* reinforces James's efforts toward moderation by challenging the courtiers to model themselves after the ideals of the king. Some of the favorites who had received large sums from James during 1611 were almost certainly among the masquers. Through the intricate "motions" of the dances, they are symbolically freed from their bondage to Plutus and taught how to demonstrate the royal lesson of moderation through their own behavior about court.

Robin's intervention has made the masque possible, but it is the presence of James himself that revives Love so that the form can flower into art. *Love Restored* is, above all, a celebration of the king as reviver and regulator of the theater. James's excesses may have forced the masque into uncharacteristic spareness, but his power also "redeems" it so that it can reattune audience and participants to cosmic principles of order, perhaps even extend goodwill beyond the court and "to the very country," where both Robin and the king's collectors of privy seal loans had found Plutus enjoying dangerous eminence.

Jonson may have meant *Love Restored* as a more specific tribute to the king as artist since it is structurally similar to the masque written by James himself. James's masque, which Jonson is likely to have seen in manuscript, has no "spectacle" to speak of, and gives prominent place to a bumpkin much like Robin Goodfellow, a character named Agrestis who speaks in a folksy, rural idiom and personifies rude country fellowship. Agrestis journeys to court to see the "game and glee" of the "gentles" and praises the king's renown for "Martiall games, and pastymes braue and faire."[24] James's masque, like Jonson's, establishes delight in such sport as an honest and praiseworthy trait ingrained in country folk and demonstrates an essential kinship between country pastimes and more lavish festivities at court. But the parallels between the two masques, if noticed, would challenge James as much as they praised him by pointing out the distance between elaborate shows at the Jacobean court and the king's own art of the masque. In *Love Restored,* the power of James I is a wondrous force for good, but only when exercised in the proper spirit and to the most laudable ends.

* ii *

Bartholomew Fair is even more pervasively grounded than *Love Restored* in contemporary controversy over theatrical arts and traditional pastimes and more trenchant in its commentary upon those Plutuses—Puritan or otherwise—who made it their "lawful" calling to challenge the authority of the king. The play has inspired fine commentary from a number of perceptive critics. But opinion has divided sharply over whether it is (to use one of its own recurrent puns) a foul play or a fair one—a dark indictment of human irrationality and moral decay or a celebration of the rejuvenating energies of folly and festival disorder.[25] A study of its "occasion" will demonstrate that Jonson fully intended to have it both ways. He immerses his audience in the seamy squalor of Smithfield and exposes the vice and blasphemy which can lurk behind noble ideals like law and religion and education. The shabby, tinsel world of Bartholomew Fair seems to slough off higher cultural forms as irreconcilable with its nature. But Jonson's fair is not all foulness, and those who would have it so must reckon with some awkward incongruities.

In the Prologue to the king, Jonson warns James not to expect too much from his fair but nevertheless promises "sport" and for a "fairing," the gift traditionally offered by those returned from a fair, "true delight."[26] James would presumably have been amused by the fair's grotesques and, beyond that, would have found rare "sport" in the play's unmasking of what he habitually identified as two major species of rebel against his authority: the Puritan who uses religion as a cloak for personal aggrandizement and the judge who argues for the supremacy of law, meaning by that the supremacy of himself. But the true delight Jonson proposes is a wider pleasure than the sport of seeing one's enemies exposed. The play carries too many echoes from contemporary defense of public mirth, echoes even from the Anglican liturgy for the Feast of Saint Bartholomew, an official holiday of the Church, for its "fair" festival side to be discounted. Unlike some of his sons, Jonson was seldom one to romanticize popular sports—he does not allow his audience to lose contact with their raucous, gritty earthiness. There is considerable tension in the play between the "fair" and the "foul" levels of its argument. But in *Bartholomew Fair,* as in *Love Restored,* the author's ambivalence, or at least some of it, is channeled into defense of the king. The "fairing" offered King James is the "true delight" of seeing one's cherished beliefs about the potential functioning of plays and pastimes reflected in the uncommon looking glass of a play about plays and pastimes.

In both the Induction to the Hope audience and the Prologue to King James, Jonson adamantly denies that *Bartholomew Fair* is meant to satirize individuals. In the Induction he wards off any "state-decipherer, or politic picklock of the scene" so "solemnly ridiculous as to search out" models for the personalities who wander his fair, and in the Prologue to James he again protests that he writes "without particular wrong, / Or just complaint of any private man / Who of himself or shall think well or can" (*Fair,* 23, 33). This formulation effectively shields *Bartholomew Fair* against accusations of slander. If any individual is so rash as to protest that he has been singled out for reflection in the unflattering mirror of the play, it will be because he cannot think well of himself. His protest will be motivated (according to the standard theory) by secret recognition of his own culpability and will therefore amount to a confession that he needs the play's tart correctives. And yet Jonson's pious caveats against politic picklocking have the effect of whetting our curiosity for precisely the activity he warns us against. Several modern critics, suspecting that the poet doth protest too much, have set out to identify historical figures as the butts of Jonson's satire and found striking parallels among his contemporaries. The Lord Mayor of London in the year 1614, like Adam Overdo, ferreted out dens of iniquity through spies and went "himself in disguise to divers of them"; he also seasoned his discourse with references to classical authors, much in Overdo's style. The famous Banbury Puritan William Whately, known as the "roaring boy of Banbury," habitually preached at fairs, as Zeal-of-the-Land Busy does, to gather a "fairing of souls" for God. Bartholomew Fair was a favorite time for Puritan invective against the drama because the crowds of fairgoers visiting London filled the playhouses to overflowing.[27]

Jonson almost certainly expected a similar picklocking on the part of his contemporary audience, but that does not mean that his warnings against it are entirely disingenuous. When the poet steers us away from attempts at specific identification he is not denying that parallels with contemporaries can be found, but advising us not to dwell on them at the expense of larger issues. Many Puritans preached at fairs; several Lord Mayors played detective. Overdo's bustling in search of "enormities" and his grave distress over the corrosive effects of puppetry and poetry also recapture the attitudes of a number of contemporary Justices of the Peace, whose court records are full of similar opinions and long lists of "notable outrages." There are even intriguing parallels between Overdo and Chief Justice Edward Coke, the king's principal opponent in issues of royal prerogative.[28] But we are not encouraged to stray in search of particulars. Jonson's characters are composites, representative of contemporary anticourt attitudes and argumentative styles; his play analyzes tendencies they have in common, especially their worship of law.

For a play about holiday license, *Bartholomew Fair* is curiously permeated with legalisms. Before it even gets underway, the Hope audience is invited to accept a formal contract granting them lawful right to criticize the work in proportion to the price of their tickets; they are authorized to sit in judgment on their "bench" like justices of the King's Bench (*Fair,* 31). The play itself teems with legal authorities: Busy, Overdo, Wasp, and Littlewit all see themselves as lawgivers in their respective realms of religion, secular government, education, and poetry. There is much talk in the play of licenses and warrants—proofs of legitimacy without which little can be accomplished. At the height of the fair's swirling madness, Trouble-all requires legal sanction even for the act of losing a cloak or downing a pint of ale. There is also much talk of license in the opposite sense of freedom from the authority of law—a liberty which the fair's hostile observers find licentious. Words like *liberty, law, license,* and *judgment* seem forever to be sliding out of meaning in the chaos of Smithfield, so that our sense of what *is* lawful is seriously impaired. Most of those making it their business to enforce some legal system end up in the stocks, like common transgressors of law; the legal documents juggled at the fair finally authorize actions contrary to what they first specified as lawful. One of the play's overriding themes is the *tu quoque*— let him who is without sin cast the first stone. Taken literally, this precept would undo all human capacity to penalize breaches of law.

Bartholomew Fair's emphasis on legalisms has struck a number of readers, but we have failed to recognize how Jonson's *tu quoque* applied to contemporary circumstances.[29] *Law, license,* and *liberty* were loaded words in 1614, as thick in the air about London as they are in the vapors of Bartholomew Fair. Jonson deliberately clouds the atmosphere of his play with legalistic obscurities in order to undercut what he saw as a contemporary tendency to worship legal authority. His target is not the law itself, but the abuse of law. Beneath its surface of folly and obfuscation, *Bartholomew Fair* is a lucid and elegant defense of royal prerogative, particularly the king's power to "license" plays and pastimes, against those contemporaries who grounded their opposition to such "licentious enormities" in the doctrine of the supremacy of law.

The play is aimed specifically at two parallel areas of contemporary dispute over law and license: the drama, under the authority of the king, and the pleasure fair of St. Bartholomew, under the authority of the London Corporation. In his Induction to the Hope audience, Jonson playfully establishes the identity of two things: his play, performed under license by the king's Master of Revels in the newly opened Hope Theater, Bankside, on the night of 31 October 1614 and the fair of St. Bartholomew, allowed by royal charter and proclaimed annually in Smithfield by the Lord Mayor of London from the twenty-fourth to the twenty-sixth of August. Jonson acknowledges that some of his more literal-minded viewers may, like the Hope stage keeper, object to the play's lack of such fine fixtures of the fair as the juggler and "well-educated ape"; nonetheless, Jonson assures us, his "ware" is precisely the same. He has even observed a "special decorum" as regards unity of place, the Hope Theater "being as dirty as Smithfield, and as stinking every whit" (*Fair*, 34). This "special decorum" serves an important rhetorical function. It forces us to see the similarities between the two and therefore points out the inconsistency of those contemporaries, particularly in London, who damned the "license" of the king's theater on all sorts of high moral grounds but managed to tolerate their own fair. The *tu quoque* of *Bartholomew Fair* is aimed especially at them.

For decades, as any student of theatrical history knows, the City fathers had opposed virtually all dramatic activity in and about London, as the king's old enemies, the Kirk, had in Edinburgh and for many of the same reasons. But the patents issued by James I to his own acting companies specifically exempted them from local restrictions. Although privy council records for the period have not survived, we know from numerous other sources that the years just before 1614 were a time of tug of war between the king and his privy council on one hand, and the Mayor and the City Corporation on the other. The king claimed power to license plays and players in and around London, and to override local ordinances against them; the City claimed the right to curb the royal monopoly within its liberties through enforcement of its own and parliamentary ordinances.[30] But what the City fathers condemned when it produced revenue for the king, they found considerably less objectionable when it produced revenue for themselves. Bartholomew Fair had two parts and it is important that we keep them straight. There was, first of all, the cloth fair, mostly business, which took place within the walls of St. Bartholomew Priory; its revenues went to Lord Rich, owner of the priory. Secondly, there was the pleasure fair outside the priory walls; Jonson's play deals almost exclusively with the pleasure fair, whose profits went to the London Corporation.[31] The area of the pleasure fair had not become part of the liberties of London until 1608. In that year, reportedly in return for funds to build a new Banqueting House, the king offered the City a new charter which specified that the "circuit, bounds, liberties, franchises, and jurisdictions" of London be extended to include the area around the priory, noteworthy for its annual fair, and Blackfriars and Whitefriars, noted for their theatrical connections.[32] Just as he was asserting royal control over the culturally marginal institution of the theater, he invited the City to try its hand at coping with the fair. However, while City fathers applied their new authority over Blackfriars and Whitefriars to curb the drama as much as they could, they showed less zeal in Smithfield. There was a notable "reform" in 1614: the muddy swamp of the fairgrounds was paved at City expense and made a "clean and spacious walk." The impetus for this improvement came from the king, who sent a letter to the Lord Mayor ordering it done. The Lord Mayor obeyed only after considerable protest.[33]

It is easy to see how these inconsistencies could be viewed by unsympathetic observers. So long as the City Corporation allowed in their fair the same liberties they condemned in the theaters, their high-sounding arguments about law and morality could appear purely self-serving. We need not, of course, agree with this prejudiced assessment. The king was acting as much in his interest as Londoners were in theirs. But the king's supporters would have drawn additional ammunition from the subsequent history of the fair. Bartholomew Fair was not suppressed during the Interregnum. When plays and traditional holiday pastimes had been banished from all of Britain by act of Parliament, similar frivolities were still allowed at the fair. Even its puppet theater, with its plays of "patient Grisel," "fair Rosamond," and Suzanna survived, as diaries and pamphlets from 1648, 1651, and 1655 record.[34]

Jonson's equation between fair and play therefore functions as an indictment of the king's London opposition, but an indictment tempered with mercy. He advises its grave citizens and judges not to carry on about the "enormities" of the royal monopoly of the drama until they have curbed the "enormities" of their own fair. In the process, they will come to recognize that they themselves participate in the imperfection for which they castigate others. At the end of the Induction, Jonson asks his viewers to judge the "ware" of his play by precisely the same standards that they would the wares of the fair; otherwise, the poet will "justly suspect that he that is so loth to look on a baby or an hobbyhorse here, would be glad to take up a commodity of them, at any laughter, or loss, in another place" (*Fair,* 34). That "other place" is Smithfield. Sober sorts who shrink from the vanities of the playhouse while allowing themselves to profit from the vanities of the fair, are counseled to look to their motives.

If Jonson's case against the City of London is to gain conviction, however, he must demonstrate his proposition that the "ware" of the play and the "ware" of the fair are in fact the same. On the most obvious level, he accomplished this by making the two events coterminous. The fair is the play and the play, except for its opening scenes, is the fair. Any objection to the scurrility of one is at once an admission of the foulness of the other since the two are indistinguishable. Both are episodic in structure: the Induction enumerates the "sights" of the play as though they were a succession of spectacles at a fair and the visitors to the fair watch its changing scene as they would the scenes of a play. Like a play, the fair has its "prologue" of a cutpurse and "five acts," its "orations" and its "tragical conclusions," and a player (Wasp) who is "Overparted" (*Fair*, 91, 96, 100). But Jonson is considerably wittier than that; the landscape of the fair symbolically recapitulates aspects of the Hope Theater, particularly those features its enemies found most reprehensible.

The poet sets us along the path of interpreting his work by pointing out a first element of correspondence between the two—their foulness—Smithfield and the Hope being equally "dirty" and "as stinking every whit" (*Fair*, 34). But the two locations have other physical features in common. The stage at the Hope was not the usual fixed platform, but a movable scaffold resembling the street stages used at fairs.[35] A major contribution to the Hope's stench was that it also served as a Bear Garden and the animals were stabled nearby. On alternate days its scaffold stage was removed and bearbaiting took the place of plays. After 1616 the theater was given over exclusively to bearbaiting, another monopoly of the king's and a frequent form of entertainment at court. City authorities opposed the sport as a danger to public order. In 1583 when a Paris Garden scaffold had collapsed during a Sabbath baiting, the Lord Mayor and other authorities had attributed the catastrophe to the wrathful hand of God, and the sport was not permitted in London.[36] But the City's own fair nevertheless boasts its own holiday bearbaiting: Ursula, the gargantuan brawling "enormity" at the heart of it, has a name signifying *little bear* and she is forever being baited by the other characters. Knockem calls her "my she-bear" and she disdains the "lion-chap" with which he snaps at her (lions did in fact bait bears—a variation on the sport introduced by King James himself). But her encounter with Knockem is a mere opening skirmish. When Quarlous and Winwife enter her booth, the baiting begins in earnest. They snap at the "she-bear," seeking to wear her down with wit, and she roars back with epithets which turn them into her dogs: "dog's-head" and mongrel "trendle-tail" (*Fair*, 80). She begins to tire, but after a brief mêlée and a scalding, she emerges the wounded but triumphant "Ursa major," as bears against dogs generally did.

Jackson Cope has pointed out that Jonson associates Ursula with the standard symbols of Ate, goddess of mischief and discord.[37] However Londoners may rail against royal bearbaiting as a source of riot and disorder, they harbor an equivalent manifestation of the Goddess Discordia in the center of their own fair. Just as the Hope Theater, in the Liberty of the Clink and safely out of their jurisdiction, was transformed into a bear ring every other night, so the "theater" of the fair becomes a ground for the baiting of Ursula. We know that puppet plays were sometimes performed after the baitings at Paris Garden, and the same custom was probably continued at its successor the Hope. If, as some critics have suggested, Ursula's booth was either adjacent to or actually tranformed into the puppet theater for act 5, then the imitative sequence is even closer. The scene of the fair becomes in turn a bear garden and then a puppet stage, as the Hope Theater did in 1614.[38]

Once Jonson's symbolic equivalence is established, it is easy to recognize how the particular types of foulness which surface in his fair parallel the vices City fathers berated in the theater. They condemned plays as the "occasyon of frayes and quarrelles" and argued that tolerance for the theater had brought the fall of Rome,[39] but their fair harbors equal disorder. In act 4, with its complicated and pervasive wrangling, any remaining semblance of social coherence breaks down into lawlessness. They complained that the theaters were a favorite resort of cutpurses and suppressed the jigs at the end of plays ostensibly for that reason in 1612, but at Bartholomew Fair, cutpurses do a thriving business under the very noses of the authorities. They condemned plays as "very hurtfull in corruption of youth with incontinence and lewdness" and the "alleurynge of maides" into debauchery,[40] but their fair is equally rife with sexual laxity and in a more organized form. Even upstanding citizens like Win and Mrs. Overdo are easily enlisted among "my Lord Mayor's green women" (*Fair,* 146).

Plays, according to City authorities, were reprehensible even when they did not spawn worse forms of vice because such mere tinsel and trifles foolishly wasted "the time and thrift of many poore people." The fair is also crowded with cheap allurements and the promise that drums and rattles can transform a life. "What do you lack?" its vendors cry to all comers, and Bartholomew Cokes, a young person notably poor in judgment, heeds their cry, loading himself up with baubles more obviously superfluous than anything he would find at the theater. As Jonson may have known, Bartholomew Fair had been founded by a notable trifler, the court jester of King Henry I.[41] For Jonson's most unsympathetic contemporaries, plays were nothing less than madness: "What else is the whole action of Playes, but *well personated vanity,* artificiall folly, or a lesse Bedlam frenzie?"[42] Yet the madness of the stage yields nothing to the "frenzie" of the fair, which boasts its traditional resident maniac Arthur O'Bradley, which teems with fools natural and "artificiall," and where the very notion of sanity threatens to dissolve altogether.

Jonson's portrait of the fair also speaks to antitheatrical arguments of an overtly Puritan stamp. Extremists among the Puritans likened play-houses to hell itself, calling them "devil chappels" and evoking lurid visions of the actions on stage as the machinations of demons, half-hidden in the stychian smoke of tobacco.[43] The same can be said of the fair. It is shrouded in noxious "vapors" and its center, Ursula's booth, is its bottomless inferno, belching forth fire and fumes. "Hell's a kind of cold cellar to't, a very fine vault" (*Fair,* 65), or if not Hell itself, then the hellish fires of paganism. Some of the most avid play-scourgers con-demned drama on account of its heathen origins and its association with Roman fertility rituals and sacrifices, an argument which receives satiric short shrift in Jonson's own *"Execration upon* Vulcan" when he describes Puritan reaction to the burning of the Globe Theater in 1613:

> The Brethren, they streight nois'd it out for Newes,
>   'Twas verily some Relique of the Stewes:
>   And this a Sparkle of that fire let loose
> That was rak'd up in the *Winchestrian* Goose
>   Bred on the *Banck,* in time of Poperie,
> When *Venus* there maintain'd the Misterie.
>
>   (*Jonson,* 8:209)

But as Jonson and other contemporary classicists knew, fairs, festivals, plays, (and even brothels), had been closely related cultural forms in classical times, found together as part of the same ceremonial structures. Jonson steeps his fair in paganism. It has its resident deities and heroes, an "Orpheus among the beasts," a "Ceres selling her daughter's picture in ginger-work," its Neptune and its Mercury, its "oracle of the pig's head," its overlay of fertility symbols and blessings for increase, its leafy pagan bowers (the fair booths), and its ritual sacrifices with fire "o' juniper and rosemary branches" (*Fair,* 76, 93). Eugene Waith suggests that the staging of the play may have been designed to emphasize the fair's connection with medieval and classical conventions: "The booths recall the mansions of the old mysteries, and more dimly, the houses of Plautus and Terence" (*Fair,* 217).

But Jonson's strongest argument for the hypocrisy of City authorities comes from the fact that all the dramatic arts they declaim against when supervised by the king, they permit in debased form as major attractions of the fair. The Smithfield area had lingering theatrical associations of its own. The royal office of the revels, which prepared masques and plays for court, had until 1607 been located near Smithfield, and Inigo Jones himself had been born in Saint Bartholomew Parish. Jonson certainly had this fact in mind, despite his disclaimers, when he created the character of Lanthorn Leatherhead, whose booth peddles the debased shards of masquing—puppets and tinsel baubles.[44] But the only masque contemplated at the fair is the forty-shilling wedding masque for Bartholomew Cokes—a travesty of the noble spectacles at court—to be scrapped together out of Leatherhead's fiddles and toys, Nightengale's doggerel, and Joan Trash's gingerbread. Smithfield was also associated with plays. The old interludes performed at Skinner's Well, some of them probably in connection with the Feast of St. Bartholomew, the patron saint of Skinners, had died out—perhaps as late as the 1580s[45]— but puppet plays, some of them with religious themes, were allowed at the fair. Near Smithfield there was also a theater, the notorious Red Bull, derided by contemporaries for catering to the lowest citizen tastes and noted from time to time for its attempts to stage opposition plays.[46] Appropriately then, the reigning dramatic authority at the fair is John Littlewit, who stands upon the supremacy of law (his own) in the kingdom of wit. His wife is as well dressed as any of the wives of the players, and the local Justices of the Peace are on his side. While those "pretenders to wit" the "Three Cranes, Mitre, and Mermaid men" are dependent on "places" at court for their livelihood, he can "start up a justice of wit out of six-shillings beer, and give the law to all the poets and poet-suckers i' town" (*Fair,* 37).

But Littlewit's "dainty device" of a bawdy puppet play stands up rather poorly alongside the work of his rivals the "Three Cranes, Mitre, and Mermaid men." His puppet play has all the external trappings of a regular stage play: "motions" and other visual effects, elaborate costumes, and an audience with the usual complement of dimwits who fail to understand the nature of dramatic illusion. In Littlewit's play, however, there is precious little *but* scurrility and illusion. Through the puppet play, Jonson cleverly exposes Smithfield theatrical tastes, which ran from empty spectacle to simplified rehash of the classics.[47] As Leatherhead explains, to play by the "printed book" would be "too learned and poetical for our audience" (*Fair,* 164). City moralists were tireless in condemning the "license" of the great theaters about London, yet allowed puppet plays at the fair—a drama deprived of noble essence and shabbily jumbled together like baubles from Leatherhead's stand.

Bartholomew Fair does have its would-be correctors: Humphrey Wasp, who buzzes against it out of some secret and incomprehensible wrath; Adam Overdo, who tolerates the fair in theory but seeks to curb its enormities in the name of civic zeal; and Zeal-of-the-Land Busy, who declaims against plays, fairs, toys, and every sort of sport on grounds of Puritan principle. On the face of it, this acknowledgment of reforming efforts by contemporary magistrates and religious leaders would seem to blunt the force of Jonson's indictment. If the opponents of the king's public mirth were simultaneously working to redress kindred evils under their jurisdiction, then they were not easily accused of hypocrisy. But they all fail. At the end of the play, they have been disarmed and silenced while the fair continues unabated. And they all fail for the same basic reason: they are so blinded by their own unrecognized faults that they cannot discover what lies beyond. In the mirror of Jonson's play (which is simultaneously the fair) they unwittingly see themselves and their own secret vice. Each learns that the *tu quoque* applies to him.

As Richard Levin has pointed out in his study of the structure of *Bartholomew Fair,* the three chief reformers of the fair constitute a moral hierarchy. They are punished in strict accordance with the level of their pride and presumption, and silenced in order, with the most dangerous, Overdo, being last.[48] The illiterate educator Wasp is the least consequential of the three and the first to be disarmed. Like a trapped insect, he stings whatever he lights on, buzzing about frantically in an imaginary bottle and perceiving things about him as similarly confined. Cokes's head is "full of bees" and the marriage contract is a "bee in a box." John Littlewit is a "Hornet" who must hold his tongue (*Fair,* 49, 54, 48). As we would expect of a creature who breeds in dung and feeds upon offal, Wasp's oath is "turd i' your teeth"; his world is bounded by the limits of a barnyard or dustbin—urine, spit, straws, feathers, and cobwebs. But Wasp's insectine worldview harms nobody but himself, and he is the first to absorb the *tu quoque.* Having been unmasked as fallible, he gives up his helpless and indiscriminate rage to avow, "he that will correct another must want fault in himself" (*Fair,* 168). If, as Jonas Barish has suggested, Jonson's portrait of the would-be educator is partly self-satire, since Jonson had just recently extricated himself from the position of tutor to the son of Sir Walter Raleigh,[49] then the silencing of Wasp gains a rueful pungency. The shrill pedagogue must come to terms with the inefficacy of his instruction, at least upon minds as impenetrable as that of Bartholomew Cokes.

Jonson's portrayal of Zeal-of-the-Land Busy and Adam Overdo is more extended, for these two "authorities" over the fair are not just petulant but genuinely seditious. In laying bare the principles which underly their ostensible ideals and motives, Jonson makes a statement about the limits of law and liberty in general. Before discussing the two authorities in detail, therefore, we would do well to step back briefly for a wider view of Jonson's 1614 "occasion" and examine the struggles over law and prerogative of which the controversy about plays and pastimes formed a single part.

1614 was a year of unprecedented political and economic crisis in the reign of James I. In the years since 1611 when he had dissolved the last Parliament, his financial situation had grown more precarious. He was forced to become increasingly dependent upon income from monopolies and other schemes; by the end of 1613 the court suffered an extreme lack of money despite the abundance of new projects.[50] The king devised several plans for trimming the wealth of London. He failed in an effort to take over "waste lands" within its liberties when the courts upheld the City against him, but eventually succeeded in collecting a tax on all buildings erected since his proclamation of 1607 outlawing new urban construction, in spite of vehement protest that the king could not use his proclamations to declare unlawful something that had been legal before.[51] These conflicts over financing came down to the issue of common law versus prerogative. The king would make a proclamation or grant licenses extending his power into areas over which Parliament, the London Corporation, or some other governmental body claimed jurisdiction. They would protest in the name of their "ancient liberties" protected by common law and fight the king through the courts on the grounds that he was subject to God and the law. He, in turn, would bridle at the notion that his policies could be circumscribed by any judicial authority and attempt to get around common law prohibitions by operating through the High Commission and ecclesiastical courts.

James consistently maintained that he was above the law, accountable for his actions to God and God alone. In a celebrated 1609 speech before Parliament he had stated that "Kings are iustly called Gods, for that they exercise a manner or resemblance of Diuine power vpon earth: . . . they make and vnmake their subiects: they haue power of raising, and casting downe: of life, and of death: Iudges ouer all their subiects, and in all causes, and yet accomptable to none but God onely."[52] James went on to acknowledge that any ruler who did not govern according to the law would be a "Tyrant" and pledged to bind himself within its limits. But he nearly always called the law *his* law. The power to legislate and judge, even in cases of common law, was a branch of his prerogative which he had given some among his subjects to exercise in his place; they did not have the right to turn this borrowed authority against its very source. As it would be "Blasphemie" to "dispute what God may doe" so, he claimed, "is it sedition in Subiects, to dispute what a King may do in the height of his power." James was often willing to bend these high ideals in practice, but seldom in theory. As he often emphasized, however, his freedom from judicial curtailment did not exempt him from responsibility. He was more bound than any of his subjects for he was answerable to God, the most exacting taskmaster and the severest judge.[53]

In early 1614 when the king's financial difficulties forced him to call a new Parliament, his theories received a severe test. He was desperate for money and inclined to be conciliatory. In his speeches before the new lawmakers, he christened them a "parleamente of love" which would reaffirm the mutual affection binding him and his people: "as the laste [Parliament] begane with discorde and ended so, so this maye begine with concorde and love, and contynue so." Borrowing a tactic from Queen Elizabeth I, he insisted that he would rather have the members' love than their money. He likened himself to God, the first gift-giver out of love, and pledged to give Parliament the gift of not insisting upon his prerogative if they in return would grant him the gift of their love.[54] Their financial support would presumably follow as a matter of course.

But the 1614 Parliament was to be no "parleamente of love." Its members had been elected amidst strong anticourt feeling in London and the counties; many were educated landowners inclined toward Puritan sentiments, openly critical of the king's fiscal extravagance, and distrustful of royal support for "popish" rituals and pastimes. The House not only failed to respond to the king's appeal for love, they passed "an act for the keeping of the Saboathe, to restrayne morisdance, beare baytinge on the said deye." Worse yet, they criticized royal expenditures and flouted the established church by refusing to take communion in Westminster Abbey "for feare of copes and wafer cakes."[55] Parliament and the king were quickly at a stalemate with Parliament asserting sabbatarian principles and the supremacy of common law over royal proclamations and the king determined to stop their meddling with royal pastimes and to preserve his prerogative as a power not subject to limitation by the courts. In his speeches before the group James reaffirmed his respect for the common law and insisted, "[I] do not beleeve I am so tendere of my prerogative as some have rumored me; I desyre to keepe also that meane, as I wolde not loose any [of] the honores and floweres of my crowne." But he termed "trayterous" the view that the king could not "proclayme and bynd by it" until his proclamations were ratified by parliamentary statute.[56] Such attacks on his prerogative were, for James, plain rebellious license cloaked as reverence for law. Only two months after it had convened, James dissolved the "Addled Parliament." Not one of its bills had met with the king's approval; he, in turn, had been thwarted in his attempts to obtain financing. It was 1620 before James was willing to risk calling another Parliament.

49

The strong sabbatarian cast of the Addled Parliament was shared by a number of the king's own Justices of the Peace. Limiting ourselves to Middlesex, which included the area around Bartholomew Fair, and to the period immediately preceding 1614, we find recorded a number of "notable outrages"—one Agnes Tedder was brought before the justices "for keepinge of Play at peigonholles one the Saboth day and in the devine seruice"; James Wilson and a number of gentlemen were indicted for the "outrage" of gathering in a field to play "a certain unlawful game called footeball." Three people named South were indicted for "keeping misrule in their house" on the Sabboth Day. There was also the famous order to suppress all "Jigges, Rymes and Daunces" after plays because, as a result of "certayne lewde Jigges songes and daunces vsed and accustomed at the play-house called the Fortune in Gouldinglane divers cutt—purses and other lewde and ill disposed persons in greate multitudes doe resorte thither at th'end of euerye playe many tymes causinge tumultes and outrages."[57] Although the records are by no means complete, they show a distinct upsurge in activity against plays and pastimes on the part of local constables and justices of the peace in the years immediately preceding Jonson's *Bartholomew Fair*. This judicial harassment reinforced the assault on royal prerogative that had emanated from the Addled Parliament. After the dissolution of Parliament, James appealed to popular devotion as he had earlier, asking for "free gifts" as a demonstration of his subjects' love, but met with widespread balking. There were mutterings from the counties about Magna Carta and the ancient liberties of Englishmen; Chief Justice Coke was willing to give privately but called the king's appeal unconstitutional.[58] James claimed his upstart judges were no better than papists who quoted the Bible and insisted it had to mean only what they said; so the judges would cite those statutes which happened to support their preconceived views and insist that only their interpretation was correct.[59] The same sleight of mind vitiates the arguments of the judges in Jonson's *Bartholomew Fair*.

Through his exposure of the secret motives of those who stand upon law, Jonson constucts a critique of the king's 1614 opponents. Zeal-of-the-Land Busy, like the Sabbatarians of the Addled Parliament, has set himself resolutely against "maypoles, morrises, and such profane feasts and meetings" (*Fair*, 45). Like some of the king's vocal parliamentary critics, he hails from Banbury, a stronghold of Puritan sentiment, where iconoclasm had reached such a pitch a few years before that all the town's crosses, including the Banbury cross of nursery-rhyme fame, had been demolished and scattered about Banbury Fair.[60] Like some of the parliamentary Puritans, Busy mutters darkly (but with careful obscurity) against profanation in "high places," obliquely suggesting the court.

The king's Master of Revels, who has licensed the puppet play, he renames the "master of rebels" (*Fair*, 179). But he utterly fails to perceive the "high place" where his egotism has placed him, let alone the irrationality of his position. He and his brethren in the faith need not observe the rigid Old Testament strictures which they impose on everyone else: they alone can pass through the vanities of the fair unscathed and find it "lawful" to eat the abomination of pig without endangering their sanctity.

Zeal-of-the-Land Busy declaims against the pastimes of Bartholomew Fair on the basis of his own frenzied, incoherent version of the standard Puritan argument against paganism—drama, church ritual, and traditional pastimes were all unacceptable to Christians because they were remnants of heathen and Roman Catholic idolatry.[61] Busy abhors the sacrament and institutions of the Anglican Church for that reason. Even a line of manuscript read at a Bishop's court is a "long black hair, kembed out of the tail of Antichrist" (*Fair*, 40). But in Jonson's portrayal, Busy himself is the chief idolater at the fair. He needs to surround himself with pseudo-sacramental foodstuffs. When we first encounter him, he has just devoured a "cold turkey-pie" with "a great white loaf on his left hand, and a glass of malmsey on his right" (*Fair*, 58). By this ritual repast he is cleansed and edified; malmsey is his *"aqua coelestis"* (*Fair*, 40). Busy identifies Bartholomew pig as a "spice of idolatry" like that consumed in the "high places" of paganism (and there were in fact contemporaries who argued against the eating of pork on grounds of Old Testament prohibition).[62] But it is Busy who feels that the eating of roast pig and the drinking of ale confer miraculous powers. Having discovered a rationalization for his gluttonous instinct, he vows, "I will eat exceedingly and prophesy" (*Fair*, 60). His repast in the "tents of the wicked" breathes into him a new spirit with which to proclaim the downfall of the idols of the fair.

In Busy's superstitious eyes, simple, innocuous objects become sinister and organize themselves into elements of a vast demonic landscape: a collection of pipes, drums, and rattles delineates the abhorrent figure of the Beast. The most colorful Puritan antidramatic tracts evoked similarly horrific visions.[63] Jonson suggests that such perception originates in deficient self-knowledge. Busy believes that people who participate in abominations like plays or Bartholomew pig do so from the same superstitious motives he avoids recognizing in himself. What he rails against in others is his own covert interpretation of reality.

In attempting to rid the world of everything popish or pagan, Zeal-of-the-Land Busy has, in effect, undertaken the disestablishment of history. Anything dating back to pre-Reformation times is automatically suspect. His brother in the faith, Deacon Ananias, takes the same extreme position in *The Alchemist:* "I hate *Traditions* . . . They are *Popish,* all" (*Jonson,* 5:345). But Busy's attempts to eradicate the past only mire him more deeply in it. If he were not so ignorant of the history of the fair and of its patron saint, he would recognize that the roles he adopts in Smithfield reinstate some of the very traditions he is zealous to destroy. He scorns anything smacking of "popish" legends: even Joan Trash's "nest of images and whole legend of ginger-work" are an abomination (*Fair,* 118), presumably because they resemble the miniature replicas of saints sold in booths at Catholic fairs and shrines. But Busy himself in his role as iconoclast unwittingly recreates events from the life of St. Bartholomew as recounted in "popish" medieval legends. St. Bartholomew had been what Busy tries to be: a powerful preacher against the idols of the heathen and a destroyer of false temples.[64]

The Puritan's grand debate with the puppets revives another "popish" custom. Within the memories of living Londoners, Bartholomew Fair had been the occasion for formal scholastic disputation. John Stow recalled, "I my selfe in my youth haue yearely seene on the Eve of S. *Bartholomew* the Apostle, the schollers of diuers Grammer schooles repayre vnto the Church-yard of S. *Bartholomew,* the Priorie in Smithfield, where vpon a banke boorded about vnder a tree, some one Scholler hath stepped vp, and there hath apposed and answered, till he were by some better scholler ouercome."[65] When he debates Puppet Dionysius, therefore, Busy unknowingly resurrects an institution of late medieval scholasticism. As in the old holiday debates in honor of St. Bartholomew, the man bested by his adversary must stand down. Busy's main argument that the "male among you putteth on the apparel of the female," is refuted by a flick of Dionysius' garment (*Fair,* 181). Through his portrayal of Busy's role at the fair, Jonson makes the standard Anglican point that you cannot abolish the past. Things like plays and fairs and festivals which happen to predate the Reformation are not necessarily and for that reason bad. As Busy's unwitting transmission of medieval tradition demonstrates, to repudiate the past is to be engulfed by it. The fair, ironically, is more "reformed" then he.

Part of the reason Busy fears history is that he fears human nature. Like some of his actual contemporaries who opposed plays and pastimes, he has no faith in human restraint and discrimination. The only fairgoer we meet who conforms to Busy's pessimistic assessment of human nature, aside from Busy himself, is Bartholomew Cokes, a true "child of the Fair" who is indeed incapable of resisting the profane blandishments of drums, rattles, and gingerbread, and would indeed be better off (at least in pocketbook) if kept from the idols of the fair. Cokes, however, is not Everyman, but a singular case of stunted human development. His lamentable figure plays an important symbolic function in Jonson's case against extreme Sabbatarians in that he stands for human capacity as they take it to be—so hopelessly weak and gullible that its only hope for salvation is to shrink from every vanity which has ever led anyone astray.

As we might expect, Busy is a very poor reader of the texts by which he castigates others. The sacred writ upon which he bases his holy war against the fair frequently boomerangs against him because his fanatical preoccupation with a few limited precepts blinds him to their context. In condemning the pagan sacrifice of the fair, Busy borrows from passages like Isaiah 65:2–3 (King James Version), in which Jehovah proclaims "I have spread out my hands all the day unto a rebellious people, which walketh in a way that was not good, after their own thoughts; A people that provoketh me to anger continually to my face; that sacrificeth in gardens, and burneth incense upon altars of brick." But the continuation of the text applies better to Busy himself than to the rest of the fairgoers. He is one of the "rebellious people" Jehovah condemns "which eat swine's flesh, and broth of abominable things . . . in their vessels; Which say, Stand by thyself, come not near to me; for I am holier than thou" (Isaiah 65:4–5). Busy even gets the *tu quoque* backward. In the opening flourish of his argument against the puppets he calls the idols of the fair "a beam in the eye, in the eye of the brethren; a very great beam, an exceedingly great beam; such as are your stage-players, rhymers, and morris-dancers, who have walked hand in hand in contempt of the brethren and the cause, and been borne out by instruments of no mean countenance" (*Fair*, 178). But in the scriptural original, the self-righteous man with the beam in his eye is more severely handicapped than the brother he presumes to correct: "How wilt thou say to thy brother, Let me pull out the mote out of thine eye; and, behold, a beam is in thine own eye? Thou hypocrite, first cast out the beam out of thine own eye; and then shalt thou see clearly to cast out the mote out of thy brother's eye" (Matt. 7:4–5). Once the beam *is* cast out of Busy's eye, he is silenced. The fair and its puppets shed their malevolent aura once he is brought into contact with the malevolent side of himself.

Justice Adam Overdo is a more complex character than Busy and possesses real power at the fair; he is also much easier for an audience to identify with. For these reasons, he is more dangerous than Busy, and the last to assimilate the *tu quoque*. Busy is instantly recognizable by his small ruff and rhetorical style, but the justice steps in and out of identities, donning a series of disguises for the good of the republic. Overdo's grave civic humanism is on the surface a much more attractive ideology than Busy's fanatical iconoclasm, but it turns out to be yet another disguise, a notably slippery one, to cover his unacknowledged motives. Overdo's law is not the law of Israel, but the law of England; nevertheless, he is as prone as Busy to confuse his own interest with the ideals he claims to represent. Like Chief Justice Coke and other opponents of royal prerogative, he professes himself the loyal servant of James I, but he consistently places the law before the king and assumes that he is its only true interpreter. The triune motto which rules his conduct at the fair would have declared his position unequivocally for Jonson's contemporaries: justice always comes first and James only second. "In justice' name, and the King's; and for the commonwealth! defy all the world" (*Fair*, 61). And yet his reverence for law finally comes down to reverence for himself and his "high place." If his person is held in proper esteem, then he has performed his duty: "I am glad to hear my name is their terror, yet; this is doing of justice" (*Fair*, 64).

Meanwhile, of course, he is neglecting his genuine obligations. As Chief Justice of the Court of Pie-powders he had final "authority" over legal squabbles growing out of the trade at the fair. Even the king could not overrule decisions made in that ancient court.[66] But the Court of Pie-powders has not even met: he is too gratified by his bustling about in search of situations that will redound to his glory to be bothered with the humdrum dispensing of justice. And the constables he relies on to keep order are even more unruly. They brag openly about their freedom from royal authority. When Trouble-all calls them "the King's loving and obedient subjects" Bristle indignantly corrects him: "His loving subjects, we grant you; but not his obedient, at this time, by your leave; we know our selves a little better than so; we are to command, sir, and such as you are to be obedient" (*Fair*, 122). This sturdy independence is not matched by uprightness, however. As Littlewit demonstrates, their "command" over the fairgoers can be bought for a shilling.

Like the contemporary Middlesex justices of the peace with their long lists of "outrages," Overdo travels the fair in search of "enormities" which he duly marks down for correction. His guides in this endeavor are the best classical authors, whom he regards as bosom companions, and he carries out his task of reforming the fair in the name of their stoical precepts about justice, measure, and sobriety—ideals that frequently graced the London Lord Mayor's pageants and other civic ceremonies. But these ideals are mere words to him; he has not internalized their essence. Although he thinks he acts out of altruism, his primary motive is the secret delight of titillating his own ego. He imagines that he wants to rescue Nightengale from the dangers of evil companionship, but his main purpose in counseling the youth is self-gratification. To appear a wise, greyheaded advisor of the young raises him in his own eyes and (he hopes) in the eyes of others. His cheerful stoicism in the stocks "will beget a kind of reverence toward me hereafter, even from mine enemies" (*Fair*, 123). Similarly, when he overhears the constables complain about his unreliability on the bench—"When he is angry, be it right or wrong, he had the law on's side ever"—Overdo soberly cautions himself to observe greater compassion, not because doing so is right, but because it "becomes" a justice (*Fair*, 125). All of these weaknesses, we will note, fall within James I's own analysis in *Basilikon Doron*, in which he warns his son that the law must be enforced "onely for loue to Iustice, and not for satisfying any particular passions of yours, vnder colour thereof," personal anger and other such "vnrulie priuate affections" being incompatible with the administration of justice.[67]

And yet, even as Jonson indicts Overdo on the basis of royal precept, he constructs a character who uncannily echoes some of the most famous utterances of the king. Readers of *Bartholomew Fair* have been puzzled by the fact that Overdo, who generally sets himself against royal authority, nevertheless travels the fair lecturing in the person of Mad Arthur O'Bradley against the evils of tobacco much as James himself had in his *Covnter-blast to tobacco* (London, 1604). A partial way out of this enigma can be found in the fact that James's own position toward the foul weed had altered since the writing of the tract. In 1612, importation and distribution of tobacco had been declared a royal monopoly.[68] In railing against tobacco, Overdo usurps royal rhetoric and directs it against a source of revenue for the king. At the same time, however, the judge stands to profit handsomely from another royal device for raising revenue,—one James claimed to be willing to abolish if alternate sources of money could be found—the infamous Court of Wards. Overdo abuses his wardship over Grace Welborn by plotting to marry her off to Cokes and thus keep her money under his control.

And yet this explanation doesn't quite explain. At the very least, Jonson's device exposes the inconsistency of James I along with the avarice of Overdo. If tobacco was indeed as harmful as the king had claimed, his proposed monopoly was hard to justify. Adam Overdo, who wanders the fair disguised in a madman's version of the rhetoric of the king, is a distorted shadow of James, an echo, perhaps, of James's own misrule, subtly instilling an awareness of the monarch's kindred weakness insofar as he can be considered a mere mortal. Jonson does not abstain from such double-edged maneuvers even in a play designed to bring "true delight" to the king.

If James did see himself in Jonson's portrayal of Overdo, however, that recognition would help to mitigate the force of the resemblance, for

Overdo has no such self-awareness. As we would expect of one so narcissistically bounded by his own interest, Overdo is as bad a reader of his Latin texts and as ignorant of their deeper import as Zeal-of-the-Land Busy is of the Bible. Overdo's chosen model Junius Brutus was in fact no paragon, but a bad judge, noted like Overdo himself for inflexibility in office. Several of the classical texts which Overdo tosses off with easy familiarity bounce back on him. His fond reference to "my Quintus Horace" and the "Epidaurian serpent" (*Fair*, 61) comes from a passage in which Horace offers a Roman version of the *tu quoque,* satirizing men for remaining blind to their own faults while they spy out the failings of others.[69]

Overdo is as bad a reader of reality as he is of literature. Like Busy, he is so enraptured by his *idées fixes* that he cannot evaluate the plainest evidence set before him—a fatal shortcoming for a judge. He takes cutpurses for innocents, "an honest zealous pursuivant for a seminary, and a proper young Bachelor of Music for a bawd" (*Fair*, 62). The lunatic Trouble-all he judges, at least initially, to be a "sober and discrete person," no doubt because Trouble-all displays due respect for Overdo's exalted office. What Cokes is to Busy, Trouble-all is to Overdo—he represents human nature as it would have to be in order for the justice's ideology to function as he wishes. Through the plight of the madman, Jonson invites his audience to recognize the twisting of human nature which can result from overvaluing judicial authority. Trouble-all, who has been ousted by Overdo from the Court of Pie-powders, takes the judge at his own high estimation. He is a god and Trouble-all his "ragged prophet"; he is the comfort of those who fear, and his warrant is the "warrant of warrants"; his guiding purpose is to "quit us all, multiply us all" (*Fair,* 130). Nothing can be done without his formal authorization, not even the giving of a blow. Trouble-all's fanatical language rings like a mad descant upon the arguments of contemporary justices in defense of the common law, justices who saw themselves as protecting that ancient institution and the liberties it sanctioned against royal encroachment. But the sad case of Trouble-all demonstrates that the law can enslave just as surely as it can liberate. His exaggerated reverence for the law has not freed him or preserved him against mistreatment by those in "high places"—quite the contrary, he has utterly lost his reason and become the tool of a justice not worthy of the name.

As Zeal-of-the-Land Busy is the chief idolator of the fair, so Overdo is its chief "enormity." The one thing he cannot tolerate is to appear foolish. It is for him to castigate the follies of others. At the beginning of the day, he dons a cloak of folly to hide his sober endeavors for the good of the commonwealth. But the fair has an uncanny way of turning him into what his disguise proclaims him to be. He is beaten as a thief, kicked about as a halfwit, mistaken by his own wife for a "lewd and pernicious enormity," and finally and most humiliating of all, exposed in front of everyone as a cuckold and a simpleton at the very moment when he has come forth in glory to discover the vices of the fair. Even his language betrays him. He orders, in the highflown Ciceronian rhetoric character- istic of the courts of common law, "Now to my enormities: look upon me, o London! and see me, o Smithfield! the example of justice and mirror of magistrates, the true top of formality and scourge of enormity" (*Fair,* 184). But his words turn against him "like swords"—the enormi- ties he has exposed are in fact "his" enormities. In asking his audience to look upon him, he unwittingly invites them to discover the chief enormity of the fair, which Quarlous proceeds to do, methodically reducing to rubble his case against the fair people and setting to rights his tangled misapplications of justice. The justice has known himself least of anyone at the fair. By the end of the play, Overdo's disguise is revealed as his identity. He has been mere flesh and blood after all, "a certain middling thing between a fool and a madman" (*Fair,* 69).

Both Busy and Overdo depend heavily on Old Testament texts to support their veneration for law. Each has managed to confuse himself with some manifestation of the God of Judgment. Busy swoops upon the idols of the fair with the wrath of Jehovah thundering against the false gods of the Israelites. Overdo conceals himself in the cloud of his disguise like the God of Exodus appearing in a pillar of cloud to guide the Chosen People out of bondage, or like the God of Revelation, who comes in a cloud to judge the quick and the dead.[70] Jonson's contempo- raries were making similar claims as part of their case against the drama. According to one tract, "Magistrates are sent of God, I. *Pet.* 2. 14. for the punishment of euill doers, and for the praise of them that do well. And as the Ministry is, so is the Magistracy the ordinance of God; to which he hath added the good lawes for instruction & the sword for correction. But hath God instituted any such authority and liberty to Players?" The answer, of course, is no.[71] But a defender of the drama might have answered, "Yes, no less an authority than the King of England himself."

The moment of Adam's silencing is a pivotal point in the play in that it forces us, along with frail Adam, to reevaluate the fair from a new perspective. Smithfield swirls with madness and disorder, but it is a madness that cures the mad. By bringing lost souls back to reason, the fair in fact recapitulates a specialty of its namesake St. Bartholomew, who was noted above all as a healer of the mad. At the moment of Adam's humiliation, the judges' Old Testament veneration for law is suddenly placed within a Christian context, and the burning question of what the law requires loses some of its urgency. For in a Christian universe there can be no such thing as supremacy of law. The ideology of the fair's lawgivers is pre-Christian: under the law of Jehovah, which they have appropriated to themselves, they themselves would be lost. Their time amidst the hurly-burly of Smithfield teaches them that the law is not absolute but limited, and that they themselves fall within its limits. Beyond the law, they have seen only immorality and license, but there is also Christian liberty—a positive freedom from law without which every Adam would stand condemned.

At the climax of *Bartholomew Fair,* fanaticism for law gives way to charity and Christian liberty, and the lawgivers rejoin the common run of men. Overdo abandons his self-serving hunt for abuses and freely invites all present to dinner, where the divisive "memory of enormity" will be drowned "in his bigg'st bowl" according to old holiday custom. In general, Jonson's play reinforces the king's appeals for charity and unanimity, appeals of the sort James had made before the Addled Parliament in 1614 when he called upon them to give up their proud wrangling over law and precedence and become a Parliament of love. The theme of justice and mercy was a favorite with the king. He used it often himself and seems to have liked to see it reflected in works presented at court.[72] But he would have found something else reflected in the play. By the end of it, if not considerably earlier, Jonson's contemporary audience would have recognized, perhaps with a bit of a jolt, that its humbling of judges recapitulates a major liturgical theme from the feast of St. Bartholomew.

The liturgy for the feast day of St. Bartholomew is built upon the theme of the limitation of law. The gospel for the day is Luke 22:24–30, Christ's words to the apostles:

> Now there was a strife among them, which of them should seeme to be the greatest. And he sayd unto them, The Kings of the Nations, reigne ouer them, and they that haue authority vpon them, are called gracious Lords: but yee shall not so bee. But hee that is greatest among you, shall be as the yonger, and he that is chiefe, shall be as he that doth minister. For whether is greater, hee that sitteth at meate, or he that serueth? Is it not he that sitteth at meate? but I am among you as one that ministereth. Yee are they which haue bidden with me in my temptations. And I appoint vnto you a kingdome, as my Father hath appointed vnto me, that yee may eate and drinke at my table in my kingdome, and sit on seates iudging the twelue tribes of Israel.[73]

The action of Jonson's play reacquaints Busy and Overdo with Christ's lesson of humility. The judges have striven for greatness and "high place" in the kingdom, forgetting that the king of the nation reigns over them and that their highest role can be but to minister. The kingdom over which they may sit in glory as judges is not the kingdom of this world. By inviting everyone to dinner in a spirit of contrition, Adam demonstates that he has learned to be as one that doth minister—his hospitality toward the fairgoers, however inappropriate the parallel may appear at some levels, becomes an imitation of Christ.

Other texts from the feast of St. Bartholomew are also about the humiliation of lawgivers: the first lesson proper for matins urges wiser judgment upon the foolish elders; the second recounts the conversion of St. Paul from Acts 22. Like Overdo and Busy, St. Paul had been a man "taught according to the perfect manner of the law of the fathers" and "zealous toward God" before his conversion (King James Version, Acts 22:3); he had persecuted multitudes and presided over the stoning of St. Stephen before he "saw the light" and repented. Adam Overdo even after his "conversion" is, of course, no St. Paul. Nor is Zeal-of-the-Land Busy,—Jonson's echoes from the festival lessons do not require us to identify the lawgivers of the fair with their New Testament prototypes but reenforce our sense of the distance separating them from these potential models. The poet does not insist too strongly on the liturgical echoes, but they are unmistakably there, adding weight and authority to the silencing and conversion of the lawgivers. If we have seen the shadow of James I in the person of Adam Overdo, at the moment of Adam's conversion the shadow dissipates as we are brought into contact with a godlike presence that overarches the frailty of the fair. The awesome power of Church and crown looms over Smithfield, operating almost imperceptibly but to powerful effect, reclaiming the "church robbers" and the "thieves of prerogative" from their blindness, healing the wounds they have caused, forging the "unity of brethren" and "love of neighbors" called for in the St. Bartholomew liturgy—and also, significantly, in the liturgy for All Saints' Day, when the play was performed at court—out of the carping litigiousness of the fair.

Bartholomew Fair has suffered from a vacuum of authority: its judges lack judgment and its reformers fail to reform. Since Londoners cannot manage to curb the vices of their own fair, they are disqualified as censurers of its equivalent, the theater. By demonstrating that the major contemporary arguments against the drama apply equally to the fair, Jonson dilutes their force against either. The ultimate power to criticize, license, and order the drama, and by extension the fair as well, is left to the King of England.

Having unmasked the would-be "authorities" over English plays and pastimes during the five acts of *Bartholomew Fair,* in his Epilogue to James I, Jonson gracefully restores final authority over such observances back to the king:

> Your Majesty hath seen the play, and you
>   Can best allow it from your ear and view.
> You know the scope of writers, and what store
>   Of leave is given them, if they take not more,
> And turn it into licence. You can tell
>   If we have used that leave you gave us well;
> Or whether we to rage or licence break,
>   Or be profane, or make profane men speak.
> This is your power to judge, great sir, and not
>   The envy of a few. Which if we have got,
> We value less what their dislike can bring,
>   If it so happy be, t'have pleased the King.
>
> *(Fair,* 187)

For this particular performance at court, as always, James had the best seat in the house—perfectly centered and above the rest—so that in a very literal sense he was best qualified to judge the play's merit because he could see and hear it most distinctly.[74] But the king's privileged position in this particular audience was symbolic of the general position he asserted in relation to the arts: he is the only man in England who is not merely a man, who is able to see from a more than human perspective, and who is therefore not bound by the *tu quoque* which the play has imposed on everyone else. The Epilogue is steeped in language from the debate over monopolies. The king, not the magistrates and constables of London, is the one who has defined the "scope of writers" and players, first through his royal patents which granted them leave to perform and defined the limits within which they were allowed to do so; and secondly through the censorship of his servant the Master of Revels, who was charged with the task of discriminating between acceptable liberty and "licence" in the play's handling of contemporary issues and personalities, and who was also charged with the task of determining whether a given play was "profane" or made "profane men speak," in which case, of course, it was not to be allowed. *Bartholomew Fair* itself—full of "rage," "licence," perhaps even blasphemy, depending on one's individual judgment, and yet licensed by the king—is a deliberate test case which swells out toward the limits of the permissible in order to create a new clarity about how those limits are defined.

Jonson's Epilogue appears after the end of the text on the last page—in precisely the spot where the Master of Revels would ordinarily stamp his license permitting the work to be acted. In praying "leave" and "licence" for the performance of *Bartholomew Fair,* therefore, Jonson offers his own submission as poet to the royal monopoly, and to the king as judge—judge of this particular evening's entertainment and of plays and pastimes generally, but also, by implication, the final judge of the larger issues of law addressed in his play, despite the "envy of a few" about London and the counties who would arrogate such power to themselves. The royal "licence" is great, but so, it goes without saying at this point in the discussion, is the royal responsibility. Jonson's handsome compliment is also a challenge to personal and political reform.

As performed at the Hope Theater, *Bartholomew Fair* did not include the Prologue and Epilogue to the king. But Jonson's Induction stirs up some of the same issues surrounding law and contract for the benefit of the audience at the Hope by offering them a mock contract to which they signal their assent by having purchased their tickets and applauding the Scrivener's speech. This contract, with its quasi-legal talk of covenant, freewill, and license, sounds like a garbled version of contemporary theories of contract and patent law propounded by Sir Edward Coke and other experts in common law. By granting his audience "licence" to judge his play, the author, like James I according to the advocates of common law, has "departed with his right" to override the judgment of those to whom he has granted the license. Jonson's quips about the "bench" where his critics sit in judgment calls to mind the King's Bench, from which Coke and his associates delivered their verdicts against James's attempts to override laws and contracts.[75]

Jonson's contract, however, is a suspiciously absolutist document: it sets strict limits upon the audience's freedom to judge. First of all, they can censure only to the extent to which they have been put out of pocket in order to support the performance at the Hope. No one who has paid a mere sixpence for his ticket dare censure a "crown's worth." Jonson is being quite sly here: if individuals are allowed to judge plays according to the level of their financial backing, then the crown's license will override all others since James was far and away the most lavish supporter of the drama. It was widely believed about London that he himself had paid for the sumptuous rebuilding of the Globe earlier in 1614 in addition to his usual support for theatrical performances at court.[76]

Secondly, Jonson's audience is licensed to judge only insofar as they "remain in the places their money or friends have put them in" and keep their verdicts free of unsettledness, inconsistency, ambition, or outside influence, especially from their fellows on the bench (*Fair,* 30–31). The terms of the contract suggest that money and friends are the usual road to judicial office and thereby challenge the disinterestedness of those who sit on benches higher than those at the Hope Theater. Jonson's restrictions upon the contract curb the powers of his judiciary just as James I sought to curb the judiciary of England and for the same basic reasons. Both poet and king have serious doubts about the settledness and impartiality of their judges and reserve the right to override judicial authority if it exceeds its proper jurisdiction.

Jonson's monarchy over his own play is, of course, drastically limited, not absolute. As its author he has submitted to licensing by James I and must defer to royal judgment; unlike a monarch, Jonson lacks any power for enforcing his own views on his "populace." His contract with his audience is a comically desperate attempt to contain reactions which he knows are beyond his control. Furthermore, as performed at the Hope, the play lacked the Epilogue bounding its "licence" within the judgment of the king. But there was still the hope—a faint hope—that the play would work on its audience according to the standard conservative theory. If Adam Overdos among the playgoers violated the terms of Jonson's contract, they might nevertheless pick up the liturgical echoes that called for a humbling of judgment; they might soften their scorn against its author's considerable "licence" and refer their verdicts to a power beyond mere flesh and blood.

Jonson's "Apology" for *Bartholomew Fair* has, alas, been lost. But whether as a result of the play's own argument or of its author's subsequent defense, at least some contemporaries understood Jonson's work as both a vindication of the royal monopoly and a tart invitation to further artistic reform. Indeed, Jonson's play may have had considerably more impact than prose tracts or satiric characters which struck some of the same blows for "authority." The modern editor of Heywood's *Apology for Actors* and I[ohn] G[reen]'s *A Refutation of the Apology for Actors* (1615) notes that Green's tract, an attack on the royal monopoly which argues that overseeing plays should be the task of local ministers and magistrates, was entered in the Stationers Register two years after Heywood's defense of the king, but only three months after the appearance of Jonson's play. That suggests that Green's reply may have been hastened or even precipitated by Jonson's defense of the king.[77] Both pro- and antitheatrical tracts regularly alluded to *Bartholomew Fair,* especially by alluding to Zeal-of-the-Land Busy. In *Jonsonus Virbius* (1638), Henry Ramsay, one of the contributing authors, used a sophisticated interpretation of the play—even an imitation of its *tu quoque*—as the basis for a much more general defense of Jonson against his enemies, who apparently had thrown Jonson's *tu quoque* back at him and accused him of the very blindness toward his own faults that he had satirized in the play. Ramsay mockingly asks for proof, "What are his faul[t]s (*O Envy!*)," and attributes to Jonson's detractors the same unacknowledged sedition that Jonson had uncovered in the play:

> That He expos'd you, *Zelots,* to make knowne
> Your *Prophanation,* and not *his owne?*
> That *One* of such a *fervent Nose,* should be
> Pos'd by a *Puppet* in DIVINITIE?
> Fame write 'em on *his Tombe,* and let *him* have
> Their *Accusations* for an *Epitaph:*
> Nor thinke it strange if such thy *scoenes* defie,
> That erect *Scaffolds* 'gainst *Authoritie.*
> Who now will *plot* to *cozen Vice,* and tell
> The *Tricke* and *Policie* of doing well?
> Others may please the *Stage, His* sacred *Fire*
> Wise men did rather *worship* then *admire:*
> His *lines* did relish *mirth,* but so severe;
> That as *they tickled, they* did *wound* the *Eare.*
> Well then, such *Vertue* cannot die, though *Stones*
> Loaded with *Epitaphs* doe presse *his Bones:*
> *Hee* lives to *mee;* spite of this *Martyrdome:*
> BEN, is the selfe same POET in the *Tombe.*
>   You that can *Aldermen* new *Wits* create,
>   Know, JONSONS *Sceleton* is *Laureate.*[78]

It is particularly interesting that Ramsay perceived *Bartholomew Fair* as both defending "authority" and tickling and wounding the wise. He seems to have understood Jonson's work as challenging its readers or viewers in proportion to their capacity to comprehend it. The play, like the festival it portrays, demands a sophisticated tolerance for paradox: the ability to acquiesce in the "licence" and "liberty" of holiday while at the same time exercising one's judgment with unusual speed and acuteness, searching the mirror of the fair for contemporary abuses and their remedies, but also for reflections of oneself.

III

The Court Restored to the Country:
The Vision of Delight, Christmas His Masque, and
The Devil Is an Ass

The Fenchurch Arch for James I's coronation pageant displayed the monarch "incarnate" in London. Atop the arch was a magnificent panorama of the City, at the bottom, a representation of the River Thames, and in between, an allegorical depiction of British Monarchy with the Genius of the City beneath, set off against City buildings and flanked by spectators gazing in wonder at the image of kingship in their midst. A frieze over the gate proclaimed, *Par Domvs Haec Coelo, Sed Minor est Domino,* echoing Martial and implying, according to Ben Jonson, "that though this citie (for the state, and magnificence) might (by *Hyperbole*) be said to touch the starres, and reach vp to heauen, yet was it farre inferior to the master thereof, who was his Maiestie; and in that respect vnworthy to receiue him."[1] The pyramid below the cityscape figured forth the authority that supported it, the king being physically present in London that day, but also immanent in London, the *camera regis,* like a soul within a body, so that the city's splendor was a mere outward expression of his power and magnificence. The pageant hailed James I as a second Caesar who had conquered the city anew and transformed it through his indwelling power. When he approached the Fenchurch Arch, a veil covering its middle portion opened to display the royal essence of London—the British Monarchy—beneath the facade of city buildings. The pageant portrayed London as submissive, subordinate to the indwelling principle of monarchy, yet an inexhaustible source and showcase for the wealth and magnificence of the king.

Londoners seem to have regarded the extravagant rhetoric of the coronation pageant as a ceremonial gesture in honor of that one day, when the king was actually proceeding through their streets. But James and some of his close advisors regarded it instead as an expression of perpetual reality. As we have already noted, James's proprietary behavior often created friction with the City. And how far was James willing to carry his identification of the City's burgeoning commercialism with his own regal glory? As time went on and it became obvious that the City was not willing to be subservient and all-giving, James strove to distance himself from it. But the interdependence between City and crown was too complete to be successfully erased. London was essential to the court's conspicuous consumption, a source of massive loans to the crown, of projects and monopolies—a whole range of fiscal

The Fenchurch Arch from Stephen Harrison, *Arches of Triumph* (1604).
Photograph courtesy of the Henry E. Huntington Library, San Marino, California.

and material "evils" that the king and his advisors relied on desperately yet preferred to disavow.

Throughout his reign, but particularly from 1614 onward, James tried to circumvent the awkward problem of London through policies designed (at least in theory) to reduce her size and influence while restoring strength and population to the countryside. He issued frequent proclamations prohibiting new building in London and ordering gentry and aristocrats back to their country estates. We have little information as to the efficacy of such orders, but we know that some London merchants objected, complaining that a depopulation of wealthy city dwellers would severely damage their trade. That, presumably, was precisely what James intended—a reduction of London wealth and a corresponding enrichment of the countryside. There were also protests from lawyers and judges who argued that the king could not use his proclamations to declare illegal something that had been legal before. Chief Justice Coke called the royal project unconstitutional.[2] Here, however, we will concentrate not on the actual repercussions of the Stuart dream of restoring a vanished agrarianism, but on modes of artistic representation. The year of 1616 was an *annus mirabilis* for Jonson's celebration of the king. During that year, all three of his major dramatic productions grew out of a major policy statement by the king. The celebrated 1616 speech in the Star Chamber first chastised the common law judges (again) as a prelude to stripping Chief Justice Coke of office, then constructed a vivid analysis of the wider ills besetting the nation, and called upon the upper classes to return to their proper place in the country. C. H. Herford and Percy and Evelyn Simpson have placed *The Vision of Delight* among Jonson's most successful masques because it avoids "the disintegrating attractions of comedy, personal satire, and topical allusion" (*Jonson*, 1:71). On the contrary, it and its companion piece, *Christmas His Masque*, are as carefully grounded in "present occasions" as anything he ever wrote. That they do not *appear* mired in topicality is a tribute to Jonson's talent for distilling "removed mysteries" out of his "present occasions."

Jonson's two masques for the 1616/17 season could not appear more dissimilar. *Christmas His Masque*, despite its title, has not usually been considered a masque at all. But the two works display two sides of the same royal policy. In *The Vision of Delight* the court is restored to the country; in *Christmas His Masque* the City is humbled and urged to return to its neglected "public mirth." Jonson's play for 1616, *The Devil Is an Ass*, is by no means the most artistically felicitous of the three productions, but it is perhaps the most interesting. Jonson argues for the wisdom of the royal program to repastoralize England by offering Squire

Fitzdotterel as a case study in the danger of giving up rural life for London. In *The Devil Is an Ass*, unlike the masques, topical allusions and personal satire are indeed "disintegrating attractions." Yet the play is fascinating as an example of the breakdown of Jonsonian panegyric. It displays the poet at stalemate with himself and royal policy. The work is structured to demonstrate the urgency of saving the upper classes from the money-hungry "devils" of the City, yet implicates James so thoroughly in the vice he ostensibly opposed that the poet's praise is nullified. The play's world of demonic commercialism is like an antimasque run on past its limits, without any saving device akin to the main masque that symbolically reasserts the king's capacity to encompass his own misrule.

* i *

The Vision of Delight was performed twice, on Twelfth Night and on 19 January 1617. The masque opens with *"a street in perspective of fair building discovered"* (*Masques*, 245). Delight appears from *"afar off"* to present the first antimasque, a *"she-monster delivered of six burratines that dance with six pantaloons."* Then Delight calls upon Night to rise and transform the scene. Night, in turn, invokes Fant'sy, creator of dreams and visions. Fant'sy offers two "dreams": the first is an antimasque of *"phantasms"* which Fant'sy somewhat apologetically introduces in a long, rambling, topsy-turvy speech which has mystified commentators; the second is a contrasting vision of Peace descending upon the verdant spring bower of Zephyrus. Wonder and the choir admire this beautiful but apparently ephemeral sight. Then the bower of Zephyrus opens and Fant'sy's vision becomes reality. The masquing courtiers are revealed as "the glories of the spring" and King James is discovered and hailed as the power "whose presence maketh this perpetual spring" (*Masques*, 253). Dances and revelry follow; finally in the epilogue, day approaches and the choir admonishes, "as night to sport, day doth to action call" (*Masques*, 255).

For the Oxford editors, as we have seen, *The Vision of Delight* is among Jonson's happiest and most unified productions. Other perceptive readers, however, have disagreed, finding the antimasques and Fant'sy's long tirade, which comprises no less than one-fourth of the spoken lines of the work, "disintegrating attractions" indeed and difficult to incorporate into the design of the whole. Enid Welsford noted Jonson's unusually strong debt to continental sources in the antimasques and took Jonson's emphasis on burratines, pantaloons, and phantasms as a condescending submission to popular taste for things foreign and grotesque.[3] More recently, Stephen Orgel has argued persuasively against Welsford's theory and defended the antimasques as "beautifully apt and structurally necessary." But even Orgel notes the masque's unusual eclecticism and its "attenuation of structure" by Jonsonian standards (*Masques*, 11, 34–36).

To read *The Vision of Delight* with its "present occasion" clearly in mind, however, is to recognize that it is put together with a great deal of care and economy. Jonson shaped the work, even the curious personages of its antimasques and Fant'sy's topsy-turvy harangue, to echo the very language and imagery of James I's Speech before the Star Chamber on 20 June 1616. In that year *The Workes of the Most High and Mighty Prince, Iames* appeared in folio, a publishing event of such magnitude that it could not possibly go unnoticed by anyone so appreciative of James's learning as Jonson was, particularly since Jonson's own folio *Works* appeared the same year. *The Vision of Delight* is one author's commemoration of the triumph of another. James and his editors obviously regarded his speech before the Star Chamber very highly. Although it was printed separately shortly after it was delivered, it was also included as the final item in the volume of his works after only four other speeches. Jonson designed his masque to give concrete form to the most important policy sections of James's address and thereby paid his chief patron a fine double compliment: the king is exalted as author and as center of creative political energy for the kingdom.

The king's long-awaited speech before the Star Chamber was orchestrated as a display of royal power. He arrived at the court in formal procession, garbed in his official robes and carrying his jeweled sword, preceded by trumpeters and other ceremonial figures. Like a sermon, his speech was based on a biblical text: "GIVE THY IVDGEMENTS TO THE KING, O GOD, AND THY RIGHTEOVSNES TO THE KINGS SONNE." Appropriately, given the place of its delivery, the royal "sermon" was designed to curb his wayward judges. The king charged himself to "imitate GOD and his Christ, in being iust and righteous" and to purge the law of "Incertaintie and Noueltie." Then he commanded the judges of the land to keep justice from overflowing its proper boundaries, particularly in matters concerning "the mysterie of the Kings power." He called upon the rest of his subjects as well to avoid "new Puritanicall straines, that make all things popular" and to respect the "ancient Limits" of English law and custom.[4]

In the last section of his speech, James applied his caveats against innovation and overpresumption to the changing economic and social conditions in London and the countryside. He defied the judicial opposition to his policies by calling for even stricter measures to prevent new building in London: "And for the decrease of new Buildings heere, I would haue the builders restrained, and committed to prison; and if the builders cannot be found, then the workemen to be imprisoned; and not this onely, but likewise the buildings to bee cast downe." In addition, he restated and amplified a 1615 proclamation commanding all gentry and nobility without special business in London to return to their country estates "to maintaine Hospitalitie amongst their neighbours; which was equiuocally taken by some, as that it was meant onely for that Christmas: But my will and meaning was, and here I declare that my meaning was, that it should alwayes continue."[5]

James perceived the population shift to London not as part of a gradual evolution in the composition of British society, but as a disease, a dangerous unbalancing of the ancient, healthy harmony of the whole body politic: "like the Spleene in the body, which in measure as it ouergrowes, the body wastes. For is it possible but the Countrey must diminish if *London* doe so increase, and all sorts of people doe come to *London?*"[6] The city was swelling in corruption and the countryside withering away. James attributed the onset of this disease to the over-weening pride of the upper classes, particularly women, and their craving for suspiciously un-English novelties. He prescribed as its only remedy a return to the old humbler pattern:

> One of the greatest causes of all Gentlemens desire, that haue no calling or errand, to dwell in *London,* is apparently the pride of the women: For if they bee wiues, then their husbands; and if they be maydes, then their fathers must bring them vp to *London;* because the new fashion is to bee had no where but in *London:* and here, if they be vnmarried, they marre their marriages, and if they be married, they loose their reputa-tions, and rob their husbands purses. It is the fashion of *Italy,* especially of *Naples,* (which is one of the richest parts of it) that all the Gentry dwell in the principall Townes, and so the whole countrey is emptie: Euen so now in *England,* all the countrey is gotten into *London;* so as with time, *England* will onley be *London,* and the whole countrey be left waste: For as wee now doe imitate the French fashion, in fashion of Clothes, and Lackeys to follow euery man; So haue wee got vp the Italian fashion, in liuing miserably in our houses, and dwelling all in the Citie: but let vs in Gods Name leaue these idle forreine toyes, and keepe the old fashion of *England:* For it was wont to be the honour and reputation of the English Nobilitie and Gentry, to liue in the countrey, and keepe hospitalitie; for which we were famous aboue all the countreys in the world; which wee may the better doe, hauing a soile abundantly fertile to liue in.
>
> And now out of my owne mouth I declare vnto you, (which being in this place, is equall to a Proclamation, which I intend likewise shortly hereafter to haue publikely proclaimed,) that the Courtiers, Citizens, and Lawyers, and those that belong vnto them, and others as haue Pleas in

Terme time, are onely necessary persons to remaine about this Citie; others must get them into the Countrey; For beside the hauing of the countrey desolate, when the Gentrie dwell thus in *London*, diuers other mischiefes arise vpon it: First, if insurrections should fall out (as was lately seene by the *Leuellers* gathering together) what order can bee taken with it, when the country is vnfurnished of Gentlemen to take order with it? Next, the poore want reliefe for fault of the Gentlemens hospitalitie at home: Thirdly, my seruice is neglected, and the good gouernment of the countrey for lacke of the principall Gentlemens presence, that should performe it: And lastly, the Gentlemen lose their owne thrift, for lacke of their owne presence, in seeing to their owne businesse at home. Therefore as euery fish liues in his owne place, some in the fresh, some in the salt, some in the mud: so let euery one liue in his owne place, some at Court, some in the Citie, some in the Countrey; especially at Festiuall times, as Christmas and Easter, and the rest.[7]

The Vision of Delight follows the king's analysis closely and creates through art the transformation his policies were intended to produce in reality. The masque moves from a corrupt and disordered city environment out to an idealized, revitalized countryside. As Orgel has perceptively noted, *The Vision of Delight* stands at the point of a major shift in the presentation of the pastoral in not only Jonson's but all Stuart court masques. In the early Jacobean masques, "when a pastoral scene appears as part of a sequence, contrasted with cities or palaces, it invariably comes at the beginning and embodies the wildness of nature or the untutored innocence that we pass beyond to clear visions of sophistication and order, usually represented by complex machines and Palladian architecture." After "about a decade," that pattern is reversed: "When pastoral settings appear they come at the end, and embody the ultimate ideal that the masque asserts." Orgel links this shift generally to the "developing movement toward autocracy" and a gradual widening of the sphere over which the ruler claimed control.[8] But given the close correlation in time between James's proclamations ordering the landed classes back out into the country and the new exaltation of pastoral over court and city life in the masque, we can suggest that there may have been more specific reasons for the sudden change in structure. The new idealization of pastoral in the masque precisely parallels the shift in Jacobean policy by which the king enforced a return to the ancient simplicities of the countryside at the expense of urban sophistication.

The Vision of Delight begins in the "here and now" of a daytime city street meant to suggest London. Delight's invitation to revelry runs contrary to the rejuvenating decentralization James planned for England and follows the prevailing upper-class impulse to focus everything on

London and the court. The king complained that "now in *England*, all the countrey is gotten into *London*." Delight calls upon Grace, Love, Harmony, Revel, Sport, and Laughter to do just that—to "turn every sort / O' the pleasures of the spring / To the graces of a court" (*Masques*, 245). Wonder, significantly, remains apart—the pleasures Delight proposes are too commonplace to arouse Wonder to a response. And too inconstant as well, for their ruling principle is the giddy desire for incessant novelty which James's speech castigated in the English upper classes. James compared London to an overgrown spleen; Jonson gives her inhabitants the impulsive changeability associated in the seventeenth century with an overdominance of spleen:

> Let your shows be new, as strange,
> Let them oft and sweetly vary;
> Let them haste so to their change
> As the seers may not tarry.
>
> (*Masques,* 245)

The first antimasque of a huge "she-monster" who gives birth to grotesque Italianate offspring—burratines and pantaloons—brings wittily to life the king's disparaging view of London, a city swollen with corrupt humors. The she-monster suggests as well a caricature of English women puffed with pride who have "got vp the Italian fashion" and given up the traditional "old fashion of *England*." The word *burratine* could refer not only to a grotesque character from the Venetian carnival, but also to one of the "new deuised names, of Stuffes and Colours" (*Jonson*, 10:571), a new-fangled fashion to which female pride had recently given birth.

The city grotesques banished, Delight turns from the everyday world of the streets to a new realm of night and fantasy which suggests the royal court and its revelry. The choir calls upon Fant'sy to create for the masque's audience a "waking dream" of harmony to counteract the monsters of the city streets, but Fant'sy protests, in effect, that novelty and change are still in the ascendant. Jonson's masque is much more explicit than King James's speech in linking these vices to the court. Fant'sy's long satiric tirade, in its pith and earthiness, is an imaginative descant upon the king's own "diagnosis" of ills besetting England. James ordered, "Therefore as euery fish liues in his owne place, some in the fresh, some in the salt, some in the mud: so let euery one liue in his owne place, some at Court, some in the Citie, some in the Countrey." Fant'sy argues, similarly,

> The politic pudding hath still his two ends,
> Though the bellows and bagpipe were nev'r so good friends;

> And who can report what offence it would be
> For the squirrel to see a dog climb a tree?
>
> (*Masques*, 248)

The irrational, free-associative turns in Fant'sy's speech suggest the irrational and restless tastes of England's upper classes and those aspiring to such exalted position. James decried their lust and pride; Fant'sy reduces them to mere plumes and codpieces. As James lamented their imitation of "the French fashion, in fashion of Clothes, and Lackeys" so Fant'sy ridicules the ludicrous significance they attach to French trifles:

> For say the French farthingale and the French hood
> Were here to dispute; must it be understood
> A feather, for a wisp, were a fit moderator?
>
> (*Masques*, 247)

For Fant'sy, as for King James, the feathers and wisps of outlandish taste exemplify in miniature the malaise of the kingdom as a whole. Order and decorum are all of a piece. To abandon them on one level is to create chaos on all levels:

> Open that gap,
> And out skip your fleas, four and twenty at a clap,
> With a chain and a trundle bed following at th'heels,
> And will they not cry then, the world runs a-wheels?
> As for example, a belly and no face
> With the bill of a shoveler may here come in place,
> The haunches of a drum with the feet of a pot
> And the tail of a Kentishman to it—why not?
>
> (*Masques*, 250)

The second antimasque of phantasms is not described in Jonson's text, but presumably the phantasms were just such fragmented and partial creatures as Fant'sy deplores. The drawing supplied by Stephen Orgel and Roy Strong as a possible study for the second antimasque of *The Vision of Delight* shows two inchoate forms, one vaguely Chinese, the other half-bird, half-man (*Inigo*, 1:270). They are the comical yet lamentable result of human art and ingenuity misapplied.

Even Jonson's difficult reference to the dueling of "the crab and the ropemaker" at the end of Fant'sy's harangue gives emblematic form to James's 1616 analysis of what was wrong with England. As Orgel points out, the crab is associated in Alciati's emblems with gluttons, parasites, toadies—like those flocking to Jacobean London in search of bonanza, but even more like the idlers hanging about court. The ropemaker, who appears with the crab in Alciati, "is Ocnus, a mythological figure represented as endlessly weaving a rope which is then devoured by an ass standing nearby. Classical commentators explain that the ass is Ocnus' spendthrift wife, and take the scene as a warning against marrying unfrugal women. But Renaissance writers, observing that the name Ocnus (oknos) means sloth, stressed the vicious aspects of misguided industry. . . . Alciati's sixteenth-century commentator Claude Mignault (or Claudius Minos) even managed to reconcile Ocnus' name with his industriousness by explaining that 'he is slothful, no matter how much he labors, who misplaces his resources and puts them to wholly unnecessary uses' " (*Masques*, 488).

The antimasques give light, form, and motion to James's description of abuses in contemporary London and at court. Considering the king's strong objection to English aping of continental fashions, we can recognize how rhetorically appropriate Jonson's extreme eclecticism in the antimasques is. He borrowed heavily and obviously from foreign masques and spectacles in order to give additional thrust to his satire of foreign things. James scoffed at French and Italian fashions; Jonson's first antimasque is imported directly from France, the second from Italy. As Welsford has pointed out, the first antimasque is an obvious imitation of the first part of the *Ballet de la Foire St-Germain* "in which the midwife brought various groups of dancers out of the huge wooden female figure representing the Fair." This ballet-masquerade was known well enough in England to be imitated again shortly after *The Vision of Delight* in a masque at Gray's Inn. Jonson's second antimasque and certain elements of the masque proper are heavily indebted to the Florentine *Notte d'Amore* (1608). In both works "Night is invoked, Phantasms are summoned to perform grotesque dances, an Hour appears, great wonder is expressed at all the glories of the time" and both pieces end with Aurora dismissing the audience to the next day's work. The Florentine phantasms were monstrous unfinished forms closely akin to those described by Fant'sy. They danced "an extravagant dance imitating various actions; but always starting another movement before they had finished the first."[9]

In addition, the opening street scene for *The Vision of Delight* was copied directly out of two drawings by Sebastiano Serlio: its strongly Italianate architecture was a particularly apt reminder of the Jacobean building craze to which both James and Jonson (in "To Penshurst") objected. London was literally being transformed from Tudor to Italianate since many of the offending new winter residences for the nobility and gentry were being built in the newly fashionable Italianate style.[10] The masque's music, too, demonstrates an unusual dependence on continental forms. It was performed by twelve French musicians, and

Delight's initial invitation to city pleasures was sung *in stilo recitativo*—very probably the first use of the Italian recitative in England.[11] We can speculate that Inigo Jones, assuming with Orgel and Strong that he was the designer for *The Vision of Delight*, may have had some difficulty stomaching the anticontinental bias of the antimasques. But Jonson's intent was not to condemn *all* borrowing. Rather, he sought to impose rationality and order on a situation which had gotten out of hand and to reeducate courtiers and gentry along the lines set out by James about the proper use of art.

Fant'sy occupies a pivotal position in *The Vision of Delight*, first demonstrating through satire the folly of one sort of dream, then, having shown the audience their folly, inspiring them with a vastly superior dream worthy of their emulation. Fant'sy shifts roles in eight beautifully modulated lines that move from the jogging anapests of the frenzied antimasque world to a smooth iambic pentameter appropriate for introducing Peace and the bower of Zephyrus:

> Why, this you will say was fantastical now,
> As the cock and the bull, the whale and the cow;
> But vanish away; I have change to present you,
> And such as I hope will more truly content you.
> Behold the gold-haired Hour descending here,
> That keeps the gate of heaven and turns the year,
> Already with her sight how she doth cheer,
> And makes another face of things appear.
>
> (*Masques*, 250–51)

In the antimasques, the various attributes are at war: art perverts nature, all is frenzied haste, and nothing satisfies. By contrast, as Peace descends on the bower of Zephyrus permanence and change, art and nature are reconciled. The character of Fant'sy in its dual roles is Jonson's tribute to the creative imagination of James I, who was able both to diagnose abuses and to propose noble and harmonious correctives. We need to notice, however, that Fant'sy is implicated in the very vices it castigates. Its long carnivalesque tirade is a sample of the swollen and overheated imaginings it tirades against. The dreamlike phantasms of a court given over to novelty are the inchoate imaginings of Fant'sy itself, who can produce "dreams that have wings, / And dreams that have honey, and dreams that have stings" (*Masques*, 247). Indeed, as we shall observe more closely later on, King James took a keen interest in the very continental fashions he condemned in his Star Chamber speech. James I both produces the disorders of the antimasque and, at the point of the shift in Fant'sy's language, moves on to correct them.

The figure of Peace, the Hour who brings in the New Year's vision of pastoral springtime, alludes to James in his favorite role of peacemaker. The frontispiece of his 1616 *Workes* displays *Pax* and *Religio* in harmony under a crown. *Pax* bears an olive branch in one hand and a cornucopia of fruit and flowers in the other. On the opposite page James is depicted holding an emblem of the world with his motto *Beati pacifici* above his head.[12] As the king brings peace to the world on the emblematic frontispiece to his works, so his creative Fant'sy transcends its own disorder to confer Peace in *The Vision of Delight*. In the masque, as on the frontispiece, Peace is closely tied to fertility. Wonder, silent until the revelation of the bower of Zephyrus, is finally aroused to awed response by the bower's organic fusion of art and nature, which "grow" indistinguishable there, and by the miraculous appearance of spring's "fruitful dew" and flowers in the midst of winter (*Masque*, 251).

The theme of rebirth and reawakening in the midst of winter appears frequently in the court masques for Epiphany and has obvious theological overtones (we will recall the revival of Love in *Love Restored*). Wonder proposes gods from classical mythology who might have worked such a marvel, but Fant'sy promises even greater marvels: the bower opens out to become a larger pastoral landscape which represents all of Britain. Wonder notes verdant fields and trees, flowing meadows, calm seas and smooth rivers, frisking lambs, grazing sheep, caroling birds and, most important of all, the masquers themselves displayed as the "glories" of this spring paradise. The final vision of *The Vision of Delight* is precisely the fertile, healthy countryside which the king proposed to restore in his 1616 speech by limiting the size of London and returning the gentry and nobility to their proper rural spheres of action.

This final and most beautiful stage in the masque's progression from perverse artifice to perfected nature goes beyond praise for the king's creative vision to celebrate his godlike power to make that vision reality. When Wonder asks, "What power is this, what god?" Fant'sy reveals the monarch in his own person among the audience:

> Behold a king
> Whose presence maketh this perpetual spring
> The glories of which spring grow in that bower,
> And are the marks and beauties of his power.
>
> (*Masques*, 253)

King James is England's Favonius, father of the spring—the god who, with God's grace, can work this miraculous epiphany upon the nation. In his 1616 speech James had admonished his subjects not to "take away the mysticall reuerence, that belongs vnto them that sit in the Throne of

God." Jonson's depiction of Fant'sy takes away some of that "reuerence," but then bestows it again by celebrating James and his policies as the channel by which divine blessings are conferred upon the land. The dances of the main masque, in greatest contrast to the overblown and frantic futility of the antimasques, imitate the balanced, orderly motion of nature and of Zephyr (Favonius) and Flora whose union gave birth to the mildness and beauty of spring: "In curious knots and mazes so / The spring at first was taught to go." Through the dances, the pattern of the masque is brought full circle. At its opening, Delight proposed to bring spring to the court but managed only to produce monstrous perversions of nature. The king is able to succeed where mere Delight failed by reversing Delight's proposal: nature is not brought to court, but the court is inscribed within an idealized revitalized nature.

By the time the masque has ended, the courtiers, and presumably the audience as well, have completed their education in the proper uses of art and festivity. What remains, as the masque's epilogue admonishes, is for viewers and participants to carry this lesson back into everyday life, to defer to the mystery of royal power and help translate the masquing vision of a night into a perpetual English reality. Such a translation might involve real sacrifice. In the case of all those who held no place at court and could not justify their presence in London by pleading urgent necessity, it would mean no less than to give up their city ambitions, submit to the king's wise cure for the diseased imbalance of the nation, and "get them into the Countrey."

* ii *

We do not know the precise date during the 1616–17 festivities on which *Christmas His Masque* was performed, very likely Christmas Day itself. Even more than *The Vision of Delight*, *Christmas His Masque* has proved a puzzle to modern readers, partly because there seems so little of it. [13] It is not words which are missing in *Christmas His Masque*: the text is approximately the same length as Jonson's other masques. But *Christmas* seems to be little more than a truncated mummers' play. It lacks Jonson's standard division between masque and antimasque; it lacks the characteristic transforming visions; and most important of all, it lacks the participation of the courtiers or any unifying interaction between masquers and audience through dances.

Why, given its radical departures from Jonson's usual form, did its author even call *Christmas His Masque* a masque? Its manuscript title was *Christmas his show* (Masques, 233). Assuming that Jonson himself was responsible for the changed title, he may have had in mind the connection he had drawn in *The Entertainment at Althrope* between masquing and traditional holiday morris dancing (*Jonson*, 7:129, 10:397n), but his purpose was more complex than merely to draw analogies between rude and refined entertainments. *Christmas His Masque* fails to become a full-blown masque, or even a complete mummers' play, because of the lack of devotion in its hypothetical producers, the citizens of London.

James's 1616 speech before the Star Chamber called, among other things, for the proper celebration of Christmas: the landed classes were to live in the country and "keepe hospitalitie" in the traditional English fashion, "especially at Festiuall times, as Christmas and Easter, and the rest." As *The Vision of Delight* satirizes the overblown humors of the upper classes and educates them in the wisdom of royal policy, so *Christmas His Masque* castigates the London citizens for their stubborn ineducability. The upper classes had failed to keep Christmas in the country, but Londoners, many of them at least, were not keeping Christmas at all. Christmas, along with all other religious holidays, was under strong attack in London by the very "Puritaines and Nouelists" who were chided in James's 1616 speech.

In great country houses, the keeping of a traditional Christmas involved collective feasting and merriment under the reign of Misrule, dancing, dicing, and very likely also mumming and St. George plays performed by local villagers. In London, similarly, the citizens had traditionally paid their holiday respects to the king and royal family in residence by offering gifts and elaborate civic pageantry. In 1377, for example, the Commons of London rode "on mumming" to make "sporte and solemnity to ye yong prince" Richard II. Bringing dice cleverly designed so that the courtiers would always win, the citizens initiated a game of chance. They "set before the prince's mother, the D. of Lancaster, and ye other earles euery one a gould ringe and ye mother and ye lordes wonne them. And then ye prince caused to bring ye wine and they dronk with greate joye, commanding ye minstrels to play and ye trompets began to sound and other instruments to pipe &c. And ye prince and ye lordes dansed on ye one syde, and ye mummers on ye other a great while and then they drank and tooke their leaue and so departed toward London." Similarly in 1401 the men of London "made a gret mummyng to [the king] of XII Aldermen & here sones" at Christmas time.[14] During Tudor times holiday civic pageants became even more elaborate. They were still a very prominent feature of Queen Elizabeth's reign but declined rapidly with the advent of the Stuarts. London pageantry came to center more and more on the Lord Mayor's shows, while court entertainments became more and more isolated from the citizenry. Part of the reason for this decline and separation was that King James disliked civil pageantry intensely and played his role in the festivities with poor grace.[15] But another part of the problem was the growing alienation of London citizens from the crown.

Londoners, already burdened with taxes which went in part to finance such costly, unsound business propositions as the Stuart court masques, resented the expenditure of yet more hard-earned money on obligatory city shows for the king. They often went to rather elaborate lengths to get out of the responsibility. In 1613, for example, James called upon the Lord Mayor to arrange an entertainment in honor of the wedding of the Earl of Somerset. The Lord Mayor sent back apologies that his house was too small. The king countered that he "might command the biggest hall in the towne." Trapped, the mayor and City council grudgingly agreed to hold the required entertainment at the City's expense. Londoners had gotten so far out of hand (at least from the royal perspective) that when a court masque included the presentation of a lavish gift to the king by his courtiers or the common people to demonstrate to foreign emissaries the "loving support" of Englishmen for their king, the gift had to be paid for in advance out of the royal treasury.[16]

Economics, however, was not the only issue. Many Londoners objected to the support demanded by the king on grounds of Puritan principle: pageants, masques, Christmas games, and other holiday festivities were relics of paganism and therefore anathema among reformed Christians. King James's habitual response to this historical argument was the *reductio ad absurdum*. In the 1616 speech before the Star Chamber he quoted a pagan sentence, *A Ioue principium,* in a Christian context and then pointed out with elaborate mock deference to Puritan sensibilities, that "though it was spoken by a Pagan, yet it is good and holy."[17] In *Basilikon Doron,* which had just been republished in his *Works,* he indirectly refuted Puritan arguments against the old festivals by drawing a parallel between fasting, which many Puritans did not object to on principle, and other old customs to which they did object. For the king, as we have seen, Puritan dissent was never a matter of religious scruples but always fundamentally political, a symptom of unacknowledged sedition.[18]

Given James's stated policies, the obstinate refusal of Londoners to keep a proper Christmas was an open defiance of authority. Especially in the 1616–17 Christmas season, when the gentry and nobility were presumably less numerous about town than in previous years, it would be particularly seemly for the citizens to return to their traditional obligations and fête the king and court. This they were not likely to do. Happily however, when a king's subjects failed him, a masque writer could be called in to fill the gap. *Christmas His Masque* purports to be a revival of a traditional English mummer's show performed by lowly

London apprentices and shopkeepers. After numerous interruptions Christmas manages to explain the purpose of his coming to court:

> Now their intent is about to present,
>   With all the appurtenances,
> A right Christmas, as of old it was,
>   To be gathered out of the dances.
>
> (*Masques*, 239)

Christmas and his merry boys and girls are striving to please the king and demonstrate London's obedience by keeping Christmas in the proper traditional fashion. And yet, as several jokes in the masque remind us, these simple, loyal, old-fashioned Londoners are themselves actors hired by the king to play their parts. *Christmas His Masque* is built upon a central irony. Whatever the hired players perform serves to point up the failure of their London counterparts. The masque's demonstration of City loyalty and its protestations of love for the king highlight the absence of such amiable sentiments in the real citizens of London.

At the beginning of the masque, Christmas swaggers in in traditional garb and expansive mood, incredulous that anyone should attempt to keep him out. He is the incarnation of a traditional London Christmas: "Christmas, old Christmas . . . Christmas of London, and Captain Christmas" (*Masques,* 233)—the very type of Christmas which contemporary Londoners with Puritan leanings were in fact keeping out. His jests about the proper time of his arrival relate not to the adoption of the Gregorian calendar, as the Oxford editors have implied, but to an important issue in contemporary controversy. Some seventeenth-century Puritans argued that relatively sober cheer at Christmas might be acceptable, particularly in great houses, so long as the holiday did not fall on the Sabbath, in which case the celebration would have to be moved to another day.[19] Old Captain Christmas ridicules such equivocation: "A good jest, as if I could come more than once a year." His next remarks are also a specific response to Puritan objections: "Why, I am no dangerous person, and so I told my friends o' the guard. I am old Gregory Christmas still, and though I come out of Pope's Head Alley, as good a Protestant as any i' my parish" (*Masques,* 233). As we have seen, contemporary Puritans claimed Christmas celebration was "dangerous" because it descended directly from pagan and popish customs: the very name of Christ-mas included reference to a popish abomination, the mass.[20] Old Gregory Christmas defends himself against such charges by pointing out, as King James and his bishops so often felt obliged to, that the mere fact of his popish origin does not keep him from being a worthy Protestant custom.

Even his mysterious name Gregory, which has stymied recent editors, can, I think, be best explained with reference to contemporary controversy. When pamphleteers and preachers sought to demonstrate the paganism of contemporary English festivals, they turned invariably to the direct testimony of Pope Gregory the Great. His missionaries in England at the time of England's conversion to Christianity wrote that their efforts were being hindered because the English continued to cling to remnants of their old heathen religion. Pope Gregory ordered the missionaries to permit heathen temples and heathen festivals to remain, but reconsecrated to the Christian God.[21] As a result of the noxious policies of Pope Gregory, according to Puritan controversialists, customs derived from *"Roman Saturnalia, and Bacchanalian festivals"* crept into the Church—among them the *"dancing, Masques, Mummeries, Stage-players, and such other Christmas disorders now in use with Christians."* The pagan derivation of such disorders "should cause all pious Christians eternally to abominate them."[22] For King James, however, such an argument was one of the very "Nouelties" his 1616 speech was designed to curb; Christmas was worth keeping precisely because of its ancient status as a good "old fashion of *England*." When Jonson's Christmas claims "I am old Gregory Christmas still," he means he is invariable in his essence—the same ancient set of customs which had existed in England at the time of Pope Gregory. The mere fact of his durability throughout the ages is no proof that he should be neglected and despised in the present, particularly since to "abominate" old Gregory Christmas would be to violate the king's express commands.

Christmas is rather apologetic about the limitations of the entertainment he is about to present. It was originally meant for a guildhall and has been touched up quickly with the help of the Groom of the Revels to make it acceptable for court. Even so, his masque is not quite the usual court production: "another manner of device than your New Year's night" (*Masques*, 234). Appropriately, old Chrstimas's show begins as a faithful reproduction of a traditional folk drama, amalgamating features from the mummers' and sword dance plays. Fish and Friday are banished as they usually are in feast-day entertainments. Christmas prays for the audience, presents the actors along with their places of origin, and specifies the purpose of the show as the leader does in the introduction to the conventional folk plays. His cry for quiet "Mum! Mum!" as the dancers are brought in, the circling of the dancers, the meter and rhyme of their carols—all are conventional.[23] Even the scrambling of actors for last minute props and their occasional bumblings comically reproduce the flurries of discomfiture simple tradesfolk or villagers must often have displayed in the unaccustomed role of performers.

The names of Christmas's dancers, however, are not at all characteristic English mumming names, with the exception of Minced Pie.[24] Rather, Jonson's mummers, the sons and daughters of Christmas, are each one of the customs necessary to make a "right Christmas, as of old it was": Misrule, Carol, Minced Pie (who stands for Christmas feasting), Gambol, Post and Pair (a card game), New Year's Gift, Mumming, Wassail, Offering, and last of all, Baby Cake, a special cake eaten at Epiphany. Each custom is at the same time a London personage who hails from a street punningly suitable to his or her profession. Minced Pie, for example, is a cook's wife out of Scalding Alley, where meat purveyors actually lived; the name of her street suggests the scalding required in the preparation of a good mincemeat pie. Offering is a Christmas custom "that in every great house keepeth," the traditional custom of holiday offerings to the poor in the houses of the nobility and gentry. Appropriately for the one who is to collect the offerings, he is named Little-worth and hails from Penny-rich (Peneritch) Street. Christmas's introduction of the dancers is full of clever and elaborate jokes, many of which are probably unrecoverable. The important point, however, is that the list welds London people, places, and holiday pastimes into an inseparable unity dedicated to Christmas revelry before the king—in much the same way that *The Vision of Delight* had concluded with a vision of organic unity in the countryside. Christmas's witty catalogue suggests that the keeping of Christmas is, or ought to be, just as indigenous and intrinsic to "little London" as the pattern of her streets and the occupations of her population.

Christmas does his best to present a proper old-fashioned show for the king. But through no fault of his own, he fails. In the first place, he cannot find enough customs in all of London to make up the twelve requisite dancers, one for each day of Christmas. His apologies that he has only mustered up ten sons and daughters could perhaps be a joke about some shortage of actors in the company which performed the show, but it also suggests a rather severe dearth of holiday spirit in the City of London. A more serious problem is the inadequacy of Cupid, whose task it is to lead and inspire the Christmas dancers. Cupid is hilariously garbed like a City apprentice *"in a flat cap and a prentice's coat, with wings at his shoulders"* (Masques, 234)—by no means a standard image for that familiar allegorical figure. His dress, though, is entirely appropriate for his specific function in *Christmas His Masque*. This prentice Cupid stands for "the Love o' the city" (Masques, 240), that is, the City's love for the king. The masque's performers have been drawn by Cupid to court, "Drawn here by Love," in order to present their entertainment. Christmas is careful to inform the audience that even when Cupid is not actually leading the dancers he continues to lead them in spirit (*Masques*, 240). Their performance will be an actualization of his influence, a proof of their love for King James. If Cupid fails to inspire them, the whole enterprise will fail as a demonstration of London's devotion.

The crucial moment in the entertainment comes when Cupid is called upon to address the royal audience, to begin an interaction between the king and his City subjects:

> You worthy wights, king, lords and knights,
>   O queen and ladies bright,
> Cupid invites you to the sights
>   He shall present tonight.

> *(Masques, 242)*

The commencement of Cupid's speech suggests that the show has barely begun—there are to be "sights" and perhaps further speeches which will give *Christmas His Masque* a more elaborate form closer to the usual court masque. Even the mummers' and sword dance plays always included the enactment of a combat, death and revival—a folk analogue to the Epiphany theme of revival in the masque.[25] But Cupid stumbles, falters, and forgets his lines: the Love of the City is not strong enough to bring the promised entertainment into existence. Christmas complains, "This it is to have speeches" and his show limps lamely toward a conclusion with nothing but the dances.

Even Cupid, though quite small and timid, might have proved equal to his task of guiding and inspiring the evening's entertainment were it not for the alien, meddling presence of his mother Venus, a *"deaf tire woman"* who intrudes upon the show without the slightest comprehension of its specific purpose or of dramatic art in general. If Cupid represents London's love for the king, timid and faltering in the present yet potentially an inspiration for considerable feats of loyalty, his mother Venus embodies all the perverse London attitudes that work against any strengthening of City love and devotion. Venus is, as critics have noted, a close relative of the meddling wife in *The Knight of the Burning Pestle* whose silly ignorance of the nature of dramatic illusion nearly destroys the play.[26] Venus, however, is a more disruptive figure, comical yet maddening in her pigheaded incomprehension. She is deaf to the caroling of Christmas's children, pushy and ambitious, and willing to ruin the whole show in order to promote her own son's fortunes. Her occupation of "tire woman" is appropriate for one concerned only with showy externals. When she bursts onto the scene, the sons and daughters of Christmas are infected with her own ambitious acquisitiveness; they break rank and start clamoring about newly discovered inadequacies in their costumes and appurtenances. Venus's concern that her son Cupid show himself off to best advantage makes the poor lad so self-conscious that he loses his powers of speech entirely. Worst of all, like the typical citizen, this London Venus is extremely preoccupied with money. She is so far from understanding the masque's purpose as a demonstration of love for the king that she can think only of how much his majesty will pay *her:* "How does his majesty like him, I pray? Will he give him eight pence a day, think you?" (*Masques,* 243). This crass reversal of the masque's intent proves to be its kiss of death. Christmas gives up on Cupid altogether and motions him and his disruptive mother aside. Venus has not only exposed the central fiction of the masque in that the hired actors are revealed as actors; her narrow-minded literalism destroys the masque's functioning even as art, as a symbolic restoration of the love of his majesty's subjects.

The allegory of *Christmas His Masque* is a more pessimistic reworking of several of the themes of Jonson's *Love Restored.* Robin Goodfellow, like old Gregory Christmas, had spoken against "Nouelty" and on behalf of old-fashioned English customs. He had unmasked a false Cupid, the god of money, so that the genuine Cupid Love-in-Court could return from his icy exile. In *Love Restored,* as in *Christmas His Masque,* Cupid had led and inspired the dances: through the harmonious motions of the masquers the restoration of Love-in-Court was made manifest. In *Christmas,* however, love is never quite restored. Venus comes perilously close to defeating the whole endeavor. In *Christmas,* too, perhaps because of Cupid's failure to initiate an interaction between dancers and audience, the presence of the king fails to work the usual miracles of transformation. It would seem that Jonson found Love-in-Court, the love of the courtiers, more responsive to the revivifying powers of the monarch than the Love of the City.

Christmas His Masque closes not with the paeans to royal power usual in the Jonsonian masque, but with old Christmas's advice to the king about how to bring that power to bear on the lost devotion of Londoners. The sons of Christmas have displayed their loyalty through dancing but will practice it through the holiday "exercises of armes" the king's *Basilikon Doron* had called for. Such displays of the martial arts necessary for the kingdom's defense were another traditional custom which had greatly declined among Londoners.[27]

> Nor do you think their legs is all
> The commendation of my sons,
> For at the artillery-garden they shall
> As well (forsooth) use their guns.

> And march as fine as the muses nine
>> Along the streets of London,
> And i'their brave tires to gi' their false fires,
>> Especially Tom my son.
>
> Now if the lanes and the alleys afford
>> Such an ac-ativity as this,
> At Christmas next, if they keep their word,
>> Can the children of Cheapside miss?
>
> (Masques, 243)

If all of London were equally devoted to such sports and "ac-ativity" (*activity* is a word from the mummers' plays referring to mummers' dancing and gymnastics), then by the next holiday season, the sorry condition of London loyalty would improve and the king would find no dearth of entertainment at court by his citizens. But, Christmas suggests, the basic problem is that Londoners are too wealthy and proud. Too many of them, like Ralph the grocer-knight in *The Knight of the Burning Pestle,* act and dress beyond their stations in the silk and gold of the nobility:

> Though, put the case, when they come in place,
>> They should not dance but hop,
> Their very gold lace with their silk would 'em grace,
>> Having so many knights o' the shop!
>
> (Masques, 244)

Christmas's advice to King James is severe beneath its joviality. "Little London" should be reduced back to his own (and the king's) premodern image of it, its overweaning citizens kindly relieved of some of the excess capital which has caused them to outreach their place in the social hierarchy. Rich Londoners are not so overburdened with taxes as they complain, but simply unwilling to spend their "pelf" on the king or indeed on anyone but themselves and their own bellies:

> But were I so wise I might seem to advise
>> So great a potentate as yourself,
> They should, sir, I tell ye, spare't out o' their belly,
>> And this way spend some of their pelf;
>
> Aye, and come to the court for to make you some sport
>> At the least once every year,
> As Christmas hath done with his seventh or eighth son
>> And his couple of daughters dear.
>
> (Masques, 244)

Jonas Barish has suggested that Jonson sometimes built the bourgeoisie into the rhetorical scheme of his masques and prominent London citizens may well have been in attendance for the performance of this particular entertainment.[28] Christmas's advice may have left Pudding Lane Venuses and grocer-knights among the audience uncomfortable in their silks and rather more uncomfortable with the masque's stern call for humility. Taken together, Jonson's 1616–17 masques make a significant statement about England, both in its present malaise and in an idealized state of health. London is brought down and the country revitalized just as King James had called for them to be in his 1616 speech before the Star Chamber.

* iii *

The Devil Is an Ass, Jonson's play for 1616, was performed by the King's Men at Blackfriars in October, November, or December, at most a few months before *Vision of Delight* and *Christmas His Masque.*[29] Although the play has had some recent defenders, it has generally been seen as the first of Jonson's "dotages," a lamentable demonstration of its author's faltering talent for construction and characterization.[30] With its perplexed demons and grandiose schemes for monopoly, it may appear a creation of quite a different order than the holiday masques. Nevertheless, it shares their major themes. Like *The Vision of Delight* but in a more realistic vein, *Devil* shows the wisdom of keeping the gentry safely in the country. Squire Fitzdottrel, who has journeyed to London from his native Norfolk to amass a vast fortune, adopts all the latest fashions and cultivates a modish looseness in his spouse. He is a "fish" (or rather bird) out of "his owne place" who nearly loses both wife and estate in consequence. Like *Christmas His Masque, Devil* puts down the pride of Londoners by revealing the crass motives behind their contempt for old pastimes. Rural customs like the devil play and the antics of Pug are crowded out by the corrosive vices of London, whose citizens pile up vast and illicit fortunes so that they can buy up the countryside and plunder its "fair lands" and "rich Manners" for their profit.[31] The financial world of *The Devil Is an Ass* is like a giant, overblown antimasque depicting the actual mechanisms by which, as James put it in his speech before the Star Chamber, "now in *England,* all the countrey is gotten into *London;* so as with time, *England* will onely be *London,* and the whole countrey be left waste." The play's country folk are diminished by fraud and their own folly while the city folk proliferate and "plant" their offspring in the country (*Jonson,* 6:212). Jonson's play demonstrates the nation's urgent need for the reordering policies announced in 1616 by the king through its portrayal of this unbalancing process at work.

Readers of *The Devil Is an Ass* have frequently been troubled by the incoherence of its central character Squire Fitzdottrel, a man so lacking in steadiness that he can scarcely be said to possess a character at all. But inconsistency and change were meant to be his essence. Like the victims of spleen in James's speech and the frantic, half-formed creatures of *The Vision of Delight*'s second antimasque, Fitzdottrel is forever redefining himself through his impulsive aping of changing London fashion. His very name proclaims his kinship with the fantasies of the masque. Jonson's contemporaries linked the bird with the personality type just as he does. The Fantastic "alters his gait with the times, and has not a motion of his body that (like a dottrel) he does not borrow from somebody else," and the dotterel is a bird "so ridiculously mimical, that he is easily caught, or rather catcheth himself by his over-active imitation. As the fowler stretchetch forth his arms and legs, stalking toward the bird, so the bird extendeth his legs and wings, approaching the fowler till he is surprised in the net."[32] Merecraft and his cohorts repeatedly capture Fitzdottrel in precisely that way—by arousing him to imitate their own exaggerated schemes and thus luring him deeper into their trap.

Jonson's play is kinder to women than James's 1616 speech. While James blamed the "pride of the women" for the gentry's descent upon London, Fitzdottrel's wife is rather the unwilling victim of her husband's search for novelty. Unlike Lady Tailbush and Mrs. Eitherside, monsters of female vanity who are obsessed with the latest foreign fashions and therefore conform to James's hostile view, Mrs. Fitzdottrel resists continental contamination and preserves an ability to see beyond surfaces. She recognizes in Wittipol a grace "beyond the newnesse" and is attracted to him partly for that reason (*Jonson*, 6:193); for her, Fitzdottrel's wild schemes for wealth and novelty are "strange phantasies" and she never quite succumbs to them herself (*Jonson*, 6:198). The Squire scornfully calls her *"Niaise"* because she balks at compromising her honor in the manner of the great houses of France, and the Oxford editors have regretted Jonson's explanatory gloss—*"a young Hawke, tane crying out of the nest"*—as a superfluity that demonstrates the poet's declining powers (*Jonson*, 6:151–52, 178). But he probably included the gloss to emphasize the play's theme of a gentry out of place. Ironically, Mrs. Fitzdottrel can properly be termed a *"Niaise,"* not because she clings to her chastity and other quaint rural virtues, but because she has been snatched from the protection of her country nest and exposed to modern London, where such virtues are difficult to maintain.

Fitzdottrel risks losing his lands, but his wife is his fairest piece of unspoiled rural property. "Wee poore Gentlemen, that want acres, / Must for our needs, turne fooles vp, and plough *Ladies,*" quips Merecraft (*Jonson*, 6:222). Wittipol praises the landscape of Mrs. Fitzdottrel's beauty: its "braue promontory" and "valley" filled with "crisped groues" and bounded by "banks of loue" (Jonson, 6:203); then he moves into the exquisite song,

> *Haue you seene but a bright Lilly grow,*
> *Before rude hands haue touch'd it?*
> *Haue you mark'd but the fall of the Snow,*
> *Before the soyle hath smuch'd it?*
>
> (*Jonson*, 6:204)

Wittipol appears unaware that these wholesome, delicate beauties only exist insofar as they remain undespoiled. In seizing this bountiful "territory" from its rightful owner, he would destroy the very innocence and perfection for which he loves it.

Fitzdottrel's demonic counterpart is Pug, a country spirit perhaps to be identified with the trickster Robin Goodfellow. Pug is as dangerously out of his element in London as his master the Squire is. Unlike Fitzdottrel, Pug quickly sees his peril—only a few hours' exposure to the vices of the city cause him to lament the folly of having abandoned his rural sphere of action. Among the ladies of London he is helpless, tormented by their academies and catechisms of fashion and deprived of even his name, which they have gallicized to De-Vile. "All / My daies in *Hell,* were holy-daies to this!" he laments (*Jonson*, 6:243). Bakhtin has pointed out that devil lore was one of the most persistent of traditional carnival motifs.[33] *The Devil Is an Ass* starts out as an old fashioned devil play dominated by its traditional Vice character, Old Iniquity, and his playful proposals for mischief. He promises Pug an expedition to London where the two of them will dance about the streets encouraging the citizens to drink, dice, and swear. But old vices stand no more chance in the modern City than old virtues do. Their "misrule" is easily quashed and their devil play disintegrates into nothing. W. S. Johnson, among others, has complained about the resulting imbalance in the structure of *The Devil Is an Ass:* "The fanciful motive of the infernal visitant to earth was found to be of too slight texture for Jonson's sternly moral and satirical purpose. In the development of the drama it breaks down completely, and is crowded out by the realistic plot. Thus what promised at first to be the chief, and remains in some respects the happiest motive of the play comes in the final execution to be little better than an inartistic and inharmonious excrescence."[34] But this "crowding out" of the old rural conventions is precisely Jonson's point. Just as the profit mongering of City lawyers and projectors has obliterated London devotion to traditional pastimes, so the realistic London scenes overwhelm the framing device of the old devil play. The resulting lopsidedness in dramatic structure causes considerable uneasiness to readers and viewers of the play by frustrating our desire for closure. Jonson makes deliberate use of this discomfort to suggest the unwholesomeness of a similar disequilibrium in the nation. The play, like England, needs the harmonizing powers of the king to restore a lost balance between city and country.

The theme of London overcrowding also appears in the prologue to the play, where Jonson offers his usual hints as to how his viewers may become understanders. He jokes at some length about the problem of overpopulation. James's vision of a London swollen with proud gentlefolk is represented in microcosm at Blackfriars by a stage so overstocked with grandees that *"this tract / Will ne'er admit our* vice, *because of yours"* (*Jonson,* 6:163). The grandees regard themselves as the day's most interesting performance. Their proud display of plumage before the assembled crowd hinders the appearance of Jonson's Vice character so that here too, new forms of iniquity have crowded out the old. Within the play, Fitzdottrel longs to place himself among the fops at the theater, and he has risked his wife's honor for a new cloak with which to catch the admiring gaze of the multitude. The play he proposes to attend is this very play, *The Devil Is an Ass,* so that his own vanity will contribute to the overcrowding which hinders its performance—a witty condensation of art and London reality which reinforces the poet's message. Fitzdottrel and his fellow fantastics go to the theater not to see, but to be seen—to show the world their magnificence. In demanding that they give up their self-preoccupation at least long enough to watch the play, Jonson guarantees himself a relatively receptive audience. Either they will have tamed their vices sufficiently to be capable of attending to the performance, or the play will not go on.

Fitzdottrel is obsessed with the theater. If he is bent on going, "no feare, no, nor authority, / Scarcely the *Kings* command" can keep him back (*Jonson,* 6:182–83). But Merecraft succeeds where the king himself might fail. Because of the pressures of the projector's schemes, the squire is obliged to give up his plans to attend *The Devil Is an Ass* and is therefore available to become its central character. Poor Fitzdottrel is condemned to learn the lesson of Jonson's play by living its plot and suffering its reverses. By the end of the action, he has at least begun to distrust the seductive fancies of London. The one character who has been who he claimed to be is Pug, the country devil, and he has also had the sense to return to "his owne place." Discovering Pug's genuineness helps the squire see the falsity of the money men who have duped him and unclouds his mind to the extent that he may now pay greater reverence to "authority" and the "*Kings* command" than to the demands of City projectors. The play ends with a bit of unfinished business. Fitzdottrel is still in London, the London of 1616, in defiance of the king's proclamation ordering him and the rest of the idle gentry back to their estates. There is hope now that he may be steady enough to heed the orders of the king, profit by Pug's example, and return to the safety of Norfolk. What the dimwitted Fitzdottrel has learned, anyone can learn, so there is hope, too, that those grandees lucky enough to have watched Jonson's play instead of living it may recognize the folly of remaining in the City where they risk becoming fodder for the ambitions of its citizens, and instead "get them into the Countrey."

We have yet to account for some of the play's major motifs. Even its preoccupation with urban forms of demonism can be understood in terms of its rhetorical *schema,* since conjuring and related arts, however venerable their history, had recently become all the rage about London, yet another newfangled fashion to which the City had given birth and which King James was attempting to suppress. A number of witchcraft trials had become the talk of the town, particularly the case of Mrs. Anne Turner, a shady individual rather like Jonson's Lady Tailbush. Turner had been a fashion advisor and confidante to the notorious Lady Frances Howard, a young woman who, contemporaries remarked, would have been much better off if she had never left her proper place in the countryside for the vice-ridden world of London. Abetted by the conjurer Dr. Forman, Mrs. Turner had attempted to destroy the sexual powers of Lady Howard's despised first husband, the Earl of Essex, through witchcraft and had also conspired in the murder of Sir Thomas Overbury in the Tower. During her public trial in November 1616 various scrolls and magic images were produced as evidence; while these were being examined before Chief Justice Coke, a scaffold crowded with spectators suddenly cracked loudly, causing those in attendance to believe the devil himself had "chosen this method of testifying his displeasure at the disclosure of his secrets." At the end of these sensational proceedings, Chief Justice Coke delivered a celebrated charge to the jury calling the accused the "daughter of Forman, the foreman of the divell," a strumpet, bawd, sorcerer, conjurer, and papist possessed by the seven deadly sins; the jury was to decide whether she was a murderess as well.[35] In sentencing her to death, Coke ordered that she wear yellow starch at her hanging since she had been one of the promoters of that odious fashion. As she stood on the scaffold in her yellow starch, Mrs. Turner confessed that she had indeed been in the hands of the devil, but was now redeemed from him.[36]

The Devil Is an Ass is full of references to the Overbury trials and other recent cases of demonism. Fitzdottrel is attracted to London largely by the fame of its conjurers: "I, they doe, now, name *Bretnor*, as before / They talk'd of *Gresham*, and of Doctor *Fore-man*, / *Francklin*, and *Fiske*, and *Sauory*." Most of these men were implicated in the Overbury affair (*Jonson*, 6:169; 10:225–27). To Fitzdottrel's disappointment, however, despite their "rings, / And virgin parchment, and their dead-mens sculls, / Their rauens wings, their lights, and *pentacles*," none of these noted experts has been able to conjure up the devil for him (*Jonson*, 6:169). During his pretended fit in act 5, Fitzdottrel raves in fragments from the case of Mrs. Turner. His devil is obsessed with the word yellow. "That's Starch!" cries Judge Eitherside, linking yellow starch with demonic possession as Coke had before him: "The *Diuells* Idoll of that colour. / He ratifies it, with clapping of his hands" (*Jonson*, 6:266). Fitzdottrel is therefore "possessed" by the vice of a newfangled London devil.

The Devil Is an Ass alludes also to a move by James I to suppress London conjurers, although editors of the play have not to my knowledge caught the reference. In 1615, as a result of the Overbury trials and their exposure of the black pursuits of the fashionable London conjurers, James "as well to show his Christian zeal as to manifest his detestation of such proceedings," had commanded the Archbishop of Canterbury to "require the Lord Mayor to apprehend such persons, that they might undergo the penalty of the law [the 1604 statute against conjuring which had not until then been rigorously enforced], or at least to certify their names and the names of those who resorted or were suspected of resorting to them to the writer or the Bishop of London, that such punishment might be inflicted upon them as in Ecclesiastical censure should be held fit [since conjuring without license by a bishop was also forbidden by a 1604 canon of the Church]."[37] When Fitzdottrel expresses his disappointment that Merecraft cannot show him the devil, Ingine blames the king's order suppressing conjurers "I thinke he can, Sir / (To tell you true) but, you doe know, of late, / The State hath tane such note of 'hem, and compell'd hem, / To enter such great bonds, they dare not practice" (*Jonson*, 6:185). James's 1615 order curbing London conjurers functioned in tandem with his 1616 proclamation ordering a cessation of new building and the return of the gentry to the countryside. Both acts sought to put down the dangerous new vices of London and lessen its allure for country gentlemen like Fitzdottrel (or aristocrats like

Lord Essex and Lady Frances Howard), who flocked to the City only to hazard their honor and estates.

As G. L. Kittredge pointed out over a half century ago, however, *The Devil Is an Ass* contains a much more significant reference to James I's activities against contemporary traffickers with Satan. The scene of feigned possession in act 5, presided over by the ponderous but mistaken sapience of Sir Paul Eitherside, commemorates a recent triumph of the king. Jonson's text mentions this event: when Merecraft instructs Fitz-dottrel in the art of faking demonic possession, he reassures the squire, "be confident, / 'Tis no hard thing to⟨o⟩ 'out doe the *Deuill* in: / A Boy o' thirteene yeere old made him an *Asse* / But t'other day" (*Jonson*, 6:259). This "Boy o' thirteene" was John Smith, the twelve- or thirteen-year-old heir of a prominent Leicestershire gentry family. His pretended fits had brought about the conviction of nine local women for witchcraft; they were executed 18 July 1616. The women had been tried before two close associates of Chief Justice Coke: Sir Humphrey Winch, Justice of the Common Pleas, and Sergeant Randal (or Ranulph) Crew. A month after the execution of the women, King James visited Leicester during his summer progress. Although he was there for only one day, he questioned young Smith and soon found that the boy was faking, although Smith's fits had utterly convinced the judges. James's timely exposure of the imposture saved the lives of six more women accused by Smith and scheduled for trial in October; the king's cleverness also thoroughly discomfited the two justices whose haste and credulity had brought nine innocents to the gallows.[38]

Ben Jonson may well have heard of the Leicestershire events as early as August, when the king examined Smith. By October, if not sooner, the king's feat was known about London. John Chamberlain reported on 12 October "Justice Winch . . . and Sergeant Crew are somewhat dis-countenanced for hanging certain witches in theyre circuit at Lecester, wheras the King comming that way found out the jugling and imposture of the boy that counterfeyted to be bewitched: yt seemes some yll planet hangs over our Judges heades here as well as in other places, that so many in so short time fall in disgrace."[39] Significantly, the Prologue to *Devil* omits Jonson's usual caveats against identifying his characters with contemporary persons. His portrait of Sir Paul Eitherside resembles the discountenanced Judges Winch and Crew in a number of particulars and was openly calculated to remind his 1616 audience of the king's victory "but t'other day" over the hanging judges in Leicestershire. Both judges were close associates of Lord Chief Justice Coke, whom James I had suspended for insurbordination after his Speech in the Star Chamber. Indeed, had Coke not been suspended from office, he himself rather than

Crew would have presided over the Leicester witchcraft trials, and it was rumored about court that Crew would succeed Coke as Chief Justice.[40] Coke was renowned as a prosecutor of witches. Partly as a result of his influence, there had been a high rate of convictions for witchcraft in the years before 1616. One contemporary asked rhetorically (and approvingly), "Doth not every Assize almost throughout the Land, resound of the arraignment and conviction of notorious Witches?"[41] We might suppose that James I, as the author of *Daemonologie*, would have approved of all this activity. But in fact, he tried to defuse it, not only through his exposure of the Leicester imposture but on numerous other occasions when he uncovered the tricks of false demoniacs. Even those hostile to the king confessed him the *"Promptest Man Living"* when it came to *"Discovering an Imposture."*[42] An "ill planet" did indeed hang over common-law judges during 1616 in the form of royal wrath. James's ready detection of the Leicester imposture was an opportune triumph for the monarch in that it displayed in spectacular fashion the superiority of the "mysterie of the Kings power" over the fallible opinion of judges.

Thus far we have found three topical motifs operating in *The Devil Is an Ass:* the related policies of limiting London growth and reviving old pastimes, and the episode recalling the king's exposure of sham demons in Leicestershire. Kittredge has speculated that Jonson added the possession scene only as a last-minute afterthought, sacrificing the unity of his play in order to compliment the king.[43] But given the close contemporary ties between the witchcraft trials and other struggles over prerogative, we can understand why Jonson chose to cap *The Devil Is an Ass* with the scene of feigned possession. The main body of the play commemorates the king's policies toward limiting London growth by demonstrating how much they are needed—the City devils are bent on making the country "all London" and their pride and acquisitiveness are the moral equivalent of this geographical usurpation. The last act then defuses the judicial opposition to James's policies by suggesting that his opponents in the courts are part of the very blight which James was seeking to eradicate.

Sir Paul Eitherside is allied for his own gain with City devils like Merecraft and Guilthead; his eagerness to pervert the workings of law result in part from this shady partnership. His name Eitherside suggests his opportunism and lack of principle: like Sir Humphrey Winch and many others among the judiciary, he works with both sides in a way which could easily suggest self-interest to a hostile observer.[44] Judge Eitherside speaks in the name of the king, the name to which he owes his pride of office, but exerts his authority solely through almighty conscience. His refrain is "I will discharge my conscience, and doe all / To the *Meridian* of Iustice" (*Jonson*, 6:267). Even before he has seen Fitzdot-trel, he is already bent on a verdict. He instantly accepts Merecraft and Everill's evidence for the prosecution, but refuses even to hear Manly's self-defense. Like a number of contemporary judges and Puritan exor-cists, and like the Sabbatarian London and Middlesex juries about whom the Great Devil warns Pug before sending him to earth (*Jonson*, 6:164–65), Sir Paul views an addiction to games, plays, and poetry—all of them pastimes encouraged by the king—as infallible signs of possession. But above all, it is Fitzdottrel's disrespect for the judiciary itself which proves he is lost to demons: when the squire raves that he will feast the devils within him on a *"Iustice head and braines"* Sir Paul concludes triumphantly, "The *Diuell* loues not Iustice, / There you may see" (*Jonson*, 6:267).

Eitherside's blindness makes him a close cousin of Adam Overdo. His certainty as to the genuineness of Fitzdottrel's "evidence" is based solely on his preconceived and very global notions of what constitutes the demonic. His tastes are narrow in the extreme, and whatever violates them is the work of the devil. Jonson slyly points out the foolish circularity of Eitherside's method by having Fitzdottrel, in the height of his fits, taunt Sir Paul, *"My wife is a whore, I'll kisse her no more: and why? / Ma'st not thou be a Cuckold, as well as I?"* The judge responds, "That is the *Diuell* speakes, and laughes in him," assuming that any such aspersion could only be the work of the Evil One (*Jonson*, 6:264). We, however, know that Fitzdottrel speaks the truth, at least as regards Eitherside. We have heard Mrs. Eitherside sigh in her jaded, fashionable way, "As I am honest, *Taylebush*, I doe thinke / If no body should loue mee, but my poore husband, / I should e'en hang my selfe" (*Jonson*, 6:238).

As a result of Sir Paul's irrational "discharge of conscience," Manly and Wittipol, the only decent men in the diseased London of the play, are very nearly condemned as sorcerers. No wise monarch enters and sets all to rights. Manly and Wittipol are saved only by a timely and symbolically appropriate accident—the partial destruction of *"Iustice Hall"* through the departure of Pug for hell. Sir Paul, like Adam Overdo, proves salvageable. He vows to make honorable amends for his "solemne, serious vanity" (*Jonson*, 6:269). But no one arraigns the City devils. So far as we can tell, Merecraft, Everill, and Ingine are left free at play's end to pick up the broken pieces of their plots and go to work on a fresh set of gullible squires from the country. This omission, along with Squire Fitzdottrel's continuing presence in London, makes the play's conclusion incomplete and unsatisfying—an effect that is surely deliber-ate. By leaving a gap in Authority at the end of the play, Jonson suggests a need for the attentive presence of the king to bring down the commercial devils of London. Sir Paul cannot divine the wickedness of Everill and Merecraft because he has been their creature, retained as their solicitor, and "possessed" by their unbounded hunger for money and power. As royal authority alone was able to redress the errors of the judges of Leicestershire, so the king alone is capable of exorcizing the projectors of London and completing the action of Jonson's play so that genuine justice prevails.

Ben Jonson was by no means the first of his time to use a devil play to examine the conflict between traditional rural ideals and the new spirit of commercialism. In his prologue, he invites his public to compare his play with two earlier works, both of which had been printed in 1612: the anonymous and perennially popular *Merry Devil of Edmonton,* which was frequently performed at court, and Thomas Dekker's less successful *If This Be not a Good Play, the Devil Is in It.* Since both plays had recently been acted and printed, there was a good chance that they would be familiar to Jonson's 1616 audience.[45] He bids his viewers applaud his play, show it *"but the same face you haue done / Your deare delight, the* Diuell *of* Edmunton," but if his play *"doe not like,"* it will be because the *"Diuell is in't,"* a jesting allusion to Dekker. There is a point to this double reference beyond the obvious matter of relative popularity; for the two earlier works had taken opposite views of demonism, the law, and traditional pastimes. In asking his audience to give his play the "same face" as they have *The Merry Devil,* Jonson suggests they prefer that work's positive portrayal of the function of old pastimes over Dekker's play, which is a thinly veiled attack on Jacobean "public mirth." Jonson's play owes much of its subject matter and even some of its language to Dekker's but recasts Dekker's materials in a way that at least partially redeems King James from Dekker's daring indictment. Through his joking reference to *If This Be not a Good Play,* Jonson in effect claims that if his own play *"doe not like,"* the devil Dekker will be *"in't."* Dekker's hostile analysis of James's impact on the nation will have poisoned Jonson's audience against the more favorable treatment of Jacobean policy in *The Devil Is an Ass.*

In *The Merry Devil of Edmonton,* a benevolent conjurer—the sort who might summon up a Pug—uses his talents to further the cause of Merry England. The laws are somewhat neglected, but love, fertility, sport, and feudal hospitality triumph over a crabbed devotion to lucre. The play's action, like the first scene of *The Devil Is an Ass,* is set back in pre-Reformation times. Sir Richard Mounchensey is an old knight who has consumed his estate through generous hospitality. He is opposed by Sir Arthur Clare, a knight of newer stamp whose main interest in life is "foggy gain" and who therefore seeks to break off a match he himself had originally sought between his daughter and Sir Richard's son, on grounds that "the riotous old knight / Hath o'rerun his annual reuenue / In keeping iolly Christmas all the yeere."[46] Meanwhile the two young people have fallen in love. Their match is saved through the antics of some unlikely allies: the innkeeper Blague who serves up fine ales and fellowship and poaches a bit on the side in defiance of "all the Justices of Hertfordshire"; Sir John, a robust priest whose guiding motto is the survivalist creed of "Grasse and hay! we are all mortal; let's liue till we die, and be merry; and theres an end"; [47] and Peter Fabel, a Middlesex magician who can conjure up hoardes of merry devils to dance jigs, teach nuns to play leapfrog, and otherwise interfere with Sir Arthur's ethic of cold sobriety. In the end, as a result of their madcap adventures, Sir Arthur is reconciled to his daughter's match, Sir Richard's hospitable estate is saved from ruin, and all the merrymakers are forgiven their peccadillos against the law.

Dekker's *If This Be not a Good Play, the Devil Is in It* takes the side of law against the devotees of merriment. The play is the last and most explicit of a series of works by Dekker which criticize James for his neglect of English common law.[48] According to its 1612 title page, it was "lately Acted, with great applause, by the Queenes Maiesties Seruants: At the Red Bull." Dekker's dedication to the company intimates that the play was performed more than once, first oppressed by the "blinde pride" of *"Fortune,"* later with success.[49] Evidently Dekker (and perhaps his company as well) felt slighted by the powers that be, for his epistle dedicatory is bitter and defensive in tone, beginning with the complaint, *"Knowledge* and *Reward* dwell far a-sunder. *Greatnes* lay once betweene them. But (in his stead) *Couetousnes* now." His play illustrates the parsimony of *"Greatnes"* toward the deserving, but at a safe distance from England: most of the action is set in Naples, where a new king, Alphonso, has just ascended the throne. The first scene, however, takes place in hell. Charon complains of a decline in his income because the damned nowadays, called by Pluto "Diuells brauer and more subtill then in Hell" (*Dekker,* 126), have found new paths to perdition and no longer require Charon's services as boatman. In order to overcome this dearth and preserve the hospitality of hell—"crowne our bord with Feasts / Of blacke-eyde-soules"—Pluto sends three agents to corrupt the three estates of Naples. Rufman is assigned the job of court devil: his task is to poison the lofty mind of the new king with "tast / Of things most sensuall." Shackle-soule is ordered off to the strictest friary to "sow / Seedes of contention" and ruin the church. Lurchall is given the task of City devil and ordered to seize courtiers' estates and further the rapacious cause of "politicke banck-ruptisme" (*Dekker,* 127).

Already in scene 1, pastimes and abundant hospitality are associated with the denizens of hell. In scene 2, we see how the court devil is able to use pastimes to debase the king. When we first encounter Alphonso, he has just been crowned and is free from corruption or any notion of royal absolutism. His courtiers kneel down "as to God, (all Kings being like to him.)" but Alphonso protests that he will be no king "of Ceremonie" looked on with "superstitious eyes," and admonishes his court, "Pray mocke not mee with such Idolatry, / Kings, Gods are, (I confesse) but Gods of clay. / Brittle as you are, you as good as they" (*Dekker*, 129). To the admiration of most of the court, Alphonso vows to restore the "Golden worlde" by basing his reign on goodness and "loyall hearts," not money. First he announces that the Sabbath will be set aside for God: "Sacred is that and hye; / And who prophanes one houre in that, shall dye" (*Dekker*, 131). Each weekday he reserves for a necessary administrative function. Just as he is about to plan his Saturday, however, Rufman enters disguised as one Bohor, a courtier of Helvetia. King Alphonso asks him how foreign monarchs spend their leisure time so that he can pattern Naples on their example. Bohor replies, "How, but in that, / For which they are borne Kings? (Pleasure:) euery mans ayme" (*Dekker*, 134). Instantly taken with Bohor's vision of kingship, Alphonso sets Saturday aside for pastimes:

> Pleasure (the slaue of Kings) shall then be our slaue,
> Lords let there be a proclamation drawne,
> What man soeuer (strange or natiue borne,)
> Can feast our spleene, and heigthen our delight,
> He shall haue gold and be our fauorite.
> Tilts, turneys, masques, playes, dauncing, drinking deepe
> Tho ere noone all *Naples* lye dead-drunke a sleepe.
>
> (*Dekker*, 135)

Before long, the dissolute among his courtiers have convinced him to play all week long and Alphonso begins to alter his previous notions about the responsibilities of power: "Had I (as first I did begin) gon on, / I like a Schoole-boy should haue worne my crowne, / As if I had borrowed it." He vows, "Ile be a Sea, (boundles.)" and "laugh, tho the whole world mournes," and his courtiers obligingly reflect his burgeoning absolutism: "Thou art a sunne, / And let no base cloudes muffle thee" (*Dekker*, 136). Soon he has thrown out all the good laws on which he had vowed to base his rule, "that booke of statutes, were enacted / In the high Parliament of thy roiall thoughts / Where wisedome was the speaker." He begins to "physicke" the nation with proclamations that plunge the court and nation into an orgy of maygames, shows, and banquets

(*Dekker,* 144–45). But Bohor persuades the king that he should aspire to more refined arts: those who appeal to Alphonso to advance learning, arms, and trade, "the triple wall / That fortifies a Kingdome," are slighted in favor of rare displays of fireworks dispatched directly from hell, "Various delights" that die in an instant so that "fresh may rise," and feasts of "strange Mirth" (*Dekker,* 151).

In the meantime, the other two devils have made serious inroads in church and city, enmeshing King Alphonso in their schemes. As the church crumbles into greed and contention, Alphonso furthers its decline by plundering its resources for his favorites. He collaborates with the city vultures to ruin the nobility by insisting on his share of the profits from their financial manipulations, no matter how demonic in origin. When his subjects protest the illegality of his arbitrary power and pleasures, Alphonso orders the lawbooks burned. Finally, by the last act of the play, his kingdom is close to ruin. As he surveys the wreckage and begins to understand how his oppressive policies and susceptibility to flattery have hardened the hearts of his people, he despairs and plans to take his own life, aided by the promptings of the court devil. But at the last minute, he remembers divine mercy and extricates himself from Bohor's influence. He courageously rededicates himself to his original austere laws and sets out to right the wrongs his policies have brought to the nation. The three devils and the profligacy they have inspired are banished back to hell and the golden age heralded at the beginning of his reign promises to come into being.

It requires no great skill at political lockpicking to discern the striking parallels between Dekker's King of Naples and James I of England as seen by his Puritan and parliamentary adversaries. Like Alphonso, James on first coming to England had been hailed as the bringer of a new golden age and had impressed observers with his sage plans for government, then had quickly gone astray. He had promoted a strict ordinance for keeping the Sabbath holy, then compromised it with his encouragement of public pastimes and Sunday revelry at court. James spent weeks on end "at his sports" to the detriment of administrative business and, like Alphonso, justified lavish expenditure for masques and "strange Mirth" at Whitehall on the grounds that such displays were "mirrors of state" that had to equal the splendor of foreign courts if England were to be respected. Alphonso's view of his prerogative sounds very much like James's, and the symbolism he uses is also quite similar. And like Alphonso, James used royal proclamations to "legislate" his policies toward pastimes and circumvent existing laws. Hostile contemporaries accused James of plundering the church for his favorites just as Alphonso does in the play. James was also accused of encouraging the corrupt monopoly system by taking his share of its profits, as Alphonso does. Even in his contempt for women, James resembled Dekker's King of Naples: as his addiction to revelry increases, Alphonso loses interest in his fiancée; so James was widely perceived as slighting his queen out of frivolous attachment to his male favorites.

Dekker's play ends happily with the regeneration of monarch and nation, but only after the king has recognized the folly of his unlimited thirst for diversions. In portraying pastimes as the inspiration of the devil and the ruin of a kingdom, Dekker comes close to the rhetoric of contemporary Sabbatarians. To dissociate his play from that group and from the suggestion of political rebellion, he constructed a final scene returning his audience to hell, where Guy Fawkes, the would-be assassin of James, and Ravillac, assassin of Henry IV of France, are shown in torment along with other undesireables like a city projector and a "prodigall" who has rioted away his ancestral lands. A lame and crooked Puritan seeks entry into the netherworld, ostensibly to "reform" it, but is denied by Pluto on the grounds that he is dangerous even to the public order of hell. However, this final scene, for all its castigation of rebels and regicides, by no means undoes the argument of the play. *If This Be not a Good Play, the Devil Is in It* is remarkable for the daring outspokeness with which it employs the drama—a royal monopoly and pastime—to condemn the system of monopolies and the king's devotion to pastimes. Indeed Dekker may have exceeded the "license of the players" and incurred displeasure with it. *If This Be not a Good Play* was followed by seven long years during which its author remained silent.[50]

The Devil Is an Ass owes a great deal to the "Rogue" Dekker, as Jonson was to characterize him to William Drummond of Hawthornden (*Jonson*, 1:133): the play's depiction of city financiers who outdo the devil; the names and attributes of several of Jonson's characters; various tidbits of demon lore; and even its song of seduction. Jonson's exquisite lyric ending "O, so white! O, so soft! O, so sweet is shee!" triumphantly recasts the seduction song from Dekker:

> Will you haue a daintie girle? here tis:
> Corrall lippes, teeth of pearle: here tis:
> Cherry cheekes, softest flesh; that's shee;
> Breath like *May*, sweete and fresh; shee shee.
> (*Dekker*, 186)

We can imagine the satisfaction with which Jonson exposed the inferior artistry of his rival through his own lyric. But resemblances between the two plays go deeper than such externals, for many aspects of Dekker's play accord with Jonsonian precept.

Dekker's play was performed and published in 1612, that year of exceptional dearth for the king. The play's criticism of a spendthrift monarch is much like Jonson's analysis in *Love Restored* during the same period and much like Jonson's own distrust for elaborate entertainments and pastimes. In *Love Restored,* which was probably nearly simultaneous with Dekker's play, and in *The Vision of Delight,* we have seen Jonson cleansing the court of just such "spleen," "strange mirth," and evanescent delights as Dekker's work deplores.

But unlike Dekker, Jonson distinguishes among varieties of "mirth." According to Dekker's analysis, all the troubles of the nation stem directly or indirectly from King Alphonso and his addiction to pastimes. His laxity allows these corruptions to enter the kingdom and proliferate almost overnight; his restoration to health and sobriety allows him to banish them just as quickly. Dekker's devils all come from the same hell and have the same goal of sending Naples to perdition. All their proposals are equally injurious to the nation. Maygames, feasting, court masques, contention among clerics, crooked financial deals, and money lending are but diverse and parallel means by which the devils promote their cause. Jonson identifies a different source for the evils troubling the nation. It is not pastimes themselves which are at fault, but excessive and misdirected pastimes. The poet distinguishes between two rival schools of demonism: there are the old-fashioned devils who respect hierarchy and function within a traditional Christian framework, whose carnivalesque pranks are fairly innocuous and often promote good; and there are their rivals, or rather masters, the City devils, an entirely separate breed, self-spawned, who exist outside time-honored conventions, whose universe is amoral and without boundaries, and who rail against the vices of the old-fashioned devils with puritanical zeal but devise their own mercenary recreations. The king's policies are allied with the former and set off against the latter. In *The Devil Is an Ass,* the old vices are not necessarily to be emulated—here as always in his Jacobean works, Jonson treats carnival with ambivalence. But the humble communal society to which they belong is far preferable to the atomized new urban world of individual self-aggrandizement that preys upon older forms. Jonson also reverses Dekker's argument about law. In Dekker's play, the laws are an absolute, an image of ideal national order, and the king's dishonoring of law a symptom of moral decline. But in Jonson the law has become tainted, its workings corrupted by the City devils and in need of the king's higher power to restore it.

The Devil Is an Ass generates a single rhetorical pattern which operates in the three areas of demonism, pastimes, and urban growth: royal power is felt through its absence, through the play's vivid portrayal of the diseased condition of England without it. Jonson's 1616 audience, familiar with the king's most important recent pronouncements and guided by hints in the structure and language of the play, were invited to identify the royal decisions which would redress the artistic imbalances of the work they were viewing and the corresponding social and economic imbalances of the England in which they lived. Dekker's devil *is* in a fourth area of the play, however. When it comes to the subject of monopolies and projects, Jonson breaks his own pattern. *If This Be not a Good Play, the Devil Is in It* implicates the King of Naples in the machinations of City devils; if Jonson had wished to rescue James from a similar entanglement in *The Devil Is an Ass*, we might suppose he would have taken his usual pains to separate such accusations from the king. But he does not. In fact, he takes note of the king's involvement. Merecraft's description of the project for recovering drowned lands spells out the extent of royal participation:

> The thing is for recouery of drown'd land,
> Whereof the *Crowne's* to haue his moiety,
> If it be owner; Else, the *Crowne* and Owners
> To share that moyety: and the recouerers
> T'enioy the tother moyety, for their charge.
>
> (*Jonson*, 6:187–88)

Merecraft is, of course, lying about his actual intentions, but he does describe the usual arrangement by which the king shared in the profits from monopolies and projects.[51] What is more, the king had recently become involved in a project very like that delineated by Merecraft in the play. There had been several attempts in the early seventeenth century to reclaim the fens, the most recent of these a grant to Sir Robert Carr and Thomas Reade recorded in the Docquet 11 August 1614 for sole draining of the king's drowned lands.[52] There were no fewer than three Robert Carrs about court, the favorites of the King, Queen, and Prince Charles respectively; the Sir Robert given the right to drain the king's drowned lands was not the Earl of Somerset, but almost certainly the Sir Robert Carr who was "powerfull" about the prince.[53] Not only does Jonson's play tie royal finances to the amoral manipulations of City money men, but in his specific choice of project he satirizes a scheme actually granted a court favorite by James I.

In theory, James opposed most such proposals. He had gone on record as disallowing all monopolies not justifiable by the advantage they would bring the nation. In 1603 he had withdrawn all the grants still in operation from the reign of Queen Elizabeth, and in 1610 he had issued his *Book of Bounty,* which forbade all suits for royal favor which would impoverish the crown or its subjects and all monopolies except "Proiects of new inuention, so they be not contrary to the Law, nor mischieuous to the State."[54] Royal monopolies like the drama were presumably acceptable on grounds of their utility to the nation. But in practice, James himself was an Eitherside, drawn into a wide variety of schemes by his pressing need for funds. Many projects licensed by the crown were economically useful, but others were simply frivolous, and some were of benefit only to the narrowest of private interests.[55] Simply by tying the City devil Merecraft to the "Crown" in connection with shady schemes which resembled actual contemporary projects, Jonson echoes Dekker and other critics of the king's financial dealings.

Beyond that, Jonson's play subtly points to ways in which James's tolerance for monopolies undermines his most cherished policies. Merecraft's plans for the Office of Dependencies provide a case in point. True to his motto *Beati pacifici*, James had always abhorred contests of honor. In 1614 he had issued a proclamation outlawing duels, and the play takes note of the State's "writing, and their speaking, against *Duells*."[56] Through the Office of Dependencies, however, and with the blessings of the "State," Everill plans to enrich himself from fines exacted against would-be combatants, landed gentlemen and aristocrats in particular, who fail to abide by the Office's arbitration. It is easy to see how this project will become an efficient machine for fleecing the gentry. The king's license will thus contribute to the fattening of Londoners at the expense of the landed classes—a process at odds with his policy of limiting London expansion and restoring the countryside.

We see the same negation more explicitly in the project for drowned lands. On the surface, this scheme looks like a worthy proposal. It will make new land arable and solidify the Fitzdottrel estate. But Merecraft's actual intent is to impoverish the squire, along with the hapless Londoners who have invested in the project, and enrich himself and his cohorts. Merecraft's various propositions are not, of course, genuine proposals but chimeras designed to dupe Fitzdottrel into parting with his money. But if they were genuine, it would scarcely make a difference. As Jonson depicts them, all the grand designs of the City financiers are equally mad and fantastical, a spinning of gold out of nothing, yet another symptom of the splenetic frenzy afflicting the inhabitants of London. And this form of the London disease is not frowned upon but favored by the king through his tolerance for monopolies.

Through this curious deviation from the rhetorical pattern of his play, Jonson probably intended, as usual, to "educate" the king, show him how his policies were being abused and reinforce his theoretical opposition to injurious monopolies against his weakness for them in practice.

In that case, the play would be a challenge to reform, urging James to move against the spreading evil of monopolies with the same zeal he had shown against the pride of London and the arrogance of judges. By withdrawing his tacit support and disentangling his finances from the machinations of City devils, the king would topple their fragile empire of illusion and remove the most seductive allurement which drew the country gentry to London—the promise of easy wealth. By realigning his own policies, the king would also permit the poet to realign the inconsistent rhetoric of his play. Instead of undercutting the work's implied praise of the king, Jonson's treatment of monopolies would then reinforce it by running parallel to it and demonstrating in yet another area of English life how the "mysterie" of royal power could restore lost national equilibrium.

If Jonson's purpose was to counsel the king, however, he aimed his play at rather a small audience, perhaps an audience of one. For a larger public like the grandees at Blackfriars or even for readers of today, Jonson's treatment of the monopoly question fatally undermines the rhetorical pattern of the play. As he so often does in the masques, Jonson plays James off against himself by linking an abuse to the king. But in *The Devil Is an Ass,* alone among the works we have discussed thus far, there is no structural mechanism for a return to order. Although Jonson's play deals with a number of festival motifs, it does not have a festival occasion. Its vice and disorder are not bounded, as they are in *Bartholomew Fair,* for instance, by a holiday framework that contains the potentially subversive energies unleashed by festival topsy-turvydom. All royal panegyric requires a suspension of disbelief. Kings are mortal, even if divinely inspired, and can be expected to be less than infallible in the day-to-day conduct of affairs. When Jonsonian panegyric succeeds, it works not by declaring itself blind to all faults in the monarch but by displaying the king's ideals as noble, harmonious, and self-consistent, strong enough to triumph over the defects and vicissitudes which forever threaten to compromise them. Its thrust is thus to bridge the painful gap between ideals and realities, even the reality of a monarch's fallibility, by displaying royal policy as a vehicle for genuine reform. In *The Devil Is an Ass,* by contrast, royal policy is itself less than harmonious and resists assimilation into a self-consistent whole. The necessary distinction between present malaise and potential order is therefore blurred. Uncomfortable facts flood in and overwhelm the praise. As though by contagion, all Jonson's "present occasions" begin working against the play's ingenious argument *per contra* for obedience to the rebalancing energies of the king.

In the area of demonism, for example, we are shown a situation of faked possession like the one in Leicestershire where James triumphed over the judges, and we are reminded by it of James's shrewdness in uncovering false demons. But if the play allows us complete "license" to weigh royal practice against principle, all the Overbury material becomes problematic, for it reminds us how close the demonism of that affair had come to the king. James himself had forced the Essex divorce upon his unwilling Archbishop, George Abbot, and argued then for the reality of demonic charms. Lady Frances was thus freed to marry the king's favorite Robert Carr, shortly to become the Earl of Somerset, and the stage was set for the Overbury scandal. James had removed Coke as chief prosecutor in the Overbury trials in late 1615, and it was rumored about London that the Chief Justice had come too close to privities of the crown, so that the king could be seen in that sordid affair as a concealer of real devils rather than a revealer of false demoniacs.[57] Sir Thomas Overbury had been a good friend of Jonson's. We cannot but wonder what effect the Overbury murder and its many links with royal favorites had on Jonson's esteem for the king.

The same destructive mechanism can be set into motion in other areas of the play, such as its counterpoising of foreign fashion against the "old fashion of England." *The Devil Is an Ass* supports the king's declarations against newfangledness by demonstrating the degenerative effect of fads from the continent on traditional English morals. But if we are free to set James off against himself, we may be tempted to note the extent to which the king, through his insistence on modeling his court after the splendor of foreign princes, was encouraging the very mania for foreign things which he complained against. As we have seen, *The Vision of Delight* alludes to the king's complicity in the "newfangledness" of French and Italian fashion. But Jonson's satire in the play is directed against the even more excessive fashions of Spain—a variety of foreign corruption the king had neglected to condemn. James was very keen on a Spanish match for Prince Charles in 1616 and negotiations were underway. That is a major reason why Spanish styles were all the rage about court and pro-Spanish factions like the Howards in ascendancy.[58] Jonson's subtext therefore associates James with a stronger dependence on foreign things than most of the groups the monarch inveighed against in defense of the "old fashion of England." And the same damaging associations are covertly stimulated by Jonson's handling of other topical materials in *The Devil Is an Ass*.

Jonson's play in fact "did not like" at the time of its performance, perhaps because there was too much of Dekker's devil in it. The 1631 text of *The Devils Is an Ass,* which we read, is not Jonson's original version. As he remarked to Drummond in 1619, he had been "accused" upon the play: "Πάρεργως is discoursed of the Duke of Drown land. The King desyred him to conceal it" (*Jonson,* 1:144). The most likely reason for "concealing" the side business about drowned land is that it glanced at the royal favorite who had been granted the right to reclaim the king's drowned lands only two years before. Or the king may have objected more generally to Jonson's treatment of monopolies. It may be, on the other hand, as G. E. Bentley has suggested, that the king took Jonson's part against accusers who saw themselves too clearly in the mirror of the play and that James advised the suppression of overexplicit references out of concern for Jonson himself.[59] Since we do not have Jonson's original text, we have no way of judging the extent of his revisions or the degree to which the changes desired by the king may have altered the original structure of his argument.

It seems unlikely, however, that even the intrepid Ben Jonson would have *increased* his emphasis on material damaging to the king or royal favorites as a result of the king's request for revision. We are left with the problem of why Jonson built the play in such a self-consuming fashion, so that the deviations from his praise for James devour the praise itself. *The Devil Is an Ass* can serve as a paradigm for Jonson's difficulties as a court poet, difficulties that came about either because he failed his occasion and did not manage to make the most of his materials or because his occasion failed him, and the royal policies he was attempting to honor were impossible to depict as honorable. Both sorts of failure cloud Jonson's achievement in *The Devil Is an Ass.* He seems to have had more trouble than usual in bringing order out of the welter of contemporary events, and he was dealing with more than usually intractable materials. Rather than viewing the play as a symptom of impending "dotage," however, we can more fruitfully view it as the expression of a Jonsonian stalemate: the moralist fatally and fundamentally at odds with the milieu within which he was required to function as court poet. Jonson's response as a dramatist was to retreat back to the masque. He continued as a fairly prolific masque writer after 1616, but set aside the drama as a vehicle for royal panegyric until 1625. When he did return to the drama in *The Staple of News,* he took several steps back from the realism of *The Devil Is an Ass,* relying heavily in his portrayal of London on allegory and other distancing devices that had served him well in the masques.

As defense of James I, *The Devil Is an Ass* is considerably less effective than the holiday masques for that year. Indeed, Jonson may have hoped that the glowing idealism of *The Vision of Delight* and the biting satire in *Christmas His Masque* would help to mitigate the devastating subtext of the slightly earlier play. But *The Devil Is an Ass* was a noble experiment, fascinating for the way it uses its own defects to cast light upon contradictions in royal policy. In a backhanded way, Jonson's play is therefore praise after all, for it suggests through its maimed art, as some of Jonson's more polished works do through their perfection, that the poet depends for the harmony of his own creation on the higher political artistry of the king.

Pleasure and Virtue Reconciled:
Jonson's Celebration of the *Book of Sports*,
1618 and 1633

In 1618, James I finally declared himself unequivocally on the matter of English sports and pastimes by producing, in his usual manner, a long and fairly colorful public document. The Jonsonian masques and plays we have considered thus far relate to the prehistory of the *Book of Sports*. James had made his support for old holiday customs abundantly clear but had not yet dealt officially with the tricky matter of their containment, the drawing of firm boundaries between acceptable and unacceptable forms of festival. In 1617 and 1618, after negotiating a series of policy dilemmas based on that very question, he finally did set limits by placing the old customs within the context of Anglican worship. The *Book of Sports* "licensed" traditional holiday pastimes to the extent that they could be made to buttress the liturgy of the Anglican Church. Jonson's lost pastoral *The May Lord* was in in all likelihood written to commemorate the royal declaration. It was a highly experimental work in which, as he told Drummond, "contrary to all other pastoralls, he bringeth the Clownes making Mirth and foolish Sports" (*Jonson*, 1:143). But in the commemorative work that has survived from 1617/18, Jonson's masque *Pleasure Reconciled to Virtue,* country jollity is curiously absent, almost completely subsumed under the liturgical. The poet could claim royal "license" for his own artistic choice in that *Pleasure Reconciled to Virtue* reproduces the royal dialectic in ecclesiastical affairs that had led up to the *Book of Sports*. But Jonson constructed this masque, like the earlier *Vision of Delight,* to indict carnival excess at court even as he praised royal mediation in the countryside. As on several previous occasions, his boldness got him into trouble. He recanted his most pointed criticism by rewriting the masque as *For the Honor of Wales.* But this time, perhaps as a result of its author's accumulated frustration,

Jonson's festival art appears to have been permanently chastened by the disapproval from on high. Thereafter he never gave his masques quite the satiric bite he had earlier in reforming royal misrule. As Dale Randall's analysis of *The Gypsies Metamorphosed* has demonstrated, Jonson's later works for James I continued to show the court its failings but with an accommodation of imperfection, a space for tolerance, that some of his earlier masques had not allowed. His artistic motives may have been as morally zealous as ever, but he allowed King James and his favorites more latitude for complacency about the vice they saw mirrored in his masques.[1]

After the publication of the *Book of Sports*, elements from the controversy surrounding the royal document quickly became literary commonplace: there was always at least an implicit political dimension to such seemingly frivolous subject as "Clownes making Mirth and foolish Sports."[2] Here, however, we shall conclude our discussion of Jonson by looking briefly at only a few of his later works, the cluster of plays and entertainments he wrote in 1633 and after to commemorate Charles I's renewal of the *Book of Sports*. In these final productions, Jonson was as experimental as ever, searching for ways to create the same revitalizing festival transformations in the Caroline court as he had for the Jacobean. But Jonson's Caroline works reverse his Jacobean pattern. *Pleasure Reconciled to Virtue* had deemphasized country pastimes and centered on James's defense of the liturgy. But in the entertainments for Charles, the liturgical is scanted in favor of festival jollity. If the Jacobean court had erred on the side of misrule, the court of Charles had set itself at too great distance from it. Jonson was trying to bring carnival back to the court—reinject it with the sort of earthy country realism that Robin Goodfellow had embodied in Jonson's earlier *Love Restored*—and for a similar purpose, to restore the fruitful reciprocity that was, in the poet's view, always lost when the refined arts of the court strayed too far from a larger community.

Jonson's final works offer by far the happiest and least equivocal celebration of holiday mirth of any he ever wrote, but they are no less admonitory for that. What the poet was reacting against was a tendency noted by other contemporaries as well and by modern cultural historians—the increasing insularity of the official culture during the period of Personal Rule, the court's tendency to close itself off through rarefied arts and entertainments, to define itself away from the popular with the danger that it might lose contact with vital elements of the national life.[3] He knew that his attempt to broaden court aesthetics was almost certain to fail, that Caroline refinement would allow small space for the raucous and carnivalesque. But he thought the effort was worth making anyway, perhaps on grounds of principle, perhaps also at the urging of his chief patron during those years, the Earl of Newcastle, who followed the old Jacobean line and continued to argue for the old calendar customs on grounds of their political usefulness in keeping up order and degree. Of course the country "realism" of Jonson's final works was itself an idealization, a deliberately nostalgic portrayal of lost holiday communalism. Charles I showed Jonson some favor in 1633 and 1634 and was clearly willing to tolerate the poet's corrective "medicine" on more than one occasion, if only because Jonson's art reflected his own official stance toward the old holiday customs. But the poet was trapped in the Caroline ambivalence whereby the king tolerated rude pastimes in theory but kept them at distance from himself. Jonson's *The Tale of a Tub* was performed at court on 14 January 1634. As we shall see, the play echoes some of the skirmishes leading up to the republication of the *Book of Sports* in 1633 just as *Pleasure Reconciled to Virtue* had events leading up to the document's publication. Yet having been called for at court, in performance Jonson's comedy was not "liked," and he knew full well it would not be. Whether as a result of the degree of royal approval he did achieve, however, or of his own and his patron's convictions, we find Jonson at the very end of his life attempting again to devise an entertainment that would reinfuse court culture with the popular. In his unfinished *Sad Shepherd*—and it is perhaps a comment on the feasibility of Jonson's Caroline strategy that the work never was finished—he sought once again to break open the enclosure of the court.

* i *

Pleasure Reconciled to Virtue was performed on Epiphany 1618. The previous year at court had been rather bleak, plagued by the usual financial difficulties and overshadowed by the Overbury scandal. James I's most important domestic achievement had been his long progress to Scotland from late March until September 1617. King James undertook this journey for several reasons. When he left Scotland to take the English crown, he had promised to revisit his Scottish subjects, a promise he had not yet kept. Then too, it would appear that James wanted to escape his pressing fiscal problems and avoid French emissaries who were pushing for an explanation of James's apparent preference for Spain. The trip's most important purpose, however, was to further his project for the creation of Great Britain by reconciling the differences that divided England and Scotland. In ecclesiastical affairs, he sought to make the Act of Union a reality by bringing the Scotch Presbyterians into conformity with the Anglican Church. King James hoped through his presence as head of the Church to "warm those cold Countreys with the beams of Majesty" and settle the spirits of the *"factious* Presbytery" in obedience to the episcopal hierarchy.[4]

Before he set off from England, James had dispatched a troop of choristers from the Chapel Royal at Whitehall to conduct services at Holyrood House. The royal chapel at Edinburgh was to become a showcase of Anglicanism: James also sent religious figures, paintings, organs and carved choir stalls, reportedly designed by Inigo Jones, to aid the general effect of Anglican comeliness. Before the king even arrived in Scotland, this "popish" decor had aroused local Presbyterians to mutter *"That Images were to be set up; The Organs were come before, and after comes Mass."* The king expressed anger at such ignorance and sent word that his northern subjects should learn to distinguish *"betwixt Pictures intended for Ornament and Decoration, and Images erected for Worship and Adoration."*[5]

The objections over chapel furnishings, however, proved to be only a prologue. After the royal party arrived in Scotland, accompanied by several high officials of the Anglican Church, there were numerous other clashes. One contemporary's report will provide sufficient illustration. A member of the guard who died in Edinburgh was buried "after the English manner" and the Dean of Paul's called upon the assembly to "recommend with him the soule of theyre deceased brother into the handes of Almighty God," a sentiment which sounded suspiciously like a "popish" prayer for the dead and "was so yll taken that he was driven to retract yt openly and to confesse he did yt in a kind of civilitie." When the body was to be lowered into the grave, exception was taken to William Laud's donning a surplice. At communion, even the Scottish dean of the king's own chapel was so scandalized at the notion of kneeling to receive the sacrament that he refused to kneel beside the king.[6] Joseph Hall, who accompanied James to Scotland and was, almost alone among the ecclesiastical entourage, fairly popular with the Scottish ministers, found his position so uncomfortable that he asked to return home early. James denied his request and later ordered him to atone for his lukewarmness by writing a defense of royal policy toward the Church of Scotland.[7]

When it came to the imposition of Anglican church government upon the Scottish Kirk, King James was hardly more successful than he was with his "model liturgy." He claimed prerogative, "power innate," to reorder the externals of Scottish church policy but was unable to bring the Presbyterians around to his view. A prayerbook corresponding generally to the *Book of Common Prayer* had been adopted in theory but not put into use. While in Scotland, King James pressed the Five Articles of Perth upon the General Assembly. These articles called for the observance of the chief Christian holidays, kneeling at communion, confirmation by bishops, and other standard Anglican practices. The articles encountered severe opposition in the Assembly and, though grudgingly agreed to well after the king's departure, were never put into effect.[8]

The king's visit to his native soil proved to be much less than the triumphal victory for Anglicanism and Anglo-Scottish union that he had hoped for. But his problems with nonconformity did not cease upon his recrossing the Tweed. England, too, had its Puritans and Presbyterians. In Lancashire on his progress back south there was another series of incidents, closely tied to the question of church ceremonies and church holidays, which led to one of the most important domestic policy decisions of the reign, James's promulgation of the *Book of Sports.*

James had advised his son in *Basilikon Doron,* "teach your people by your example: for people are naturally inclined to counterfaite (like apes) their Princes maners."[9] His Scottish journey was designed to teach not only Anglican ceremony but also the observance of traditional holiday sports and traditional country hospitality. Puritan opinion against dancing, mumming, and holiday revelry was making significant inroads in the countryside. Nicholas Bownde's *The True Doctrine of the Sabbath,* in particular, had a very wide impact, partly because it demonstrated contradictions in the king's own policy toward the traditional sports.[10] As we have seen, James had already issued a series of proclamations ordering the nobles and gentry back to their country estates to watch over local conditions and keep hospitality in the traditional "old fashion of *England.*" Shortly after departing for Scotland, he announced this policy yet again.[11] Along the route of his progress northward, he made his court a mirror of "public mirth" by "Feasting, Masking, and Dancing" to encourage answering sports and festivities on the part of his subjects along the way. Courtiers interacted with local country folk. "In some of these Pastimes several Counties excelled, and to entertain community with their Mirth, the Court Progresses, took delight to judge of their wagers, in their journey to *Scotland,* which the people observing, took occasion to themselves to petition the King in his return [from Scotland] for freedome, and leave to be merry."[12]

In Scotland itself, however, as in many areas of England, the old customs had been severely curtailed by law: there was almost no "freedome and leave to be merry." The king encountered precious little hospitality on the part of his own citizens of Edinburgh. The universities put forth verses in praise of his return and William Drummond wrote his "Forth Feasting" in praise of the "Melodie . . . Ioy and Sport" of the king's progress northward—this was the poem Jonson wished he had written himself because it had pleased the king.[13] But the City of

Edinburgh, astonishingly, omitted the civic pageantry which ordinarily would embellish so important an occasion as the return of a long-absent king. Part of the reason for this omission was undoubtedly the city's poverty, but a much more important reason was that the Presbyterians opposed "vain shows" on the same grounds as they opposed the Anglican liturgy. "For Pageantes they hold Idolatrous thinges and not fitt to be used in soo reformed a place."[14]

However, James also had to concede that public sports could get out of hand. When he reached Lancashire on his way back south, he had to contend not only with Puritan suppression of "public mirth" but also an opposite problem—too much hospitality, dancing, and merriment at the expense of Anglican observance. Lancashire was a county noted for recusancy and addiction to traditional pastimes. Four years before the king's visit, a despairing observer had complained that piping "put down preaching . . . . For one person which we have in church . . . every piper (there being many in one parish) should at the same instant have many hundreds on the greens."[15] The local bishop Thomas Morton supported public pastimes in general but considered this behavior part of a popish plot "to keep the people from Church by danceing and other recreations, even in the time of divine service, especially on holy dayes, and the Lords day in the after noon: By which meanes they kept the people in ignorance and Luke warmnesse, and so made them more capable to be wrought upon by their emissaries." In 1616 local Justices of the Peace had attempted to stem all such recreation by issuing a series of orders prohibiting violation of the sabbath; clergy were required to read these orders from the pulpit once a quarter, in defiance of the bishop.[16] Clearly a battle was brewing.

While the king was in Lancashire, the group that favored the sports decided to flout local ordinances and conduct a demonstration to assert their "freedome to be merry." Taking the king's own policies as encouragement, a group of merrymakers piped and danced the morris so rowdily outside a church during Sunday services that Anglican worship was totally disrupted. When informed of this licentious behavior, the king "disavoued any thoughts or intention of encouraging such prophaneness." The piper was "laid by the heeles" as an example to the rest.[17]

By countenancing the piper's punishment, however, the king appeared to ally himself with the Sabbatarians. Local magistrates with Puritan sympathies had worked hard to suppress the sports, and the king seemed to be advocating precisely their position. Some sort of clarifying action obviously had to be taken. With the aid of Bishop Morton and ecclesiastics within his own entourage, James drew up the document which came to be known as the *Book of Sports,* a royal declaration which attempted to impose order and uniformity upon the whole confused subject of country pastimes by defining their proper limits within the Anglican community. The text of this document is worth quoting in some detail because it shows the king in the process of reconciling pleasure with virtue, of establishing the standard of mediation between traditional pastimes and religious duties which Ben Jonson was to celebrate in *Pleasure Reconciled to Virtue.* The declaration was issued locally in Lancashire in 1617 and published nationally on 24 May 1618. I quote from the 1618 version:

> Whereas We did iustly in Our Progresse through Lancashire, rebuke some Puritanes & precise people, and tooke order that the like vnlawfull cariage should not bee vsed by any of them hereafter, in the prohibiting and vnlawfull punishing of Our good people for vsing their lawfull Recreations, and honest exercises vpon Sundayes and other Holy dayes, after the afternoone Sermon or Seruice: Wee now find that two sorts of people wherewith that Countrey is much infested, (Wee meane Papists and Puritanes) haue maliciously traduced and calumniated those Our iust and honourable proceedings. . . . Our County of Lancashire abounded more in Popish Recusants then any Countie of England, and thus hath stil continued . . . . [A recent report of] growing amendment amongst them, made Vs the more sory, when with Our owne Eares Wee heard the generall complaint of Our people, that they were barred from all lawfull Recreation, and exercise vpon the Sundaye afternoone, after the ending of all Diuine Seruice, which cannot but produce two euils: The one, the hindering of the conuersion of many, whom their Priests will take occasion hereby to vexe, perswading them that no honest mirth or recreation is lawfull or tollerable in Our Religion . . . ; The other inconuenience is, that this prohibition barreth the common and meaner sort of people from vsing such exercises as may make their bodies more able for Warre . . . . And in place thereof sets vp filthy tiplings and drunkennesse, and breeds a number of idle and discontented speaches in their Alehouses.

The king ordered bishops to offer religious instruction for the Catholics and to force Puritans to conform to Anglican ritual or leave the county:

> so to strike equally on both hands, against the contemners of Our Authoritie, and aduersaries of Our Church. And as for Our good peoples lawfull Recreation, Our pleasure likewise is, That after the end of Diuine Seruice, Our good people be not disturbed, letted, or discouraged from any lawfull Recreation; Such as dauncing, either men or women, Archerie for men, leaping, vaulting, or any other such harmelesse Recreation, nor from hauing of May-Games, Whitson Ales, and Morrisdances, and the setting vp of Maypoles and other sports therewish vsed, so as the same be

had in due and conuenient time, without impediment or neglect of diuine Seruice.[18]

The *Book of Sports* sought to contain festival by keeping it within the bounds of state religion. Papists who refused to convert were to be barred from participation in all the old pastimes. The "freedom to be merry" was a privilege available only to faithful adherents of the English Church.

James I's *Book of Sports* aroused an immediate furor among Puritans. In Lancashire, where it was commanded to be read in churches in place of the earlier antisport ordinances, several ministers were reported for failing to comply and justifying their action on the grounds of Calvinist principle. The declaration became known among its enemies as the "dancing Book," a Churchmen's *"Maskaradoe"* in the "Dances that these Times were guilty of."[19] King James, with a caution his son Charles I was not to share when the *Book of Sports* was reissued in 1633, did not seek to enforce the declaration nationally but did see to it that some of the offending ministers were called in for questioning.[20] As usual, his chief concern was with the maintenance of order. The old pastimes were not only acceptable in themselves and an important symbol of royal author- ity, they were a crucial means of "keeping up" the Anglican Church.

While the king was in Scotland in 1617, it was remarked about London that Ben Jonson had vowed, no doubt out of zealous emulation of his chief patron but also for his "profit," to retrace James's journey, though Jonson humbly proposed to travel on foot (*Jonson,* 1:76). He did in fact walk to Scotland in the summer of 1618, with the king's approval. But before Jonson set off in imitation of James's stately progress, he wrote a masque commemorating its major policy achieve- ments and depicting emblematically the Lancashire events which had moved the king to formulate the *Book of Sports.* Ben Jonson himself had recently been "reconciled" to Anglicanism. *Pleasure Reconciled to Virtue* is his tribute to the comely *via media* of the Anglican Church and the king's attempts to preserve it against the extremes of Popery and Puritanism.

Pleasure Reconciled to Virtue opens with the mountain Atlas, a hoary old man who suggests the mountainous northern reaches of Scotland and Lancashire from which the king had returned less than four months before the masque was presented. In Lancashire, the king had been forced to conquer two opposite evils which had arisen to plague him, first the licentious, popish prosporters who disrupted Anglican services, then the presumptuous Puritans who had challenged royal authority by railing against all sports. Hercules in the antimasques represents King James in action, first curbing those who carry sport too far, then stifling those who refuse to allow it altogether. Hercules was an appropriate figure for the king on several grounds. As contemporaries were well aware, he was believed to have founded the Olympic Games and was therefore associated with the promotion of state pastimes. Through his labors he was also associated with the dividing of vice from virtue, himself given to excess, according to the Ovidian tradition, but capable of triumphing over it. He was, according to one tract, the "type of a good king, who ought to subdue all monsterrs, cruelty, disorder, and oppression in his kingdom, who should support the heaven of the Church."[21] Like James in Lancashire, Hercules in the masque operates dialectically, defining his own position by setting limits on one, then another extreme.

As the masque opens, Comus, *"god of cheer, of the belly"* (*Masques*, 263), rides onto the scene in triumph amidst his raucous crew. Just as the Lancashire prosport demonstrators drowned out Sunday services with their dancing and rowdiness, so Comus and his followers make a "hymn" and religion of their debauched pleasures, refusing to recognize any higher obligations. Their cry, "Room, room, make room," the traditional opening line of English mummers' plays, was also used by morris dancers about to perform, and suggests the pushy intrusiveness of the Lancashire morris men. Significantly, one of Comus's drunken retinue carries Hercules' bowl and claims to serve him, just as the Lancashire promoters of "public mirth" claimed the king's support for old pastimes as justification for their brawling. As James I reproved this disruptive faction in Lancashire, so Hercules appears on the scene and condemns Comus and his followers with fine scorn:

> What rites are these? Breeds earth more monsters yet?
> Antaeus scarce is cold: what can beget
> This store?—and stay! such contraries upon her?
> Is earth so fruitful of her own dishonor?
> Or 'cause his vice was inhumanity,
> Hopes she by vicious hospitality
> To work an expiation first? and then
> (Help, Virtue!) these are sponges, and not men.
> Bottles? mere vessels? half a tun of paunch?
> How? and the other half thrust forth in haunch?
> Whose feast? the belly's? Comus'? and my cup
> Brought in to fill the drunken orgies up?
> And here abused? that was the crowned reward
> Of thirsty heroës after labor hard?
>
> (*Masques*, 266–67)

The *Book of Sports* allowed the traditional sports only after church on Sunday and only for those who had demonstrated their loyalty to the king by attending the Anglican liturgy. Hercules, similarly, protests that the rites of hospitality and good cheer are deserved only after they have been earned. Comus and his crew have done just what the king's declaration warned against—they have neglected the practice of arms and similar active sports and "in place thereof set vp filthy tiplings and drunkennesse." The first antimasque, appropriately, is a dance *"by men dressed as bottles and a cask"* (*Masques,* 266). Jonson's first antimasque does dwell on gluttony more than would be necessary to suggest the license of the rioting Lancashire Catholics; the poet does that, I think, to make a specific point about the court which will be taken up later in the discussion.

Once Hercules has performed the labor of banishing Comus and his rioters, Atlas undergoes a transformation; Comus's grove of revelry disappears and the *"whole music"* is discovered *"sitting at the foot of the mountain, with Pleasure and Virtue seated above them"* (*Masques,* 267). The Choir invites Hercules to rest. But his task is not yet complete: no sooner is excess banished than dearth and parsimony appear on the hillside. On the level of political allegory, Antaeus and his pygmy "brothers" represent the proud, inhospitable spirit of Puritanism as encountered by King James in Scotland and then in Lancashire. The mythic giant Antaeus refused hospitality and tried to destroy those who came in search of it, just as the proud Scotch Presbyterians scorned to make their own king welcome and attempted even to turn him from his Anglican "errors." At the beginning of the masque, Hercules had just destroyed Antaeus ("Antaeus scarce is cold"), as James had "vanquished" the inhospitable Scots. But after the defeat of Comus, Antaeus' brothers rise up to do battle, just as Lancashire Sabbatarians had. The pygmies correspond closely to Jame's habitual characterization of the Puritans as mean men, a "sect rather then Religion," who acted not out of principle but rebellious self-interest and a desire to topple those in authority.[22] Their size is small, but their rhetoric is lofty and their ambitions are grandiose:

> Antaeus dead! and Hercules yet live!
> Where is this Hercules? What would I give
> To meet him now? Meet him? nay three such other,
> If they had hand in murder of our brother?
> With three? with four? with ten? nay, with as many
> As the name yields? Pray anger there be any
> Whereon to feed my just revenge, and soon:
> How shall I kill him? Hurl him 'gainst the moon,
> And break him in small portions? Give to Greece
> His brain, and every tract of earth a piece?
>
> (*Masques,* 268)

The resemblance between their rhetoric and that of contemporary Puritans is admittedly oblique, perhaps for "reasons of state." If Jonson had made the identification too obvious, he would have touched off dangerous speculation among the foreign diplomats present for the performance of the masque. James may have hated the Puritans at home, but he supported the Huguenots in France. When English Puritans were "openly flowted and abused" in court entertainments, some found it "unseemly and unseasonable, specially as matters stand now with those of the religion in Fraunce." Earlier masques that *had* "abused" the Puritans—like *Christmas* and *Love Restored*—were almost certainly performed without foreign dignitaries present.[23]

Jonson's text does not make clear who actually banishes the pygmies, Hercules himself or the Choir.[24] The poet probably wanted to suggest that the two act in close conjunction and harmony. Merely to notice the pygmies is to destroy them: they are not real adversaries, but dreaming dwarfs who scurry into holes after their first encounter with real power and authority. Once he has vanquished both disordered extremes which have impeded the reconciliation of Pleasure and Virtue, Hercules is rewarded with a crown of poplar and finally allowed to rest. The mountain undergoes a further transformation from inhospitable crag to a peaceful, more pleasant landscape. Orazio Busino, chaplain to the Venetian embassy in London, reported that after the pygmies had scurried off, Atlas "opened by the turning of two doors, and from behind the low hills of a distant landscape one saw day break, some gilded columns being placed along the sides to make the distance seem greater."[25] At this point the masque's symbolic embodiment of royal power shifts from Hercules, "the active friend of Virtue," to Hesperus, a force of nature who stands outside time and circumstance as Hercules does not. Hesperus is, of course, another representation of King James. Given the recent events in Lancashire, the extreme west of England, it is particularly appropriate that King James should be depicted as Hesperus, the western star. According to Busino, the king was symbolically linked to the world of the masque by a green carpet which extended from his throne at the front of the audience up to the proscenium.

Jonson's distinction between the king as actor in the realm of events (Hercules) and as a force of nature (Hesperus) is very close to the standard seventeenth-century concept of the king's two bodies: one a "body natural," mortal and dependent upon contingency like the struggling Hercules; the other a "body politic," immortal and unchanging like God himself.[26] The promulgation of the *Book of Sports* in Lancashire had grown out of the king's mastery of a series of difficult situations, like the labors of Hercules. Antaeus was "suffocated" and Comus "beat from his grove"

(*Marques*, 270). But on a higher level, the royal edict was preordained, part of a grand scheme for order which the king in his immortal body as Hesperus could effect through his mere presence. A climactic speech by Mercury, the son of Maia and therefore associated with Maying pastimes himself,[7] celebrates the *Book of Sports* as a manifestation of universal law. As the western star presides serenely over the reconciliation of the quarrelling Pleasure and Virtue in the Land of the Hesperides, so James has presided over a similar reconciliation in the "other world" of Britain:

> But now
> The time's arrived that Atlas told thee of: how
> By unaltered law, and working of the stars,
> There should be a cessation of all jars
> 'Twixt Virtue and her noted opposite
> Pleasure; that both should meet here in the sight
> Of Hesperus, the glory of the west,
> The brightest star, that from his burning crest
> Lights all on this side the Atlantic seas
> As far as to thy pillars, Hercules.
> See where he shines: Justice and Wisdom placed
> About his throne, and those with Honor graced,
> Beauty and Love. It is not with his brother
> Bearing the world, but ruling such another
> Is his renown.
>
> (*Masques*, 270)

As Richard Peterson has pointed out in his detailed study of the masque's classical backgrounds, Jonson makes clever use of the two rival traditions of an inhospitable and a hospitable Atlas.[28] The north country of Britain has been transfigured from icy wilderness to an inviting and sunny prospect through the power of James I.

It would be a mistake to argue the Mercury's speech commemorates *only* the *Book of Sports;* by alluding to that declaration, Mercury praises James I for a favorite role which the king played particularly well on the occasion of its formulation, his role of peacemaker and mediator. James himself claimed, "I am euer for the *Medium* in euery thing. Betweene foolish rashnesse and extreame length, there is a middle way."[29] In Lancashire, he had negotiated a middle way between pleasure which had degenerated into license and a virtue so stern and inhospitable that it no longer deserved the name. As the masque is being performed, the royal *via media* acts upon the court itself, which, illuminated by the shining light of Hesperus, becomes a Hesperidean garden, a place for virtuous pleasures. The main masque's "distant landscape" of pastoral felicity is brought home to Whitehall and made a living reality. The twelve masquing courtiers, chief among them Prince Charles, the son of Hesperus, are called forth from Mount Atlas to demonstrate their own mastery of the king's *via media* in the reconciliation of Pleasure and Virtue.

Critics have frequently noted the prominence of rituals in Jonson's masques, rituals which sometimes seem to assume a liturgical form and significance. In *Pleasure Reconciled to Virtue,* the twelve princes descend from the hill to the music of a hymnlike song by the Choir. As Orgel has perceptively noted, the masque from this point on "moves almost ritualistically through a series of invocations, ceremonies, and what, if we were speaking in religious terms, we would have to call benedictions."[30] The masquers were apparently led down to the masquing floor by both Virtue and Daedalus, the prototypical artisan who symbolizes the arts in *Pleasure Reconciled to Virtue.* What Busino saw at this point in the masque is quite interesting: "then came a musician with a guitar dressed in a long robe, who played and sang some trills, implying that he was some deity; and then came a number of musicians dressed in the long red robes of high priests, with golden mitres, and in their midst was a goddess in a long white costume." The first musician was undoubtedly Daedalus and the goddess in white, Virtue. The mitred priests accompanying Virtue do not appear in Jonson's text, but on the level of political allegory they were certainly intended to represent Anglican bishops, who did in fact wear red robes for processionals on at least some occasions.[31]

Modern readers have been uncomfortable with the idea that the Stuart court masque could be used to celebrate Anglican religious usage, but that is precisely what Jonson meant the ritualistic final portion of *Pleasure Reconciled to Virtue* to do. By the Caroline period, such "daring" condensation of state and ecclesiastical ritual would become commonplace, with King Charles himself leading the rites.[32] As the victories of the antimasques in *Pleasure Reconciled to Virtue* emblematize the king's victories in Lancashire, so the patterned order of the main masque's songs and dances commemorate the king's "showcase" of Anglican comeliness in Edinburgh. The language of the songs reinforces the liturgical feeling of the final portion of the masque: Daedalus has composed his dances according to the laws of sacred harmony. It is significant that as the dances are about to begin, Hercules reawakens to question Daedalus, assures himself of the divine origin of the artist's precepts, and then places his benediction upon the dances. So King James himself, when he assumed the English crown, had tested and placed his approval upon the "beauty in holiness" of Anglicanism, a uniform set of ritual practices embellished by human arts. Hercules has banished the "false rites" of Comus and Popery, with their misused artifice and excessive appeals to the senses. The Choir in this particular masque seems to embody the function of music in Anglican rite: Hercules and the Choir together defeat the base pygmies who can boast no rites and no art at all. Finally, as King James tried to bring Anglicanism to Edinburgh and the Scots, Daedalus and Virtue together create a patterned ritual harmony that shuns dangerous extremes and serves as a secure guide through the complex "labyrinth or maze" of life.

In Scotland, the king's decorated chapel furnishings, organ, choristers, and the Anglican liturgy itself had been widely rejected as popish abominations and remnants of pagan idolatry. English Puritans and Scotch Presbyterians tended to condemn all dancing—to call the *Book of Sports* the "dancing Book" was no compliment. Echoing Calvin's condemnation of the Catholic mass, they scorned Anglican bowing, kneeling, and moving ceremoniously before the altar of God as a particularly idolatrous form of dance.[33] The king's use of religious images, similarly, was a worship of idols. Jonson designed the songs of Daedalus to support James's position toward the place of the arts in religious worship and symbolically restore the respect they had lost in Scotland. What the Anglican chapel services at Holyrood House had failed to teach the Scots, Jonson teaches his audience through the masque, a form itself created, in the poet's view, to impart virtue through the arts of poetry, dance, and picture. If contemporary Puritans called the prosport bishops dancers in the *"Maskaradoes"* of the times, Jonson felt no breach of decorum in using mitred masquers to symbolize bishops. Daedalus defends the dance in his first song as "an exercise / Not only shows the mover's wit, / But maketh the beholder wise, / As he hath power to rise to it" (*Masques,* 273). He implies that if contemporary Puritans inveigh against dancing, their hostility merely demonstrates their own incapacity for wisdom and virtue. The actual dancing that follows his speech proves his proposition for those who *are* capable of "wit." The first dance "figures" Hercules' (and James's) dialectical negotiation of the *via media,* with the dancers appearing to double back on themselves as they traverse the maze, while in actuality they are defining a path of measure and wisdom.

Daedalus' second long song defends the pictorial arts as King James, in yet another manifestation of his role as mediator between extremes, had recently been forced to defend them in Edinburgh:

> And now put all the aptness on
> Of figure, that proportion
> Or color can disclose.

That if those silent arts were lost,
Design and picture, they might boast
From you a newer ground,
Instructed to the height'ning sense
Of dignity and reverence
In your true motions found.

(*Masques*, 273–74)

Through observation of the dancers, the viewers will not commit idolatry but will learn the power of "Design and picture" to teach virtue. The songs of Daedalus and the dances over which he presides demonstrate the value of Anglican ritual in itself, but they also "show" how its beauty in holiness can order the conduct of all of life. Jonson's message was emphasized through costume. Red in the masque is the color of Pleasure—Comus's cupbearer wore red. White is the color of Virtue. When Virtue in her white robe appears between the bishops in red to escort the princes down the hill, together they symbolize the Anglican *via media*. The costumes of the twelve princes carry out the same symbolic motif: they wore mingled crimson and white.[34] In the last part of the second song and in the third song about love, Jonson skillfully turns his subject back to the motif of the court as Hesperidean Garden and provides a proper mythic context for the inclusion of court ladies in the dances. If the princes have learned the proper balance between the red of Pleasure and the white of Virtue, they can negotiate even the labyrinth of love without danger. James's negotiation of the labyrinth of British church politics has provided a pattern by which they may tread their mazes successfully. The princes, as the concluding song by Mercury admonishes, must always remember the place of art and Pleasure in the larger scheme of things and keep them reconciled to Virtue. Mercury warns them that this task will not be easy. As the masque's night of revelry draws to an end, the place of the princes is similar to Hercules' at its beginning. They reascend the hill, it closes, and Atlas is once again the forbidding wilderness of the masque's first scene, ready to try the strength and talents of a new set of Herculean heroes.

Pleasure Reconciled to Virtue is such a finely wrought tribute to the king's recent achievements that we might suppose he would have been greatly pleased by the masque's rhetoric and artistry. Apparently, however, he was not. According to Busino, during the last dance, "because they were tired [the masquers] began to lag; and the King, who is by nature choleric, grew impatient and shouted loudly, 'Why don't they dance? What did you make me come here for? Devil take all of you, dance!' At once the Marquis of Buckingham, his majesty's favourite minion, sprang forward, and danced a number of high and very tiny capers with such grace and lightness that he made everyone admire and love him, and also managed to calm the rage of his angry lord." There are many possible explanations for the king's show of temper. The court was generally dull that holiday season, the queen was sick and the king depressed, the masque started late, the room was hot, and the dancing probably not up to standard; Englishmen generally had a hard time appreciating the subtlety of Inigo Jones's staging.[35] In addition, if the king was attending closely to Jonson's allegory in the masque, instead of complimenting him for his success in Lancashire, it may have succeeded only in reminding him of his humiliating Edinburgh failures. It is possible, however, that the king may have attended too well to another strain of Jonson's rhetoric, a strain which implied criticism of some of James's favorites and indirectly of the king himself. If the rioting Lancashire Catholics exemplified the abuse of country pastimes, the royal court itself was the best contemporary example of the abuse of traditional feasting and hospitality. Jonson's theme of proper and improper hospitality, especially his treatment of Comus the belly god, evokes not only the licentious conditions prevailing in Lancashire, but also a similar license which currently governed culinary fashion at court.

The subject of feasting is extremely prominent in contemporary commentary about court life in 1617. In that year the king's perennial favorite Lord Hay, having recently returned from a diplomatic mission in France, introduced a lavish new style of banqueting to the English aristocracy. While in Paris, according to a contemporary report, Lord Hay "among many other great bankets made him had three wherof the least cost £ 1000 sterling, the rest £ 1300 and £ 1500." Part of the extraordinary cost of these feasts could be attributed to their "monstrous waste."[36] One hostile and incredulous contemporary left a vivid description of the new French fashion in dining as Hay and others practiced it in England after his return from France:

> [T]he Earle of Carlile [Lord Hay] was one of the quorum, that brought in the vanity of ante-suppers, not heard of in our forefathers time, and, for ought I have read, or, at least remember, unpracticed by the most luxurious tyrants. The manner of which was, to have the board covered, at the first entrance of the ghests, with dishes, as high as a tall man could well reach, filled with the choycest and dearest viands sea or land could afford: And all this once seen, and having feasted the eyes of the invited, was in a manner throwne away, and fresh set on to the same height, having only this advantage of the other, that it was hot. I cannot forget one of the attendants of the king, that at a feast, made by this monster in excesse [Hay], eat to his single share a whole pye, reckoned to my lord at ten pounds, being composed of amber-greece, magisteriall of perle,

musk, &c. yet was so far (as he told me) from being sweet in the morning, that he almost poysoned his whole family, flying himselfe like the satyr from his own stinck.[37]

This description of the new style of feasting, though exaggerated perhaps in a few of its details, is corroborated by other contemporary reports. Lord Hay reportedly kept thirty master cooks. When he entertained the French Ambassador in February 1617, the occasion for which Jonson wrote *Lovers Made Men,* the food alone cost over £ 600; for Lord Hay's wedding, the banquet came to £ 1000. Hay, along with other courtiers, accompanied James I on his progress to Scotland and kept on banqueting: "The like feasting he kept during his abode in Scotland, where his ordinary rate for his table was £ 300 a week besides feasts, which were very frequent, both to the counsaile, our clergie and chaplains, the household, the pensioners, the guard, the chappell, and his own countrie nobilitie and gentrie."[38]

A significant difficulty with all this largesse was that, however complimentary to the king and others, much of it was paid for directly or indirectly out of the king's own pocket: he gave Lord Hay £ 10,000 simply as a wedding present. Upon James's return from Scotland, his frantic advisors managed to convince him of the necessity for reform: royal household expenses were severely curtailed and the number of courses at royal dinners significantly reduced. According to one contemporary, the king proposed to eliminate "every third dish from the tables for diet." But according to the same source, this project failed through "opposition."[39] On 3 January 1618, three days before the first performance of *Pleasure Reconciled to Virtue,* the king's new favorite Buckingham, who had also spent several years in France before coming to court and had just been created Marquis, gratefully feasted the king at a great supper managed "after the French" and reported to have cost over £ 600: "You may guesse at the rest of the cheere by this scantling, that there were saide to be 17 dousen of fesants, and twelve partriches in a dish thoroughout, which me thincks was rather spoyle then largesse."[40]

By urging his gentry and nobility to "keep hospitality" in the "old fashion of *England,*" James had probably not intended to unleash such monsters of continental excess. In *Basilikon Doron* he had gone on record in favor of moderate dining. He counseled his son,

serue your appetite with few dishes, as yong *Cyrus* did: which both is holesommest, and freest from the vice of delicacie, which is a degree of gluttonie. . . . Let all your food bee simple, without composition or sauces; which are more like medecines then meate. The vsing of them was counted amongst the ancient *Romanes* a filthie vice of delicacie; because

they serue onely for pleasing of the taste, and not for satisfying of the ne-
cessitie of nature; abhorring *Apicius* their owne citizen, for his vice of delicacie and monsterous gluttonie. . . . beware the vsing excesse of meat and
drinke; and chiefly, beware of drunkennesse, which is a beastlie vice.[41]

James's attempt to limit the number of dishes at court banquets was
compatible with his own advice in *Basilikon Doron*. Moreover, we will
remember his castigation of French fashion in a proclamation of the
previous year. Quite clearly, his own favorites were undercutting his
attempts to curb his own indulgence and create an English *via media* in
hospitality. It is suggestive that one of Comus's attendants in the first
antimasque of *Pleasure Reconciled to Virtue* bears the cup of Hercules; for
within days of his arrival at court Buckingham himself had been made
cupbearer to James I. According to the Earl of Clarendon, the king's
"inclination to his new cupbearer" caused him to allow Villiers "frequent occasions of discoursing of the Court of France, and the transactions there, with which he had been so lately acquainted that he could
pertinently enlarge upon that subject, to the King's great delight."[42]
Might they have talked of banqueting? In the masque, the cupbearer, by
attending upon Comus, is being false to his real master Hercules. In
reality, James himself was all too susceptible to the belly-God hospitality of his favorites.

According to reports about the Lancashire incidents that led to the
Book of Sports, some of those same courtiers, "too favorable" to the
papists, had also attempted to undermine the king's policy toward
country pastimes. There were strong hints that members of the court had
encouraged the prosport demonstration by the Lancashire morris dancers
and even tried to get King James's support for such unbridled
merriment.[43] It is extremely appropriate, then, that Comus and his crew
as depicted by Jonson are excessively immersed in the spirit of holiday
license *and* excessively preoccupied with the belly. Through *Pleasure
Reconciled to Virtue*'s opening scenes of revelry, Jonson sought to reform
the courtiers according to the king's own stated principles of moderation. As the king had imposed a mean between the extremes of excess
and dearth in the area of pastimes, so the masque teaches a middle way
between the prodigal feasting of the courtiers and the equally undesir-
able alternative of no banqueting cheer at all. Comus and his followers
eat as only the very wealthy could. The hymn of his retinue to their
"father of sauce, and deviser of jelly," with its lists of delicacies and
catalogues of modes of preparation, suggests the culinary "idolatry"
committed by courtiers like Lord Hay and Buckingham, who were
indeed making a god of the belly. The Bowl-bearer's speech suggests

that these revelers have become so engrossed in feasting that they have forgotten all the old holiday sports. The martial arts and dancing that the *Book of Sports* encouraged have been distorted into aspects of gluttony; farts are the only "ordnance" discharged on festival days (*Masques*, 265); the only dancers are a tun and bottles. The tipsy Bowl-bearer claims that "men that drink hard and serve the belly in any place of quality (as The Jovial Tinkers, or The Lusty Kindred) are living measures of drink," referring on one level to the king's condemnation of idle tippling in alehouses in the *Book of Sports*. But the poet's mention of "any place of quality" obliquely suggests the court and again we are reminded of Buckingham, who had just granted the infamous monopoly on alehouses to his relative Sir Giles Mompesson.[44] Hercules's scornful speech against the "vicious hospitality" of Comus and his crew becomes a condemnation of court excess as well as country license. In language which parallels the king's own condemnation in *Basilikon Doron*, Hercules calls any gluttonous Comuses among the courtiers back to a more rigorous life of action in which feasting is not all of existence but a reward for heroic labor.

In the main masque, the twelve princes choose an active life: they dance through potentially dangerous labyrinths instead of basking forever in the sloth of overmuch feasting. *Pleasure Reconciled to Virtue* closes on a didactic note of warning unusual at the end of Jonson's masques:

> These, these are hours by Virtue spared
> Herself, she being her own reward,
> But she will have you know
> That though
> Her sports be soft, her life is hard.
> You must return unto the hill,
> And there advance
> With labor, and inhabit still
> That height and crown
> From whence you ever may look down
> Upon triumphèd Chance.
>
> (*Masques*, 275)

The very pattern of the verse suggests the act of climbing a mountain— to have a place at court becomes a rigorous responsibility rather than an excuse for luxury, as much a hill of Atlas as a Garden of Hesperides. The world of the masque and the world of the court have merged; through their actual reclimbing of the mountain, the masquing courtiers symbolically enact their choice of the hard path of Virtue, a choice which their subsequent behavior about court will presumably make manifest.

In his attempt to reform the courtiers along the pattern set by King James, Jonson himself was treading a rather dangerous path. The roles of the twelve virtuous princes of the masque were performed by some of the very courtiers who had recently been carrying on like Comus. Lord Hay had at one time been scheduled to dance a role but apparently did not, though he was probably involved in the masque's preparation (*Jonson*, 10:575–77). The king's new favorite Buckingham, who had just given the court a huge and excessive feast "after the French" *was* one of the dancers being called to conquer vicious hospitality and aspire to Virtue's crown. Jonson's handling of excess implicated James as well, insofar as he permitted his courtiers to defeat his attempts at fiscal reform and allowed himself considerable overindulgence. Jonson tactfully omits from the masque any reference to the myths about the drunkenness of Hercules, but the tradition was familiar enough to lurk beneath the surface of the masque.[45] It is (barely) possible that James on this occasion was in complicity with Jonson, using the masque as an oblique vehicle for reforms he was too weak to enforce himself. If so, however, he allowed the poet to become his scapegoat. On the night of Epiphany 1618 the king's sympathies were obviously with the offenders against moderation rather than with Jonson's correctives. After his choleric outburst against the tediousness of the masque, James was restored to good humor by a few capers from Buckingham.

We may wonder how Jonson the moralizer reacted to yet further evidence that evening of his art's failure to teach virtue. Busino reported that after the masque was over,

> His majesty rose from his chair, and taking the ambassadors along with him, passed through a number of rooms and galleries and came to a hall where the usual supper was prepared for the performers, a light being carried before him. He glanced round the table and departed, and at once like so many harpies the company fell on their prey. The table was almost entirely covered with sweetmeats, with all kinds of sugar confections. There were some large figures, but they were of painted cardboard, for decoration. The meal was served in bowls or plates of glass; the first assault threw the table to the ground, and the crash of glass platters reminded me exactly of the windows breaking in a great midsummer storm. The story ended at two hours after midnight, and half disgusted and exhausted we returned home.

Comus the belly god had once again triumphed at court.

When Jonson rewrote *Pleasure Reconciled to Virtue* to make it more acceptable to its audience for the second performance 17 February 1618 under the new title *For the Honor of Wales,* he gave up the dangerous business of "venturing upon Venter." Part of the purpose of the new

Welsh antimasques was to give more prominence to Prince Charles and his recent investiture as Prince of Wales. But it is extremely likely that Jonson also meant to smooth ruffled feelings at court by eliminating the episode of Comus altogether. In doing so, of course, he also had to leave out much of the material which had made *Pleasure Reconciled to Virtue* a celebration of specific incidents in James's recent trip to Scotland. *For the Honor of Wales* still takes note of the trip: his majesty's Welsh subjects clamor for the honor of a similar visit to their territory. But in place of *Pleasure Reconciled to Virtue*'s heroic triumph over the dangerous opposites of Puritanism and popery, *For the Honor of Wales* offers humor and palliatives. The satire against overfeasting and drinking is abandoned for praise of plain Welsh food and drink and an invitation to James to feast in Wales; instead of an antimasque of boasting pygmies, whom the Welsh claim to scorn, there are dances to the music of the "ancient Welse harp" by proper British men and women; to take the place of the antimasque of tuns and bottles, the Welsh present "a properly natural device" of mountain goats dancing to grave measures (*Masques,* 288–89). The point of all this combined foolery and seriousness is clear. In Wales, the king will not find the alternating dearth and excess which troubled his peace in Scotland and Lancashire, but he will find humble devotion to himself and his family, proper preservation of the old pastimes he encouraged through the *Book of Sports,* and measured feasting of the sort he commended in his *Basilikon Doron.* The antimasque closes on a rather elevated note. One of the Welshmen comes forward to laud Wales as a seedbed of talent for the entire kingdom and more particularly, with a sidelong glance at the rebellious Scots, as a bulwark of British loyalty and customs: "Though the nation be said to be unconquered, and most loving liberty, yet it was never mutinous, an't please your majesty, but stout, valiant, courteous, hospitable, temperate, ingenious, capable of all good arts, most lovingly constant, charitable, great antiquaries, religious preservers of their gentry and genealogy, as they are zealous and knowing in religion" (*Masques,* 291).

By closing the antimasque only a few lines after this praise of Welsh zeal for religion, Jonson provides a smooth transition to the main masque, which opens at precisely the point in *Pleasure Reconciled to Virtue* when the twelve masquers descend the mountain to dance their grateful tributes to the "beauty in holiness" of Anglicanism. *For the Honor of Wales* salvages much of the earlier masque's compliment to James on his recent policies, but expresses it through easy positives instead of strenuous and challenging negatives. No Herculean labors are required to prepare the way for the reconciliation of Pleasure and Virtue since the two exist already in indigenous harmony in the hills of Wales, as rocky as any in Scotland or Lancashire but much more hospitable. In *For the Honor of Wales,* there is no real conflict between the world of the antimasques and the world of the main masque. Through their comely dances the twelve princes simply raise the rough, humble capers of the Welshmen to a civilized level of art.

Even as he obligingly reworked his allegory, however, Jonson could not resist a few digs at those who had failed to comprehend his original masque. The literalistic Welsh castigate the poet for putting "the Prince of Wales in an outlandis mountain" (*Masques,* 279), not recognizing that Atlas himself was meant to represent the mountainous north of Britain. They fail also to comprehend the satiric function of Jonson's original antimasques. Comus, Jonson's embodiment of the profanation of human arts, is criticized for being insufficiently artistic: "There was neither poetries nor architectures nor designs in that belly-god, nor a note of musics about him"(*Masques,* 284). We will note that even as he pokes fun at the original version of his masque, Jonson slyly manages to remind his audience of its stronger satiric message. By ridiculing those who had not understood him, he restates his original message for those who had understood him too well.

For the Honor of Wales was nonetheless a capitulation on Jonson's part to prevailing taste and opinion. The moralist was forced to narrow the scope of his teaching so as not to offend those Comuses most in need of it. Such education, it would seem, was more acceptable at a distance: although the court disliked *Pleasure Reconciled to Virtue* when it was presented in early 1618 and had few kind words for its creator, the next holiday season, when Jonson was in Scotland and therefore unable to provide his usual masque, his absence was "regretted" (*Jonson,* 1:71). The revision of *Pleasure Reconciled to Virtue* marks the end of the most strenuous phase of the poet's efforts to "wound the wise" at the court of James I. Thereafter, his criticism was rather more leavened with praise, or at least with tolerance. But even praise, for Jonson, was theoretically a form of instruction—an encouragement for those mirrored in his art to emulate their own idealized image. If Jonson overestimated the educability of those at whom his reproof was aimed, he could at least fall back on intent:

> I have too oft preferr'd
> Men past their termes, and prais'd some names too much,
> But, 'twas with purpose to have made them such.
>
> (*Jonson,* 8:159)

* ii *

In 1633, Charles I made his own pilgrimage to Scotland in an elaborate progress designed to replicate his father's journey of 1617. Despite the sixteen years that had passed since James's visit, the Stuart plans for Scotland were still hanging in suspension. The Union of the Kingdoms had not been effected nor the Scottish Kirk assimilated into the liturgical and hierarchical structure of Anglicanism. Charles had not yet been crowned King of Scotland. So consciously was the progress of 1633 fashioned to recapitulate and fulfill the progress of 1617 that Charles's advisors got out the lists of those who had accompanied King James in order to select Charles's retinue. He, like his father, was attended by a number of bishops, most prominently William Laud, who had also gone to Edinburgh in 1617. As before, the royal progress was orchestrated as a display of Anglican comeliness designed to win the stubborn Scots away from their resistance to Anglican church government and ceremonies. Along the progress northward the court paused in various places to order ecclesiastical affairs; the cathedrals of York and Durham were restored to their "ancient beauty," and Puritan lecturers were put down.[46]

In Edinburgh itself, there was the predictable outrage among the Calvinist clergy at the "popery" of the Chapel Royal and Laud's preaching in defense of the liturgy but much less overt resistance than in 1617 to the imposition of the *Book of Common Prayer*. There was also the predictable outpouring of royal panegyric and, as though in recompense for the grievous omission of 1617, a coronation pageant in Edinburgh to welcome Charles back to his people. This entertainment, devised by William Drummond of Hawthornden, emphasized the liturgical dimension of the royal visit by depicting Religion in triumph over Superstition and urging the loyal citizens of Edinburgh to look upon their monarch as upon a piece of ecclesiastical art: "Gods sacred picture in this man adore." One of the arches commemorated the Stuart defense of traditional pastimes: it was labeled in "great Characters HILARITATI PVBLICÆ" and depicted "men, women, and children, dauncing after diverse postures with many Musicall Instruments."[47] As though to emphasize his ceremonial repetition of his father's progress, in connection with the event Charles reissued Jacobean proclamations designed to restore the countryside: the *Book of Sports* and the order commanding gentry and aristocrats back to their rural estates to keep hospitality in the traditional fashion. But perhaps the most obvious way Charles's progress replicated his father's was in its ostentatious banqueting. There was the same public feasting en route and in Scotland itself. Londoners noted that the only court news coming from Scotland was of "feasting."[48] At one banquet, given Charles by the Earl of Newcastle at Welbeck, "Both King and Court were received and entertained by the Earl . . . at his own proper expense, in such a wonderful manner, and in such an excess of feasting, as had never before been known in England" (*Jonson*, 10:703). The entertainment for this prodigious occasion was provided by that old Venturer upon Venter, Ben Jonson, who had so ably and fearlessly commemorated the progress of 1617. Even when it came to the choice of poets in 1633, Charles's journey recapitulated the past.

The King's Entertainment at Welbeck is both a celebration of the renewed *Book of Sports* and a tribute to the superior culture of the court. It was liked by the king and demonstrates that Jonson was quite capable of working within the official Caroline ambivalence toward traditional pastimes. In the entertainment, the carnivalesque is both aired and repudiated, allowed its brief time of flourishing then curbed and silenced by the severe presence of the king. Jonson's work is a piece of anti-quarianism, a conscious replication of the popular pastimes that had embellished a royal entertainment more than fifty years earlier, the "solemn *Brydeale*" and "cumly Quintine for featz at armz" performed before Queen Elizabeth I at Kenilworth in 1575. The Queen's entertain-ment had itself been nostalgic in that it had made a case for the restoration of old customs suppressed under Protestanism. It included, for example, a plea by men of Coventry that their old mystery plays be allowed again, the suppression of their drama being the fault of learned preachers "sumewhat too sour in preaching awey theyr pastime."[49] Jonson's entertainment revived the spirit of the old Elizabethan show but for timely reasons. *The King's Entertainment at Welbeck* commemo-rates Charles's role in the Somerset skirmishes of 1632 that had issued in the republication of the *Book of Sports*. It melds recent history into a primordial pattern of mirth and country festivity.

The Somerset imbroglio had centered on church ales—the traditional parish sales of beer and other intoxicating substances for the church's annual feast of dedication, or at Whitsuntide, or as part of the celebra-tion of a marriage. Local justices of the peace had systematically sup-pressed the church ales as a source of drunkenness and disorder and their efforts had been seconded by Chief Justice Richardson, who issued an order suspending the ales on his regular itinerant visit to Somerset. But the official policy of King Charles and Archbishop Laud was to support the ales as "neighbourly meetings and recreations of the people." Laud himself suspected that the Puritans were behind the suppression: "The Humourists increase much in those parts, and unite themselves by banding against these feasts." He ordered the local bishop to make an inquiry and received the following report of the sentiments of the "better sort" of clergy in Somersetshire:

> I. That those feasts have been kept as long as they have lived in their several parishes without any disorders. II. That on the feast days the service of the church has been more solemnly performed, and the church better frequented, than upon any other Sunday in the year. III. That they have not known of any disorders in the neighbouring towns where the like feasts are kept. IV. That the people very much desire their continuance. Lastly. All those ministers are of opinion that it is fit they should be continued, for a memorial of the dedication of their churches, for the civilizing of people, for their lawful recreations, for composing differences by meeting of friends, for increase of love and amity as being feasts of charity, for relief of the poor, the richer sort keeping them open house, and for many other reasons.[50]

One of the "other reasons" was that the wakes and ales were a major source of parish revenue. The Somerset controversy gives us a particularly vivid glimpse of how the politics of mirth was envisioned as furthering the fiscal prosperity of the Church and respect for the crown as well. According to one report, "when the constables told their neighbours that the judges would put down these feasts, they answered that it was very hard if they could not entertain their friends once a year, to praise God for his blessings, and pray for the King under whose happy government they enjoyed peace and quietness." Charles I forced Chief Justice Richardson to revoke his order suppressing these "decent and sober recreations" and the Justice, eventually removed from office and well nigh broken by the experience, protested with reference to Laud's part in the affair that he had been *almost choaked with a pair of Lawn Sleeves.*"[51]

In Jonson's entertainment before Charles, the very customs the king had supported strongly in Somersetshire are chastised and banished from his presence. *The King's Entertainment at Welbeck* was performed on 21 May 1633 around Whitsuntide. The entertainment served as a frame for the Earl's "wondrous" feasting of Charles I, with a prologue sung just as His Majesty was "set at Dinner." The prologue hails Charles as the informing spirit behind the May Day of the performance. He has quickened all of nature and its creatures unite to praise the royal presence that *"makes the time"* and the season. After the banquet, that unprecedentedly sumptuous feast, Charles I was interrupted in his leave-taking by a less elevated episode, the performance of a Whitsun Bride-Ale complete with its traditional games under the supervision of a comic pedant and the "learned *Antiquarie*" of Sherwood Forest. The Bride-Ale is earthy and comical, featuring the display of a holiday martial art like those advocated in the *Book of Sports*—riding at the quintain—and a rustic groom and his bride, an "old *May-Lady,* with Skarfes and a great wrought Handkerchiefe, with red, and blew, and other habilliments" (*Jonson,* 7:799–800). Their bridal feast winds on, embellished with clownish dances, the dividing of the *"Bride-Cake,"* and other popular customs, very much in the manner of Queen Elizabeth's Bride-Ale at Kenilworth.

The Welbeck Bride-Ale is the lowerclass counterpart of the king's Whitsun feast just completed, its native English dances comically preferred by the country louts over the French dances of the court. Given Jonson's earlier attitudes toward overdelicate feasting, we may wonder whether the implied parallel carried a hint of reproof at the king's prodigious banqueting. The Bride-Ale faithfully captures the spirit of country jollity and solidarity that Charles's *Book of Sports* was designed to restore. And yet, having aired the old customs, a representative of the Earl of Newcastle repudiates them lest they offend the monarch, even though the Earl himself was known to be one of the staunchest supporters of all such popular forms:

> Give end unto your rudenesse: Know at length
> Whose time, and patience you have urg'd, the *Kings!*
> Whom if you knew, and truly, as you ought,
> 'Twould strike a reverence in you, even to blushing,
> That *King* whose love it is, to be your Parent!
> Whose Office, and whose Charge, to be your Pastor!
> Whose single watch, defendeth all your sleepes!
> Whose labours, are your rests! whose thoughts and cares,
> Breed you[r] delights! whose bus'nesse, all your leasures!
> And you to interrupt his serious houres,
> With light, impertinent, unworthy objects,
> Sights for your selves, and sav'ring your owne tast's;
> You are too blame! Know your disease, and cure it.
> Sports should not be obtruded on great Monarchs,
> But wait when they will call for them as servants,
> And meanest of their servants, since their price is
> At highest, to be styl'd, but of their pleasures!
>
> (*Jonson,* 7:801–2)

This speech is a variation upon the traditional formula whereby peasant sports give way to the dances of the gentles—we shall see John Milton using it in *Comus.* But in Jonson's 1633 entertainment, the curbing of the countryfolks' holiday is much more severe than the usual formula would allow. The king is portrayed as the fosterer of their merriment, his "cares" breeding their "delights," but himself too severe, too exacting, to tolerate festival's intrusion upon his life of solemn duty. The rest of the speech praises Charles I for his progress to Edinburgh and his attention to such essential national business as the Union of England and Scotland. Charles is at once the source of the Maying season, its merriment and holiday pastimes, and the severe censurer of the mirth he has brought into being.

In 1634 Jonson was again called upon to produce an entertainment for the Earl of Newcastle, and again in *Love's Welcome at Bolsover* he used the successful formula of airing "Holy-day" briefly then dismissing it in favor of something less unworthy, in this case a chaste "Schoole of Love" inspired by the king and queen and conducted in the usual manner of Caroline court Platonism. Incongruously, the earthy sports are brought in and coached by Colonel Vitruvius, a caricature of Inigo Jones, who was in fact one of the animating spirits behind the *refinement* of Caroline pastimes. In Jonson's entertainment, that Italianate Englishman is humbled and brought back to his origins in the popular. We will recall his birth in the clothworker's quarter glanced at in *Bartholomew Fair* and the alienating effect of his stage machinery on Robin and the court in *Love Restored.* These repeated attacks on Inigo were not merely a venting of personal spleen, although there was certainly an element of that.[52] Jonson was attempting to nudge the court out of its refined self-insulation from the popular. The same pattern is much more visible in *A Tale of a Tub.* For Jonson the figure of Inigo Jones exemplified the alienation of the court, a hypocritical disavowal of origins. Jonson himself was much like Jones in that he too had suppressed his menial origins and passed himself off as a gentleman. But unlike Jones, Jonson tried, with considerable ambivalence, to retain some contact with the popular. *Love's Welcome at Bolsover* transforms the master artisan back into a director of homely country sports and thereby brings the court of Charles back to the humble arts they scorned.

King Charles was apparently not offended by the entertainment's needling parody of the arts at court. Yet we may wonder what message he received about his own equivocal stance toward the old holiday customs. When Ben Jonson wrote his contribution to *Annalia Dubrensia,* the 1636 volume of verses commemorating Robert Dover and his still flourishing Cotswold Games, the poet effaced Charles I as a promoter of traditional pastimes in favor of his father James. The "EPIGRAM TO MY IOVIALL Good Freind *Mr. Robert Dover*" gives a capsule version of the standard Stuart argument for the *Book of Sports* but places James and his "glory" at the center despite Charles's recent reissuing of the declaration:

I Cannot bring my *Muse* to dropp (her) *Vies*
Twixt *Cotswold,* and the *Olimpicke* exercise:
But I can tell thee, *Dover,* how thy *Games*
Renew the Glories of our blessed *Ieames:*
How they doe keepe alive his memorie;
With the *Glad Countrey,* and *Posteritie:*
How they advance true Love, and neighbourhood,
And doe both *Church,* and Common-wealth the good,
In spite of *Hipocrites,* who are the worst
Of Subiects; Let such envie, till they burst.

(Jonson, 8:415–16)

King James had been overly lenient toward holiday "license," too immersed in his own "misrule," but Jonson seems to have found that extreme more attractive—at least in retrospect—than the austere isolation of Charles.

Like Jonson's 1633 and 1634 entertainments for the royal progresses, *A Tale of a Tub* is deliberately and overtly antiquarian—doubly anachronistic in that it is a quasi-Elizabethan "festive comedy" set back in the Catholic times of Queen Mary. It is also somewhat peculiar in its claim to historical realism. The play's action oscillates among known towns and villages of Middlesex, yet the central characters speak in a West Country dialect, the dialect of Somerset.[53] This disjunction calls attention to the play's engagement of events of the recent past: again, as in *The King's Entertainment at Welbeck,* we are presented with a homely Bride-Ale and attendant skirmishes, recalling the king's 1632 triumph in Somerset over the enemies of parish festival. The play revives one of the major themes from *Bartholomew Fair*—the conflict between holiday "license" and the law—but without the earlier work's virulence against the enemies of royal authority. In *A Tale of a Tub,* as in rural Somersetshire, a series of malapert local officials abuse the law in order to prevent the enactment of an old holiday custom, Audrey's marriage lottery in honor of St. Valentine's Day. For a time disorder reigns, but eventually their legalistic strategies cancel each other out and holiday triumphs over all attempts to suppress it in the interest of private gain. Audrey ends up matched to a different mate than the drawing of lots had given her—the irrepressible energies of festival operate outside even its own mechanisms for containment—but no harm is done. Fertility and well-being win the day, and the play ends with the beginnings of a Bride-Ale feast, a "neighbourly meeting and recreation of the people" that cements community according to the doctrine of the king's supporters in Somerset, with the "richer sort" Lady Tub and her son keeping open house according to traditional custom. In its unambivalent celebration of the transforming energies of popular festival, the play is unlike anything Jonson had produced earlier, utterly unlike the caustic satiric pieces he had produced during the heyday of festive comedy in the late 1590s.[54]

The poet's prologue for the court performance 4 January 1634 suggests, however, that there may be more afoot than just a happy, comical paean to holiday. Jonson invites his audience to measure the world of his play against the court itself:

> No State-*affaires, nor any politique* Club,
>   *Pretend wee in our Tale, here, of a* Tub.
> But acts of Clownes *and* Constables, *to day*
>   *Stuffe out the* Scenes *of our ridiculous* Play.
> A Coopers wit, *or some such busie Sparke,*
>   *Illumining the* high Constable, *and his Clarke,*
> And all the Neighbour-hood, *from old Records,*
>   *Of antick Proverbs, drawne from* Whitson-Lord's,
> And their Authorities, *at* Wakes *and* Ales,
>   *With countrey precedents, and old Wives Tales;*
> Wee *bring you now, to shew what different things*
>   *The* Cotes *of* Clownes, *are from the* Courts *of* Kings.
>
> (Jonson, 3:10)

On the surface, this disparaging prologue fuels the court's tendency to define itself away from the popular. The play is a mere tale of a tub, a piece of nonsense; the audience's act of measuring will show them their elevation above the rudeness of Turf and his fellow rustics—how far their court taste is from the "Cotes *of* Clownes." But on another level, the prologue debunks Caroline art, specifically its notions of pastoral, the polite fiction that works such as William Montagu's *The Shepherd's Paradise* or John Fletcher's *Faithful Shepherdess,* both performed at court during 1633 or 1634, have anything to do with the actual rural world they purport to represent. The invitation to discover differences carries disturbing implications that work against Caroline aestheticism even as they appear to reinforce it. King Charles and his courtiers are confronted with the stuff of their own policy but without the structural mechanisms for distancing that Jonson had obligingly provided at Welbeck.

At the same time, Jonson's challenge uncovers a disquieting likeness. When it comes time for the play's climactic wedding masque, Lady Tub welcomes her guests, "Neighbours, all welcome: Now doth *Totten-Hall /* Shew like a Court: and hence shall first be called so" (*Jonson,* 3:88). Her claim is, of course, ludicrous as the ensuing "Masque of the Tub" makes clear, yet containing a grain of truth that calls the court back to the original popular forms of its own refined entertainments. Totten-court, like Charles's court, has its master-artisan In-and-In Medlay, Architect, Cooper, and Headborough of Islington. Despite Medlay's debasement of the form, his masque does "Shew like a Court" in its reproduction of the ritualized milieu surrounding masques at Whitehall. There is the proper hierarchical seating of dignitaries in attendance, the usual careful attention to the reaction of the exalted personage in whose honor the work is presented, and even an appropriate regard for topicality, in that the literal-minded masque comically reproduces the action that has gone before. Squire Tub's masque is, like a masque at court, immersed in its "present occasions," displaying its central figure in heroic conquest over a series of difficulties that figure forth recent events. Inigo Jones took offense at the play's portrayal of him, and the satire we have is presumably much tamer than Jonson's original version. But the poet's jibes are not merely based on personal animus. The parody of Inigo Jones and his exalted masques at court works to diminish the distance between high and low forms of festival.

The court was not amused. Squire Tub himself speaks the play's epilogue, recounting yet once more his tribulations under the legal authorities of the countryside: *"Slie Iustice arts, with the High Constables briefe, | And brag Commands."* For all his artistic naïveté, the squire has a canny instinct for ferreting out ambiguities; he closes by suggesting that there is more than one way to understand his play. Its climatic (or anticlimactic) masque has been offered,

> *That you be pleas'd, who come to see a* Play,
> *With those that heare, and marke not what wee say.*
> *Wherein the* Poets *fortune is, I feare,*
> *Still to be early up, but nere the neare.*
>
> (*Jonson,* 3:92)

Squire Tub articulates Jonson's usual distinction between viewers and understanders but also forecasts pessimistically that the play will not succeed. Its author's efforts have, as usual, gone for naught, early up but "nere the neare." And, of course, the squire was right. The play was not liked at court, and for all its rollicking merriment, it was not meant to be likeable, at least not in that setting. If it had any effect at all, it would work by creating discomfort, prodding its disapproving audience into greater sensitivity to the discontinuities between Caroline policy and practice, between official art and neglected areas of the national life.

The Sad Shepherd was almost certainly Jonson's last play, still unfinished at the time of his death in 1637. Like *A Tale of a Tub* it makes a surface gesture toward the prevailing taste at court. It is, unlike all of

Jonson's other extant productions, a pastoral, with yearning lovers, rustic haunts, and some of the elegaic quality of pastoral at the Caroline court. But unlike court pastoral of the 1630s and in all probability like Jonson's own lost *May Lord, The Sad Shepherd* is steeped in the homely realism of popular rural customs. The prologue calls attention to Jonson's greater fidelity to native English forms, which he hopes will commend themselves to his audience as readily as the *"Fleece"* of classical Arcady:

> And though hee now present you with such wooll,
> As from meere English Flocks his Muse can pull,
> He hopes when it is made up into Cloath;
> Not the most curious head here will be loath
> To weare a Hood of it; it being a Fleece,
> To match, or those of Sicily, or Greece.

(Jonson, 7:9)

The play itself is a feast within a feast, full of country rituals associated with late spring and summer holidays and offered in a spirit of "good neighborhood." It centers on Robin Hood and Marian's threatened banquet in the greenwood. Like Jonson's other final works, *The Sad Shepherd* uses nostalgia for the lost spirit of holiday to strike blows against overrefined taste in the present. The work is offered as a refutation of the Caroline *"Heresie of late let fall; / That Mirth by no meanes fits a* Pastorall." Even as it paints a portrait of innocent rural pastimes—the golden world of community advocated through the Stuart politics of mirth—it bears a covert kinship to *The Devil Is an Ass* in that it points out hidden alliances between court fashion and a chilling subculture of economic individualism that would appropriate the public benefits of holiday for the private uses of a few. Jonson's delicately crafted pastoral is a parable of rural exploitation that, even in its unfinished state, suggests disquieting parallels between "sour" antifestive sentiment in the countryside and the enclosed world of the court.

Robin Hood and Maid Marian live in a premodern English Eden, a "Landt-shape of Forrest, Hils, Vallies, Cottages, A Castle, A River, Pastures, Heards, Flocks, all full of Countrey simplicity" (*Jonson*, 7:7). But there is trouble in paradise: the rural sports of Maying and Midsummer have fallen into disuse. Robin asks,

> Why should, or you, or wee so much forget
> The season in our selves: as not to make
> Vse of our youth, and spirits, to awake
> The nimble Horne-pipe, and the Timburine,
> And mixe our Songs, and Dances in the Wood,

And each of us cut downe a Triumph-bough?
Such are the Rites, the youthfull *Iune* allow.

To which Clarion answers him,

> They were, gay *Robin,* but the sowrer sort
> Of Shepherds now disclaime in all such sport:
> And say, our Flocks, the while, are poorely fed,
> When with such vanities the Swaines are led.

Friar Tuck serves much the same role in the play as a Laudian churchman in the actual seventeenth-century countryside. He serves as master of ceremonies for the upcoming feast and defends old custom against the "sowrer sort" on the standard conservative grounds that its enemies are merely envious of its felicity and warped by "Covetise and Rage" for private gain (*Jonson*, 7:15). Once the stage is set in terms of the familiar antagonisms surrounding the *Book of Sports,* we are acquainted with the disasters that threaten the woodland feast. All of the misfortunes can be traced to Maudlin "The Envious," a Wise-Woman or witch who lives in a shadowed vale of "humorous" melancholy and spends her time brewing up devices to prevent communal festivity. Maudlin has imprisoned Earine, a Flora figure whose name means Spring and who is associated with flowers and fertility. As a result of her kidnap, Aeglamour, the leader of the country sports and dances, is pining away and refuses to play his role; the "Mirth, and Musicke" of the day cannot go forward. Not content to spoil the festival, Maudlin impersonates Marian in order to appropriate its largesse for herself. Having stolen the venison intended for everyone, the witch, in language that eerily echoes the Stuart calls for holiday feasting of the poor, assumes the guise of a humble suppliant grateful for Marian's bounty. Jonson's portrayal of the witch is fascinating in that it suggests a connection between necromancy and the denial of traditional communal responsibilities. Twentieth-century historians and anthropologists have offered two competing theories of the social dynamics of seventeenth-century witchcraft: one, that the witch was likely to be an old woman denied the traditional alms from wealthier members of the community; the other, that the witch was more often identified with the prosperous villager who denied hospitality on the basis of a new ethos of individualism.[55] Jonson overlays one explanation with the other. Maudlin is ostensibly the former, presenting herself as a deprived suppliant, but in fact the latter, using her disguise of poverty to mask her greed for private gain. Her son is as acquisitive as she is. In contrast to Robin, Marian, and the shepherds, who enjoy the forest in common, Lorel brags about his estate, his renters, his "Large heards, and pastures," and his private fields closed off from collective use (*Jonson,* 7:28). Like the "City devils" of *The Devil Is an Ass* he and his demonic mother prey upon older collective forms, his planned rape of Earine the amatory equivalent of his mother's "rape" of the holiday banquet. They have even enlisted Puck the country devil to abet their schemes for self-aggrandizement. Unlike *The Devil Is an Ass,* however, *The Sad Shepherd* was probably meant to close in reconciliation and restored community. When Maudlin's plots are unmasked, the bickering and dissention she has caused soon dissolve and the way is cleared for an appearance by Reuben, "The Reconciler," a "devout Hermit" probably planned to recall the hermit figures from the old Elizabethan Accession Day Tilts and perform a similar festival function.[56]

Thus far, Jonson's pastoral may appear a straightforward expression of the social and economic theory behind the *Book of Sports*. But there is one way in which Maudlin and her son closely resemble the Stuart court. They share its enclosing aestheticism. While the free spirits of the greenwood accept all comers to their homely festival, their table roughly fashioned of "greene sword" and seats "laid in / With turfe," their taste simple and accommodating enough to encompass the whole community, Maudlin and Lorel mimic the Stuart court's disdain for the popular. The witch steals the communal venison on the grounds that it is too good for its intended recipients, "these course rustick mouthes that cannot open, / Or spend a thanke for't. A starv'd Muttons carkasse / Would better fit their palates" (*Jonson,* 7:24). Her son, in marked contrast to Robin and Marian in their open "Jolly Bower," enjoys his pastimes apart, piping within a private enclosure on his own estate where he is shaded by "An aged Oake, the King of all the field" (*Jonson,* 7:28). His pleasures are not for public imitation, not for the common eye. Maudlin and her son are the characters within the play who most resemble the aesthetes attacked in Jonson's prologue, those who refuse to acknowledge that pastoral can (and should) be anchored in collective mirth. The poet asserts that his humble tale of country life is no less intrinsically worthy than the sophisticated, declamatory pastoral of the court:

> But that no stile for Pastorall *should goe*
> Current, but what is stamp'd with Ah, *and* O;
> *Who judgeth so, may singularly erre;*
> *As if all* Poesie *had one Character.*
>
> (*Jonson,* 7:10)

By linking the "enclosure" of art with economic exploitation and divisive individualism, the poet undercuts the play's argument as a defense of Stuart ideology. Again, as in *A Tale of a Tub,* the audience is confronted with a joyous holiday collectivity like that endorsed by the court but simultaneously disavowed through Whitehall's avoidance of the common. We cannot be certain that *The Sad Shepherd* was intended for performance at court, or how Jonson intended to resolve his play. We cannot be sure even whether the work was left unfinished because of the poet's death, or as a result of the sort of artistic stalemating that led him to end *The Devil Is an Ass* without a satisfactory sense of closure. What we can recognize is that even at the end of his life, Jonson was developing fascinating new strategies for defending "public mirth" while at the same time "wounding" and teaching the "wise."

Churchman among the Maypoles:
Herrick and the *Hesperides*

Over one hundred years after his death, Robert Herrick was still remembered in the parish of Dean Prior for having taught a pet pig to drink out of a tankard. His verses were remembered too—they had been passed down orally from parent to child, and some of the villagers could recite whole poems by heart. We have no direct evidence that Herrick set up maypoles in Devonshire or encouraged Sunday bowling, dancing, and church ales in the manner of some Laudian advocates of the *Book of Sports*. But the Somerset imbroglio over parish wakes came close to his doorstep. In calling for the reinstatement of suppressed wakes and revels in Somerset, Charles I ordered the "same care" to be "taken for Devon and Cornwall, where, as he is informed, there is observed a great hurt and general disheartening to the people for want of their due and accustomed recreations."[1] The "Argument" of *Hesperides* announces just such "recreations" as one of Herrick's major subjects:

> I SING of *Brooks*, of *Blossomes*, *Birds*, and *Bowers*
> Of *April*, *May*, of *June*, and *July*-Flowers.
> I sing of *May-poles*, *Hock-carts*, *Wassails*, *Wakes*,
> Of *Bride-grooms*, *Brides*, and of their *Bridall-cakes*.[2]

Within the garden of his verses, the "Argument" suggests, the suppressed customs will be brought back to life for the "heartening" of his readers, perhaps also for the "heartening" of villagers at Dean Prior, where even a century and a half later, Herrick's poems were still remembered.

In *Hesperides*, as in Stuart England, the guiding force behind the "harmless" revelry is the monarchy. Herrick makes this clear in his dedicatory poem to Prince Charles, who was strongly associated with

spring pastimes on account of his birth in the maying season on 29 May
1630. The nativity of the "May prince" was accompanied by the appearance of Hesperus, the evening star, at midday—a phenomenon hailed in
court circles as proof of divine favor upon the royal family and its support
for traditional pastimes.[3] The poems of *Hesperides,* according to Herrick's
dedicatory verses, will be inspired and "come forth" as lesser lights, the
children of Charles's Hesperian light, so that the holiday customs listed
in Herrick's "Argument" become an efflorescence of the glory of the
prince (*Herrick,* 3). The connection between the verses and their royal
"source" was emphasized on the 1648 title page through the metonymic
device of a large, elaborate crown.[4]

In fact, however, Herrick's collection is far more diverse and equivocal than the opening panoply of prosport rhetoric would suggest. A
relatively small percentage of its thousand-odd poems are actually about
the old customs, and even in those, collective mirth is elusive. Herrick
envisions himself as praying to Father Ben for guidance in his own poetic
enterprise, but in *Hesperides,* festival does not have the same irrepressible, almost menacing energy that it does in Jonsonian works like
Bartholomew Fair. In *Hesperides,* holiday has to be made to happen. The
poet sometimes contemplates traditional observances in melancholy
retrospect, as though grieving for their passing; but more often, he
proposes and "stage-manages" them through authorial directives to an
imagined audience.

Part of the reticence of holiday in *Hesperides* can be attributed to the
shifting of the times. Although some of Herrick's poems were composed
during the 1620s or earlier, many were written after the poet's "exile" to
Devonshire in 1630. In Caroline England, as a result of the political
polarization created by the *Book of Sports,* the old holidays were celebrated more sporadically, or at least more self-consciously, than they had
been earlier. Then too, Laudian sponsorship of festival required its
attenuation. When Thomas Laurence set up maypoles and feasting at
Bemerton, or when Giles Widdows preached a 1631 open-air sermon at
Carfax, Oxford, in defense of maypoles, church ales, and the *Book of
Sports,* then "confirmed his doctrine with his practice" by walking to a
maypole and joining a dance around it, such intervention was meant
both to encourage holiday "mirth" and to dampen its potential for
disorder.[5] In *Hesperides,* holiday is similarly performed and regularized
under the direction of the poet-priest.

However, Herrick presents himself in his verses as a Cavalier as well.
Hesperides is remarkable for its accommodation of sexual energies that the
Laudians often overlooked. If Herrick is a jolly parson, teaching his
villagers the value of festive mirth, he is also an Ovid, tasting the joys of

license himself, creating his record of traditional festivals from the
banishment of Dean Prior as Ovid had revised the *Fasti* during his exile
in barbarous Tomis.[6] A recurring idea in *Hesperides* is "cleanly-
Wantonnesse," a sexual liberty "licensed" by its enclosure within a recurrent cycle of sacred events, just as the seeming insouciance of the
collection's "Argument" is qualified and contained by its final verses: "I
write of *Hell*; I sing (and ever shall) / Of *Heaven*, and hope to have it after
all" (*Herrick*, 5). Even Herrick's insistent classicizing of native English
customs, I will argue, needs to be understood within the context of
contemporary debate over the *Book of Sports*. Like Jonson in *Bartholomew
Fair*, Herrick steeps his pastimes in paganism in order to affirm their
primordial, indigenous nature. But in *Hesperides*, holiday is fragile.

A repeated motif of *Hesperides* is the assertion that traditional pastimes
have magical efficacy against economic and other misfortunes. In "The
Wassaile," for example, some carefree wassailers sing blessings upon the
house before which they stand:

> GIVE way, give way ye Gates, and win
> An easie blessing to your Bin,
> And Basket, by our entering in.
>
> (*Herrick*, 178)

As they wait, they wish prosperity upon all parts of the estate—its
larders, dairies, crops and hives, ducks, poultry, and plows. If they are
allowed entrance, the house will always get more than it spends, even if
"a thousand, thousand eat." But the wassailers remain shut out, denied
even the traditional "Ale or Beere" before the door, and their holiday
cheer suddenly dissipates. As though for the first time, they notice that
the estate shows signs of neglect, its chimneys cold, its servants hungry,
its doors bound with "Rust and Cobwebs." There is no mention of the
owners. Might they be absent in London? Or have they simply lacked the
means to keep up their decaying property? If so, their poverty provides
no excuse because, in the perception of the wassailers, the estate's failing
condition can never be a cause, but only the effect of hospitality denied.
The "easie blessing" of wassailing is infallible, guaranteeing the house
increase so long as it spends itself in traditional obligations like the
entertainment of holiday suppliants. The wassailers leave empty-
handed, warning,

> The time will come, when you'l be sad,
> And reckon this for fortune bad,
> T'ave lost the good ye might have had.
>
> (*Herrick*, 179)

This threat defies logic: if the estate already shows the effects of the failure of holiday reciprocity, how is it that such "fortune bad" will become evident only in the future? Herrick's deceptively simple poem portrays a collective mechanism for dealing with the breakdown of a system of communal obligations. According to some social historians, just such imprecation against those who refused to perform traditional almsdeeds could lead to accusations of witchcraft against the petitioners.[7] But in the perception of the wassailers, the decay of the estate is instead the effect of festival "magic" repudiated. Offering hospitality would have undone the conditions that make hospitality seem impossible.

The perceptual disjunctions in "The Wassaile" point to a sophisticated understanding on Herrick's part of the fallacies underlying such an explanatory system. But that insight did not prevent him from repeatedly asserting the power of festival magic. In *Hesperides* Herrick constructs what we can perhaps call an "economics of festival" by which traditional customs do not merely "keep up" institutions in a political sense but also insure basic subsistence and well-being. Usually in *Hesperides*, festival magic is not analyzed, but simply prescribed, in the form of verse instructions for achieving its effects. Trees bear fruit in direct proportion to the amount of wassailing they are given:

> WASSAILE the Trees, that they may beare
> You many a Plum, and many a Peare:
> For more or lesse fruits they will bring,
> As you doe give them Wassailing.
>
> ("Another," *Herrick*, 264)

Drinking and playing on "Psaltries" while the Christmas Log is lighted will bring "sweet luck" ("Ceremonies for Christmasse," *Herrick*, 263); relighting the log on Candlemas and laying up coals for the fire next Christmas will keep the house safe from the fiend ("The Ceremonies for Candlemasse day," *Herrick*, 285). Holiday greenery, renewed with the cycle of the seasons, will have "grace" to renew the house as well. Herrick's "Ceremonies for Candlemasse Eve" mimics the round of a holiday dance, ordering the decorations in accordance with the sequence of the seasons: holly must be put up for Christmas, boxwood from Candlemas to "dancing Easter-day," then yew, then birch and flowers for Whitsuntide (*Herrick*, 285).

Implicit in such formulations is the idea that festive practices associated with a religious holiday participate in the "grace" of the holiday itself. But rather than emphasize the divine origin of his festival magic,

Herrick usually stresses concreteness—the precise placement of ritual elements to achieve the desired effect. Even ecclesiastical law and ceremonial are assimilated into Herrick's economics of festival. Holy bread placed beneath a pillow will preserve a child against night perils ("Charmes," *Herrick*, 284); holy water mixed with spittle and meal will keep off the "evill Sp'rite" ("The Spell," *Herrick*, 258). Tithing to the Church, like holiday hospitality, will paradoxically increase one's wealth. The poet counsels a miser who, like many actual contemporaries, was withholding his obligation to the Church:

> MUCH-MORE, provides, and hoords up like an Ant;
> Yet *Much-more* still complains he is in want.
> Let *Much-more* justly pay his tythes; then try
> How both his Meale and Oile will multiply.
>
> (*Herrick*, 73)

"Pray and Prosper" makes the even more extravagant claim that incense and prayer in the fields will confer fertility:

> FIRST offer Incense, then thy field and meads
> Shall smile and smell the better by thy beads.
> The spangling Dew dreg'd o're the grasse shall be
> Turn'd all to Mell, and Manna there for thee.
>
> (*Herrick*, 143)

This brief poem evokes an actual ceremony practiced just before the Feast of the Ascension. The priest and parishioners in rural areas would process into the fields on Rogation Day to "beat the bounds" of the parish and pray for divine blessings upon the crops. But in Herrick's version, it is the ceremony itself, with ecclesiastical incense an essential adjunct to the prayers, that brings down blessings upon the fields. Incense must come "FIRST" for the "beads" to be effective.[8] Repeatedly in *Hesperides*, Laudian Anglican forms are woven into a quasi-magical system for insuring rural prosperity.

For Herrick and other ecclesiastical advocates of old pastimes, the *Book of Sports* controversy went beyond a few maypoles or even the policies of an individual monarch. It was a struggle to preserve a vanishing way of life. As Christopher Hill has pointed out, support for the *Book of Sports* implied support for a feudal or immediately postfeudal mode of social and economic organization in which the Church was bound up with communal agrarian subsistence. The medieval Church, at least at the parish level, had accommodated its ritual to the crucial need for securing agricultural increase. There were formulae for blessing the crops. Making the sign of the cross was an accepted way of frightening off evil influences. Even the sprinkling of holy water on the fields was permitted for aiding the success of the harvest.[9] That is very much the way ecclesiastical forms and traditional charms are put to use in *Hesperides,* except that Herrick was not a medieval Catholic. The Reformation had precipitated a questioning of all such "popish" formulas, along with the rural superstition that made them appear efficacious. Seventeenth-century "Precisians" who opposed wassailing and other traditional pastimes on religious grounds usually opposed post-feudal communalism as well. They tended to be tradesmen, merchants, independent farmers—those who stood to profit economically through the expansion of competitive trade and the disintegration of the traditional agrarian structures that the monarchy and Laudian wing of the Church sought to revive.[10] Herrick himself, the son of a family of prosperous London goldsmiths and apprenticed as a goldsmith in his youth, was no stranger to the world of competitive commerce. But in his poetry, that urban world and its values are systematically undermined in favor of a rural "economics of festival" in which prosperity is tied to the preservation of late medieval traditions. In arguing for a return to all manner of ritual magic in the interest of collective well-being, Herrick was performing a deliberate act of cultural revival not unlike the political program of the *Book of Sports* itself—broadening the scope of Anglican "liberty" in order to shore up a traditional system against the inroads of newer forms.

According to Puritan reformers, there were many people in England who would have been susceptible to such an amelioration of established religion. In the 1590s William Perkins made a list of some of the benighted opinions rife amongst his countrymen:

> That God is serued by the rehearsing of the ten commandements, the Lords Prayer, and the Creede.
> That none can tell whether he shall be saued or no certenly.
> That merry ballads and bookes, as *Scoggin, Beuis* of *Southhampton,* &c., are good to driue away the time, and to remooue heart-qualmes.
> That ye know all the Preacher can tell you.
> That drinking and bezeling in the ale-house or tauerne, is good fellowship and shewes a good kinde nature, and maintaines neighbourhood.
> That it was a good world, when the old Religion was, because all things were cheape.[11]

Over sixty years later, Richard Baxter constructed a similar list. The "ungodly crew" held that "it was never a good world since there was so much religion, and preaching, and preciseness, and so much ado about serving God! It was a better world, when we had but a short service read on Sundays, and played and merrily talked together the rest of the day!

There was more love and good neighbourhood then amongst men than there is now. There was not then so much deceit, and cozening, and oppressing, and covetousness in the world; there was more peace and plenty, and a better world it was than now."[12] Both lists end with assertions about economic prosperity: the land was more prosperous under the "old Religion," or in some unspecified past before the rise of Puritanism, when people could get along merrily without undue anxiety about the state of their souls, or even about the well-being of their bodies, because "all things were cheap." Whether this "merry world" had ever existed is doubtful; some of the power of such nostalgia derives from the indefiniteness of the time that is preferred to the present. But to some degree in the sixteenth and seventeenth centuries, complaints about the decline of "neighborhood" registered a perception of actual change—the breakdown of a communal agrarian system under the pressure of a new kind of "economics" that stressed individualism and autonomous labor.

Herrick himself was well acquainted with newer ideas about how to achieve prosperity. But his early immersion in urban commerce, his distance from the old agrarian model, seems to have aided him in delineating precisely how it functioned and what its unarticulated assumptions were. As Raymond Williams has noted, of the many seventeenth-century poems in praise of that virtually moribund institution, the late feudal country estate, Herrick's "The Hock-cart, or Harvest home" is easily the most specific depiction of the relationships which had traditionally sustained it. The lord provides the land and tools which allow his laborers to feed themselves and him. Their mutual dependence is based on the fruitful agrarian cycle of planting and harvesting and celebrated through communal feasting at important points in the cycle. This is the pattern recent social historians have termed *survivalism:* economic relationships are inseparable from the natural rhythms of the seasons and from seasonal festivities.[13] Except that, as usual in *Hesperides,* the poet has to intervene and "stage-manage" a festival in order to make it happen.

In "The Hock-cart," the speaker of the poem first addresses country laborers who have brought in the crops, inviting them to celebrate their traditional "harvest home":

> COME Sons of Summer, by whose toile,
> We are the Lords of Wine and Oile:
> By whose tough labours, and rough hands,
> We rip up first, then reap our lands.
> Crown'd with the eares of corne, now come,
> And, to the Pipe, sing Harvest home.
>
> (*Herrick,* 101)

But who is talking? By what right does he place himself among the landed classes? "We," he claims, "are the Lords of Wine and Oile." And why is he at such pains to point out to the laborers the connection between their own hard work and the prosperity of the "Lords" of the harvest? It is not the Lord of the manor who speaks, for he is the next person addressed and invited along with the "Sons of Summer" to become part of the collective merriment. The poet's stance in this poem is precisely that of the Laudian village priest, himself a "Lord" of the harvest in the sense that part of it must be tithed to the Church and therefore to his support, who acts as a community go-between, bringing the top and bottom of the social hierarchy together for the increase of "good neighborhood." "The Hock-cart" does not mystify the source of the wealth. It is through the "toil" of his tenants that the Lord enjoys his prosperity and even his social rank: their labor *makes* him what he is. In that sense, "The Hock-cart" can be taken as a decoding of the festival "magic" worked by customs such as wassailing in other poems of *Hesperides*. Part of the "magic" is simply rural labor, performed by actual rustics, who are more likely to work industriously if they are kept contented. Festival in *Hesperides* does not substitute for work but facilitates it by absorbing it into a continuously self-regenerating cycle. The estate's well-being arises not out of individual initiative, but through conformity to primordial collective patterns reaffirmed through holiday observances.

However, the magic of Herrick's "economics of festival" will work only if the Lord does his part as well. He cannot play absentee landlord, as many contemporaries were, but must remain close to the round of rural festivals and obligations on his country estate. Herrick invites the magnate to "come forth" and preside over the triumphant entry of the decorated Hock-cart, to observe the antics with which his laborers welcome it. Amidst the raucousness of the holiday, there is a curious semblance of religious devotion upon which the Lord is invited to look with benevolence:

> Some blesse the Cart; some kisse the sheaves;
> Some prank them up with Oaken leaves:
> Some crosse the Fill-horse; some with great
> Devotion, stroak the home-borne wheat.
>
> (*Herrick*, 101)

Some commentators have explained these apparently pagan observances as an overlay of Roman festive practice such as we might expect from an English Ovid or Tibullus: Herrick's rout of seventeenth-century peasants is also a group of Roman rustics, engaging in customs that would logically accompany the bringing in of "Wine and Oile," those notably un-English crops.[14] But Herrick's peasants are English as well as Roman, and practicing a time-honored English tradition. Pre-Christian veneration for natural things had by no means died out in remote areas of the country, as reformers bitterly complained. In some parts, country-folk still worshiped the sun and the moon and believed that doing homage to the harvest would insure a good crop next year.[15] By inter-mingling Roman and native English forms, Herrick suggests a tie between paganism of old and surviving peasant superstition. Here again, as elsewhere in *Hesperides,* a magical practice is revived, assimi-lated to the economics of festival, and surrounded with a diffuse aura of religiosity. Those who stroke the home-bound wheat are engaged in a traditional festival practice, but they are also at their "Prayers" (line 24).

Then the poet turns back to address the "Harvest Swaines, and Wenches," inviting them in to feast at the "Lords Hearth" and at the Lord's expense:

> for your mirth,
> Ye shall see first the large and cheefe
> Foundation of your Feast, Fat Beefe:
> With Upper Stories, Mutton, Veale
> And Bacon, (which makes full the meale)
> With sev'rall dishes standing by,
> As here a Custard, there a Pie,
> And here all tempting Frumentie.
> And for to make the merry cheere,
> If smirking Wine be wanting here,
> There's that, which drowns all care, stout Beere.
>
> (*Herrick,* 101)

Even here, there are subtle references that define the economic function-ing of the system being described. What is affordable is also the most acceptable. The plain, abundant fare promised the laborers is less costly than "smirking Wine" and culinary delicacies would be but more to the tastes of its recipients. Again, as in "The Wassaile," offering hospitality is an "easie" way to receive blessings. Those present are invited to drink freely to the health of all parts of the agrarian community—the Lord, the plow, the maids in "Wheaten Hats"—and this collective well-wishing and solidarity will further their common enterprise. But just as the feast is about to "drown" in drink and lose all semblance of order, the poet interrupts his invitation to license to remind the celebrants of its limits. The next turning in the fertile cycle of reciprocity will be up to the laborers themselves. They have fed and grown "fat" but must imitate their Lord's generosity, pass the prosperity down to their inferiors, the farm animals, if the collective prosperity is to continue. They must also return to their everyday labor so that the crops will not fail at the next harvest season. Herrick's language at this point in the poem becomes a blunt, almost jarring curb to holiday liberty:

> Feed, and grow fat; and as you eat,
> Be mindfull, that the lab'ring Neat
> (As you) may have their fill of meat.
> And know, besides, ye must revoke
> The patient Oxe unto the Yoke,
> And all goe back unto the Plough
> And Harrow, (though they'r hang'd up now.)
> And, you must know, your Lords word's true,
> Feed him ye must, whose food fils you.
> And that this pleasure is like raine,
> Not sent ye for to drowne your paine,
> But for to make it spring againe.
>
> *(Herrick,* 102)

The word "paine" is sharply equivocal. *Pain* can simply mean effort, but in the poem, "paine" is counterpoised against "pleasure" and therefore also suggests the cost of that effort in human suffering. Even the suffering is equivocal, however, in that it is assimilated into a survivalist pattern of renewal. The lord of the manor is identified with the heavens, from which precipitation falls to insure the fertility of the fields. Through his hospitality, holiday "pleasure" rains down upon dormant "pain," causing new effort, new suffering to "spring" up, but also causing a renewed seasonal "spring" of life and fertility. The laborers, too, are assimilated to the natural cycle. They become almost indistinguishable from their own animals—like them, needing their "meat," like them, destined to return on the morrow to the plow. This is a more extreme form of the organicism we have noted in some of Ben Jonson's works, in which festival has a similar capacity to meld individuals into their natural surroundings and into a larger collective entity. But Herrick's poem is more graphic about the mechanisms by which such collectivity is created and also far more provisional. The detailed scrutiny that allows Herrick to recreate the dynamics of holiday also exposes its vulnerability. In "The Hock-cart," holiday is performance. If either the Lord or his laborers refuse to play the parts that the poem sets out for them (and from a twentieth-century perspective, at least, the laborers are shown good reason not to), the festival and its magic will fail.

In "The Wake," the breaking of holiday becomes a "feare" acknowledged within the poem. As we have noted, contemporary Justices of the Peace were suppressing just such parish feasts on the grounds that they fostered disorder. In Herrick's poem, by contrast, the wake is an effective means for contenting the "ruder sort" and creating "good neighbor-hood." The poet stands outside and above the festival, portraying its buffooneries with amused condescension, but at the same time, planning to do "as others do" and join the follies himself. There will be "Tarts and Custards, Creams and Cakes," morris dancers and Maid Marian, a "Mimick," "Base" traveling players who strut about to impress the "incurious Villages," and as the festival wears on, more violent entertainment:

> Neer the dying of the day,
> There will be a *Cudgell*-Play,
> Where a *Coxcomb* will be broke,
> Ere a good *word* can be spoke:
> But the anger ends all here,
> Drencht in Ale, or drown'd in Beere.
> Happy Rusticks, best content
> With the cheapest Merriment:
> And possesse no other feare,
> Then to want the Wake next Yeare.
>
> (*Herrick*, 255)

This account is subtly shaped to defend the parish wake against the charge that it provoked disorders. Herrick acknowledges the wake's potential for violence: rage and physical injury are sure to be part of the *"Cudgell*-Play." But the outbreak will be contained within a larger structure that promotes community solidarity. Hostilities are first allowed release, then smoothed over as neighbors drink together in mutual reconciliation: "The anger ends all here, / Drencht in Ale, or drown'd in Beere." The wake thus functions normatively, in accordance with the "escape valve" theory of festival, easing tensions which might otherwise threaten the structure of the community.

As Herrick portrays it, the wake is also a sound business proposition. Like the harvest home, it offers merriment that is inexpensive, easy to provide, yet preferred above all else by the "Happy Rusticks." In the poem's sixth line, "Where the businesse is the sport," Herrick indirectly acknowledges the wake's financial function, which was to raise money for church repair and other parish necessities through the sale of beer and ale.[16] But this "businesse" is inseparable from the cyclical rhythms of survivalism. Herrick defuses newer ideas about how profit and labor are related by reintegrating commercial language into a larger structure in which profit is not measured primarily through money. The wake promotes collective prosperity as much through its strengthening of "good neighborhood" as through its financial benefits to the Church; it should therefore be recognized as an irresistible bargain by anyone interested in maximizing profit with minimal outlay for labor and materials. But the threat of disruption hangs over the wake nonetheless. There is only one "feare" of "want" that Herrick's economics of festival cannot allay in the minds of its participants—the fear that the wake may be wanting "next Yeare" and that the holiday may be discontinued.

To the extent that they were kept up, seventeenth-century wakes and Whitson Ales tended to occur along with Maying ceremonies, as in Herrick's "The Wake," in which morris dancing and "Pagentrie" of Robin and Maid Marian are promised among the feast's attractions. May Day itself was an official festival of the Anglican Church—the Feast of Philip and James the Less—but Maying customs were not restricted to May 1. They were practiced on and off throughout the "Maying season," beginning on May Day, clustering particularly around Whitsuntide, and ending about Midsummer, the Feast of St. John the Baptist, in late June. More than any other concrete vestige of late medieval culture, the maypole was a figure for the festival "license" allowed by the *Book of Sports*. Maypoles were thrust up defiantly against the opposition of local magistrates, churchwardens, and others—not all of them Puritans—who looked upon the poles as focal points for disorder. And in fact, May Day violence erupted with predictable regularity, especially in London, where threats of unusually severe rioting by apprentices and others in the year before the first publication of the *Book of Sports* caused authorities to impose such strict controls that the would-be Mayers "durst not adventure."[17]

Puritans were particularly troubled by the structural similarities between English maying customs—the erection of the pole, the dancing about it, the raucous games that followed—and the pattern of pagan idol worship. In Puritan tracts, the maypole was frequently likened to the golden calf around which the idolatrous Israelites had danced or to the false gods of Roman and Greek antiquity. Once the maypole is erected, complained Phillip Stubbes, country folk "straw the ground rounde about, binde green boughes about it, set by sommer haules, bowers, and arbors hard by it. And then fall they to daunce about it like as the heathen people did at the dedication of the Idols, whereof this is a perfect pattern, or rather the thing itself." During the iconoclastic phase of the Edwardian Reformation, London's most majestic maypole had actually been chopped up and burned as an "Idoll."[18] Although maygames were briefly restored along with Catholicism under Mary Tudor, they became increasingly embattled under Elizabeth. Even the moderate Edmund Spenser used maygames in the May Eclogue of his *Shepheardes Calendar* to symbolize the dangerous follies condoned under Catholicism.

Those who advocated the suppression of May Day frequently cited Lactantius's account of the holiday's obscene origins. The Roman Floralia, like the English May Day, had been a spring festival associated with flowers, fertility, and also with sexual license. According to Lactantius, the Floralia had begun not according to the charming Ovidian legend of Chloris and Zephyrus, but in a less idyllic fashion—as an annual orgy of debauchery dedicated to perpetuating the memory of a Roman prostitute. St. Augustine corroborated that the Floralia were "reckoned devout in proportion to their lewdness" and that even more sober pagans like Cato the Censor had deplored them. The English maygames that the Stuart monarchs were so anxious to revive were therefore "Revels and disorders" which "sprung from the Pagans *Saturnalia*, and from them came to the Papists, and so to us," preserving throughout their long, inglorious history the idolatry, sexual license, and anarchy of the heathen original. [19] In *A Divine Tragedie Lately Acted, or . . . Gods Judgements upon Sabbath-breakers* (1636) Henry Burton cited a series of calamities stemming from the republication of the *Book of Sports* in 1633. Villages burned as a result of rude revelry; a maypole in Glastonbury fell and killed a child; a "tall lusty maid" chosen as Lady Flora was struck by lightning; another unfortunate heard the king's declaration, went out dancing, was immediately seduced, and was later put to death for murdering her bastard infant. According to contemporaries, bastardy rates did indeed rise in connection with the holiday since some ignorant folk evidently considered sexual license in the forest an essential element of May Day observance. [20] One of the reasons May Day was viewed as particularly threatening to public order, we can speculate, was that a key element of its observance—the trip to the woods to gather greenery—required an escape into uncontrolled territory, where all manner of abuses could be hidden from the eyes of watchful authorities.

Sexplay in the forest did not come under the category of "harmless" customs allowed by the *Book of Sports*. But at least one defender of royal policy before Herrick took the somewhat irregular step of incorporating the sexual license associated with May Day into an idealized account of the holiday's functioning. One of the earliest and most irreverent defenses of the *Book of Sports* was *Pasquils Palinodia*, published in 1619 and attributed to Nicholas Breton or William Fennor. After a printer's preface acknowledging the probable displeasure of *"the peeuish, puritanicall, and meager* Zoilist," the author takes his muse on a somewhat wine-sodden tour of that Puritan stronghold, the City of London. He castigates the pride and acquisitiveness of City tradesmen and lawyers and stops for a moment to contemplate the maypole in the Strand, a "signe" of the "harmelesse mirth and honest neighbourhood" England had enjoyed before the encroachment of political factionalism and competitive commerce. In that idyllic past, "all the Parish did in one combine, / To mount the rod of peace," without the opposition of "*capritious Constables,*" Justices of the Peace, or "peevish" Puritans. In that "Happy" age of "true loue and amity," maypoles were raised in every village, "And *Whitson-ales,* and *May-games* did abound." There was dancing for the young, feasting for the poor, and as in Herrick's "The Wake," the reconciling of differences among locals who might otherwise resort to more divisive measures for the redress of grievances:

> Then raign'd plaine honest meaning, and good will,
> And neighbours tooke up points of difference,
> In *Common lawes* the Commons had no skill,
> And publike feasts were Courts of Conscience.

For our purposes at present, the poem's most important stanzas are those describing the functioning of May Day license within the larger community:

> The Lords of Castles, Mannors, Townes & Towers
> Reioyc'd when they beheld the Farmers flourish,
> And would come downe unto the Summer-Bowers
> To see the Country-gallants dance the Morrice,
>   And sometimes with his tenants handsome daughter
>   Would fall in liking, and espouse her after
>   Vnto his Seruing-man, and for her portion
>   Bestow on him some farme, without extortion.

> But since the Summer-poles were overthrowne,
> And all good sports and merriments decayd,
> How times and men are chang'd, so well is knowne
> It were but labour lost if more were said. . . .[21]

Most of Pasquil's arguments in defense of the *Book of Sports* customs will be recognized, by this point in the discussion, as Stuart commonplace. But Pasquil is, to say the least, unusual in his open nostalgia for what is essentially the feudal *droit du seigneur.* The Lord would come down to view village festivities, very much as Herrick's "Hock-cart" prescribes that he should, but would have more in mind than showing his solidarity with tenant mirth. As Pasquil depicts it, the Lord's seduction of one of the village maids was a form of holiday "license" that was good for all concerned. The young woman he chose would, consequently, be married off above her station with a farm as her dowry, thus increasing the flourishing of the rural community. The logic operating here seems to be that sexuality under the happy aegis of festival is preferable to more modern forms of exploitation, such as the "extortion" practiced by less scrupulous landlords or by the profit-mongerers of the city, because it helps to build up the rural community rather than tearing it down. It is an outrageous position to take and one that few supporters of the *Book of Sports* would have countenanced, at least in public. Contemporary churchmen, in particular, were intent on defusing May Day's association with rampant sexuality. Maygames performed under the benevolent authority of the village priest would, it was hoped, be far more decorous than otherwise.

But what if, as in Herrick's *Hesperides,* the village priest appears half Cavalier himself and does not always stand apart from the libertine ethos of sexplay in the forest? Herrick deals with the sexual license of May Day by confronting it directly, even celebrating it, but at the same time incorporating it into the ritual structure of survivalism, where it waxes and wanes in accordance with the seasons and is made "honest" by the timely intervention of the Church. One of Herrick's most wittily outrageous poems is "The May-pole," in which the pole itself becomes the locus of festival "magic." A major Puritan objection to the maypole was that, like its ritual equivalents in the Roman Floralia, it served in the minds of its devotees as a fertility charm—indeed a rather potent one if Puritan complaints against maygames as a "nursery of bastardy" carry any credence. In "The May-pole," as in Herrick's many other poems offering ritual formulas for prosperity, heathen magic is channeled into an acceptable role within the parish community. The poem is itself a fertility charm, a piece of mimetic magic, with its author in his usual pose of a benevolent, somewhat condescending director of village "mirth." He orders a cup to drink to the "erection" of the maypole; the veneration of this phallic object will encourage fruitful marriages for the young women who have encircled it with garlands:

> The May-pole is up,
>   Now give me the cup;
> I'le drink to the Garlands a-round it:
>   But first unto those
>   Whose hands did compose
> The glory of flowers that crown'd it.
>
>   A health to my Girles,
>   Whose husbands may Earles
> Or Lords be, (granting my wishes)
>   And when that ye wed
>   To the Bridall Bed,
> Then multiply all, like to Fishes.
>
> (Herrick, 239)

There can be no question that Herrick's phallic symbolism was intentional: the maypole was commonly viewed so in his day, not only by Puritan controversialists, but also by Thomas Hobbes, who made a list of Roman holidays along with Anglican equivalents. As the Romans had their "Procession of *Priapus*; [so] wee our fetching in, erection, and dancing about *Maypoles*." The author of *Pasquils Palinodia* jested at some length about the fact that maypoles were used as weathercocks in order to hint at their association with a different sort of cock.[22] In "The Maypole," however, fertility has to wait for marriage. The situation being described is similar to that which led to the May Day seduction in *Pasquils Palinodia,* and we may detect more than a hint of voyeuristic interest, or perhaps vicarious participation, in the poet's hearty toast to the fertility of his "Girles." But their blossoming sexuality is regulated and tied to the higher functions of the Church. The dance of the flower-laden maids about the pole symbolically anticipates the marriage act—carefully specified as taking place in the "Bridall Bed," not out in the freedom of the forest—by which they will fulfill the Biblical injunction to "be fruitful and multiply."[23]

Some of the maying poems of *Hesperides* are much more decorous. "The meddow verse or Aniversary to Mistris Bridget Lowman" is addressed to the daughter of a Dean Prior gentry family and purports to commemorate a specific occasion—Bridget Lowman's appearance as May Queen for the second year in a row. Whether or not the poem was written for an actual maying celebration, it elevates the ritual in much the way that Robert Dover refined his Cotswold Games to make old pastimes more acceptable to the gentry.[24] "The Meddow Verse" is far more refined and reticent than "The May-pole," carefully elevating Bridget Lowman to a "neat distinction" above the rest of the celebrants, addressing her with delicacy and deference, giving her an etherialized version of the standard role of May Queen (she will be the Lady of "Fairie land"), promising her "full mirth," but nothing that will cause a "blush" to anyone:

> COME with the Spring-time, forth Fair Maid, and be
> This year again, the *medows Deity.*
> Yet ere ye enter, give us leave to set
> Upon your Head this flowry Coronet:
> To make this neat distinction from the rest;
> You are the Prime, and Princesse of the Feast:
> To which, with silver feet lead you the way,
> While sweet-breath Nimphs, attend on you this Day.
> This is your houre; and best you may command,

Since you are Lady of this Fairie land.
Full mirth wait on you; and such mirth as shall
Cherrish the cheek, but make none blush at all.

(*Herrick*, 140)

In the companion poem to "The Meddow Verse," however, it becomes clear that even this civilized, attenuated ritual may be on the verge of extinction. In "The Parting Verse, the Feast There Ended" Herrick depicts the celebrants as returning home in melancholy, not knowing whether they will meet again for the festival next spring. The effect is rather like that of the regretful epilogues that closed masques at court, but far more intense. The poet himself is, like Bridget and her Nymphs, melancholy, full of "cares / And griefs," in part, perhaps, over the uncertain future of the feast, in part because he is aging and may not last out the year. The verses establish a strong subliminal connection between the life of festival and the life of the poet, as though to suggest that he may die along with the maygames. And if he lives, so will they. The poet, the meadows, the "meddow-verse" will all renew themselves as part of the same natural cycle:

but if fates do give
Me longer date, and more fresh springs to live:
Oft as your field, shall her old age renew,
Herrick shall make the meddow-verse for you.

(*Herrick*, 140)

The poet's vision of his own life as merged into the endless self-regeneration of the meadows will exist only if he remains alive. In that sense, the poem exposes a fallacy in the mentality of survivalism, which insulates the poet against noncyclical changes but cannot undo their effects. By extension, the poem casts doubt on the power of festival "magic": its one great flaw is its vulnerability to forces that are independent of its own explanatory system, as in the threat from outside that hangs over "The Wake." In all of Herrick's poems of holiday "mirth," extinction is preferred to disjunction. The poet describes the "drowning" of individual consciousness, even his own, with remarkable cheerfulness. In fact, he fairly revels in it, imagining his own death with considerable complacency so long as it is kept within a pattern of ritual observance.[25] Being wrenched out of the insulating cycle of survivalism is far more painful a prospect than mere extinction.

"Corinna's Going a Maying" is Herrick's most daring treatment of holiday sexual license in that it unites an argument in defense of the *Book of Sports* with a frank attempt at seduction. But it is also the poem of *Hesperides* most thoroughly steeped in the ecclesiastical side of May Day.

By the end of it, the paganism and "license" of the feast day have been drawn into the sacramental order of the church. For many Laudian churchmen, the mirth of the maying season *was* sacramental in the sense that it was an outward manifestation of the descent of the Holy Spirit. John Cosin argued of Whitsunday (Pentecost), "This *Day* hold we *holy* to the *holy Ghost* by whom all *holy Dayes,* all *holy Persons,* & all *holy Things* whatsoever are made *Holy.*" He explained that "ancient Christians" had clothed themselves in white on Whitsunday and its attendant holidays in order to express the "*Joy* they had, and the *Festivitie* they held for the visible descent of the *Holy Ghost* upon the Church at first, as for his mysterious descent now in The blessed Sacrament of *Baptisme.*"[26] Since all holiday "*Festivitie*" derives from that one sacramental font, all holiday customs, even dancing around a maypole, are in a very broad sense sacramental in that they manifest the descent of the Spirit. If contemporary Puritans condemned May Day dancing by likening it to that of the Israelites about their pagan idols, Laudians could respond with more positive Biblical precedents. Particularly after 1633, there was an outpouring of treatises in defense of the *Book of Sports* that cited David's dance before the Ark of the Covenant as proof that dancing could be a form of praise. King David had not only leapt and danced before the Lord, he had also prescribed dancing in his psalms, for "many good psalms began with *exaltate,* which ought not to be translated *rejoice* (for so *gaudete* signifies) but *dance ye,* for it cometh of *ex* and *salto.*" If the English wished to have "Manna rained downe" upon them, they had to give up their strict "*Sabbath*" and keep Sunday and holidays with dancing, feasting, and rejoicing.[27]

We will note that such formulations go far beyond the *Book of Sports* itself, which had merely required that holiday customs not be hindered. As they were sacramentalized by some of the Laudians, the traditional customs become a high religious obligation. Heaven itself was part of the cycle of holiday reciprocity. Prayer and praise went up to God in the form of feast day observances; in return, God sent down blessings and a renewal of holiday grace that permitted the cycle to begin anew. Churlishly refusing to participate in holiday thus became tantamount to refusing God proper "hospitality." In accordance with the traditional mechanisms for dealing with the breakdown of communal obligations, such a denial might call down God's curse—not only upon the ingrate who broke the cycle of reciprocity, but upon the community as a whole. The magic behind Herrick's "economics of festival" is finally the magic of the Holy Ghost, which operates through natural things like rain and dew, through humble people like rural laborers, but must be returned to God in the form of holiday mirth.

"Corinna's Going a Maying" is perhaps Herrick's most overtly sacramental poem; it is not, however, a religious poem. Rather, it is a poem in which religious duty and festival liberty are joyously one and the same. In "Corinna," as frequently in *Hesperides,* contemporary festival forms are interlayered with their classical or medieval precedents in order to elide two great cultural boundaries—one between paganism and Christianity and the other between the medieval and the post-Reformation church. Such erasure of cultural discontinuities was a common strategy among contemporary churchmen interested in preserving older communal forms. Bishop Corbett regretted the vanishing of the fairies along with the "old Profession" that had fostered belief in them; Richard Mountagu, chaplain to Charles I and later Bishop of Chichester, publicly endorsed the idea that the sign of the cross could render spells and sorcery ineffectual and also favored the use of religious images and other "popish" forms on grounds that they had been permitted in the "ancient Church"; John Cosin composed an Anglican Book of Hours which resurrected the "old godly" canonical hours of the medieval church in order to ease the conversion of Catholics to Anglicanism.[28] Ecclesiastical conservatives responded to Puritan complaints about the "paganism" of such revivals by conceding the opposition's major premise. Numerous customs tolerated in the Anglican Church were indeed "relics of paganism," yet innocent despite their origins. As Robert Sanderson argued in 1639 in a sermon before Charles I, the very primitive church which Puritans longed to restore had often "fetched" practices "from the very dregs of paganism" and cleansed them for Christian use. The only customs unlawful among Anglicans were those specifically forbidden by apostolic doctrine. All others, however similar to paganism or popery, were validated by their antiquity, by the very fact of their perpetual observance since the time of the primitive church. The pagan origins of a particular English custom, then, could demonstrate its acceptability in the present by proving its "long continuance."[29] That is the way paganism functions in *Hesperides.* Herrick's extreme ritual eclecticism does not undercut the traditional pastimes he celebrates, but rather helps to sustain them by asserting their participation in a sacramental pattern of "long continuance."

In the poem's early stanzas, May Day appears predominantly pagan. As the poet invites Corinna to become more deeply immersed in the festivities, they gradually move closer to Christian ritual but do so without breaking the continuum of observance. Finally, by the end of the poem, in a tactic Herrick could have borrowed from Jonson's *Bartholomew Fair,* the poet's language and argument unmistakably echo the Anglican liturgy for May Day. Even the apparent heathenism of the early stanzas is retrospectively amalgamated into an all-embracing pattern of worship. The poem enacts the "cleansing" of pagan pastimes described in ecclesiastical arguments for "long continuance." As the scope of the ritual expands, the landscape of the poem becomes "all country": May Day abolishes the divisions between town and countryside, between urban and rural values, by absorbing everything into its own ritual structure, which is finally inextricable from the ritual of the Church.

In the first stanza of "Corinna's Going a Maying," Herrick describes a rite of distinctly heterogeneous nature. By urging Corinna out of doors, he appears to be plunging her into heathen "idol" worship within a temple of nature that is inscribed with Anglican ritual forms. He points out to Corinna that the flowers have bowed toward the East (like Laudians before an altar); the birds have said "Mattens" and sung their "thankfull Hymnes." Yet the object of this liturgical devotion appears to be the rising sun, associated with the pagan Apollo, the "god unshorne." Herrick's reference calls to mind Puritan objections against the Laudian north-south placement of the altar on grounds that it required the priest to bow idolatrously toward the East, as though in worship of the rising sun.[30] But for the moment, that flicker of possible meaning is not engaged. The poet contents himself with admonishing Corinna that, when all of the world outside is charged with such glorious life and motion, she "sins" by remaining indoors. One objection contemporary Sabbatarians made against maygames was that the racket of profane mayers and morris dancers outdoors hindered family devotions indoors,[31] but Herrick turns their language back upon them: "'tis sin / Nay, profanation to keep in." Paradoxically, Corinna would sin not by joining the "pagan" sun-worship outside, but by staying home in obstinate singularity and refusing the collective mirth.

In the poem's second stanza, heathen and Christian practices are again counterpoised in a way that suggests they are mutually exclusive. Corinna is envisioned as emerging into the natural world, where she is immediately transformed into part of it. She is, like the Roman goddess Flora, the spirit of spring, but also a "flower" decked with dew and greenery:

> Rise; and put on your Foliage, and be seene
> To come forth, like the Spring-time, fresh and greene;
>   And sweet as *Flora*. Take no care
>   For Jewels for your Gowne, or Haire:
>   Feare not; the leaves will strew
>   Gemms in abundance upon you:
> Besides, the childhood of the Day has kept,

Against you come, some *Orient Pearls* unwept:
Come, and receive them while the light
Hangs on the Dew-locks of the night:
(*Herrick*, 68)

The stanza is bathed in Maydew and Corinna is repeatedly enjoined to come forth and "receive" it, as though it has special significance. Traditionally, on May Day villagers would go out in the fields and wash themselves in maydew, much as Corinna is invited to do, because it was believed to have curative and restorative powers. Even Oliver Cromwell tried it as a remedy for the gout.[32] But the poem still preserves an apparent distinction between the "magic" of the maydew and orthodox religious observance. Corinna must scant her prayers in favor of the natural "bespangling" outside: "Few Beads are best, when once we goe a Maying."

What happens to Corinna in the second stanza of the poem happens to the entire landscape in the third. Corinna is invited to discover the greening of the town, which now appears a country grove or garden: "Come my *Corinna,* come; and comming, marke / How each field turns a street; each street a Parke / Made green, and trimm'd with trees . . ." The poet is describing a traditional English custom whereby huge boughs were brought in from the countryside and set up before each doorway so that an English town on May 1 did literally resemble a park. But he is also implying something about the function of May Day festivities—their tendency to draw participants out of the urban world and back into the survivalist cycle. The town, a center of commerce and economic individualism, is reabsorbed into the country. In this stanza, there are no specifically pagan references, although the customs being described had their pagan equivalents. According to Polydore Vergil and other standard sources, the English practice of decorating houses and churches with boughs had derived from the practice of "Heathen people, which decked their Idols and houses with such array."[33] (We will recall the leafy "pagan" booths at Jonson's *Bartholomew Fair.*) But the parallel Herrick cites within the poem is Hebraic rather than pagan. By terming the traditional bower "An Arke a Tabernacle," he ties contemporary maying customs to the ancient Jewish agricultural festivals characterized by a similar pattern of action: the Feast of Tabernacles, when the Jews went out to collect foliage and arrange it into temporary dwelling places, and Shuvuos, the Jewish Pentecost, when homes and the sanctuary containing the Ark were decorated with green.[34] The Hebraic references bring maying customs into a cultural milieu less alien from orthodox Christianity than that of pagan Rome and also provide a context for

Herrick's evocation of the "law" of May in the lines immediately follow-ing. Just as the Jewish Feast of Tabernacles was dedicated to rejoicing in the law of Moses, so English maying is portrayed as obedience to another injunction:

> Can such delights be in the street,
> And open fields, and we not see't?
> Come, we'll abroad; and let's obay
> The Proclamation made for May:
> And sin no more, as we have done, by staying;
> But my *Corinna*, come, let's goe a Maying.

The "Proclamation made for May" could be taken to refer to the observances the May Queen requires of her dutiful subjects; but in Herrick's poem, Corinna herself is invited to take on that role. The authority she is admonished to obey is higher than her own. In the context of Herrick's collection as a whole, this call for obedience to the "Proclamation made for May" is an unmistakable allusion to the *Book of Sports*, which was not only issued in May but also "made" to encourage May Day customs. The Jewish law associated with the Feast of Taberna-cles thus becomes a precursor of Stuart "law" for the preservation of English May Day. Herrick's method is akin to that of Biblical typology: the "type" of the law of the Tabernacles gives way to the "truth" of the royal proclamation. In this stanza, the center stanza of the poem, May Day festivities receive the validating imprint of scriptural and royal authority.

At the same time, however, a new form of "heathenism" enters the poem as Herrick's persuasion to May Day observance begins to take on sexual overtones. Even as he acknowledges the "Devotion" that has created the leafy "Arke" and "Tabernacle," Herrick perceives another purpose to which these edifices could be put:

> Made up of white-thorn neatly enterwove;
> As if here were those cooler shades of love.

The flowering whitethorn, gathered from the woods that very morning or the night before, evokes the place of "love" and license where it originated. In the poem's fourth stanza, the implied landscape expands even further as the poet urges Corinna off with him to the freedom of the forest, where all the other youths have already played out the sex games associated with the holiday:

> There's not a budding Boy, or Girle, this day,
> But is got up, and gone to bring in May.

> A deale of Youth, ere this, is come
> Back, and with *White-thorn* laden home.
> Some have dispatcht their Cakes and Creame,
> Before that we have left to dreame:
> And some have wept, and woo'd, and plighted Troth,
> And chose their Priest, ere we can cast off sloth:
> Many a green-gown has been given;
> Many a kisse, both odde and even:
> Many a glance too has been sent
> From out the eye, Loves Firmament:
> Many a jest told of the Keyes betraying
> This night, and Locks pickt, yet w'are not a Maying.

There has been rolling in the grass and talk of keys betraying locks—altogether typical May Day behavior, except that it transgresses the officially countenanced distinction between acceptable "liberty" and "license." The boys and girls behave like the English peasants of whom Philip Stubbes reported, no doubt with some exaggeration, "that of fortie, threescore, or a hundred maides going to the wood over night, there have scaresly the third part of them returned home againe undefiled."[35] Just in the nick of time, however, the Church is brought in to redeem the disorders. The woodland sexplay culminates in the plighting of troths and choosing of a priest. Indeed, the very sequence of the poet's description "contains" the license. It is only after the mention of the priest that Herrick intimates just how far the earlier sexgames have gone. By this point, the poem has moved considerably further toward cultural amalgamation than most Laudians would have found acceptable. Even the ritualized promiscuity of the maygames is cleansed and assimilated into the order of the Church. The "license" of May Day has spread to fill the countryside but has also been encompassed within the "liberty" of the Church.

In "Corinna's" final stanza, however, Herrick appears to undo the pattern of gradual amalgamation. The poem expands once more but this time into an abrupt reminder of death. Herrick's mortalist evocation of the traditional *carpe diem* motif so strongly resembles its classical Greek and Roman analogues that he seems to be giving May Day back to the pagans. The poet and Corinna, all the "budding" mayers, will be "drown'd" in night like "fleeting" shades of Elysium:

> Come, let us goe, while we are in our prime;
> And take the harmelesse follie of the time.
> We shall grow old apace, and die
> Before we know our liberty.
> Our life is short; and our dayes run

As fast away as do's the Sunne:
And as a vapour, or a drop of raine
Once lost, can ne'r be found againe:
    So when or you or I are made
    A fable, song, or fleeting shade;
    All love, all liking, all delight
    Lies drown'd with us in endlesse night.
Then while time serves, and we are but decaying;
Come, my *Corinna*, come, let's goe a Maying.

This stanza engulfs the earlier energies of the poem in a vision of human transience that arrests the mirth of festival but also strengthens the festival's claim to legitimacy in that its mirth becomes one of the highest blessings afforded in this mortal life. However, Herrick's lines are not so exclusively pagan as they may appear. May Day and *carpe diem* were very commonly linked in literature of the period, even in folk carols of such humble origin that we cannot assume a common classical source. For all its seemingly pagan fatalism, the last stanza of "Corinna" comes directly out of the lessons and epistles proper for May 1:

> Go thy way, eat thy bread with joy, and drink thy wine with merry heart; for God now accepteth thy works. . . . Live joyfully with the wife whom thou lovest all the days of the life of thy vanity, which he hath given thee under the sun, all the days of thy vanity: for that is thy portion in this life, and in thy labour which thou takest under the sun. Whatsoever thy hand findeth to do, do it with thy might; for there is no work, nor device, nor knowledge, nor wisdom, in the grave, whither thou goest. (Eccles. 9:7–9)

> Let the brother of low degree rejoice in that he is exalted: But the rich, in that he is made low: because as the flower of the grass he shall pass away. For the sun is no sooner risen with a burning heat, but it withereth the grass, and the flower thereof falleth, and the grace of the fashion of it perisheth: so also shall the rich man fade away in his ways. (James 1:9–11)[36]

These liturgical lessons undo individualism and individual effort and restore human beings to an organic connection with fleeting natural things—the sun, whose days "run" fast away, the flower that fades and dies. We will recall the survivalist creed of Sir John, the madcap priest from *The Merry Devil of Edmonton*: "Grasse and hay! we are all mortall; let's liue till we die, and be merry; and theres an end," which like the *carpe diem* motif of "Corinna," comes straight out of the liturgy for May Day.[37] At the end of "Corinna," extinction is once again preferred to disjunction. The "drowning" of individual identity is a natural corollary of the survivalist credo by which human beings and institutions are sunk back into the green world, as the grass that "withereth" and the flower that fades away.

Once the poem's echoes of the Anglican May Day *carpe diem* are recognized, other elements of the poem can be assimilated retrospectively into the liturgical milieu established by its final stanza. If the liturgy for May Day celebrated transience, it also called attention to a power beyond the things that "pass away." A prominent theme of liturgies and homilies for the Maying season is the idea of continuous creation and divine immanence. God acts through natural powers; if He were to withdraw His sustaining grace for even an instant, the world would crumble into atomies. Through spring dew, sun, and showers, divine grace is renewed. The "pagan" ritual elements that appeared early in Herrick's poem—the rising sun worshiped in the first stanza and the magical maydew sprinkled in the second—become recognizable in retrospect as conduits for God's sustaining power. The poem's landscape is charged with spiritual intensity. Each flower, herb, and tree scatters maydew, a sacramental substance whose transforming gems "bespangle" and enrich all they touch. Herrick subtly underlines the sacramentalism of the English maying festival by tying it to Jewish and classical precursors which also emphasized water as a vehicle for divine renewal. On the eighth day of the Feast of Tabernacles, according to the standard seventeenth-century sources, the Jews brought water from Shiloah to the Temple and poured it on the altar, singing "With ioy shall ye draw water out of the wells of Salvation"; when Jesus celebrated the feast (John 7), its waters came to represent Christian regeneration. The pagan Romans used branches of herbs and trees (olive, laurel, rosemary, or pine) to sprinkle *aqua lustralis* among participants at their fertility festivals. Herrick's "Dew-bespangling Herbe and Tree" recall their classical predecessors and perform a similar ritual function.[38] In the medieval church, as we have seen, holy water, the Christian descendant of the pagan *aqua lustralis,* was scattered over the fields to insure abundant crops, and even during Anglican times, Whitsuntide was considered a particularly appropriate season for baptisms. By carrying in dew-laden branches and strewing themselves with its transforming drops, therefore, Herrick's English country folk keep alive an ancient ritual pattern that sheds divine blessings upon them. Such activities will appear "pagan" and "superstitious" only to those who refuse to take part and therefore remain untouched by the festival's sacramental power. In accordance with the laws of holiday reciprocity, maying customs do not finally compete with more orthodox forms of worship, but extend them, offering prayer and praise like that repeatedly called for in the Psalms

Proper for the maying season: "Let the people praise thee, O God; let all the people praise thee. Then shall the earth yield her increase; and God, even our own God, shall bless us" (Psalm 67:5–6).[39]

With its elaborate web of pagan, Hebrew, and Christian references, "Corinna's Going a Maying" is clearly not one of the poems of *Hesperides* that would have been accessible to simple country folk. But it might have been comprehensible in another way, in that it preserves a mode of "worship" that had not quite died out in remote parts. Some rural people still considered maying a way of insuring the "Success of the Fruits of the Earth," and also a form of divine praise. As usual, our best evidence comes from reformers who found such superstition appalling. Henry Burton describes the activity of one poor mayer who was punished for his "sacrilege": in 1634 "One good man Paul neere Stoke in Dorcetshire, rejoycinge much at the erection of a summer-pole, at a Parish cald Simsbury in Dorcetshire, & saying before one [of] his Neighbours, he would goe see it, though he went naked through a quickset hedge: which is a common proverb they use: Going with wood in his armes to cast into the bonfire, where he lived, and using these words: Heaven and earth are full of thy glory, O Lord: he was presently smitten by the Stroke of God" and died.[40] Paul's problem was that he confused the holy and the holiday. His enactment of old custom as a form of divine praise was just the sort of holiday "liberty" that *Hesperides* was fashioned to revive.

The hedges of Dorset may appear far removed from the court of Charles I, from which the *Book of Sports* had been promulgated to the nation. But that distance between the everyday life of the people and a king and church that held themselves aloof was precisely the space that Laudian sponsorship of old customs was designed to bridge. Quasi-magical ruralization of England was a regular feature of Caroline literature. Jasper Fisher's "A Morisco" (1633), for example, imagines all the natural world, humankind, and God himself moving together in the harmony of one vast morris dance or morisco and suggests that so long as the morris is danced, the quiet of merry old England will be untroubled by "foreign spite or civil fight."[41] In the Caroline masque, the transformation of town into country was often symbolically effected through a seemingly pagan or hermetic ritual enacted by the king. In *Albion's Triumph* (1632), for example, the king performs a mysterious rite by which London—chief stronghold of political resistance—is metamorphosed into a green, parklike landscape dominated by the palace at Whitehall and five personages on clouds representing "Innocency, Justice, Religion, Affection to the Country, and Concord" (*Inigo*, 2:457). But the masque that came closest to Herrick's sense of the frailty of holiday "magic" was *Salmacida Spolia* (1640), last of the Caroline "spectacles of state" before the outbreak of war (*Inigo*, 1:72). *Salmacida Spolia* begins with an antimasque of Furies who inflict political and economic discord of a clearly Puritan stamp upon an England previously blessed above all other nations. Through the "secret wisdom" of the king, the Furies are quelled and the scene is transformed to a landscape of cornfields and villages "with all such things as might express a country in peace, rich and fruitful." From the heavens appear Concord and the Good Genius of Britain, who descend "to incite the beloved people to honest pleasures and recreations, which have ever been peculiar to this nation." But their appeal to public mirth falls on deaf ears. The ungrateful people refuse to value the "easie blessing" they have received through the king's solicitude. Concord threatens to withdraw from them, creating general dearth, if they continue in their sullenness and vice:

> Should dews not fall, the sun forbear
> His course, or I my visits here,
> Alike from these defects would cease
> The power and hope of all increase.
>
> (*Inigo*, 2:731)

But new antimasques emerge, and even when the Chorus of Beloved People is finally "instructed" to the point that they will do honor to the king and queen, the praise they offer sounds an elegaic note:

> When with instructed eyes we look upon
> Our blessings that descend so fast
> From the fair partner of our monarch's throne,
> We grieve they are too great to last.
>
> (*Inigo*, 2:732)

In *Salmacida Spolia*, May Day *carpe diem* is applied to the realm of national politics, but the magical insulation it affords is a tenuous barrier against the Furies massed outside.

In *Hesperides*, the poet's "garden" of rural mirth is similarly violated by events outside its limits: poems like "TO THE KING, Upon his comming with his Army into the West," "TO THE KING, Upon his welcome to Hampton-Court," "The bad season makes the Poet sad," and "Upon the troublesome times" record the progress of the Civil War. King Charles, Prince Charles, and other members of the royal family carry with them the power of May—when they appear, the land springs magically into vitality and renewed spring fertility. But when they depart, fertility gives way to dearth.[42] The magic of the monarchy and of the old holiday customs must compete with other less optimistic assessments of the national situation from which such "easie" remedies are called into question. In that indirect way, Herrick undoes his own "economics of festival." And occasionally in *Hesperides*, holiday is revealed as "unthrifty" even for its most loyal celebrants—heaven itself appears to violate the law of reciprocity whereby hospitality is rewarded with "increase." In Herrick's enigmatic "To Meddowes" the poet chides the meadows for having "spent their stock" on Maying rituals, only to be left poor and abandoned:

1. Ye have been fresh and green,
    Ye have been fill'd with flowers:
And ye the Walks have been
    Where Maids have spent their houres.

2. You have beheld, how they
    With *Wicker Arks* did come
To kisse, and beare away
    The richer Couslips home.

3. Y'ave heard them sweetly sing,
    And seen them in a Round:
Each Virgin, like a Spring,
    With Hony-succles crown'd.

4. But now, we see, none here,
    Whose silv'rie feet did tread,
And with dishevell'd Haire,
    Adorn'd this smoother Mead.

5. Like Unthrifts, having spent,
    Your stock, and needy grown,
Y'are left here to lament
    Your poore estates, alone.

(*Herrick*, 110)

The liturgy for May Day is clearly behind this poem. Herrick contemplates the deserted meadows in terms of the "flesh is grass" motif from the Book of James. Their condition is, in terms of the May Day *carpe diem*, inevitable, yet another turning of the cycle that brings all things to destruction. But in this case, Herrick interprets holiday liberty as prodigality: the meadows have spent all and received nothing in return. It is possible to read the poet's indictment as a temporary failure of vision cancelled out by the liturgical context of the poem. Come spring, the meadows can be expected to be renewed and replenished, once again capable of offering hospitality. But the poet's depiction of their abandonment has a finality that belies such optimism. Perhaps the Mayers will not, after all, return. It is as though divine grace has been permanently withdrawn. The poem has some of the elegaic quality of *Salmacida Spolia,* in which the motifs conventionally associated with holiday's renewal instead forecast its demise. Herrick foresaw all too clearly that holiday was likely to perish—indeed, by the time the collection was published in 1647–48 the traditional festivals had been legislated out of existence through a series of Parliamentary ordinances. In one of *Hesperides'* many poems "To his Booke," Herrick tries to predict the fate of his poetry after it is printed. It may hold its own amidst the "dung-hil" of popular ballads and may even outlast all time. But it may be doomed instead to follow the fortunes of King Charles and the Star Prince, those once glorious figures whom Herrick has so frequently portrayed as the inspiration behind his verses:

> *He's greedie of his life, who will not fall,*
> *When as a publick ruine bears down All.*
> (Herrick, 155)

Milton's Anti-Laudian Masque

In early 1634 Londoners were treated to the grim spectacle of William Prynne's mutilation. He was placed on the pillory, his ears were cropped and his book *Histrio-Mastix* "burnt by the common Hangman." Contemporaries perceived Prynne's ordeal as an episode in the continuing controversy over the *Book of Sports,* which was reissued in 1633. *Histrio-Mastix* had been written before the renewal of the royal proclamation but could be seen as insulting the queen with its condemnation of "scurrilous amorous Pastorals" and women actors ("notorious whores"); worse yet, Prynne seemed treasonously to challenge the right of church and crown to foster plays, maygames, and such idolatrous customs. Prynne's detracters jeered that the enemy of dancing had "become so enamoured of it" that he would "dance a gaillarde on the losse of his ears"; his supporters claimed divine intervention when one of the government officials directly responsible for Prynne's conviction was felled by a stroke even as he stood in the crowd watching the sentence being carried out.[1]

John Milton's *Comus* was performed on 29 September 1634—a little over a year after Charles I's republication of the *Book of Sports* and only a few months after Prynne's trial and punishment. To assert a connection between the escalation of the *Book of Sports* controversy after 1633 and the major themes of Comus is nothing particularly new—the link was proposed at least as far back as 1884 and has been rediscovered periodically since then. What has been new in the last ten years is an increasing curiosity about Milton's political intent.[2] Even among seventeenth-century masques, *Comus* is unusually self-reflexive. Within its compact space, it displays an amazing range of dances, rituals, and holiday pastimes both wholesome and nefarious, from the "wavering Morrice" of the sea and the riot of Comus and his crew, to the harvest festivities of the shepherds about Sabrina, and finally to the Ludlow revelry of the Earl of Bridgewater and his guests. Milton himself was not always comfortable with such holiday forms. In his academic prolusions, he had looked kindly upon Bacchus, festival liberty and public amusements like the Floralia. In his early "Song: On May Morning" he welcomed "Flow'ry May," dancing in with the Eastern star and inspiring "Mirth" and "Warm desire." Considerably later, during the period of his antiprelatical tracts, he was more guarded, portraying the *Book of Sports* as part of an insidious plot by the bishops to keep people slavishly quiescent. But he still kept the way open for "publick sports, and festival pastimes" under the control of magistrates instead of the prelates, "that they might be, not such as were autoriz'd a while since, the provocations of drunkenness and lust," but "eloquent and gracefull enticements to the love and practice of justice, temperance, and fortitude."[3]

Clearly, the young man who wrote *A Mask at Ludlow* did not mean to take Prynne's extreme position towards sports and pastimes. *Histrio-Mastix* had called women actors whores; the central actor in *Comus* is a young girl who demonstrates her chastity. Prynne had condemned dancing as lascivious; the Earl and his family dance to celebrate their victory over intemperance. Prynne had lumped the drama, ecclesiastical ritual, and old festival pastimes into one inglorious category and condemned their essential nature; Milton's masque, in Jonsonian fashion, challenges its audience to make moral discriminations among superficially similar forms of revelry. Jonson's *Pleasure Reconciled to Virtue* had been created to celebrate James I's promulgation of the *Book of Sports* in 1617–18; Milton's masque resembles the earlier work so closely that most recent critics have assumed he knew it, either through Henry Lawes, who might have encountered a manuscript copy at court, or through the Earl of Bridgewater, whose father Lord Ellesmere had been James I's Lord Chancellor and a friend and patron of Jonson's.[4] Moreover, Milton was quite conversant with Caroline court entertainments of the 1630s, as our discussion will show. But Milton did not devise *Comus* to celebrate the power and policies of Charles I—not even in the severely qualified sense in which Jonson's masque had honored James. By the 1630s Jonson himself, in at least some of his entertainments, was displaying considerable skepticism about the court's capacity for self-transformation through art, but his dramatic works nevertheless continued to revolve around the life of the court. Milton's masque is quite another order of creation, not only refusing to celebrate royal power but symbolically undoing it.

Of course the Ludlow masque was not written for the king, nor was it performed in his presence. Its immediate occasion was the installation of

John Egerton, First Earl of Bridgewater, as President of the Council in the Marches of Wales; it was performed at Ludlow Castle on Michaelmas night in 1634 as part of the festivities surrounding the installation. But the Earl was Charles I's deputy and surrogate in Wales. The Council over which he presided was an important court of law, one of the so-called prerogative courts created by royal fiat and expected to support the crown; it was also the central government's chief administrative unit in Wales and four adjoining English counties. Charles I's 1633 instructions to the Earl of Bridgewater had greatly increased the size of the Council and had been designed to improve its effectiveness in implementing government policy. The Earl of Strafford was forging the Council of the North into an effective political instrument, and Bridgewater was expected to do the same for Wales. He was charged with suppressing riots and sedition, overseeing military and judicial affairs, collecting "benevolences" and other forced loans within his territory, enforcing Privy Council orders and royal declarations like the *Book of Sports*. Court records from the Council of Wales show that under Bridgewater there was indeed some attempt to enforce that document by prosecuting those who participated in "unlawful games."[5] So *Comus*'s exploration of "license" and "liberty" in the pursuit of old customs was timely and appropriate. Milton's audience in 1634—particularly that segment of it familiar with masques at court—may well have expected the Ludlow entertainment to celebrate Charles and the renewed *Book of Sports* through its praise of the royal deputy appointed President of Wales.

But that is not what *Comus* does. Milton deliberately arouses generic expectations about masquing structure and political strategy only to subvert them. Instead of establishing a continuum between Whitehall and Ludlow, *Comus* creates disjunctions. It sets a distance between Charles I and the Earl, between the images of authority presented in masques at court and Bridgewater's goals in Wales. *Comus* was designed to bear the type of close political reading we have made for some of Jonson's masques. If we consider Milton's work in terms of the concrete political problems faced by the Earl as he assumed his post at Ludlow, we will find that the poet emphasizes precisely those areas in which Bridgewater was in conflict with elements of the central government. Bridgewater was no admirer of William Laud and Laud's plans for ordering the Church. In fact, during the year of the Earl's installation at Ludlow, he was already engaged in a quiet, desperate struggle against Laud. *Comus* celebrates the Earl's autonomy and urges him to consolidate his position as President of Wales into an independent base of power; but it does so—and this is one of the surface paradoxes that makes Milton's stance so interesting—squarely within the liturgical context of the

Anglican Church. The masque defends "public mirth," but only insofar as it can be freed from its association with the party of Archbishop Laud.

To attempt to reduce the whole meaning of *Comus* to the political message which it may have carried for some of its contemporaries would be an unpardonable diminution of its art. But reinterpreting *Comus* in terms of its Ludlow milieu will reveal a different level of its functioning than we have understood before and may help to resolve a few cruxes—most notably the problematic double jeopardy of the Lady who, even after the banishment of Comus, remains immobile in his chair. Our endeavor may also help to dispel a notion sometimes encouraged by Milton himself in his later years, the notion that the young man who wrote *A Mask at Ludlow* was a detached recluse, politically naïve and uninvolved. That may be the way Milton portrayed himself with the benefit of hindsight; after the cataclysmic changes associated with the war, Milton's political position had galvanized into a much more sweeping indictment of received forms. But it is a notion belied by the complexity and urgency of the Ludlow masque itself.

* i *

What do we know about the Earl of Bridgewater's conduct in public affairs? Remarkably little, considering his prominence, and what we do know leads to conflicting interpretations. He was the son of the famous and influential Thomas Egerton, Lord Ellesmere, Lord Chancellor under James I. Bridgewater was, before his appointment to the Presidency of Wales, a Privy Councillor of eight years' standing, a member of the High Commission and the Court of Star Chamber. But those august bodies included noblemen of varying political and ecclesiastical views and there has, to my knowledge, been no detailed effort to assess his own political situation at the time *Comus* was performed, even though plentiful documentary evidence is available. Recent interpreters of the masque have tended to follow William Riley Parker and place Bridgewater among the moderate Puritans or as a Puritan sympathizer. But one of his twentieth-century descendents has claimed he was a die-hard royalist, and at least one historian has described him as a devoted, even sycophantic, follower of royal policy.[6] He had also been a reliable ally of the infamous George Villiers, Duke of Buckingham, and a close friend and associate of Charles's Attorney General William Noy, who had begun his political career as a parliamentary dissident but had gone on to become the architect of some of Charles's most unpopular policies. Noy and Archbishop Laud had worked together on the republication of the *Book of Sports.* Indeed, it was Noy who had been stricken as he watched the ordeal of William Prynne; the attack proved fatal and he died a few months later.

On the other hand, Bridgewater kept up alliances with contemporaries severely critical of Charles, and some of his private papers show him questioning such cornerstones of Caroline policy as the theory of royal absolutism. Bridgewater was impeached by the Long Parliament along with Laud and many other high government officials for alleged violations of the Petition of Right, but he got off with only a fine, whereas Laud and Strafford were executed. He ended up taking the parliamentary side in the Civil War, not without considerable anguish over the break with Charles. But contemporaries were confused about his allegiance. His estate was sacked by parliamentary forces in 1643, then reparations made on grounds that he was no opponent "in any kinde" to Parliament.[7] The same mixed message obtains when we consider the later history of his family. His son and heir was a royalist and Church of England man during the Civil War; in 1651 he was imprisoned briefly for his opinions and wrote in the family copy of Milton's *Pro Populo Anglicano Defensio* "Liber igne, author furcâ dignissimi." Several of the first Earl's daughters leaned in the opposite direction and ended up as Nonconformists.[8]

Despite these seeming contradictions, the Earl of Bridgewater was neither flighty nor opportunistic. He had a reputation for unusual probity and seems always to have conducted himself in office with an almost painful conscientiousness. He had received extensive legal training and was strongly interested in reform, particularly legal and administrative reform. That was one way in which he could wholeheartedly work with Charles: we find him appointed to commissions to examine excessive court fines, study conflicting jurisdictions, and arbitrate naval disputes.[9] But in political matters he tended, like his father before him, to act as an individual and not as a member of a group. He worked hard to support those royal policies with which he was in sympathy, but for his own reasons, which might or might not coincide with the motives of the originators. When his strong sense of duty to Charles came into conflict with his principles, his usual tactic was to try to forge a quiet compromise, working almost invisibly through a vast network of allies which cut across the usual political lines. He was reticent—even secretive—about his own political views. But that in itself suggests a certain sympathy with opposition causes. As Valerie Pearl has noted, much of the reformist activity in the 1620s and 1630s was carried out by "backstairs" tactics—informal meetings, verbal agreements, engines "which the world sees nothing of."[10]

In ecclesiastical affairs Bridgewater was a moderate. He had no quarrel with established ritual, even in its more elaborate forms, but he was strongly Calvinist and anti-Arminian. According to one of his daughters he had taken great care to "season" his family "against *Arminian Principles.*" The Egerton family had a long history of support for strongly Protestant causes and of opposition to Laud. In 1611 Bridgewater's father had tried unsuccessfully to block Laud's appointment to the Presidency of St. John's College, Oxford, on the grounds that Laud was too tainted with popery. The family worked against Laud indirectly by giving their own patronage to men who opposed him. Bishop John Williams, who became one of Laud's most powerful opponents at Whitehall and was noted for his tolerance toward Puritans, had started out as the Egerton family chaplain. Both the Earl's father and his stepmother the Dowager Countess of Derby had been well known for their patronage of strongly anti-Catholic authors—a family tradition celebrated, as John Wallace has demonstrated, in Milton's *Arcades.*[11] The Earl of Bridgewater himself seems to have taken fairly consistent anti-Catholic and anti-Spanish positions; during his youth, while James was on the throne, Bridgewater's name surfaces in the record in connection with Buckingham and Charles after the breakdown of the Prince's marriage negotiations with the Spanish Infanta—at just the point that the two came out most strongly against Spain and allied themselves with the "popular" party against James I.

Indeed, Bridgewater's ties to Buckingham can be partially explained in terms of his anti-Catholic and anti-Arminian principles. The Duke had first appeared in court through the sponsorship of the Earl of Pembroke and the Countess of Bedford, who wished to present James I with a new strongly Protestant favorite to counteract the pro-Catholic and pro-Spanish influence of the then favorite Robert Carr, Earl of Somerset; until almost the end of his life, Buckingham kept on cordial terms with members of the ecclesiastical and parliamentary opposition. One of his own chaplains was John Preston, Master of Emmanuel College, an outspoken Puritan leader particularly known for his talent at "backstairs" reformist politicking. Buckingham did not finally commit himself to the Arminian side until 1626.[12] Of course, before then he may have been playing the ecclesiastical factions off one another to further his own power and preserve his status as sole conduit for royal preferment. But that sort of tactic could work both ways: Bridgewater owed his earldom in part to Buckingham's intervention with King James, and like Williams, Preston, and many others, he could use his leverage with Buckingham to counterbalance the influence of Laud and his supporters.

The year 1626 may have marked the beginning of Laud's real power in England. But until 1633—so long as George Abbot, strong Calvinist and religious moderate, was Archbishop of Canterbury—Laud and his associates were not in a position to impose their views on the Church as a whole.[13] In 1633 Laud was named Archbishop and Bridgewater was appointed President of Wales. Almost immediately, the Earl faced a challenge from Laud and the High Commission. The Council in the Marches of Wales had traditionally enjoyed considerable influence over ecclesiastical affairs—all the bishops with Welsh sees were members and a bishop had sometimes headed the Council itself; Presidents of Wales had sometimes even appointed bishops to the sees under their jurisdiction. The Council could also hear and determine cases involving "popish" practices which continued to flourish in Wales—like the visiting of holy wells and eating and drinking in churches. It was even empowered to try sexual offenses—fornication, adultery, and incontinence—and to prove wills, despite the fact that the ecclesiastical courts also held jurisdiction over those matters. Before Laud, the influence of faraway Canterbury had been fairly weak in Wales. The Council in the Marches had been relatively free to supervise church business, although, if contemporary complaints are to be trusted, it had been less than diligent about doing so. As Bishop of St. David's, Laud had had the opportunity to observe the laxity firsthand. When he became Archbishop, the High Commission was greatly increased in size and administrative capacity, with the result that he could conduct efficient inquiries and visitations in areas previously neglected by the ecclesiastical authorities. Almost as soon as he was appointed, Archbishop Laud became very active in Wales. He favored bishops who would zealously further his plans for the Church, ordered visitations, and reported abuses for action, all with the goal of removing Wales from the darkness of its superstition and enforcing ecclesiastical conformity.[14]

If a man willing to work with Laud had been President of Wales, the Archbishop would have had in the Council a powerful agency for furthering his vision. The Earl of Strafford in the North was working closely with Laud, as was Attorney General Noy at Whitehall. But the Earl of Bridgewater was a man of a different spirit; he deplored Welsh backwardness and worked hard to counteract the local influence of powerful Catholic magnates like the Earl of Worcester, but he preferred to leave most matters of clerical nonconformity to the conscience of the individual. We have a clear example of his adroitness in evading what Laud would have considered his duty to the Church from the testimony of Richard Baxter, who was a curate at Bridgenorth in 1639. In that year

when the Earl of Bridgewater passed through Baxter's town on his way
north to Scotland, townspeople complained to him that Baxter "did not
sign with the Cross, nor wear the Surplice, nor pray against the *Scots*
(who were then upon their Entrance into *England*; and for which [Baxter
notes] we had no Command from the King, but a printed Form of Prayer
from the Bishops.) The Lord President told them, That he would himself
come to Church on the morrow, and see whether we would do these
things or not." So Bridgewater avoided the immediate importunities of
the parishioners. Then he sidestepped the issue by not appearing at
church but leaving bailiffs to report to him on Baxter's conduct of the
service. Baxter did indeed fail to conform and the bailiffs reported this to
Bridgewater, but the Earl still refused to take action against him, saying
"he had not the Ecclesiastical Jurisdiction, and therefore could not
meddle with us." He did not, in fact, have jurisdiction as President of
Wales since, by a set of legal anomalies, Baxter's parish was not under
the Council's authority; he did have the authority as a member of the
High Commission. But stringent action against an obviously conscien-
tious Nonconformist went against Bridgewater's principles.[15] Such eva-
sions of the Laudian policy of Thorough can be noted from much earlier.
Already in 1636 we find Laud complaining to Charles I that in the
Dioceses of Wales, "much more good might be done . . . in a church
waye, if they [Laud and his associates] were not overborne by the
Proceedings of ye Court of the Marches there. And this present yeare in
this diocese of Bangor my Commissioners for my Metropolitical visita-
tion there complaine unto me that the power which belongs to my Place
hath been in them very much wronged and impeached by that Court."
Laud beseeched the king to give his complaints against Bridgewater and
the Council of Wales a hearing, and opposite the entry is a marginal
note, probably in Charles's own hand, "I doubt not, but by the grace of
God to agree these differences by my hearing of them."[16]

Given the Earl of Bridgewater's unwillingness to work with Laud, we
may marvel that he had been appointed President of Wales at all. But he
had been promised the post before Laud's influence was at its peak, and
he had been close to Charles since the king's boyhood. Charles was well
known for his reluctance to alter his opinion of men he had learned to
trust. Then too, although he supported Laud in general, Charles may
have seen the appointment of Bridgewater as a way of keeping the
Archbishop in check (should the need arise) by counterbalancing his
powerful presence with that of an ally whose loyalty lay only to himself.
However, as it turned out, Laud was not willing to suffer Bridgewater's
opposition lightly. Since the Council did not cooperate with his efforts at
ecclesiastical reform, he set out to strip it of power in those vital areas in

which it held concurrent jurisdiction with the ecclesiastical courts. For a time in 1637, Laud managed to halt Council proceedings altogether.[17] But in 1634, when Milton wrote *Comus*, the conflict had not yet reached a crisis. Religious moderates still hoped to curb Laud and turn around the most rigorous of his policies. That, I should like to argue, is one of the things Milton designed *Comus* to do: to encourage the Earl in his resistance to Laud and the central ecclesiastical authority. For moderates in 1634, the Earl of Bridgewater must have seemed almost a last hope—one of the last high governmental officials who was both willing to work against Laud and who possessed a strong administrative base from which to do so.

In 1634, so far as we know, Milton had not yet broken with the established church. He had subscribed to the Oath of Allegiance and the Thirty-nine Articles upon his graduation from Cambridge in 1629 and again upon receiving his master's degree in 1632. Only considerably later did he declare himself to have been "church-outed by the Prelates." This shift is usually interpreted as a response to the ascendancy of Laud. The rigid policies of the new archbishop convinced Milton, or at least confirmed his decision, not to enter the priesthood. In 1634, Milton's position regarding ecclesiastical matters was probably much like the Earl of Bridgewater's own. Certainly *Comus* displays no particular reservations about ritual observance: its echoes of the liturgy for its Michaelmas occasion are so many and so strong that one critic has pronounced it "virtually a liturgical pageant."[18] But, as I shall argue, the masque turns Anglican ritual against the Anglican establishment, symbolically freeing the church from the powerful influence of Laud.

Similarity of viewpoint, however, does not necessarily imply acquaintance or intellectual indebtedness. We have no clear evidence of a direct link between Milton and the Earl. To demonstrate a personal relationship between the two men is not necessary to my argument, since anyone vitally concerned with ecclesiastical affairs could have made it his business to know what Milton seems to have known. But the overwhelming likelihood is that Milton was acquainted with the Earl of Bridgewater and that he worked with him or with some of his close political associates to develop the themes of his masque, in the same way that earlier masque writers like Jonson had worked with the monarch or with published royal proclamations. Christopher Hill has suggested that Milton's father knew the Earl, or was at least part of his large network of associates. According to early biographers and antiquarians, the Milton family rented their house in Horton from Bridgewater, either in 1632 or in 1635.[19] And of course, Milton's *Arcades* had been written for the Earl's mother-in-law, the Dowager Countess of Derby, and shows considerable familiarity with the family's tastes and circumstances. That entertainment, we think, was performed at Harefield, only twenty-five miles from Horton. Milton may have attended and so, perhaps, did the Earl. Ashridge, the Bridgewater family estate, was also close by. The leading family at Horton were the Whitelocks; Bulstrode Whitelock had collaborated earlier in 1634 with Attorney General Noy—the Earl's longtime associate—on James Shirley's *The Triumph of Peace,* performed before Charles in 1634. The musician Henry Lawes was another important link. He was acquainted with Milton and the Earl and involved in the production of *The Triumph of Peace* as well as *Comus* and the masques of Charles I. So the rings of possible contacts could be made to widen further.

Even the fact that the Earl of Bridgewater was usually reticent about his political projects might help to explain why we have no direct evidence of a connection between the nobleman and the poet. If the Earl wished to sponsor a masque defending his own position against the powerful William Laud, it made a certain amount of sense to conceal the "engine" of its genesis. The masque itself would be a relatively open display for anyone interested in deciphering its political message. But it was performed only once in a place far from court and had the power of the Earl and the Council of Wales behind it. Then too, the masque is anything but heavyhanded. Its political message is handled discretely and with careful ambiguity, and only relatively blatant attacks tended to attract censorship. Still, we can speculate, a copy of Milton's masque may well have reached Laud and exacerbated his conflict with Bridgewater. It is significant that *Comus* was published only in 1637, by which time the jurisdictional conflict between the two men had become open, irreconcilable, and very threatening for the continuation of the Council in the Marches of Wales. Further theorizing at this point would probably not be helpful. It is time we turned to the masque itself and to its strategies for establishing a separation between the official world of Whitehall and Canterbury and the Earl's milieu in Wales. Our method will be to concentrate on key passages of the work that, at least in contemporary context, seem to demand political interpretation but which refuse to yield the conventional, expected meaning. There is one area in which Milton engages specific jurisdictional issues relating to the Earl's conflict with Laud: that is in connection with the Lady's "double jeopardy." But that specific juncture is reached quite late in the masque. From the beginning, Milton prepares the way for its interpretation by engaging repeatedly in a rhetorical ploy that mirrors the larger political functioning of the work as a whole. The masque separates its audience from the power at the center of government; it does so by creating, over and over again, situations that appear to call for interpretation in terms of the Stuart "politics of mirth" but that turn out instead to "free" judgment so that traditional pastimes and the art of the masque itself no longer have to be understood as an encoding of Stuart authority.

* ii *

In most Caroline masques it is possible to identify allegorical persons who can be taken as figures for the monarch—a Hercules or Hesperus or Jove who presides over the masque's idealized image of the nation and embodies the divine, transforming energies of the king. And Charles I often made the task of interpretation easier by performing in the masques himself. In the usual royal masque it is also possible, as Stephen Orgel has so cogently demonstrated, to identify the specific vehicle of transformation from the imperfect, fallen world of the antimasques to the perfected vision of the main masque as referring to some policy pronouncement by the king.[20] Stuart masques were meant to be politically comprehensible, at least to a reasonably sophisticated audience with some knowledge of contemporary affairs.

But in Milton's masque, Charles I and his power are not so easily located. Many, if not most, of *Comus*'s Ludlow audience were acquainted with Caroline masquing conventions, as were all of its major participants. The Earl's wife and children had all danced in masques at court, the two boys as recently as *Coelum Britannicum* only six months before.[21] Of course, Milton's masque was not a court masque. It was meant to honor the Earl of Bridgewater and his family, not the king. But its occasion was a public and political one. It marked the ceremonial beginning of the Earl's authority over Wales, an authority granted him by Charles I himself. It was timed to coincide with Michaelmas, the date on which local officials traditionally took office and on which the Court of the Marches commenced its autumn sessions. Since Charles I's instructions to the Earl of Bridgewater had greatly expanded the Council, the new members, most of them high dignitaries with considerable experience at court, may well have been formally installed along with the Earl himself. Officials from the town of Ludlow were invited.[22] At least some Council officials, along with political allies of the Earl, were sure to be in attendance that Michaelmas night.

Given the public nature of the occasion, the audience at Ludlow may well have expected the masque to make some clear reference to Charles I as the source of the Earl's authority. But *Comus* does no such thing. In devising his *Mask at Ludlow* Milton took into account his audience's experience with masques at court and their probable expectations about the strategies by which masques celebrate royal power. He designed

Comus to raise generic expectations, then frustrate them. The work repeatedly tempts its audience into political misreadings—into positing an allegorical equivalence between its mythological figures and actual persons and issues associated with the court of Charles I only to befuddle these equivalences to the point that they must be abandoned. Milton's masque for the Earl of Bridgewater challenges its audience to interpret it on its own terms, not as an extension of the political rhetoric of Whitehall.

Of course the question of the poet's intent is complicated by the fact that Milton's text was altered for the actual performance at Ludlow. In light of the masque's contemporary political significance, some of these changes are interesting indeed. Our strategy throughout the discussion will be first to consider the ways Milton seems to have designed his masque to function, then to assess the significance of the alterations for performance.

All but one of the manuscript versions of *Comus* begin in a "wild wood," with the descent or entry of the Attendant Spirit and his glowing evocation of the place from which he has come:

> Before the starrie threshold of *Ioves* Court
> My mansion is, where those immortall shapes
> Of bright aëreall Spirits live insphear'd
> In Regions mild of calme and serene aire.[23]

His mansion is before a celestial "Court" and he has come from there. But the specific words he chooses suggest a possible allegorization of the relationship between Whitehall and Ludlow. Nearly everyone in the audience would have known who was speaking these lines and where he had literally come from. The part of the Attendant Spirit was played by Henry Lawes, who worked for Charles and Laud as one of the musicians of the royal chapel. He had in fact journeyed from his place at court, or with the king's summer progress, to perform at Ludlow. To an audience even slightly familiar with the strategies of masque mythography, this speech might therefore have suggested an identification between Lawes's actual journey and the Attendant Spirit's descent from the threshold of Jove—between the court of "Iove" and the court of Charles I. Charles was commonly associated with Jove in his masques. In *Coelum Britannicum,* for example, he and his queen had appeared as a higher Jove and Juno, the divine dyad Carlo-Maria, who had shown the lesser Jove how to reform his disordered realm through the example of their serene and perfected court. Just as the Attendant Spirit and Jove could, at least initially, be associated with Lawes and the king, so Milton's "starrie threshold" and "Regions mild of calme and serene aire" peopled by "bright aëreall Spirits" recall the idealized visions of Britain and the court in masques at Whitehall—realms of peace like Milton's "serene aire," which raise the masquers to the status of "bright" immortal beings and display Stuart policy in the light of the platonic ideals toward which the king was striving.

For members of the audience familiar with *Coelum Britannicum,* either with the 1634 printed version or with it as it was performed, the opening of *Comus* might have suggested an even closer link with entertainments at court. *Coelum Britannicum*'s unifying motif, as the name suggests, had been the British heavens, especially the realm of the fixed stars, extinguished and reillumined to manifest the divine beams of majesty. Lawes had helped to compose the music for the masque and probably sang the role of Eternity, who appeared in the work's splendid final apotheosis of the British court. If so, he was clothed in a garment studded with golden stars, suspended in the "middle part of the air," with stars arched above him to express the "stellifying of our British heroes." Directly over his head would have hung a star "more great and emminent than the rest" which "figured" Charles I. Lawes may have worn the same starry robe he had at his court performance in *Comus,* so that for anyone who knew the *Coelum* performance, his opening speech at Ludlow about the "starrie threshold of *Ioves* Court" would have recalled his specific role in the transcendent skies at the end of *Coelum Britannicum.*[24] As Lawes's music for *Comus* could be taken as an extension of the art he practiced at court, so his very appearance at remote Ludlow Castle could be taken as a reflection of the royal power at Whitehall. There he had appeared at the "starrie threshold" of a vision of divine monarchy. Now he was describing himself as recently come from there—an emanation from the glory at the center. Whether or not the continuity of symbolism from *Coelum Britannicum* to *Comus* was recognized, however, the opening of Milton's masque encourages an initial sense of security about the work's political interpretation. For a few brief moments, the audience was invited to experience this entertainment as an extension of theatrical arts at court and to anticipate that it would communicate the same vision of royal power.

But these initial possibilities for the masque's allegorical scheme start coming undone almost as soon as they are suggested. The first potential complication is the Attendant Spirit's depiction of the region of Jove's court as a realm quite apart from the "smoake and stirre of this dim spot / Which men call Earth." This sounds like a transition to an antimasque, but it isn't. The Spirit continues to define the serene realm from which he has come but in a way which moves it progressively farther from earth:

> Above the smoake and stirre of this dim spot
> Which men call Earth, and with low-thoughted care

Confin'd, and pester'd in this pin-fold here,
Strive to keep up a fraile, and feaverish being
Vnmindfull of the crowne that Vertue gives
After this mortall change to her true Servants
Amongst the enthroned gods on Sainted seats.

(Milton, 47–49)

While Caroline masques tended to fuse earthly and divine into images of
political incarnation, the Attendant Spirit's speech separates them out.
His "deincarnation" of conventional masquing imagery arouses uncertainty about the hypothesis his speech had encouraged moments before—that the starry threshold of Jove could be the court of Charles.

The later portions of his speech force the questioning further by
transferring attributes associated with the monarch to every Christian
soul and delaying their attainment to a time after death. An audience
familiar with masques at court might expect the "Regions mild of calme
and serene aire" to be dominated by the single crown and all-pervasive
power of the king, as the bright star representing the monarch dominated the heavens in the final vision of *Coelum Britannicum*. Milton's
Attendant Spirit talks instead of many crowns, many thrones available to
all of virtue's servants in the afterlife. The language is clearly scriptural
and poses an alternate interpretation of the Attendant Spirit's speech
which conflicts with the nascent political allegory and renders it implausible. In masques at court, royal power links heaven and earth, the
present moment and eternity. But in the universe evoked by the Attendant Spirit, heaven and earth are too unlike, too far apart in time and
space, to be bridged by a vision of monarchy. At this early stage in the
entertainment it is still possible that the political and the specifically
Christian levels of interpretation may be reconciled later in the work.
But at least for the moment, the masque is forcibly removed from the
realm of Whitehall's political rhetoric. The elements which at first seem
to carry conventional political freight are voided and set apart. Caroline
masques wrote Charles I and his policies into the heavens; Milton's
Attendant Spirit writes them out and, in doing so, begins to create
uncertainty about the political vision behind this particular entertainment.

It may be objected that the process I have described is too complicated
a transaction for a few swift lines to accomplish, even if it can be
supposed to operate subliminally. But then it is repeated. The Attendant Spirit launches into a second narrative which reinforces the operation of the first. As though to call himself back to business after having
allowed his thoughts to wander, he starts out afresh:

> But to my task. *Neptune* besides the sway
> Of every salt Flood, and each ebbing Streame
> Tooke in by lot 'twixt high, and neather *Iove*
> Imperial rule of all the Sea-girt Iles
> That like to rich, and various gemms inlay
> The unadorned bosome of the Deepe,
> Which he to grace his tributarie gods
> By course commits to severall government
> And gives them leave to weare their Saphire crowns,
> And weild their little tridents, but this Ile
> The greatest, and the best of all the maine
> He quarters to his blu-hair'd deities,
> And all this tract that fronts the falling Sun
> A noble Peere of mickle trust, and power
> Has in his charge, with temper'd awe to guide
> An old, and haughtie Nation proud in Armes.
>
> (*Milton*, 49–51)

Again, his audience is tempted into the game of political interpretation, and their earlier frustration with this activity is dispelled by the Spirit's new beginning. What Milton seems to offer here is a statement of the masque's political occasion: an allegorical chain of command which legitimates the power of the Earl of Bridgewater by placing it in relation to a central government authority and a divine source. One perceptive reader has described the speech as an efficient detailing of a traditional hierarchy, the "divinely-sanctioned power" of the monarch descending from "Sovran Jove . . . to Neptune," who represents Charles I, to the "blu-hair'd deities" and, finally, to "'A noble Peer of mickle trust and power' in whose honor the masque was written."[25] But Milton's hierarchy only appears efficient. The "Peere of mickle trust, and power" can be understood to refer to the Earl of Bridgewater—that much is clear. But when Milton's auditors attempted to establish political parallels at the higher levels, each equivalence they were likely to posit would have been undercut by the next to be stated.

The most plausible figure for Charles I in Milton's allegorical hierarchy is Neptune. Stuart masques very commonly represented James and Charles I as Neptune in recognition of Britain's island status and to compliment her seapower; such an interpretation would work nicely in terms of the Earl of Bridgewater because of his considerable experience as a Commissioner of the Admiralty. Neptune, High, and Nether Jove have divided the universe by lot and the oceans have fallen to Neptune. He has "Imperial rule" over all islands, granting the individual rulers of island kingdoms their sovereignty, which sounds rather like Stuart claims of imperial status for the British monarch. But if we equate Neptune and Charles, Milton's assertion goes too far, even by the standards of the Stuart masque. It is one thing to depict the monarch in a general sense as ruler of the oceans, as in Ben Jonson's earlier *Neptune's Triumph for the Return of Albion,* and quite another to assert for the king the right to appoint all rulers. Charles I had recently claimed sovereignty over all the waters surrounding Britain, but he had not claimed the right to appoint the monarch of every "Sea-girt Ile." So there is a certain discomfort about associating Neptune in this particular masque with Charles.

According to the Attendant Spirit, Neptune appoints rulers. We might therefore imagine that he has appointed the British king as well and identify Charles I as one of his tributary gods, those he has given leave to "weare their Saphire crownes, / And weild their little tridents." But this is a demeaning, almost comically trivial image of monarchy. And in any case the Attendant Spirit goes on to suggest that "this Ile" (Britain) has not been granted a single "tributarie god" as sovereign, but several: Neptune has "quartered" it to his "blu-hair'd deities." The image of unitary political authority which might be anticipated is dispersed to several figures and a gap appears where the audience might reasonably expect a strong image of monarchy. The idea of quartering corresponds to the four major administrative divisions of Britain, which lends the Attendant Spirit's account an appearance of great exactness, except that the blue-haired deities cannot be made to correspond with actual persons or positions within the government hierarchy. And Bridgewater's relationship to them is anything but clear—as President of Wales is he one of the deities, a deputy, or a being with some other status? The "and" of line 37 leaves that open to question.

It can be argued that Milton intended his hierarchy of power to be general because it would be passed over quickly and that the analysis just offered is a ludicrous example of overreading. But the strenuous effort required to achieve a political reading is precisely what needs to be noticed. Milton's account of the masque's political occasion creates an aura of topical specificity, yet it is remarkably obscure and defies topical reading by frustrating the establishment of parallels between elements of the masque and aspects of its occasion. Instead of offering a hierarchy of authority which delineates an orderly transmission of power from the court of Charles to Ludlow, Milton subverts that expected allegory and again, as in the Attendant Spirit's first narrative, the mythological figures are neutralized and rid of political specificity. The only clear hierarchy at this point in the masque is from Jove and Neptune—gods but not necessarily figures for the king—to the Earl of Bridgewater, to the Welsh nation "proud in Armes."

What we have been discussing thus far is what Milton *aimed* to achieve by beginning his masque as he did. Unfortunately, however, we are fairly certain that its opening was altered for the actual performance, so that the Attendant Spirit's first speech was prefaced with twenty-three lines from the epilogue, and the audience did not encounter his decentralizing narratives in quite the abrupt and challenging way I have argued as Milton's intention. The added prefatory material softens the effect of the Attendant Spirit's speech by presenting generalized images of the heavens: the gardens of Hesperus, flowery fields of "eternall summer" visited by balmy west winds, watered by Iris, drenched with Manna. These images may or may not have been taken as deliberate evocations of masquing imagery at court—certainly most of them had been used in court masques on one occasion or another. But in the revised version of *Comus,* the audience was not confronted first with an explicit reference to the court of Jove and specific parallels with *Coelum Britannicum,* the most recent masque at court; they were not invited with the same dramatic directness to construct continuities between the Ludlow masque and entertainments at court nor obliged with the same urgency to relinquish the continuities they had established.

There has been much speculation as to why the opening of the masque was altered for the Ludlow performance. Perhaps it was, in part, out of a desire for greater tact—because the opening as Milton wrote it was perceived by someone involved in the performance as too explicit in its obfuscation of the place of royal power. Whether or not Milton's tactics were clearly perceived by the masque's audience or participants, the opening as written would have created a sense of restlessness and slight disorientation for anyone who came to the masque with expectations based on court masquing conventions. The most likely perpetrator of the revision might seem to have been Henry Lawes himself, who had come to his task at Ludlow from a position at court to which he presumably had hopes of returning. He might therefore be forgiven some discomfort with the masque's evasion of expected lines of authority. But Lawes, although fundamentally loyal, was not a fanatical partisan of all aspects of government policy. He worked from time to time on entertainments critical of the central authorities and owed his place at court to the Earl of Pembroke, who was known for opposition sympathies.[26] In the version of *Comus* which Lawes had published in 1637, Milton's opening appeared in its original, more radical form, which suggests that Lawes did not think it should be suppressed. The performance version may have been altered at the wish of someone else—perhaps the Earl himself, who was usually inclined to be cautious. Even in the version performed at Ludlow, however, the masque still functions in the basic way Milton intended. Its initial tactic is to create political expectations, then disorient them—to appear to pull back from the immediacy of its political occasion into a more neutral realm. But that apparent retreat actually functions to create a space for freer political thinking about elements of *Comus*'s occasion, particularly about the standard Caroline and Laudian doctrine that sports and traditional pastimes should be encouraged as outward signs of submission to authority.

Having offered two narratives which question the Earl's relationship to a central government hierarchy, the Attendant Spirit begins yet a third narrative, this time going out of his way to suggest that no political parallels are intended. Although he claims to be explaining why he has come to earth to help the Earl of Bridgewater's children, he begins his tale of Comus the enchanter by setting the narrative frankly and firmly within the realm of myth:

> And listen why, for I will tell yee now
> What never yet was heard in Tale or Song
> From old, or moderne Bard in hall, or bowre.
>
> (*Milton,* 53)

This formulaic opening reverses his earlier tactic. This time the audience is invited to respond to the tale as a tale, even though it is a new tale; that they have been twice frustrated in their pursuit of contemporary political applications makes it unlikely that they will undertake such unrewarding activity a third time. His earlier narratives were cast in the present tense, as though describing contemporary places and circumstances: this wood, "this Ile," "this tract." But the Attendant Spirit's third narrative begins far away in the Homeric past, and here again the audience is caught unawares. The first two narratives sloughed off potential political applications, distanced what had appeared immediate; the third tale makes what at first seemed distant and obscure progressively more immediate, moving with the god Comus from the "*Tyrrhene* shore" of the Homeric period, to the Celtic and Iberian fields where Comus has more recently wandered, then finally to "this ominous wood" and the present year of 1634, in which the enchanter poses an immediate threat to the Earl's children on their way to Ludlow.

At this point the Attendant Spirit's tale reengages the issue of topicality, but seemingly on a personal rather than a public level. The children are threatened by an evil enchanter. For a number of years critics of the masque, at least on this side of the Atlantic, have interpreted

Comus's menace as essentially private. He threatens the Earl's children with alluring intemperance, and their victory over him constitutes a family ritual of purification or a family affirmation of chastity.[27] That dimension of the masque's meaning is an important one and should not be set aside. But in 1634, the private question of how to preserve one's chastity yet contribute to festival observance was a public issue as well. Milton shaped his treatment of chastity and incontinence, lawful and unlawful pastimes, within the context of the *Book of Sports* controversy and as a contribution to it. As Comus reveals more of his nature, the masque's generic potential for political statement is gradually reengaged. Part of the brilliance of *Comus*'s construction is that the work distances its audience from the court of Charles I, moves it into politically undefined territory, then reintroduces the politically charged subjects of holiday pastimes and obedience to authority in a way that puts the audience off balance and engineers an unexpected confrontation with one prominent strain of Caroline political rhetoric.

We modern readers of *Comus* are so familiar with the work that we tend to think of the enchanter in terms of the last environment in which he appears: *"a stately palace set out with all manner of deliciousnesse, soft musicke, tables spred with all dainties"* (*Milton*, 135). But it is only after Comus has the Lady in his power that the audience sees him in that ultra-civilized setting. Earlier, his base of operations had been the dark parts of the forest, and what his *"stately palace"* is doing in the middle of the Shropshire wilds is an interesting question in itself. Milton withholds essential aspects of the enchanter's nature and activities until quite late in the masque. That tactic allows the poet to forestall a politically stereotyped response and to stimulate a reconsideration of the seemingly rigid issue of proper and improper revelry as though for the first time. As the masque progresses, the figure of Comus gradually picks up political accretions until finally he can be identified as a personage not of forests and shadowy byways only, but of the center: his language and his argumentative style are those of a pro-Laudian spokesman in the manner of Robert Herrick, who advocates survivalism, sports, and the "freedom to be merry" as part of a broader fidelity to a vision of political and ecclesiastical conformity.

But by the time Comus has been associated with that current of contemporary opinion, the whole subject of rural pastimes has been opened up afresh. Comus does not "represent" Charles, or Laud, or any other historical figure. Nor can his court be precisely identified with the court of Charles I. He is rather an ideological construct, modeled, as numerous readers have noted, upon the pattern of a Cavalier gentleman and designed to generate questioning. Milton's gradual revelation of

Comus's nature allows the poet to probe the assumptions behind the arguments of the prosport party and explore the unresolved contradictions between ideals they claimed to uphold and the methods they were willing to countenance. Advocates of the *Book of Sports* liked to portray political obedience as a delightful form of liberty. But in Milton, what may appear to be liberty—a free choice of pleasure—turns out to be base submission. Through his portrayal of Comus and his retinue, Milton offers a caustic critique of the politics of survivalism. The process by which the full force of Comus is revealed is one which dismantles the pastoralizing strain of Caroline rhetoric and lays bare the stark mechanisms of power which underlie its images of rural celebration.

When the Attendant Spirit first describes Comus, the god's association with sports and pastimes is largely suppressed. As Stephen Orgel has shown, he would have been a recognizable figure to anyone familiar with the iconography of revelry, and his father is identified as berry-wreathed Bacchus.[28] But in the Attendant Spirit's account, he is like "his Mother more"—an enchanter in the style of Circe who emerges from the forest to tempt weary travelers with his glass and transform them into the "brutish forme of Wolfe, or Beare"; their debased countenances are a sign of their surrender to the "pleasure" of a "sensuall stie." The Attendant Spirit's initial description is so close to the traditional Renaissance moralization of the Circe myth that Milton's audience would probably have felt they were on familiar ground—called upon to respond with suitable moral revulsion to a figure so obviously nefarious. Who "knows not Circe"? The Spirit guides the audience's reaction to Comus's menacing presence by condemning his "hatefull steps" before he even comes into view.

When Comus actually enters and begins talking for himself, however, the flow of easy condemnation is at least briefly interrupted, for the necromancer does not quite match the Attendant Spirit's forbidding description. Instead, he sounds like a gifted courtly poet in the Cavalier mode—a spokesman for traditional pastimes—seeming at first to advocate innocent pleasures. Indeed, his invitation to revelry has much the same rhetorical structure we have already seen operating in pro-Laudian invitations to mirth like "Corinna's Going a Maying," except that his sports are exclusively of the night and of the forest. Herrick's "Corinna" begins its appeal to revelry with the eastern sky's testimony to the fitness of the time: "the Blooming Morne / Upon her wings presents the god unshorne." Comus, similarly, invokes the coming of evening, signaled by the rise of Hesperus and the setting of the "gilded Carre of Day." In "Corinna" and in the literature of Renaissance festival generally, participants are immersed in natural process. In the same way, the morris

dances and wakes appropriate to Comus's festival season of late summer
will imitate the motion of the heavens, time and the tides:

> We that are of purer fire,
> Immitate the starrie quire,
> Who in their nightly watchfull Spheares,
> Lead in swift round the Months and Yeares.
> The Sounds, and Seas with all their finnie drove,
> Now to the Moone in wavering Morrice move.
>
> *(Milton,* 61–63)

There is a sense of urgency for the celebration has already begun: fairies,
"dapper Elves," and woodnymphs already "Their merry wakes, and
pastimes keepe"; just as in "Corinna," the boys and girls are already
returned home from the woods "Before that we have left to dreame."
Herrick transforms town into country, erasing "business" and commercialism and reversing the moral judgments of the enemies of mirth. The
"sin" would be in "staying" at home on May Day. Comus similarly
applauds the absence of the "graue Sawes" of Rigor, "Strict Age, and
sowre Severitie" at his ceremonies and appeals to a holiday reversal of
"severe" morality: "Come let us our rights begin / 'Tis onely day-light
that makes Sin." "Severitie," however, is not banished but asleep; when
daylight returns, the rituals of the night will again look like sin. The fact
that Comus's secret rites are being "exposed" to the masque's audience of
judges and other government officials casts an interesting light on his
invitation. Comus's appeal is slightly off-key, slightly tipsy, and close
analysis of almost any line brings out disturbing implications—a reminder that he is not to be trusted. As one critic has amusingly put it,
once he invokes the goddess of nocturnal revelry Cotytto, "the party"
starts "getting rough."[29] But for much of his speech Comus sounds at
least on a superficial level like a charming Cavalier advocating merry
wakes and pastimes out of a love of rural pleasures, obedience to the
"time," and to a beneficent natural order.

For Milton's Ludlow audience, of course, there would have been
loathsome visual reminders of the evil Comus could do. He enters
carrying his sinister rod and glass, surrounded by a *"rout of Monsters,"*
their behavior unruly, the "measure" to which he incites them "wild,
rude, & wanton." But there still would have been an unsettling disparity
between the grim necromancer described by the Attendant Spirit and
the graceful poet appearing before the audience. The perception of this
gap sets in motion a process of measurement by which the audience is
challenged to find some way of reconciling the hateful vision they have
been cautioned to expect with the attractiveness they encounter. They

are challenged, in other words, to consider afresh the basic polarities operative in the *Book of Sports* controversy, for the conflicting images of Comus recapitulate the conflict between Puritans and conservative Anglicans on the intrinsic nature of old pastimes.

The obvious way of undoing the contradiction would be to adopt one viewpoint or the other. On the one hand, it would be possible to equate Comus's appeal to revelry with the stupefying and intemperate draught offered in his cup. His language would then be a mere verbalization of the lure of his "orient liquor." That interpretation would result in a position like William Prynne's—holiday pastimes are the blandishments of the devil—and make the Attendant Spirit a spokesman for the strict Sabbatarians. But such an extreme role seems an unlikely one for him, given the devotion to the arts which he has already expressed through his disguise as Thyrsis, a swain with "soft Pipe, and smooth-dittied Song." On the other hand, it would be possible to discount the testimony of the Attendant Spirit and trust Comus, which would approximate the prosport position. But the Attendant Spirit has established his divine origins too convincingly for his viewpoint to be dismissed so easily. So the audience is stymied in its attempt to associate the two images of Comus at this point in Milton's entertainment with the rigidly polarized positions which fueled the *Book of Sports* controversy in 1634.

By the end of Comus's speech, matters are complicated further. It becomes increasingly uncertain whether his invitation to revelry is to be taken as representative of the standard Caroline position or as a grim travesty of it. His final verses continue to parallel prosport rhetoric but sound more and more like parody. In "Corinna's Going a Maying" birds sing matins, the green bowers are sanctified, and the bringing in of whitethorn becomes an act of devotion; the sexual liaisons of the forest are blessed and legitimized by the priest, so that the Maying ritual becomes an extension of ecclesiastical observance. But Comus and his crew are "vow'd Priests" of the "mysterious Dame" Cotytto, whose associations are all demonic. Their rites, like a black mass, invert "innocent" daytime rituals of the type advocated by Herrick; their sports are not open but "concealed" solemnities, associated not with the sun god Apollo and the fertility of the fields, but with the Stygian realm of darkness. And unlike the usual Caroline poet, at least as the poets portrayed themselves, Comus is preaching his defense of holiday license to a public with no ability to choose. If the beasts he has transformed are compelled by his power and their own oblivious natures to follow his call for celebration, then why does he bother with a lavish rhetorical appeal? Again, the audience is prevented from locating the masque's portrayal of sport in terms of the contemporary polarities.

A partial way out of the interpretive quandry is provided by Comus himself. After he hears the chaste footsteps of the Lady and disperses his followers, his image seems once again to alter. He abruptly drops the dancing trochaics of his persuasion to mirth and begins to sound much more like the sinister figure the Attendant Spirit had described:

> Now to my charmes
> And to my wilie trains, I shall e're long
> Be well stock't with as faire a Heard as graz'd
> About my Mother *Circe*.
>
> (*Milton*, 67)

His invitation to revelry, he now reveals, was merely one of his "charmes." He did not promote pastimes for their own sake or out of devotion to some obscure goddess of festivity but to increase and display his own power. The Lady has heard the riots of his crew but not this declaration of purpose. At the point that Comus reveals his "ambition" to increase his herd, Milton introduces a new set of conflicting perceptions of revelry, but the issue now is not the moral valuation of pastimes in themselves but their purpose. Are they intended by their advocates as a form of genuine devotion or as a display of power? What the Lady thinks she hears when she overhears Comus's crew dancing their "light fantastick round" is remarkably like what Comus's own invitation to revelry portrayed him and his followers to be. She does not hear the hateful accents of a necromancer and his slaves but the rather less threatening noise of peasants immersed in the "ill manag'd Merriment" of a harvest festival:

> Such as the jocund Flute, or gamesome Pipe
> Stirs up among the loose unleter'd Hinds
> When for their teeming Flocks, and granges full
> In wanton dance they praise the bounteous *Pan*,
> And thanke the gods amisse.
>
> (*Milton*, 71)

It is not clear from these lines whether she considers late-night wassailing "amisse" in itself or only when it is carried to excess. But she has obviously failed to perceive the nature of the menace behind the revelry. She anticipates a possible danger to herself from the "swill'd insolence" of a bunch of drunken, unruly shepherds but decides to approach them anyway in order to seek directions. She cannot "hear" the structure behind the merriment, its high level of organization, or the nature of its leadership.

When Comus actually appears before the Lady, he is careful to further her misconceptions. She reaches the spot which had rung out with mirth only a short time before and encounters first emptiness, then a single seemingly innocuous figure, a "Gentle" shepherd whose civilized accents appear to mark him as a more high-minded forest dweller than the rude, swilling wassailers she expected. He promises to conduct her to a "low but loyall cottage" and she follows willingly:

> Shepheard, I take thy word,
> And trust thy honest offer'd courtesie,
> Which oft is sooner found in lowly sheds
> With smoakie rafters, then in tapstrie halls,
> And courts of Princes, where it first was nam'd,
> And yet is most prætended.

(Milton, 89)

However, the very terms of her acquiescence—the reference to "courts" and the "tapstrie halls" of "Princes" being somewhat incongruous in the midst of a dark forest—ironically forecast her destination. The "Gentle" shepherd leads her not to some cot but to a courtly palace where she is placed in a more deadly jeopardy than she would have faced from the forest revelers she had expected to encounter. Her trust in the humble accent and "ancient neighbourhood" of a shepherd brings her unexpectedly to a court.

Here again there is an interpretive gap, for nothing in the earlier accounts of Comus had suggested that he lived in a sumptuous palace. There had been hints of a courtly milieu: the audience had been allowed to listen in on Comus's imitation of Caroline prosport rhetoric while the Lady had not; they had seen the costly glittering garments of his crew and heard his vow to make the Lady his queen. But Milton had deliberately withheld the full revelation of Comus's sophisticated ambience until the audience was first made to perceive the hegemonic aim behind his invitation to revelry. Even in Thyrsis' account to the two brothers, the enchanter is portrayed as a creature of the forest: "within the navill of this hideous wood" he and his rout do "abhorred rites to *Hecate*" in their "obscured haunts of inmost bowres" (*Milton*, 117). It is only when the two brothers are on the verge of accosting him that Thyrsis refers to Comus's "hall," and even that term underrepresents the palace which they enter to find him and the Lady. Milton's tactic of withholding information closes off the possibility of a premature and overfacile evaluation of Comus's courtly milieu, just as a similar withholding earlier had warded off stereotyped judgments about the morality of holiday pastimes. The masque's focus shifts from pastimes in and of themselves to pastimes in their relation to power, particularly to the power of a court.

To draw a simple equation between the court of Comus and the court of Charles I would be recklessly facile. And yet there are connections. With Comus's place of residence, as with the figure of the enchanter, Milton sets up a paradigm for purposes of comparison and contrast. To a contemporary audience with even the slightest political awareness, however, the revelation that the "navill" of the wood from which Comus conducts his operations is in fact a stately palace would have given rise to an interesting set of associations. Comus's forest is not just some abstract wood but identified with Dean Forest—the forest through which travelers like the Earl's children regularly passed on their way westward to Ludlow. And Dean Forest was royal territory. It belonged to the king. The central government had recently made its presence felt in the forest through a number of unpopular measures. In order to raise revenue in the absence of funding from Parliament (which he had resolved to do without), Charles I and his ministers had recently revived the medieval forest laws and held forest courts to enforce them—measures which outraged the inhabitants of Dean. In addition, the monarch had granted several patents to courtiers for the development of mining and manufacturing in Dean Forest, including patents to the family of Sir John Coke, Charles's Secretary of State, and to the infamous Sir Giles Mompesson, derisively known as the "Lord of Hosts," onetime ally of Buckingham and purveyor of the monopoly on alehouses who kept turning up like a bad penny despite his having been banished by Parliament. To further the Dean projects, areas of the woodland were enclosed, which led to fierce rioting in protest, sometimes timed to coincide with traditional holidays. Comus's palace is itself an enclosure—a privileged island of civilization separated from the wilds but also a focal point for holiday disorders that spread from there out into the woodlands. The Earl of Bridgewater and his associates would have been particularly sensitive to such topical resonances since the unenviable task of quelling the riots had fallen to the Council of Wales, whether or not its members and President approved of the policies of the king.[30] Milton's masque creates a suggestive geographical congruence between the two types of power being felt in the Forest of Dean—the actual power emanating from the court of Charles I and the fictive power exercised by Comus.

Let it be said again—Milton is not equating the court of Comus with the court of Charles I. As we have seen, Charles I had made strong efforts to reform licentious elements at court—a policy celebrated through the reform of the lascivious heavens in Carew's *Coelum Britannicum*—so that in one way at least, Milton's portrayal of the defeat of Comus could be seen as harmonizing with the efforts of the king. But the same cannot be said for Milton's analysis of the structure of Caroline pastoralism. The literal progress of the Lady from a wood echoing with holiday merriment to an ensnaring court symbolically discloses the hidden design of Caroline prosport rhetoric as Milton conceived it. On the surface it appears to be a jolly invitation to rural festivity with the seamier elements smoothed into an appealing portrayal of humble country virtue, but it turns out unexpectedly to cement the power of a central authority with its surface of rusticity, as in the case of Comus the "Gentle" shepherd, being a mask for political designs. Milton's masque began by detaching its audience from the imagery and political rhetoric of the court of Charles I only to surprise his auditory into a new encounter with some of the same material from a different perspective. The masque's mythography is reattached to contemporary political issues but from an angle of vision not contained within or controlled by the Stuart rhetoric of power. Masques at Whitehall typically moved from court out to an idealized countryside inscribed with the revitalizing energies of royal power. Milton's masque moves in the opposite direction from a rural landscape subtly tainted with "license" back to its civilized source.

Some features of Comus's appeal to the Lady once he has her safely imprisoned in his palace are very like the conservative Anglican appeal to survivalism, especially as it was invoked in defense of the *Book of Sports*. As we have seen, Herrick's *Hesperides* and Ben Jonson's *Bartholomew Fair*, among many other such works, called for a surrender of individual striving (in the manner of Adam Overdo) and a reimmersion in community—a willingness to acknowledge human frailties and the limits imposed by time and the seasons. According to the May Day liturgical lesson of *carpe diem*, we are but as the grass that withereth or, in the capsule version offered by the madcap priest from *The Merry Devil of Edmondton*, "Grasse and hay! we are all mortall; let's liue till we die, and be merry; and theres an end."[31] According to the argument of Church of England conservatives, it is precisely this holiday abandonment of one's separate identity, and of spiritual experience conceived as a personal quest for righteousness, which brings down divine blessings upon all and enriches and restores the community.

Comus portrays a willingness to drink from his cup as much the same sort of surrender. According to his interpretation, the Lady has committed an act of spiritual pride by refusing to drink. She has "inverted" nature's covenant and arrogantly exempted herself from the limitations imposed on all humanity, "Scorning the unexempt condition, / By which all mortall frailty must subsist, / Refreshment after toile, ease after paine" (*Milton*, 139); his cup will "restore all soone" by offering her much needed refreshment and also by returning her to her proper place in the natural cycle of which Comus's community seems to be an integral part. Much of Comus's "survivalist" speech was omitted, we think, from the performance version—we may wonder whether it was perceived as too overt a reference to the Anglican mode of argument. He invokes the typical *carpe diem*, pleads with the Lady to enjoy nature's gifts while she is still young and capable, and—also typically—extends his plea for proper heed to the present moment to encompass collective pastimes:

> If you let slip time, like a neglected rose
> It withers on the stalke with languish't head.
> Beautie is natures brag, and must be showne
> In courts, at feasts, and high solemnities.
>
> (*Milton*, 147)

These lines echoing the traditional holiday *carpe diem* were, if Sprott's conjectures are correct, also omitted at Ludlow, so that what we are discussing here is in part Milton's intent rather than what was actually performed. But Comus's anchoring of his arguments in the "laws" of organized religious authority was apparently *not* cut from the version performed at Ludlow. The Lady has protested that he is attempting to purvey mere swinish oblivion; he replies, his tone suddenly darkening with an implied threat: "Come; no more, / This is meere morall babble, and direct' / Against the canon laws of our foundation, / I must not suffer this" (*Milton*, 157). *Mutatis mutandis*, his court now constitutes a religious house of some kind and the wily figure who appeared to the Lady first as a simple forest dweller, then as a sophisticated courtier, now portrays himself as an upholder of organized religion.

Readers of Milton's masque who were closer to its occasion than we are perceived these lines as a reference to the canon law of the Church.[32] The necromancer's "foundation" could be Catholic rather than Anglican or some demonic imitation of Anglican ritual like the "blessed" cup he carries in travesty of holy communion. But Milton's lack of specificity suggests that there is no significant difference. It does not really matter whether Comus is identified as a pagan, a Catholic, or a medievalizing Anglican, for in any case his call for a humble surrender to the cycle of the green world encourages a pre-Reformation stupor of ignorance leading finally to spiritual perdition. The revisions for performance helped to cloak the figure of Comus in protective ambiguity and eliminated some of the specific parallels between his arguments and Laudian rhetoric, thus making it easier to "misinterpret" the masque as condemning Catholicism alone. Even if the lines are taken to refer to the "foundation" of Catholicism, however, they still glance at the court of Charles I, with its Catholic queen and its strongly Catholic tone, and at Laud, who was showing marked favor, along with the king, to key

Catholic magnates even though such preference undermined the Laudian program for reform. To take but one example very troublesome for the Earl of Bridgewater: Laud and Charles I were granting extraordinary favors to the Earl of Worcester, who was the most powerful Catholic magnate under the Council of Wales' jurisdiction and one of Bridgewater's most dangerous rivals for political dominance in Wales. They were thereby undercutting the authority of the Council itself and encouraging the flourishing of "popery" within the vast territories under Worcester's influence.[33]

The condition of Comus's rabble—human but for their heads because they have reduced themselves to their lower natures—exemplifies the happy oblivion idealized by Catholicizing Laudians. We may think in particular of Herrick's "Hock-cart" and its peasants who feed and grow fat at the harvest home—human beings described in terms usually reserved for the oxen they drive. Except that they have the heads of various species of animals, Comus's followers are indistinguishable; their common countenance and unquestioning obedience to their "high priest" and the "canon laws" of his "foundation" are a parody of the Laudian call for uniformity as a demonstration of obedience to the Church. They perceive themselves as happy but are awash in a spiritual misery they are too deadened to perceive. They have forgotten that life's goal lies elsewhere, in the splendid heavenly mansions evoked earlier in the masque by the Attendant Spirit. Like Arminians as perceived by seventeenth-century Calvinists, they enjoy a "concord" that is dangerous because it produces spiritual stasis, a confidence that they are doing quite well in life, thank you, when in fact they are in mortal jeopardy. Milton's implications are devastating: by allowing the Church to advocate pastimes as a way of patching over dissent, questioning, and spiritual ferment—all elements that more rigorous Protestants considered essential for genuine spiritual growth—the Laudian party was shaping the Church into something quite like Comus and his crew.

Laud himself may not have been an Arminian in the strict sense of the term. Nor did he advocate spiritual obliviousness: he placed great emphasis on catechizing and other institutional means for raising individual Christians out of ignorance, but there were limits to that elevation. If awakening a believer's powers of understanding initiated a questioning of the doctrine and discipline of the Church, then intellectual curiosity had to give way to obedience. Even among the Oxford dons, Laud had prohibited controversy over ecclesiastical affairs.[34] The Laudian ideal of humble reverence toward authority is parodied in the ordered "disorderly" dances of Comus's rabble, who, like good mirthful Anglicans dancing about their maypoles, are most submissive in their revelry and never for an instant turn holiday "license" against their master's power. Their behavior expresses the basic paradox behind Stuart policy in that, as the *Book of Sports* had advocated, it turns festival license into a form of obedience—channels the potentially anarchic impulses released through holiday pastimes into a reinforcement of the central authority.

Milton's portrayal of Comus and his rabble is, of course, unlike the holiday mirth advocated by the *Book of Sports* in its tolerance for sexual license. The king's declaration had specified that the allowable pastimes were to be "lawful," "harmelesse," and "honest." But the prosport party sometimes stretched honesty a bit, allowing erotic suggestiveness to color their invitations to revelry, just as Herrick's "Corinna" is a persuasion to holiday that is also a persuasion to love. And the same slight "contamination" could be found in entertainments at court, despite the cult of chastity. John Fletcher's *Faithful Shepherdess,* for example, was revived and performed at court in 1633–34, less than a year before the performance of *Comus.* Milton's masque is so permeated with echoes of the earlier work that Annabel Patterson has suggested he set out deliberately to "rewrite" it.[35] Fletcher's pastoral is built upon the misadventures of various pairs of lovers in a forest; their liaisons are purified by the end of the play through rituals before the Priest of Pan, a figure who embodies the civilizing power of church and monarchy and whose reform of woodland "license" recalls the reforms called for in the *Book of Sports.* But along the way the entertainment offers a number of titillating episodes: there is a half-comical would-be rapist, the Sullen Shepherd, who chases virgins about and also the not unsympathetic Cloe, a nymph so ardent for a good roll in the grass that she is willing to accept anyone, any circumstances. "It is impossible to ravish me, / I am so willing." The rhetorical strategies employed by Comus call attention to a basic contradiction in the practice of much of the Caroline prosport argument in that his ploys to get the Lady to drink his cup and join the party are inseparable from his effort to seduce her.[36]

There are many ways of interpreting the immobility of the Lady, frozen in her chair by the power of Comus's wand. In terms of the *Book of Sports* controversy, she can be seen as Milton's embodiment of a personal and political dilemma that had been intensified by the rise of William Laud and his zealous campaigns against those who quarreled with his vision of the church. For if indulgence in revels and holiday pastimes was interpreted as submission to Laudian authority, then an anti-Laudian was obliged to reject the pastimes in order to make clear his or her rejection of the authority. The encounter between the Lady and Comus in the palace is yet another of the masque's reworkings of the polarities behind the *Book of Sports* controversy, with the Lady taking a strongly Puritan position. She is not a fanatical hardliner like Prynne, for whom all ways of enjoying oneself were suspect. For her, at least some of nature's blessings are acceptable when used not as baits to ensnare a brute but as rewards for virtue. Comus has misunderstood the moral economy of nature, who, "good cateresse / Means her provision only to the good / That live according to her sober laws" (*Milton,* 153). But the Lady has expressed distrust for "tapstrie halls, / And courts of Princes," and for "ill manag'd Merriment" like that of wanton shepherds in the forest. It is worth noting that at least some members of the Earl's family acted upon sentiments like those the Lady expresses here. One of Lady Alice's older sisters refused to dance in masques at court on the basis of Sabbatarian principle and another wished she had had the courage to refuse.[37] But this young lady is performing in a masque, which makes her severity particularly interesting. Many readers have found her rejection of Comus overly shrill and rigid. There are good psychological explanations for her harshness—perhaps she is fleetingly tempted by the enchanter's proposals—but there is a strategic dimension as well.

Within Comus's territory, the dichotomy between those who participate and those who refuse is absolute. Those who drink the cup taste all the pleasures and are immediately absorbed into the community of beasts; those who refuse are isolated and can accomplish nothing. Comus has all the sport and mirth while she must sit immobile—unable to participate in any of the refined arts which surround her without having drunk of the cup of "license." Her only course of action is to resolutely deny all he offers. It is Comus's power which keeps her immobile and deprives her of the artistic self-expression she had previously enjoyed. Before encountering him, she sang and her song had considerable impact even on the enchanter; now she can only speak and her musical talents are held in abeyance. The only independence she has is the freedom for verbal combat, and even that meager liberty may disappear. At the moment the two brothers enter to free her, Comus appears on the verge of forcing his cup upon her. It is not enough that he has prevented her from following her own way; she must be made to drink his "liquor," see the world as he dictates—from the same perspective as the rest of his oblivious "congregation."

Milton's portrayal of the confrontation between the Lady and the enchanter shows considerable sympathy for a Puritan dilemma in the face of Laudian power—the plight of those who were locked into rigid rejection of all arts and pastimes because those which were most culturally conspicuous seemed tainted with political and sexual corruption. It was a dilemma very close to John Milton himself; he constantly weighed and reweighed the competing claims of pleasure and virtue. But at the time he wrote *Comus,* Milton was interested in freeing the Lady and freeing the Puritan party more generally from such a limiting stance. He provides two complementary ways out of the dilemma: through the plant haemony and through the healing ritual of Sabrina. Both of these forces are associated with festival "magic."

Haemony, that mysterious weed, has given rise to much allegorical interpretation. But to the extent that it can be identified with an actual herb, it is a plant associated with traditional holiday observances. As Charlotte Otten has shown, haemony has all the botanical and magical attributes of hypericum or andros-aimon (haemony), a plant associated with the sun and gathered on Midsummer Eve, the Feast of St. John the Baptist. Appropriately, given its festival connection with light and regeneration, it had special power over the demonic: "a plant whose botanical features, stamped with the signature of the sun, enabled it to quell the forces of darkness; whose efficacy as a device able to detect sorcerers and thereby protect a virgin's chastity was universally acknowledged; and whose potency as a demonifuge was established from antiquity by herbalists and theologians and attested to by Milton's collaborator Henry Lawes."[38] Lawes himself had used the plant more than once against demons and so, no doubt, had other members of Milton's audience. What is most interesting about Otten's suggestion, from our perspective here, is the light it casts on the rescue attempted by the Lady's brothers. They banish the enchanter with haemony, associated with the sun and with the protection of virtue, but also with a traditional festival of the church. The herb bridges the seemingly impassable space between the Lady's severe "sunclad" chastity and Comus's corrupt nocturnal rituals of power. But it does not suffice in itself to free the Lady, at least not as it is used by the Elder and Younger Brother. To accomplish that, the Attendant Spirit cannot rely on haemony alone but must call upon the magic of Sabrina.

Sabrina, in Milton's account, is a divinity with her own power against natural evils. As the goddess of the River Severn, which marks the border between England and Wales, she is a boundary figure, both geographically and spiritually, a reconciler who bridges the extremes created by the corrupt power of Comus. Her influence is like that of haemony in that she offers a healing middle territory between the absolute rejection of the Lady and the extreme indulgence of Comus. But she is able to provide a much more effective antidote against his power because she has the same breadth of operation he does, only in purified and decentralized form. Like Comus, she is associated with poetry and song, rituals and magical transformations; she too is surrounded by a group of revelers and becomes a focal point for holiday pastimes. Milton provides both figures with histories linking them to the pre-Christian era, he a pagan import from the Mediterranean and the progeny of lesser Homeric gods; she more nearly indigenous as the daughter of Locrine and granddaughter of Brutus but also descended from Homeric paganism through the figure of Brutus, son of Aeneas, and associated with images of violence through her own tragic history as a victim of forced drowning. The two figures are comparable, yet utterly unlike. The difference between them is the difference between the power of virtue and the virtue of power. Comus forces his presence upon the unwary to their perdition; Sabrina comes only in response to earnest prayer; her goal is to "Listen and save." Comus incites the "wavering Morrice" of his rabble as a demonstration of his power which is staged by minions with no capacity to choose. But the essence of Sabrina is her virtue. The shepherds who "Caroll her goodnesse lowd in rusticke layes" collect about her of their own free will, out of gratitude for her healing of their flocks from the "urchin blasts" of malicious sprites (*Milton,* 163). Their "festivalls" are not engineered by any higher power but initiated by the shepherds themselves out of gratitude for her "goodnesse."

If Comus and his crew enact a travesty of the Laudian style of church government, in which individual spiritual well-being is subordinated to the preservation of power at the center and the cohesion of the whole, then Sabrina can be seen as offering an alternate paradigm for the relationship between pastimes and "authority." At her festivals, the lines of power do not move inexorably downward from a demanding and immovable center. Her relationship with the shepherds is much more fluid, flexible, and responsive to individual and localized needs. Comus and his rabble are courtiers trumped up as forest dwellers, with their glittering garments hinting at their actual place of origin even as they dance like peasants on the green. He and they are an alien presence in the woodlands. But the shepherds who praise Sabrina are genuinely rural people who live along her banks, and she is also a more indigenous figure than Comus in that she personifies the river and is modeled on Welsh legends about goddesses who dwell beneath the flood. Thyrsis invokes her aid in language of considerable sophistication and artifice—even by the "songs of *Sirens* sweet," which recall the Sirens of Comus's mother Circe—but the art surrounding Sabrina is spontaneous, closely allied to virtue, and independent of any court.[39]

Sabrina does not shun ceremonies. As Comus has his cup, so she has the drops from her "fountaine pure" which she applies according to a ritual formula in order to heal and save. The fact that Milton provides both figures with a pagan origin suggests that he was interested in countering the usual Puritan argument that all rituals traceable to paganism are suspect. Comus's rites imprison but Sabrina's create new autonomy. She offers a radically different model for the relationship between power and ceremonial observance which frees arts and pastimes from their contamination in the palace of Comus. The Laudians could have objected to Milton's unfriendly analysis on the grounds that the Archbishop too opposed empty or harmful ceremony. Ecclesiastical ritual was for him an outward sign of inward unanimity but had to be a means for "edification" at the same time. However, Laud did not believe that the demands of the collective church could genuinely conflict with the best interests of the individual Christian. If anyone perceived such a conflict, he or she was nevertheless required to conform. Sabrina's use of ritual is quite different and parallels the Earl of Bridgewater's tolerant stand toward nonconformity. She allows wide latitude for individual choice while at the same time responding with alacrity to a case of genuine need. The encounter with Comus reduced the Lady to immobility. Once freed by the healing rites of Sabrina, however, she can move outward again and take up the arts and pastimes which Comus had forced her to renounce. What matters is not the provenance of the rituals or even their past history but their use.

The liturgical framework of *Comus* reinforces its emphasis on church government and the proper use of ceremony. As William B. Hunter, Jr., noted ten years ago, *Comus* is steeped in the liturgy for its festival occasion, the Feast of St. Michael and All Angels. Many of its themes— the guardian spirit and his angelic protection of the "little ones" of God, the battle against the evil one, even its culmination in praise for a "famous" man in a position of political authority—are designed to echo the liturgy for Michaelmas. Nearly everyone in attendance at the Earl of Bridgewater's masque that Michaelmas evening would also have attended the Anglican services that day. For them the parallels would have been unmistakable and would have encouraged them to perceive the masque as an extension of the liturgical lessons.[40] Milton's trenchant criticism of a corrupt ecclesiastical power is thus cast in a framework which upholds the liturgy of the church.

Even his emphasis on the use of rites and pastimes is developed out of the liturgy for the day. The morning lesson proper for Michaelmas is from Ecclesiasticus 39:

A man need not to say, What is this? wherefore is that? for he hath made all things for their uses. His blessing covered the dry land as a river, and watered it as a flood. As he hath turned the waters into saltness: so shall the heathen inherit his wrath. As his ways are plain unto the holy; so are they stumblingblocks unto the wicked. For the good are good things created from the beginning: so evil things for sinners. The principal things for the whole use of man's life are water, fire, iron, and salt, flour of wheat, honey, milk, and the blood of the grape, and oil and clothing. All these things are for good to the godly: so to the sinners they are turned into evil. . . . All the works of the Lord are good: and he will give every needful thing in due season.[41]

Michaelmas came just after harvest. As we have seen, the masque makes several references to harvest celebrations and the passage from Ecclesiasticus is particularly appropriate for the season. Comus and the Lady debate the proper use of fecundity, but only the Lady has the liturgy for the day behind her. In speaking for Nature, "good cateresse" who offers abundant blessings but means her provisions only for the "good," she is speaking the language of the liturgical lesson which enumerates the goods of the earth in a sparing and elemental way, as though to suggest that elaborateness beyond such "principal things" is vain.[42] For all its criticism of the Laudians, Milton's masque is as tied to its festival occasion as any pro-Laudian text.

Comus's commentary on the *Book of Sports* controversy is particularly appropriate for the day. The next lesson for matins on the Feast of Michaelmas comes from the second chapter of Mark, in which Jesus chides the Pharisees about the proper keeping of the Sabbath:

> And it came to pass, that he went through the corn fields on the sabbath day; and his disciples began, as they went, to pluck the ears of corn. And the Pharisees said unto him, Behold, why do they on the sabbath day that which is not lawful? And he said unto them, Have ye never read what David did, when he had need, and was an hungred, he, and they that were with him? How he went into the house of God in the days of Abiathar the high priest, and did eat the shewbread, which is not lawful to eat but for the priests, and gave also to them which were with him? And he said unto them, The sabbath was made for man, and not man for the sabbath.
>
> (Mark 2:23–28)

This was one of the standard proof texts in the *Book of Sports* controversy, cited repeatedly by the prosport party to buttress their own position in defense of Sunday and holiday pastimes against the Sabbatarians. Its presence in the liturgy for Michaelmas helps link Milton's emphasis on pastimes and their uses with the festival occasion. And as we might expect, Milton's own reading of the passage as offered through the masque cuts across the usual political interpretations of the text, creating new ground upon which to build. The strict Sabbatarians among

seventeenth-century Puritans were like the Pharisees in that they advocated the suppression of Sunday and holiday pastimes on the basis of Old
Testament prohibitions. But Christ in this festival lesson seems clearly
to abrogate the old Mosaic code: "The sabbath was made for man, and
not man for the sabbath." The Laudian party, at least in Milton's highly
unfavorable portrayal, were advocating another version of the same
Sabbatarian error. By building a tight ecclesiastical structure requiring
rigid adherence to canon law, royal proclamations, and the traditions of
the church, they were distorting Christ's teachings in the opposite
direction from the Puritans but ending up with a similar reversal of his
warning that the sabbath was made for man and not man for the sabbath.
They were molding believers to fit the demands of the church and not the
church for believers.

Milton's masque does not advocate the overthrow of church government. It is far too immersed in its liturgical occasion to be interpreted in
so extreme a sense. But what it does is almost equally unsettling. Milton
sets the language of the *Book of Common Prayer* against one of the
dominant elements of the church, turning the liturgy against the party
of Archbishop Laud in order to shake off what was becoming a Laudian
stranglehold over the arts and old holiday observances. Sabrina operates
according to the principle that man was not made for the sabbath. By
freeing the Lady from the charms of Comus, she makes it possible for her
to move onward again toward Ludlow to become part of her father's new
court and join its "mirth, and chere" without a threat to her virtue. All
these things are good for the godly.

But there is another way, much closer to Bridgewater's conflict with
Laud, in which the process of freeing the Lady can be interpreted. On a
different but related level, it is a specific defense of the Earl of Bridgewater and the authority of the Council in the Marches of Wales against the
jurisdictional threat posed by Laud. The subject of chastity in *Comus* is
overdetermined; it can be understood on a theoretical plane as part of the
masque's exploration of the interrelationships among purity, human
volition, and divine grace; it can be linked to the Castlehaven scandal of a
few years earlier, in which the Earl's wife's brother-in-law had been tried
and executed for rape and sodomy—a series of events which in themselves would have offered sufficient reason for the Egerton family to
reaffirm its chastity. But the protection of chastity and the punishment
of sexual incontinence was also one of the major responsibilities dele-
gated to the Earl and the Council of Wales and a key issue in the
jurisdictional conflict between Bridgewater and Laud. Milton's portrayal of the predicament of the Lady echoes elements of the Earl of
Bridgewater's actual defense of the Council's authority to try cases of

sexual incontinence and reflects the Earl's view of the proper relationship between secular and ecclesiastical authority.

According to Charles I's 1633 Instructions to the Earl of Bridgewater, the Council in the Marches of Wales was given

> full power and authority . . . to hear and determine, and also to punish all manner of persons within all and evry the Limits and Jurisdictions aforesaid [of Wales and the Marches of Wales], which shall be notoriously known to live, contrary to Gods Laws and the Kings Highness Ecclesiastical Laws, in Incest, Adultery or Fornication, to the offence and dishonor of Almighty God, and to the evil and pernicious example of his Highness Subjects . . . Provided also, and his *Majesties* meaning is, that the ordinary of every Diocess, where any such Offender shall be resident or comorant, shall or may proceed for the better satisfying the Congregation, and for the more knowledge of Offendors penitency in that behalfe; according to the Laws and Censures of the Church.[43]

In December of the same year, Charles I granted Laud and the High Commission "full power and authority . . . to inquire, hear, determine and punish all Blasphemies, Incests, Adulteries, Fornications Simonies, scandalous and notorious Drunkenness, clandestine Marriages, outragious Misbehaviours and Disorders in Marriages . . . punishable or reformable by the Ecclesiasticall Laws of this our Realm, . . . any our Laws, Statutes, Proclamations or other Graunts, Priviledges or Ordinances, which be or may seem contrary to the Premisses, notwithstanding."[44] This document could, if one were so inclined, be taken as canceling out the Earl's instructions of only a few months before.

In theory, the jurisdictional conflict had existed for a long time. There had been occasional clashes between the Council and the ecclesiastical courts before 1633, but Laud's zeal to consolidate the power of the church, the High Commission, and the lower ecclesiastical courts created a new and much more serious crisis in 1634. For whatever reason, Charles I or some of his ministers seem deliberately to have set the Welsh Council and the ecclesiastical courts at odds. The church courts would attempt to remove a case of adultery or incontinence from trial in the Court of the Marches on grounds that such cases belonged to them, arguing that if the Court of the Marches were to try the same cases it would be placing defendants in double jeopardy. The Council of Wales would counter by claiming that each court system had its own proper functioning, and if the ecclesiastical courts tried and punished sexual offenders in the same way the Council of Wales did, the church was exceeding its proper authority. If the church courts were to keep within their legal boundaries, there would be no double jeopardy.

The dispute did not reach a climax until 1637 but was already brewing much earlier. Even before he assumed the Presidency of Wales, the Earl of Bridgewater was well aware of the impending threat to the Council posed by Laud's challenge to its jurisdiction.[45] Keeping the Council's authority to try sexual offenses was not just a matter of principle or of curbing the power of Laud. What was at stake was the Council of Wales's ability to survive and function with the degree of autonomy the Earl of Bridgewater envisioned for it. To lose the fines from the sentencing of sexual offenders would damage the court financially, since such revenue formed an important part of its income, but the decline in its prestige would be far more serious than that. As the Earl complained, losing the jurisdiction would "very muche damp & blemishe it . . . for if (after the Losse of so many ornaments & supplements, which did advance the state & reputation of that Counsell,) the fines be lessened, I scarcely knowe howe the house will subsist, though with disgrace & blemish, which I shoulde be Loathe to see, or to thinke what may followe after . . . . I shoulde be very sory to finde it nowe within the limits of its Jurisdiction and Instructions so bitten & crushed that it shoulde not be able to breathe or moue."[46]

In moving against the Council in the Marches of Wales, Laud may well have hoped to render it "so bitten & crushed that it shoulde not be able to breathe or moue." As we noted earlier, he perceived the Council under Bridgewater as an impediment to his ecclesiastical reforms in Wales. The legal aspects of the struggle are far too detailed to be explored here, but its general outlines will be familiar from our earlier discussion of Ben Jonson. As the Earl and his associates pointed out, the jurisdictional conflict over sexual offenses ran parallel to the related problem of jurisdiction over sports and pastimes. Again we encounter a conflict between the secular magistrates, local and parliamentary ordinances, and the common law on the one hand, and the ecclesiastical authority and canon law on the other. Since the Council of Wales was a prerogative court, deriving its legitimacy in part from the king's claim to ultimate authority over judicial affairs, we might expect it to have made its case against Laud on that basis. But the Council claimed the right to try sexual offenses on grounds of legal precedent since they could demonstrate that the body had tried such cases "Constantly and Continuallie" since its beginnings. Their most important arguments rested on the authority of Parliament, specifically, a Henrician statute which had given the king the right to determine Council jurisdiction. The ecclesiastical party, by contrast, based their case squarely on royal prerogative—the king's right to order his Church as he saw fit.[47]

According to the legal briefs prepared by the Earl of Bridgewater and his associates as part of the defense against Laud, the Council of Wales as secular authority had the right to "inflict Fine & imprisonment pro Reformatione Morum" and to remove the actual offense, while the lower ecclesiastical courts, although they had begun to impose fines and imprisonment for sexual offenses, could lawfully prescribe only spiritual penalties: "inioyne penance pro salute animae" and public humiliation for the "better satisfieng the congregation and the more knowledge of the offendors penance." If each court system kept to its proper function, there would be none of the double jeopardy of which the Church courts complained and both would "agree well togeather; the one punishment being for the offence against god, and the other as it is an offence or wrong to the partie thereby iniured, both concurrent to reforme the inward and outward man." And, as the Earl and his associates argued emphatically, the ecclesiastical courts could properly move in such cases only upon the prompting of the Council of Wales itself: even in the early days when bishops had headed the Council, they had allowed it to proceed to temporal punishment and only then caused the ecclesiastical courts to devise spiritual penance. The Earl even went so far as to cite scripture in support of his interpretation: "And as the Jurisdiction of the Courte of the Marches is Justified & maintayned by Lawe & reason, and his Majesties Power to giue that Court Jurisdiction in the matter in question fullie warranted by the Lawes of the Realme so is it also proved by the lawe of God, For when Paule was accused for Heresie hee appealed to Caesar and would not (as Festus advised him) goe to the high Priests at Jerusalem to be tryed, which appeale was allowed."[48] For the Earl of Bridgewater, such a division of responsibility was in no way a derogation of the ecclesiastical authority but rather a harmonious balancing of sacred and secular jurisdictions.

The double process outlined in the Earl of Bridgewater's briefs is precisely the division of responsibility we see operating in *Comus* to free the Lady from the enchanter. The Lady is, of course, no sexual of-fender—she stands firm against temptation—but a potential victim, subject first to the imagined perils to her chastity created by her solitude in the forest, then to the very real insinuations of Comus, which are at the least a leering invitation to the sin of incontinence and at their threatening height, intimations of sexual violence. He has imprisoned her in her chair and "offers" to force his cup of sensual delight to her lips.[49] But once we concede the dissimilarity produced by her status as potential victim rather than participant in excess, we can recognize a congruence between the double remedy which frees her and the Earl's view of the complementary functioning of the secular and ecclesiastical authority. In freeing their sister from the threat of Comus, the two

brothers are acting for their father—performing the type of duty dele-
gated to the Council in the Marches of Wales. The brothers' assault upon
Comus parallels the Earl of Bridgewater's analysis of the function of the
secular arm—they remove the actual threat to their sister by dispersing
Comus and his rout, although they are only partially successful since the
enchanter himself escapes. The secular authority, even with the aid of
the "magic" of haemony, does not suffice in itself. The Lady is still
imprisoned and in need of the spiritual ministrations of the goddess
Sabrina.

Like Comus, Sabrina is associated with the ritual functions of the
church but in freer and less centralized form. Sabrina comes at the
invocation of the Attendant Spirit and the two brothers, just as their
father argued that the spiritual remedies of the church should be applied
at the behest of the secular authority. Comus has fled and is therefore not
available to do public penance "for the good of the congregation," but
the Lady, although innocent, has suffered a ritual pollution through her
contact with the cup and chair of the enchanter. She remains immobile
and isolated until the rites of Sabrina act "pro salute animae" to restore
her to her proper place in the community of holiday celebrants who have
gathered at Ludlow. Sabrina is a powerful figure, accorded much respect,
yet curiously reticent and unassuming—quite unlike the Archbishop
who was even then attempting to strengthen the Welsh Church at the
expense of the Council of Wales. The spiritual functions associated with
Sabrina in Milton's masque are not politically subservient to the secular
authority, nor do they take precedence over it, but operate in coopera-
tion with it, "both concurrent" to restore the Lady "inwardly and
outwardly."

If we combine this specific aspect of the masque's political meaning
with the more general exploration of old pastimes outlined earlier in the
discussion, we will uncover one of the masque's most basic strategies.
The regulation of sexual offenses and of traditional pastimes had turned
into a tug-of-war between magistrates and churchmen—between the
secular and ecclesiastical authorities. Milton symbolically disarms the
Laudian Church in its challenge to secular judicial authority by showing
the Laudian party to be disqualified as agents of genuine spiritual
reform. Comus and the "canon laws" of his foundation, associated in so
many ways with the Laudian style of church government, can scarcely
provide a solution to the predicament of the Lady since it is Comus
himself who is responsible for her imprisonment in the first place.
Milton was not necessarily calling Laudian churchmen a crew of liber-
tines—a few were, most were probably not. His point is a bit subtler
than that. He suggests that a church which would rather tolerate

spiritual indolence than cope with the unsettling ferment of genuine spiritual freedom is not the institution best qualified to police public morals and improve the spiritual health of the community. Conservative Anglicans tended to cast an aura of accepting nostalgia over partially corrupt institutions, shrugging off minor vices as an inevitable aspect of human nature and stressing instead the acknowledgment of human frailty as a remedy for broken community. We will remember Justice Adam Overdo and his healing "conversion" to recognition of his own and the world's imperfection at the end of *Bartholomew Fair*. The moral style represented by the Earl himself is more strenuous and less paternalistic toward vice. He has allowed his valued children the dangerous freedom of traversing the wilderness alone. His virtue is mirrored in the masque through the uprightness of his offspring who receive guidance but must find their own way, who make no compromises with evil but fight against inner temptation and outward corruption with whatever tools are available to them. The two brothers' weapon against Comus is haemony—a plant associated with traditional holiday observance—employed not in Laudian fashion, to cast an aura of accepting nostalgia over partially corrupt institutions, but to attack vice and noxious pastimes at their very origin.

At the same time, however, Milton was not suggesting, as some of his antisport contemporaries would have, that the secular authority could operate entirely on its own to suppress sexual excess and unwholesome pastimes. Later on, in *The Reason of Church Government*, he held that public pastimes should be regulated by the magistrates.[50] But in *Comus*, the two brothers need Sabrina. Their secular intervention must be supplemented with a power associated with festival and ritual observance. Sabrina provides that function: she cooperates with secular authority but retains her own identity and her local nature. In the case of Comus the necromancer, all forms of power converge at the center. The secular merges inextricably into the ecclesiastical, the countryside becomes a court, and the court a religious "foundation." Like Charles I, Comus is the head of his church. But in Milton's account of Sabrina, the Attendant Spirit, and the brothers, the secular and sacred exist in looser association. The lines of demarcation are clearer and there is harmonious interaction rather than quasi-mystical unity.

Milton's masque began with images recalling masquing imagery at court but separated from the court of Charles I and emptied of the political connotations they would have carried in the milieu of Whitehall. Then the poet gradually reintroduced contemporary political associations but in a backhanded way which intimated connections between some aspects of royal and ecclesiastical authority and the debased rites of Comus. But the masque culminates in a vision of yet another court—the court at Ludlow Castle where the Earl of Bridgewater, his family, and friends have gathered "in state" to celebrate his installation as Lord President of Wales. Milton's masque follows the very pattern of motion from a remote pastoral landscape to a courtly and civilized center that it had earlier exposed as part of the artifice of Comus. Pastoralism, like other things, can be good to the godly. At Ludlow Castle, the *"Sun-shine holiday"* mirth and "chere" associated with the Laudian party seem to flourish. The local swains have assembled to celebrate the Earl's presence with the duckings and noddings of "Iiggs, and rurall dance," their homespun measures giving way according to traditional formula to the *"Court guise"* of the masquers and the "lighter toed" dances of the aristocrats. Their sports follow the pattern of Mercury and the *"mincing* Dryades" and demonstrate the masquers' triumph over the antimasque vices of *"sensuall Folly, and Intemperance"* (*Milton,* 177–81). At this point, Milton's work seems to follow the pattern of masques at court, particularly of Jonson's *Pleasure Reconciled to Virtue,* which also ends in victory over Comus and chaste dances performed under the guidance of Mercury. The difference is not in the pastimes themselves but in the way the lines of power are drawn.

I have resisted the temptation to draw elaborate comparisons between *Comus* and *Pleasure Reconciled to Virtue* because that has been done often and well,[51] but perhaps one observation is in order. In Jonson's masque, the pattern for the dancing is provided by the authority of the church: Daedalus is flanked by two mitred figures as he leads the masquers in the dance; their motions figure forth the ceremonial patterns which James I and his ecclesiastical officials (Laud among them) had imposed on the Scottish Kirk during the king's visit to Edinburgh earlier the same year. One power informs all levels of the reforming energies of the masque— the divine power of the king. In Milton's masque, virtue is not reflected or infused from some central authority, however benevolent, but generated inwardly through individual experience. Sabrina is there to aid those in need but does not diffuse a pattern by which all that is good manifests its participation in her. Nor does the Earl of Bridgewater. He, his court, and his power have been clearly separated from those of the central government, and the festivities in his honor move spontaneously upward toward a virtuous ideal, not downward by compulsion from a powerful center. Of course Jonson, like Milton, was interested in a virtue which was intrinsic. But Jonson's masques nevertheless tended to portray virtue as something which could be communicated by the mere presence of the king, even against the will of the unregenerate forces who attempted to resist his influence. At Ludlow, rituals and pastimes are cleansed of their usual role in Stuart political rhetoric as figures of royal power and made, instead, a way of celebrating virtue. Insofar as he argued for outward ritual forms as a manifestation of inner rectitude, Milton was being quite Jonsonian. But at Ludlow, the integrity of ritual depends on its separation from Stuart images of power.

There may have been a personal meaning in the children's victory over Comus, for in the memoirs of the family, the Earl's solicitude for the spiritual welfare of his many offspring is prominent. Not only did he "season" them against Arminianism, he would himself examine each child before communion to ensure that they had not succumbed to false doctrine.[52] He and his Lady had armed their children as best they could against the spiritual oblivion proffered by Comus, yet at the same time allowed them considerable freedom to choose their own beliefs, which may account for the remarkable diversity of religious opinion the children actually demonstrated in later life. The masque is rich in debates and disagreements—even the brothers differ over the nature and power of chastity. But all members of the family are virtuous, for all their diversity of opinion. They are praised, as Sabrina is, for what their virtue has genuinely accomplished. The victory over Comus also has a political meaning, of course. As the two brothers disperse the rout of Comus, so the Earl had already demonstrated some ability to discomfit the Laudian and Catholic forces which, to moderates in 1634, seemed to be threatening the welfare of the church. But Comus is not yet vanquished; at the end of Milton's entertainment, with the installation of the Earl and his family at Ludlow, the battle has only begun. Milton's masque celebrates the Earl and his Council for their independence from the power of the center as a new and autonomous base for reform—in much the same way the Earl and his supporters envisioned the Council of Wales themselves in the key areas of conflict with the central government.

Ludlow Castle is also established as a new and independent locus for the dissemination of arts and pastimes. As William S. Miller and others have demonstrated, the mythography surrounding the Attendant Spirit associates him with the Druids, with the Welsh Apollo Belin, and with the indigenous arts of Wales.[53] In his role as Attendant Spirit, Lawes has symbolically separated himself from the cultural center of Whitehall, at least for the space of the masque, and made himself part of a new center. He "belongs" to the house of Bridgewater, and his performance in the masque as a heavenly messenger and guide displays the power of an autonomous art that can genuinely accomplish what the arts of the Stuart court proclaimed to do—bridge political differences and elevate its audience to the contemplation of moral truth. Comus had roused his cohorts with an appeal to the "freedom to be merry," his call for freedom being, ironically, an appeal for a show of submission. But the Attendant Spirit, before he ascends back to the court of Jove (in the heavens, not at Whitehall), offers his own reformulation which seems deliberately to recast the standard Anglican call to mirth. The freedom to be merry is not necessarily freedom at all: "Love vertue, she alone is free" and when virtue is kept at the center, all manner of mirth, sports, and revelry can legitimately flourish.

* iii *

A brief and melancholy political postscript: the Earl of Bridgewater did not live up to the hopes of Milton and the other anti-Laudians that he would be able, as President of Wales, to create a strong base for countering Archbishop Laud. He was plagued by a series of personal and political reverses which commenced only shortly after the performance of the masque. His wife died and her loss seems to have been a shattering blow, he sank into debt as a result of his son-in-law's rash business ventures, and he became more and more incapacitated by illness. Laud never did manage to take away the Council's power to try sexual offenses. In 1636 he tried to force the issue by bringing one celebrated case to the attention of Charles I, but the Earl's associates in Wales were cautiously confident that their President would prevail against the Churchman. As one of them assured him, "such is his Maiesties fauour towardes your Lordshipp . . . & your own vigilance therein, as you Cannott be surprised, And then I hope your Lordshipp need not doubt of the victorye."[54] By 1637, the king had agreed to arbitrate the dispute, but Laud or someone working in the interest of the High Commission managed to procure a general stay of proceedings in the Court of the Marches until the jurisdictional conflict was settled. When Bridgewater appealed to the king, Charles assured him that the general stay had been made in error and would be corrected, but the conflict was not resolved. The Council in the Marches of Wales continued to try sexual offenses despite continuing opposition, and the matter was still pending at the point of Laud's trial and execution.[55]

So the Earl of Bridgewater managed to hold the Archbishop at bay, but he could do little more than that. Perhaps he lacked the opportunity or the political expertise. Perhaps the whole project was impossible. But at some point he did lose the confidence of Charles I. By 1640, he was quite isolated from the central government and seems to have been systematically deprived of information essential to his tasks as President of Wales. As Lord Lieutenant for the counties under Council jurisdiction, Bridgewater was theoretically in charge of military operations there but was passed over in humiliating fashion by King Charles in favor of his rival the Catholic Earl of Worcester. Painfully and slowly, he gave up most of his political allegiance to Charles, finally taking the Parliamentary side in the Civil War and dying in 1649, the same year Charles was executed. But his family considered him to have been faithful to the king all along,[56] and probably, by his own lights, he was. Through much of his political career, the Earl of Bridgewater seems genuinely to have believed that it was possible to serve Charles I well while at the same time maintaining and even acting upon his own independent principles. Perhaps Laud showed him he was wrong.

Milton's gradual disenchantment with the existing structures of church and state is considerably better documented and moved him finally far to the left of the Earl's moderate parliamentarianism. In the process, as he relinquished his plans for a career in the church, he may have felt considerable regret at the fact that the "Peere of mickle trust, and power" celebrated with such bright hopes in his masque had not accomplished more against the Laudians. In the 1637 edition of *Comus* he did not identify himself as author of the masque but did supply a Virgilian tag for the title page *"Eheu quid volui misero mihi! floribus austrum / Perditus———"* (Milton, 37). The fragment, quoted from Virgil's "Second Eclogue," can be interpreted very generally as an expression of regret that he had allowed the "flowers" of his masque to be published and so unloosed to criticism or as a complaint that he had been wasting his time and talents.[57] But perhaps he meant it also as a comment on the political meaning of the masque—his poetry had been blasted, wasted in the sense that its vision of a new political accommodation seemed further than ever from achievement. The bright possibilities of 1634 had receded and the language of political imperative had, perforce, been reduced to the meaner role of elegaic for the vision it had sought to further. As we shall see on turning to Andrew Marvell, Virgil's "Second Eclogue" provided more than one seventeenth-century poet with a storehouse of images for delineating political change and exploring the national imbalances revealed through a shift in the patterns of mirth.

Pastimes without a Court:
Richard Lovelace and Andrew Marvell

During the 1640s, as King Charles I and Archbishop William Laud were caught in the narrowing circle of Puritan and Parliamentary opposition, the rituals and old pastimes they had cultivated with such care were gradually extinguished. The theatres were closed, "the Feasts of the Nativity of Christ, *Easter* and *Whitsuntide* and all other festivall dayes commonly called holy dayes" were abolished as "Festivall or Holy dayes" by Parliamentary order; the *Book of Sports* was burnt by the common hangman; the Laudian clergy, the High Commission, and Laud's favorite "pulpit" the Court of Star Chamber were all swept away; both Laud and Charles I perished on the scaffold. After the death of the king, according to one pamphlet, there was a *Deep Sigh Breathed Through the Lodgings At Whitehall*. The old center of the nation's culture, the vital spring from which public mirth had been envisioned as flowing out to the nation, became empty and dry.[1] England in the late 1640s and early 1650s appeared—and was meant to appear—a very different place than it had been under Stuart rule. Traditional pastimes and Laudian ritual forms, a symbolic language of royal absolutism, were suppressed along with the monarchy itself.

It would be hard to overestimate the impact of these vast and relatively sudden alterations. In many quarters, the sweeping away of the outward signs of Stuart oppression was undoubtedly cause for euphoria. But even among those who were ambivalent about Stuart rule, we can identify mechanisms for blunting the suddenness of the change. To a degree that we have only begun to recognize, royalists and royalist sympathizers coped with the loss of public ritual and festivity by recasting old ceremonies in more private forms and surrounding them with cryptic language and hermetic symbolism—barriers against the intrusion of hostile outsiders. The Stuart monarchs had urged their gentry and aristocrats to "Get thee to the country"—give up the court for a more wholesome immersion in the duties and cyclical rhythms of their country estates. Out of admonitory fidelity to the rural ideal, Stuart entertainments had regularly pastoralized the court itself, assimilating it into an idealized rural pattern like that urged upon the nobles. But the Civil War turned this amiable sentiment for country life into a matter of grim necessity. The court was dispersed. Royalists fortunate enough to hang on to their rural estates at all were frequently forced into retirement, an involuntary "contentment in the country." When the joys of rural life could no longer be celebrated in entertainments at court, royalists began to inscribe images of the court upon the countryside. A very common poetic motif of the late Civil War and Interregnum period is the discovery of cryptic vestiges of the lost court and its ritualism in the midst of a country landscape. The defense of old pastimes did not disappear as a poetic motif when the pastimes themselves were suppressed; rather, it sank underground, removed from its collective public role in Stuart ideology but preserved as a form of private ritual communion with the vanished culture of the court.

It would, of course, be a mistake to suppose that all public festivity disappeared from England along with Charles I. Old holiday customs survived here and there, but the only ones practiced openly without risking suppression were those that did not reflect the image of Stuart rule. As we will recall, for example, puppet shows and kindred "abominations" were tolerated at London's Bartholomew Fair throughout the Interregnum despite the ban on stage plays. A more marginal, more interesting phenomenon was the resurgence of the anarchic side of May Day and other traditional pastimes. With the collapse of the monarchy, popular holiday observances seemed to spin off from their crumbling Stuart center as though by centrifugal force, to be taken up by radical sects and flaunted in "contempt of all authority."[2] To many contemporaries, the England of the Civil War period was itself a grim festival run rampant—a world "turned upside down" like the inverted world of carnival, overturning established hierarchies and mocking images of power—except that the topsy-turvydom failed to right itself according to the proper holiday pattern. As the revolutionary army and the radical sects took to the roads and fields, appearing to overrun the countryside with images of disorder, royalists sought shelter. In Interregnum poetry, the "public mirth" and "liberty" of open spaces are associated with anarchy and vulnerability. Orderly and ordering rituals are found rather in protective enclosures: estates, gardens, mystical groves.

Lovelace and Marvell may appear a curious set of poets to consider together—the one a darling of the court, a precocious wit granted his master's degree at eighteen by Archbishop Laud amidst the proliturgical pageantry of the king's visit to Oxford in 1636, an ardent royalist whose dashing charm and passionate self-sacrifice made his name even among his contemporaries almost synonymous with the Cavalier ideal; the other much more obscure, more reticent about his political sentiments, but never much of a Laudian so far as we can tell, despite his brief flirtation with Catholicism as a young man, and clearly identified by the time of the Interregnum with the Puritan party. Yet the two poets have major themes and major strategies in common: writing at a time when the old forms were being swept away, both were concerned with the problem of cultural survival, with discerning or creating continuities. Marvell knew Lovelace personally, perhaps well. He also knew *Lucasta* well and contributed to the volume a poem that subtly undercuts the Cavalier enterprise even as it praises the verse. Thanks to the work of Frank Kermode and others, we are well acquainted with Marvell's poetic transformation of Cavalier amatory conventions.[3] But we have perhaps not attended sufficiently to his recasting of Cavalier strategies for dealing with political disintegration. Lovelace will receive short shrift in our discussion here in that we will be more concerned with *Lucasta* as a Cavalier paradigm, a treasury of political motifs which were mined and recast by Marvell, than with Lovelace's verse in itself. Marvell's poetry may be taken on one level as a reconceptualization of the dilemma of defeated Royalism. In *Lucasta* Lovelace repeatedly imbeds rituals and symbols of the vanished court in protected rural enclosures as a way of perpetuating vestiges of the culture that was lost. Marvell's poetry echoes the pattern, but less to preserve the past than to work himself out of it and come to terms with the massive cultural transformation implied by the eradication of Stuart "public mirth."

Marvell's commendatory poem, *"To his Noble Friend Mr. Richard Lovelace, upon his Poems,"* which appeared in the 1649 edition of *Lucasta*, was written before the death of the king and before the darkest time for royalists but displays an early version of Marvell's ambivalent ways with royalist symbology. Richard Lovelace was, in the 1640s, the Cavalier par excellence, an embodiment of the finest ideals of the royalist cause. The poem testifies to a personal link between the two poets and seems initially to align its author with the political ideals of his *"Noble Friend."* Marvell praises the "candid Age" of Lovelace's artistic flourishing by contrast with "Our times," the Civil War period, in which earlier virtues have been banished: the air swarms with barbaric "Censurers" and reformers who rise against the author of *Lucasta* in the name of Presbyterian zeal and parliamentary privilege.[4]

Marvell's description of the tainted "degenerate" present seems to carry little admiration for the reformers; his invocation of the prewar virtues sounds very much like the usual royalist nostalgia for those bygone "golden days." But Marvell depicts himself as likely to be taken for one of Lovelace's accusers, at least by the flock of warlike ladies who rise in defense of their "favorite":

> They all in mutiny though yet undrest
> Sally'd, and would in his defence contest.
> And one the loveliest that was yet e're seen,
> Thinking that I too of the rout had been,
> Mine eyes invaded with a female spight.
>
> (*Marvell*, 3–4)

In comic duress, Marvell declares his willingness to die in defense of Lovelace's ladies or in Lovelace's "cause." This sounds like a declaration of political allegiance: Lovelace's "cause" was preeminently the cause of the royalists and the poem takes note of that through specific reference to the Petition of Kent and Lovelace's sequestration (*Marvell*, 239n). But Marvell's commendation of Lovelace writes him out of the contemporary political scene. He has climbed to a transcendent realm where he is safe from his detractors, his victory over time secure, his fame and his "cause" defined not through his political allegiance but by his personal attributes and requiring no "aid" on the part of the poet or anyone else for their preservation:

> O no, mistake not, I reply'd, for I
> In your defence, or in his cause would dy.
> But he secure of glory and of time
> Above their envy, or mine aid doth clime.
> Him, valiantst men, and fairest Nymphs approve,
> His Booke in them finds Judgement, with you Love.
>
> (*Marvell*, 4)

Lovelace may have been at a literal distance from his fellow Cavaliers in 1646 or 1647 when Marvell's poem was written—perhaps abroad or in prison.[5] But that possibility does not sufficiently account for Marvell's strategy. He appears to exalt the image of a Cavalier hero, as contemporary royalist verses so often did, but at the same time he voids that image of the very political resonances which would, in a clearly royalist context, have made it most worthy of admiration. Lovelace becomes an apolitical icon, encapsulated, suspended in air, separated from his "cause" so that his virtues can be reevaluated and admired independently of their political significance for the partisans of Charles I. The tactic is reminiscent of some of Ben Jonson's lyrics in that it evokes a vision of virtue which is serenely detached and strong enough to weather time and circumstance. But in Jonson, such moral imperviousness is never divorced from a social context, a shared system of values; Jonson never quite gave up the belief that, given sufficient energy and commitment, stoic detachment could become a basis for political and moral reform. Lovelace was born too late to be a "son of Ben" but not too late to absorb and transmit some of Jonson's confidence about the potential impact of good verses on the conduct of public life. For admiring contemporaries, his poetry seemed to hark back to the art and principles of Jonson: one of the other commendatory poems to *Lucasta* calls him *"another* Ben."[6] Marvell also owed much as a poet to Jonson and the sons of Ben; he strikes a Jonsonian note in his praise of Lovelace. But the effect of his poem is to divorce Jonsonian ideals from the implied social setting which had given them their urgency.

"*To his Noble Friend Mr.* Richard Lovelace" is based on a deliberate disjunction. The "candid Age" which Lovelace's "sweet Muse" and "fair Fortune chose" is envisioned as a time long gone, before the shattering experience of the "Civill Wars." But in actuality, as Marvell well knew, much or most of Lovelace's poetry had been written during wartime. It dated from the Scottish campaigns at the end of the 1630s and from the 1640s—scarcely a period which had fostered candid virtues. His Muse and Fortune may have "chosen" a happier time when art and public morality were compatible, but that was not the time during which he did his writing. Some of the other commendatory poems to *Lucasta* take note of the fact, marveling that such tumultuous years had produced so sweet a poetic voice; but those poems describe Lovelace's lyrics as continuing to perform at least a quasi-political function of providing solace to the royalists in their dark days by singing of liberty and the glories of the king from out the iron bars of defeat.[7] Marvell's poem, instead, creates an unbridgeable space between the Cavalier poet and his implied community. Lovelace is secure in the heavens—almost like a hero who had perished rather than one who was still alive and writing for the "cause." His verse inspires "Judgement" and "Love," but is bereft of its vital function as an articulation of shared social and political values. Indeed, Marvell seems to suggest, the Cavalier's adherence to bygone ideals, however admirable in themselves, has insured his isolation from the present: he himself has "climbed" to his place "secure of glory." For better or for worse, he has severed himself from history and the community whose values he meant to reaffirm.

As Marvell wrote his "*Noble Friend*" out of the political cause in which Lovelace was actually immersed, so he frequently attempted to write his own poetry, his own independent stance, out of the politically charged symbols he borrowed from Lovelace and the other Cavaliers. Time and again, we find him entertaining a Cavalier stance but transmuting it so that it becomes a way of distancing himself from ideals associated with the vanished Church and monarchy, a way of growing beyond old truths. During the Civil War period and the Interregnum, poets did not (or could not) appeal to the enactment of seasonal festivals for ritual affirmation of national timelessness and unity. Instead, they looked to the cyclical processes of nature itself and found symbols of the old pastimes inscribed within "sacred" natural enclosures. Lovelace, like many of his contemporaries, salvaged elements of the royalist programme by sinking them into the natural world and identifying them as emanations of unvarying ancient wisdom. Marvell practiced a similar immersion but for the purpose of self-extrication. The old patterns are invoked to be written through, written beyond. Marvell's adoption of images and attitudes from the poetry of Lovelace and the other Cavaliers often has the quality of a "rehearsal" in Steven Mullaney's sense—a representation whose aim is not preserving the old but rather laying it finally to rest, a ceremonious extinction of ceremony.[8]

* i *

One of the commonest, yet most enigmatic images in royalist poetry of the late Civil War and immediate postwar period is the image of a grove, not an ordinary grove, but a place charged with visionary intensity, its shape suggesting the architecture of a church or palace and harboring emblems of one or both of those institutions in their prewar form. Among the most striking of these is the grove in Lovelace's "Aramantha. A PASTORALL," the final poem of *Lucasta* and one we know to have been important for Marvell. He imitated its progression from a garden to a meadow to a mystic grove in his own "Upon Appleton House," though to radically altered effect. Aramantha is a lovelorn shepherdess who has taken to the green world in retreat from the Civil Wars, the "sad storm of fire and blood" which has set "Hydraphil," the Parliamentarians, against "Philanact," the Cavaliers (*Lovelace*, 117). Enjoying the peaceful "liberty" of her country life, she enters a garden where the flowers crown her Flora, Queen of May. They offer her "Tribute" and adorn her with themselves, preserving in their rural "*Elisium*" a "due Obedience" to Maying rituals banned from the nation at large. We will remember the natural May Day piety of the birds and flowers in Herrick's "Corinna." In Lovelace's poem as well, the observances are inherent, portrayed as intrinsic to the English countryside.

Next Aramantha wanders through a meadow, a less protected place where nature's harmony and reciprocity have been unbalanced by injurious human intervention. There she encounters a mysterious herd of cows, "rev'rend" and stately yet curiously self-sacrificing. As the garden flowers had obeyed the laws of festival, so the cows keep traditional hospitality, freely offering her their milk. Aramantha observes that the cows give far more than they get: "receive in Hay, / And pay in silver twice a Day" (*Lovelace*, 110). But despite their helpful ministrations, they are destined for eventual slaughter as a result of the "inhumanitie" of "men." That is, perhaps, the usual fate of cows, but this "God-like race" of cattle is not the usual herd; they are cast in a heroic mode and seem more human than bovine. Lovelace shapes the experience of the cows—living in openness and magnanimity but destined to perish under a harsher code—in a way that suggests the plight of the old landed classes as seen from the usual idealizing conservative perspective. The "God-like race" had shaped their peaceful rural lives in accordance with traditional patterns but found that their fidelity made them vulnerable. The wars had first impoverished them, then seemingly placed them in the hands of their enemies.

Weeping over the human cruelty that would first despoil the "God-like race" of their freely offered produce and then deprive them of their lives, Aramantha takes refuge from the cruel fields in a sheltering wood where she comes upon a "well ordered stately grove." As in the garden and the meadows she encountered remnants of the ideals of festivity and hospitality, so within the grove she discovers a well-ordered sylvan court resembling the dispersed cultural center from which those ideals had been promulgated to the nation:

> This is the Pallace of the Wood,
> And Court o'th' Royall Oake, where stood
> The whole Nobility, the Pine
> Strait Ash, tall Firre, and wanton Vine;
> The Proper Cedar, and the rest;
> Here she her deeper senses blest;
> Admires great Nature in this Pile
> Floor'd with greene-velvet Camomile,
> Garnisht with Gems of unset fruit.
>
> (*Lovelace*, 111)

This verdant "Pallace" is a reverend "Pile" adorned with sophisticated natural artifacts, such as velvet carpeting and gleaming jewels; its walls are lined with stately "nobles" as though part of a royal audience; its air is filled with the song of a consort of birds, "winged Musick of the ayre," who are allotted their daily feast in the "Pallace of the Wood" and provide in return a "gratefull *Serenade*" each evening, like royal musicians at court. The economic relationship between servants and master is no mere business proposition but a free exchange of gifts according to the old feudal pattern. The "Royall Oake" that presides over the "Pallace of the Wood" is of the arboreal species traditionally associated with monarchy, but also a symbol closely tied to King Charles I and his family. In James Howell's *Dodona's Grove* (1640), an extended and widely read allegory of court and national life, the oak represents in turn James and Charles I. Royal oak imagery became pervasive in Cavalier poetry after Prince Charles's celebrated evasion of the parliamentary armies at Worcester by hiding in an oak tree.[9] Even earlier than that, it had been an image associated with Stuart ecclesiastical policy and with the Druid forerunners of British kings and bishops—a matter to which we will return presently. The "Court o'th Royall Oake" offers Aramantha emotional solace and blesses her "deeper senses" in part because it recapitulates a set of social institutions and relationships which she has supposed destroyed.

As she lies down to rest in her consoling woodland "Pallace," Aramantha is awakened by the woeful cries of Alexis, a shepherd who, like her, has fled the firestorm of the wars and sought shelter in the woods. In *Lucasta* the name Alexis is associated with the poet Lovelace himself; Aramantha turns out to be his long-lost Lucasta. The lovers plight their troth and vow to remain forever in and near the "Court o'th' Royall Oake" where they will lead lives of pastoral simplicity. They have found their proper milieu and, in accordance with long Stuart practice, their "court" is irradiated with "Affection for the Country." In the depths of the forest, they have revived the world of court pastoral. Their chaste marriage becomes a timeless commemoration of the ongoing pastoral romance which had dominated entertainments at court—the celebrated union of King Charles I and Queen Henrietta Maria, two faithful lovers who, like Lucasta and Alexis, had been separated by the wars but could enjoy no prospect of reunion. The poet and his bride fill the void left by the absent pair and become imaginative surrogates for the king and queen. Lovelace's 1649 volume thus closes with an idealized reconstruction of Caroline culture inscribed upon a landscape and perpetually insulated from the ravages of war. The grove reunites the lovers with each other, undoes the war in that sense, but also provides them with a soothing environment which magically recaptures elements of the prewar court. Lovelace must have expected this lingering final image of a Cavalier Elysium to solace readers of *Lucasta* as well, at least those readers who were capable of sympathy for the Royalist cause.

"Aramantha. A PASTORALL" is by no means the only poem of *Lucasta* to dwell upon the image of the grove. The volume is full of

similar sheltering spaces—Orphic woods and enclosures harboring images of order. There is a variation upon the theme in "AMYNTOR'S
GROVE," probably written during 1648, a country house poem in
disguise which interprets the mansion of a celebrated arch-Royalist as
yet another grove fused with imagery of the Caroline court.[10] The
Amyntor of the poem was almost certainly Endymion Porter, friend of
poets and "public mirth," who had been responsible for the acquisition
of much of Charles I's art collection. Porter's country house was like a
miniature Whitehall in that it displayed his own smaller collection put
together in the course of his purchases for the king. In Lovelace's poem,
Endymion Porter's paintings, displayed on the walls of his country
house, define the precincts of a sacred grove which serves as a setting for a
royalist ritual of Bacchanalian transcendence. Although the king's art
collection at Whitehall was already threatened with dispersal, Porter's
"grove" is intact, graced with a noble "stand / Of *Titian, Raphael,
Georgone*" (*Lovelace*, 72) which recall the splendid canvasses displayed at
court. Within the "embroidered" walls of Porter's house metamorphosed to landscape, the company deck themselves with "Vine, / The
Poppy, and the Eglantine," drink the "Oriental bowle," kindle a "Sacrifice" of tobacco, amber, and thyme which "through our Earthen
Conduicts sore / Higher then Altars fum'd before." The ritual before the
"sacred Flame" in the grove of Amyntor removes its participants from
the harsh realities of the royalist situation in 1648 and takes them back
to a solemn-festive paganism much like the atmosphere cultivated in
entertainments at court and in prewar Cavalier poetry. Their secluded
revival of the cultural imagery of the court sparks their valor for the
tottering cause and fortifies them against impending defeat:

> So drencht we our oppressing cares,
> And choakt the wide Jawes of our feares,
> Whilst ravisht thus we did devise
> If this were not a Paradice.
>
> (*Lovelace*, 73)

In "AMYNTOR'S GROVE," as so often in the Cavalier poetry of
mirth, we encounter a problem of tone. Is this wine-drenched communion seriously meant as worship or is it mere glorified dissipation? And
here, as in our earlier discussion of Herrick, we discover that the two
categories are inseparable. The rites of Amyntor's Grove create a Diony-
siac "holy rage" familiar from the verse of Jonson and Herrick, familiar
also from the stately Bacchanals at court, but carried to a new pitch of
intensity.[11] Lovelace's poetry is both play and worship, a melange of
flippancy and political desperation in which each extreme fuels the

other. To get a clearer sense of the Anglican pattern underlying his seeming nonchalance with sacred matters, we might briefly consider a parallel case in which seriousness of intent is unquestionable and un-alloyed with complicating levity—the "sacred grove" imagery in the poetry of Henry Vaughan. Our excursus will carry us into the seemingly remote subject of Giordano Bruno and Hermeticism but will help us penetrate some of the "frivolous" mysteries of *Lucasta* and their rewritten versions in Marvell's "Upon Appleton House."

Vaughan may have been at Oxford at the same time as Lovelace or only shortly thereafter; as his early verses to "Amoret" and his *Olor Iscanus* testify, he was steeped in the same Cavalier culture. Like Love-lace, the young Vaughan was fascinated with the image of the sacred grove. *Olor Iscanus* is permeated with motifs from the myth of Orpheus, the antique poet whose powerful music could create his own sacred wood by drawing trees about him in a magic circle.[12] Vaughan forcibly repudiated the Cavalier culture of his youth when he began to write sacred poetry. But he kept his fascination with the image of the grove. The 1650 edition of *Silex Scintillans* begins in much the same way that the 1649 *Lucasta* ended, with a retreat to a sheltering sylvan edifice.

"Regeneration" delineates a pilgrimage from spiritual bondage to renewal in a sacred grove, an enclosure seemingly impenetrable from the outside but mysteriously suffused with light and vitality within, its vegetation arranged to recapitulate the structure and ritual practices of an Anglican Church. The air is "in spice" like the incense favored by Laudians, the sunlight is refracted into a "thousand pieces" as though through a stained glass window, and the bushes are decked with garlands like the nave of a prewar church on some festival occasion. The bank of flowers is its congregation, some attentively drinking in the Sun, some asleep, like the standard Laudian view of the state church as including everyone, whatever their degree of enlightenment.[13] The natural temple of "Regeneration" brings the solitary poet into sudden and mysterious contact with ritual forms banished from the nation at large. It rustles with the wind of the Holy Spirit and seems to promise an infusion of sacramental grace, a form of "regeneration" no longer available in Britain through public liturgical worship.

Vaughan's grove is a church, not a court, but it is like the groves of *Lucasta* in that it mysteriously recapitulates a prewar institution. And Vaughan and Lovelace were only two of a number of writers of the late Civil War or immediate postwar period to have used the image, among them Edward Benlowes, Mildmay Fane, and Henry More.[14] As we shall see, only a year or two after *Lucasta* and *Silex Scintillans*, Andrew Marvell described a similar phenomenon, the grove at Nun Appleton to which he retreats to escape the flood in the meadows—another enclosure "closely wedg'd" and dark from the outside but within, bright, "passable and thin." Marvell's sacred grove also forms an architectural structure, a temple with *"Corinthian porticoes"* and columns linked with both the ritual practices of Anglicanism and the hierarchy of the court. The sacred groves of Interregnum poetry are steeped in arcana, particularly the symbolism of the "Ancient Theology" of Hermes Trismegistus, but would not necessarily have struck contemporary readers as impossibly esoteric for all that. The appeal of Hermetic doctrines to religious radicals of the Interregnum is well known. But earlier in the century, Hermetic doctrine had also been important for those who wrote in defense of the Church of England. It provided them with a "historical" basis for their appeals to the ideal of Anglican unity and with magical tools for preserving the mystical community of church and state against threats from within and without. The most important prewar center for Hermetic imagery had been the Stuart court.

In Caroline masques and pastorals, groves are often religious temples and temples groves, the nexus of a British Ur-Christianity which fuses the natural and the ecclesiastical into a single structure with the monarch, the head of the Anglican Church, appearing in the figure of an ancient Roman emperor or Druid priest to preside over the sacred rites. In *Albion's Triumph*, for example, Charles I is Albanactus, emperor of Britain; the main masque reveals a *"grove of straight trees, which rising by degrees to a high place, openeth itself to discover the aspect of a stately temple; all which was sacred to Jove"* (*Inigo*, 2:456). Charles I sits in the grove. He is clad in yellow satin, adorned with golden rays like the sun—a source of light in the shadows. Then, flanked by singing Hermetic priests and sacrificers, the king descends from the place of mysteries to dance the main masque and be united with his queen, the Goddess of Britain. The sacred grove then gives way to the contemporary prospect of the royal palace at Whitehall and part of the City of London. An image of national union, which existed first in the mind of the priest-king, is conferred on the Britain of 1631 through his ancient ritual magic. Clouds open above the landscape to reveal *"Innocency, Justice, Religion, Affection to the Country, and Concord, being all companions of Peace"* (*Inigo* 2:457). The rituals of church and state are at once an outgrowth of the ancient ceremonies of the grove and a reflection of the royal mind.

As we will recall from our earlier discussion of Herrick, this identification of grove and church had a certain historical validity, at least if one credited the testimony of Gregory the Great. According to the "Ancient Theology" of Hermeticism, believed to date from the time of Moses or earlier, the oak groves of the ancient British Druids, the myrtle and laurel groves associated with the Sibylls and with esoteric pagan cults, the grove which the Magus Orpheus drew about himself through the power of his hymns—all these sacred places were holy to Christianity as well since the worship practiced within them had been proto-Christian, a pious veneration of the One God based on the reading of prophetic hieroglyphs in nature many ages before the coming of Christ. For a Renaissance Englishman thinking hermetically, natural groves could therefore become a hieroglyph of the church and, conversely, the foliated pediments of a Corinthian temple or the soaring treelike arches of a Gothic church could be interpreted as vestiges of their origin. Some of the drawings reproduced in Orgel and Strong's collection actually fuse the encircling trees of a grove to the columns of a temple as though to establish the identity visually.[15] In the literature of the Stuart court, concerned always with perserving the church and the nation against the divisive threat posed by Puritans and sectarians, Hermetic assertions about the sacredness of ancient mystery had been a powerful political tool.

A key source for Anglican Hermetic argument was, of all people, the archheretic Giordano Bruno, who had spent time in England during the 1580s and had observed the nation's religious divisions firsthand. Bruno had little good to say about the English Church. In *The Expulsion of the Triumphant Beast* (Spaccio de la bestia trionfante), published in England in 1584, he applied Hermes Trismegistus' lament for the decline of the divine cult of Egypt to the English scene. Hermes had prophesied in the *Asclepius*, "There will come a time when it will be seen that in vain have the Egyptians honoured the divinity with a pious mind and with assiduous service. All their holy worship will become inefficacious. The gods, leaving the earth, will go back to heaven; they will abandon Egypt; this land, once the home of religion, will be widowed of its gods and left destitute. . . . Then this most holy land, the home of sanctuaries and temples, will be covered with tombs and the dead."[16] For Bruno, post-Reformation England, with its doctrinal quarreling, its countryside defaced with the ruined remains of outlawed religious houses, was just such a desecrated sanctuary. Bruno's proposed remedy for this national desecration was solar magic, which would purge the British nation of the "Triumphant Beast" who had despoiled her.

Bruno's ideas were greeted, for the most part, with hostility in the 1580s. But in Caroline England, they were safer and looked more attractive. Bruno had been closely connected with the court of Henry III of France; English interest in his ideas may have been fueled by the strong current of French Platonism which arrived at Whitehall along with Queen Henrietta Maria. By whatever means, his influence upon court culture was unmistakable. In the Caroline masque, Bruno's analysis is applied to the confounding of contemporary Puritans; the seer whose solar magic will revive the ancient national and ecclesiastical unity is King Charles I. Thomas Carew's splendid masque *Coelum Britannicum* (1634), which we have already discussed briefly in connection with Milton's *Comus*, follows Bruno and the *Asclepius* very closely. The masque begins with an evocation of Roman Britain in ruins like the Egypt of old, once a "temple of the world," now decayed. But Jove has vowed to reform it by following the pattern of the divine dyad Carlo-Maria, envisioned as a sun or noonday star appearing in the darkness. Jove purges the heavens of the corrupt old constellations and installs chaste new stars in the firmament, thus making a restoration of the earth possible. This part of the masque follows Bruno particularly closely, except that all the reforms Jove envisions resemble actual political reforms initiated by Charles I in Britain of 1634.[17] Ancient Britain is revitalized, a chorus of Druids and Rivers behold the sun of divine majesty, and the scene undergoes a series of splendid metamorphoses that portray the progress of history toward the present. Finally, Religion, Truth, and Wisdom are revealed sitting in the firmament. Eternity breaks forth from a great cloud, with the new stellar deities arranged above him, the brightest representing Charles I, whose Hermetic magic has not only restored the lost temple of Britain but will also guide it throughout history by means of his and his descendants' magical influence over the stars. Thrice-great Hermes had preached that a nation whose priests knew how to use astral magic would be permanently preserved: that is what happens in the Caroline masque through the sacred power of the priest-king of England.[18]

We cannot be sure to what degree the astral magic of the Stuart masque was actually considered efficacious and to what degree it was intended merely as a symbology of royal power. The sudden eclipse of the Caroline court and the rituals of the church, followed by the execution of the sacred monarch himself, was a staggering, almost incomprehensible, blow for many Royalists and may have induced some of them to give nostalgic retrospective credence to doctrines they would earlier have viewed more critically. During the Interregnum, the irenic Hermeticism associated with the Stuart court became a crypto-language for talking about the vanished ideals and institutions. Hermes Trismegistus had foreseen the fall of the Ancient Theology of Egypt and prophesied that the "temple of the world" would be renewed through some purgative catastrophe—pestilence or fire or flood. For hermetically inclined royalists, the Civil War had been just such a catastrophe and could perhaps usher in some magical renewal of Britain. Neoplatonic astral magic had always been understood as a powerful curative for the soul; it could purge melancholy and restore the happy, sanguine temperament associated in Laudian circles with participation in the "public mirth" of old sports and pastimes. Indeed, for many of its practitioners the mystical reuniting of church and state was a project which would be carried out through the reharmonizing of individual psyches. One method favored by Bruno and others was the creation of a mental model of some perfected hierarchy or institution. Through astral magic, the mind could be healed of its divisions and made to assume the perfection of the model.[19] This is a project which we find enacted over and over again with varying degrees of sobriety in the poetry of the Civil War years and Interregnum, often through the arcane image of the sacred grove.

Henry Vaughan offers perhaps the most clear-cut example. Vaughan identified himself as the Hermetic Magus of an Anglicanism gone underground. His chosen epithet "Silurist" declares him an inhabitant of South Wales in the times of Roman Britain; even in his secular poetry, he portrays himself at least implicitly as a Welsh bardic priest and latter-day Druid who frequents the groves to find intimations of sacred unity. His devotional prose frequently echoes Giordano Bruno and earlier Platonizing Anglicans on the importance of religious unity and good works. Vaughan even laments, like Bruno, the disappearance of the medieval religious orders, venting scorn upon the malicious railers and sectaries who had destroyed the church. Vaughan also translated treatises on hermetic physick and seems actually to have practiced hermetic medicine after the wars as a country doctor in Wales. Much of his prose is designed to provide medicine for the soul and sustain his fellow Welsh Anglicans in their time of darkness by offering them works of devotion which recapture the spirit of the vanished liturgy and piece together the broken Anglican community by forging his readership into a secret community of seers. His poetry has a similar political and religious goal but it is more cryptically expressed. He seems to have intended *Silex Scintillans* to function like the grove of an Ancient Theologian, revealing hieroglyphs of the One to be gathered and interpreted by his readers for the healing of their own sufferings and for the good of the shattered church.[20]

"Regeneration" is a mysterious poem and deliberately so; it is designed to alert readers to the cryptic strategies of the collection as a whole. In this initial poem, Vaughan takes the stance of a neophyte who encounters a series of puzzling natural emblems which he is unable to interpret. The mystic book of nature is dark to him. Vaughan could certainly expect his most enlightened readers to read the hieroglyph of

the forest-church correctly; the image was commonplace in the poetry
and thought of the Interregnum. But he portrays himself as uncompre-
hending and thus places the poem's stress upon the process of learning to
read hermetically. Much of the power of his description of the grove
derives from the contrast between its dynamic, highly charged images of
light and its utter silence. The language of the grove is visual. The
poet-neophyte walks about studying its structure, striving to encompass
its meaning, but never quite enters into its mystery. What he sees in the
sixth stanza are silent natural hieroglyphs of the Anglican ritual practices
which the Civil Wars had destroyed. The quiet recapitulates the "silenced" condition of the church but also suggests hermetic silence—a
stillness in the presence of ultimate mysteries which includes within
itself all meaning. The quiet is finally broken by the weeping language of
the fountain which, in the architectural schema of the grove, can be
"read" as a baptismal font, but also embodies an unheeded sacramentalism available through the natural world. The fountain spends her music
in vain on the "dumb shades" which surround her. Then the whole grove
is set in motion by the tremendous energy of the "rushing wind"—the
Holy Spirit, certainly, but identified as it so often was in Renaissance
texts with the Hermetic World Soul, linking the many and the one.
Even at this intense moment, the poet remains outside the spiritual
experience, hearing the wind, not feeling it, praying for the healing
power of "one breath." The poem ends without a clear answer to his
prayer. Its aim is to teach how to ask. "Regeneration" vividly but
mysteriously sets forth one of the religious goals of Vaughan's collection
as a whole: to offer, through the poet's own example, a program for
"reading" the silent church and its liturgy through the visual language
of nature in everyday things like a cock crowing, a waterfall, a constella-
tion, or a flower. The Book of Nature was not, of course, the exclusive
property of Anglicans but a text recommended by devotional writers all
accross the religious spectrum. What makes Vaughan's Hermeticism
distinctively Anglican is its political specificity—its reading of an
identifiable ceremonial structure in the natural landscape. According to
the teaching of Anglican Hermeticism, the bards and prophets of old
had been a privileged caste apart, Ur-priests of Anglicanism and prototypes of the ecclesiastical hierarchy who had learned the secrets of the
groves in order to divine Christian truth long before that truth was
institutionalized in a visible national church.[21] Vaughan's Hermeticism
works backward toward the apprehension of origins to heal the survivors
of a destroyed church and to offer prophetic glimmers of its eventual
reconstruction.

Richard Lovelace was a much less devoted follower of the Ancient

Theology than Vaughan. Yet the sylvan enclosures of *Lucasta* are steeped in the Hermeticism of the Stuart court. "Aramantha" contains unmistakable references to England of the Civil War period but depicts Alexis and Lucasta as ancient Britons, pre-Christian priests of the oak grove. The political and ecclesiastical issues behind the Civil Wars are cast in ancient British form as a struggle over "BARDS Decrees, and DRUIDS rite" (*Lovelace*, 117). In the grove, Lucasta enthrones Alexis in a natural "SEE" of flowers as though he were some Druid forerunner of an Anglican bishop installed in his green diocese to preside over their marriage vows:

> And for a full reward of all,
> She now doth him her shepheard call,
> And in a SEE of flow'rs install:
> Then gives her faith immediately,
> Which he returnes religiously;
> Both vowing in her peacefull Cave
> To make their Bridall bed and grave.
>
> (*Lovelace*, 118)

As usual in the Cavalier lyric, the religious language is shot through with eroticism, yet it is recognizable as an evocation of ancient priestly rite. Alexis is both pastoral lover and a shepherd of souls. Lovelace's neopagan rituals revive the earlier state Hermeticism of Caroline masques like *Albion's Triumph* and *Coelum Britannicum*, except that in *Lucasta* the mysteries are performed in a "court" restored to the primeval rural setting in which the Ancient Theology was believed to have flourished initially. The poet Lovelace, inspired by Lucasta, becomes his own priest of the grove, a slighter replica of the king, who purges the melancholy of Royalists in defeat by offering them a model of the vanished culture as a psychic restorative, with the added intimation that the magical reharmonizing of the soul achieved through the use of the image might somehow, someday, be extended to the desecrated temple of the nation.

Like Vaughan, Lovelace invited his readers to peruse the Book of Nature: Aramantha/Lucasta demonstrates the technique in her explorations of the countryside, where she discovers remnants of prewar Stuart ideals in the behavior of flowers, cattle, and songbirds. Lovelace also composed a series of separate animal hieroglyphs that offer veiled poetic commentary on the Royalist defeat and even, at least in one case, a hidden program for undoing it. Most of these political hieroglyphs were published among his posthumous poems; at least some of them unquestionably date from the Interregnum, after the death of the king. They can receive only fleeting mention here. "The Ant" is perhaps the most accessible of them. It describes an insect embodying the commercial stereotype of the Puritan, *homo economicus*, laboring incessantly to increase his own store and making his narrow ethic "our Law" as Parliament did when it abolished religious festivals. Looking with the disapproving eye of a Cato upon the rites of Flora, the ant rides roughshod over the old pastimes: he drives on "sacred Festivals" his "Plow," never stopping for "one poor Minute" to relieve its "o're labour'd Bulk with mirth" (*Lovelace*, 135). In "The Falcon," a noble bird, "Bright Heir t' th' Bird Imperial," reenacts the fate of the Caroline ideal of sacred monarchy in the Civil War period: like a king, the bird lives first "enthroned" on high and ranging freely through the air, mediating between heaven and earth, but then is pitifully imprisoned and finally destroyed—despite a series of brilliant military and political strategies—in a cataclysmic battle with the heron (*Lovelace*, 141–45). "The Snayl" and "Another" can be read as advice for Royalists in defeat. A "Wise Emblem of our Politick World," the snail teaches the poet to bide his time, going "slowly fast," keeping within himself, his ideals, religion, and potential power "lock'd up" from prying eyes, collected about him until the ripe moment for their use against the enemy.[22]

But the best known of these elusive political hieroglyphs and the only one to appear in the 1649 volume of *Lucasta*, was "The Grasse-hopper. To my Noble Friend, Mr. CHARLES COTTON," a poem which revises the traditional Stuart call for "freedom to be merry" in light of the radically altered state of the nation at the end of the Civil Wars. Lovelace's poem reads the fate of the Stuart policy toward old pastimes through the plight of the grasshopper, vulnerable monarch of the meadows. In the iconography of the Stuart court, the grasshopper had been an emblem for "Contentment in the Country." So he appears on Inigo Jones' ornamental frontispiece to *Salmacida Spolia*, the last Caroline masque, where "Affection to the Country, holding a grasshopper" is displayed along with other emblems of Caroline policy.[23] Lovelace's grasshopper lives his summer out as one long festival in a paradise of carefree hedonism. The poet addresses him,

> Oh thou that swing'st upon the waving haire
> Of some well-filled Oaten Beard,
> Drunke ev'ry night with a Delicious teare
> Dropt thee from Heav'n, where now th'art reard.
>
> (Lovelace, 38)

Here we encounter once more the Bacchic "holy rage" of inspired inebriation. And as so often in the poetry of Cavalier mirth, the creature's festive merriment is directly linked with the heavens. Like a Bacchic reveler of old he becomes drunk each night with a celestial liquor dropped from on high, a dew with a sacramental virtue like that traditionally attributed to maydew. He enjoys the ecstasy of proprietorship like an Adam come to paradise again, possessed of all creation: "The Joyes of Earth and Ayre are thine intire" (*Lovelace,* 39). His days follow the nights in harmonious succession. Like the happy peasants of Caroline prosport poetry or some carousing Cavalier, the grasshopper begins each morning by doing homage to the sun, then passes his time in sports which make himself and others merry:

> Up with the Day, the Sun thou welcomst then,
> Sportst in the guilt-plats of his Beames,
> And all these merry dayes mak'st merry men,
> Thy selfe, and Melancholy streames.
>
> (*Lovelace,* 39)

The last line is notoriously cryptic, seeming to suggest that his revelry operates as a general panacea for melancholy, curing its "streames" wherever he encounters them. The grasshopper is the embodiment of pure festivity, swinging on his "Oaten Beard," knowing no other existence, and enjoying his sport "while he may" according to the traditional *carpe diem,*—at one with the green world and its cyclical rhythms.

However, Lovelace's poem works disturbing changes upon the traditional pattern. In the usual poetry of festival *carpe diem*, the darker side of survivalism—the inevitability of death and the passing of all things in their season—is accepted or at least acknowledged as a strong argument for enjoying the present. But Lovelace's poem refuses to submit to the limits imposed by that age-old perception of mutability. There are disquieting overtones even in the poet's account of the grasshopper's summer holiday: the allusion to the insect's death in the first stanza ("Heav'n, where now th'art reard") and the numbing draught of poppy in the second which induces a death-like oblivion each evening (and may remind us of the debilitating cup of Comus). The grasshopper's experience unfolds under the ironic shadow of a termination of which he appears unaware. He spends his long summer holiday in a mirth that knows no tomorrow, forgetting that according to the cyclical laws he lives by, festival will yield to the everyday, and life give way to death. In the fourth stanza, the poet seems to turn against the insect, chiding him for his lack of foresight. The grasshopper's joys are abruptly cut off by harvest and frost, inescapable elements of the same natural cycle which fostered his mirth initially:

But ah the Sickle! Golden Eares are Cropt;
  Ceres and *Bacchus* bid good night;
Sharpe frosty fingers all your Flowr's have topt,
  And what sithes spar'd, Winds shave off quite.

Poore verdant foole! and now green Ice! thy Joys
  Large and as lasting, as thy Peirch of Grasse.

                             (*Lovelace*, 39)

The grasshopper has fallen victim to the familiar Maying pattern from James and Ecclesiastes, the liturgical lessons we have heard echoing through the literature associated with May Day. The "verdant foole" has enjoyed his time "under the sun" and must perish like the green stalk upon which he has perched so precariously. "As the flower of the grass he shall pass away. For the sun is no sooner risen with a burning heat, but it withereth the grass, and the flower thereof falleth, and the grace of the fashion of it perisheth."

In Anacreon and other analogues to Lovelace's poem, the grasshopper is *basileus*, a fragile image of monarchy. Lovelace is careful to mute the obvious analogy with another deposed king. Yet much of the poignancy of the grasshopper's fate is derived from its resemblance to that of King Charles and of the Cavaliers as they saw themselves in hindsight. They had promoted "Affection to the Country" and basked in the pleasures of English peace while the rest of Europe was embroiled in the Thirty Years' War but had been insulated by the all-pervasive ritualism of the court from a realistic assessment of the forces that threatened them at home.[24] As the grasshopper is suddenly killed in the midst of his country pleasures, so Charles I and his adherents had been cut off abruptly from a ritualized way of life which was designed, in Selden's pithy language, to "preserve all things" as new wine is preserved in old bottles. They faced no ordinary season of privation but what Earl Miner has aptly termed the "Cavalier winter"—a sudden freezing of earlier hopes and liberties without any promise of cyclical seasonal renewal.[25]

At the point at which he turns to chide the "Poore verdant foole," Lovelace's poem appears on the verge of abandoning the politics of mirth in favor of a more providential ethic. The poem is ultimately based, of course, upon the familiar fable of the grasshopper and the ant and seems about to offer the traditional moral that one must make hay while the sun shines. But for the Cavalier party, it was already too late for such prudence. Winter was already upon them. Having appeared to distance himself from the foolishly improvident grasshopper, the poet shifts again, restoring the insect as a model for Cavalier revelry, but a revelry brought indoors. The hieroglyph of the grasshopper does not teach the poet to be providential in terms of the amassing of goods against the winter to come but rather in the way he lays up festivity to counter the abolition of festival.

The poem is, like many others in *Lucasta*, a defense of sacred enclosure. The grasshopper's folly was not in the type of life he lived but in the place where he lived it—out in the ephemeral fields under the sun, where "Golden Eares are Cropt" and all things are vulnerable to sudden shifts in the weather. The moral taught by his example is that "mirth" must be kept safe in protective enclosures, under the control of intimate groups of Royalists like the poet and his friend Charles Cotton. Festival is removed from the cyclical natural round—where it had proved to be intolerably vulnerable—and internalized through the creation of a model impervious to variations in the world outside. The fate of the grasshopper "Bid us lay in 'gainst Winter, Raine, and poize, / Their flouds, with an o'reflowing glasse" before a "sacred" hearth, yet another place of light enclosed by darkness, like the sacred grove.

As Miner has noted, the poet turns to address Charles Cotton "as if Cotton succeeds to the Grasshopper's role in the scheme of things as well as in the verse apostrophe."[26] The remaining stanzas of the poem demonstrate how the two men's indoor holiday can achieve a permanence denied to the outside world. Their sacred hearth will be kept eternally burning, like the sun that shined on the grasshopper, but under human control. Winter sports will take the place of summer—a perpetual indoor Saturnalia instead of the vulnerable Midsummer of the fields. Showers of wine and "old Greeke" will replace the grasshopper's nightly dew. December will come "weeping in," bewailing "th'usurping of his Raigne," but crowned again before the hearth and within their breasts:

> Thou best of *Men* and *Friends*! we will create
> A Genuine Summer in each others breast;
> And spite of this cold Time and frosen Fate
> Thaw us a warme seate to our rest.
>
> (*Lovelace*, 291).

Their indoor summer is a ritualism internalized and made a model of mind. There are intimations that this festival may exert some magical influence on the world outside. Lovelace claims that their day in the midst of night will restore "everlasting Day" to the heavens and reestablish a lost link to divinity. And, as in Lovelace's poems of the grove, the poet and his friend reconstitute the image of monarchy within the space they have marked out as sacred; they compensate for the loss of their king by becoming kings themselves. The "monarchs" who appear in Lovelace's poem are curiously impotent: the oblivious grasshopper and weeping December bewailing his lost authority. We may sense behind the poem a disappointment in the ideal of monarchy. How could a king theoretically invested with the sacred power of a deity prove so pathetically weak in practice? Lovelace and Cotton will rescue monarchy from its demeaning impotence by becoming strong and effective rulers. They have constructed a model of protected mirth which allows them to enjoy the freedom and power of monarchy within their miniature kingdom of the hearth, within the "restored" kingdom of the mind (*Lovelace*, 40).

Marvell read *Lucasta* with great perception. When he installed Lovelace in the secure but isolated Elysium at the end of his commendatory poem "To Mr. Richard Lovelace," he was imitating a characteristic strategy of the collection to which his poem was affixed—doing little more than Lovelace had already done through the creation of protective enclosures. The sacred insulation advocated by Lovelace for himself, his friends and fellow Royalists, curiously resembles the compelling image of "green ice" from his poem "The Grasse-hopper." They are frozen into immobility, but an immobility perpetually green, preserving an appearance of continuing life beneath the surface cold, but with no potential for creative interchange with the world that moves on outside.

* ii *

Marvell's Mower poems, which we will consider briefly before plunging into the interpretive abyss of "Upon Appleton House," "rewrite" the story of Lovelace's grasshopper. Damon the Mower is unlike the grasshopper in that he appears to be pure peasant—he lacks the aristocratic associations of the Insect-Proprietor of the Meadows. But he resembles the emblematic insect in his entrapment within the green round of survivalism. To conjure up poetic visions of country lads and lasses at their holiday sports had been a seventeenth-century commonplace. But Marvell is perhaps the only poet to have explored survivalism and its breakdown from within the consciousness of an individual peasant. In "Damon the Mower" the poet invites us in the initial stanza to hearken to the song of the Mower, then turns the poem over to him. Damon is allowed to tell his story of alienation as though in his own words. Like the grasshopper, he falls victim to the leveling vision associated with May Day. But the traditional politics of mirth takes on a markedly different quality when seen from within the consciousness of one of the "Sons of Summer" himself.

"Damon the Mower" and "The Mower's Song" offer different perspectives upon the Mower's "fall," the latter "Song" imagined as sung after the catastrophic accident described in "Damon the Mower." The two poems chart the disintegration of what we can perhaps call an original country narcissism—the carefree pride of one who has "owned" the meadows in the sense that he has perceived himself as the secure focal point of the natural processes enacted there:

> I am the Mower *Damon*, known
> Through all the Meadows I have mown.
> On me the Morn her dew distills
> Before her darling Daffadils.
> And, if at Noon my toil me heat,
> The Sun himself licks off my Sweat.
> While, going home, the Ev'ning sweet
> In cowslip-water bathes my feet.
>
> ("Damon the Mower," *Marvell*, 46).

Unlike Lovelace's idle grasshopper, Damon labors in his summer paradise, bringing in the harvest of the grass. But that difference seems almost inconsequential in that he does not perceive his mowing as work, a chore separated from the rest of his life in the meadows, but as part of one round of activity. He is as much at the center of things when he enjoys the traditional rites of the fields as when he does his mowing. The fairies dance about him as though he himself were their maypole as well as the supplier of their music:

> The deathless Fairyes take me oft
> To lead them in their Danses soft;
> And, when I tune my self to sing,
> About me they contract their Ring.
>
> (*Marvell*, 46)

He perceives his sports as a link with natural magic—dances with the "deathless Fairyes"—but appears to recognize no wider religious dimension to his maygames in the fields. He is, practically speaking, a mortalist, like many actual peasants complained of by seventeenth-century spiritual reformers—uninterested in any higher dimension to existence than the green vitality he observes around him.[27] He himself, not God, the king, or some religious hierarchy, is the focal point of the sports in the meadow. Marvell's Mower is a countryman apparently untouched by Laudian teaching as to the proper relationship between traditional country pastimes and religious observance.

We will recall the phallic associations of the maypole in the poetry of Robert Herrick. There is a similar sexual suggestiveness in Damon's image of himself as upright center about whom the fairy "ring" is contracted, and this surfaces again in "The Mower's Song" when he describes the uncut grass in strongly phallic terms: "not one Blade of

Grass you spy'd, / But had a Flower on either side" (*Marvell*, 48). But he appears unconscious of the symbolism of natural fertility that his language evokes, let alone of any connection between that symbolism and a sacramental link to divinity. In "The Mower's Song" Damon conceptualizes his original Eden as a mental state:

> My Mind was once the true survey
> Of all these Medows fresh and gay;
> And in the greenness of the Grass
> Did see its Hopes as in a Glass;
>
> (Marvell, 48)

He had lived within the insulating timelessness of survivalism, sensing himself at one with creation, the greenness of the meadow grass mirrored in his mind, his sports a participation in the naturally fertile "May-games" and good "fellowship" of the meadows. But he had lived without the accompanying consciousness of the sacred that the Laudians had tried to instill.

Lovelace's grasshopper had frozen suddenly, before he had a chance to discover that the seasons might change and his showers of divine blessing be withdrawn. But Damon the Mower is unfortunate enough to live beyond the termination of his summer holiday. The two Mower poems delineate progressive stages of his "fall" from original immersion in the meadows. In "Damon," nature seems to continue its mirroring: he perceives a fundamental congruence between his withered hopes and the withering heat of summer; in "The Mower's Song" he has suffered a more radical perceptual break from the green world, its "gaudy May-games" proceeding as usual while he has been cut down like the grass at harvest. In both poems, he dates the end of his "green" time of happy self-possession from his rejection by Juliana, a severe young maid who has obviously resisted the traditional maying invitation to a harmless roll in the hay. It is curious that his capacity for holiday mirth collapses at the point of Juliana's refusal. His sudden despair can be explained in any number of ways: through standard Renaissance psychological theory or Petrarchan convention or through allegorization of the *Song of Songs* as reflected in contemporary emblem literature. And as has frequently been noted, Marvell's portrait of the lovelorn countryman owes much to Virgil's Second Eclogue.[28] But if we view Damon's plight in terms of the traditional "laws" of May Day, Juliana appears more scapegoat than the actual agent of his destruction. At most, through her refusal to acquiesce in the "folly of the time," she has hastened the inevitable.

The fallen Mower reproaches nature for enacting its age-old cycles without consideration for him, as though the mutability of the seasons has been invented just to spite him. But all the while, behind his plaints of abandonment, we can hear the familiar echoes from the May Day liturgy. Flesh is grass and as the grass it withereth, "For the sun is no sooner risen with a burning heat, but it withereth the grass, and the flower thereof falleth." The most Damon can expect from the shifting world of the meadows is an ephemeral joy appropriate to the season. But he demands that the seasons conform to him—dutifully reflect the emotional alterations he himself has suffered. He reproaches the green fields as though they have failed in their traditional holiday duties toward him, but their crime has been rather to keep up holiday—continue their "gawdy May-games" while he lies "trodden under feet." He has discovered that he himself is not the center of holiday observance.

A proper Laudian Anglican response to that perception would, of course, be the traditional festival submission—a humble acknowledgment of his individual inadequacy, a recognition of the vastness of the political and religious design of which he is a part. But Damon's reaction is quite different. His discovery of his impotence against the relentless cycle in which he has been imbedded breeds a rage of injured narcissism. He reestablishes his sense of domination over the impassive round of festival by taking on its destructive energies himself, becoming a "leveler" who mimicks the leveling vision associated with May Day, but a leveler out of season, an agent for general destruction:

> But what you in Compassion ought,
> Shall now by my Revenge be wrought:
> And Flow'rs, and Grass, and I and all,
> Will in one common Ruine fall.
>
> (*Marvell*, 48)

Never having assimilated the melancholy side of May Day, its message that all flesh is but as the grass, Damon is doomed to inscribe its holiday message upon his own body: "By his own Sythe, the Mower mown." From his point of view, at least, the universe is empty; there is no sustaining sacramental vision to compensate for the discovery of individual powerlessness.

What Marvell describes in these enigmatic poems is a mental process by which an original sense of well-being in the countryside converts to anarchy and violence. As the Mower is "pre-Laudian" in his unawareness or indifference to the sacred dimension of "public mirth," so he is prehierarchic in his understanding of his place in the universe. He is autonomous, his own landlord, unaware of the existence of an authority beyond himself. He takes part in the "gawdy May-games" and good "fellowship" of the meadows like a proper Caroline countryman ("The

Mower's Song," *Marvell*, 48) but without any consciousness that his sport might be interpreted as a sign of submission to authority. Marvell's portrait of the Mower probes the age-old connections between holiday and violence that the Laudian prosport policy had been designed to suppress. The poet was analysing an actual contemporary pattern—the mental mechanisms which turned displaced villagers and other marginal people from holiday sport to violence. Marvell's pastoral poems explore politically charged holiday motifs as they press upward from the bottom of the social hierarchy, not down from the top.

In Marvell's poetry generally, May Day motifs are a focal point for political and religious differences. Always, the poet undermines the standard Laudian position by subtly altering the perspective from which old pastimes are considered. "Clorinda and Damon" reverses the Cavalier pattern of seduction. Clorinda tries to entice Damon into a grassy plot where "*Flora* blazons all her pride," but Damon turns the usual May Day *carpe diem* into a rejection of May Day sexuality: "Grass withers; and the Flow'rs too fade." He invites her to transform her familiar May Day music into a chaster praise for Pan, god of shepherds, and for his transcendent "*flowry Pastures*" (*Marvell*, 19)—give up the ephemeral for the eternal instead of achieving some chaste mediation between the two in the usual Laudian fashion. In "A Dialogue between Thyrsis and Dorinda" on the other hand, maying is the permanent condition of Elisium, an achingly sweet vision of the afterlife, but radically unlike the Laudian model in its repudiation of all hierarchy:

> There, birds sing Consorts, garlands grow,
> Cool winds do whisper, springs do flow.
> There, always is, a rising Sun,
> And day is ever, but begun.
> Shepheards there, bear equal sway,
> And every Nimph's a Queen of *May*.
>
> (*Marvell*, 21)

The vision of a perpetual egalitarian May Day is so powerful that it inspires the two shepherds to hasten out of life by drinking wine and poppy. The death they find so seductive is remarkably like the nightly oblivion of Lovelace's grasshopper except that it is irreversible. What Thyrsis and Dorinda long to achieve in the afterlife, Damon the Mower had once enjoyed on earth—a prelapsarian peasant "Eden" in which he was his own master, an Original Man, with liberty to use the fields and his pastimes as he wished. Of course the lovely picture is painted from hindsight since Marvell leaves open the possibility that Damon's country narcissism is more nostalgic fantasy than reality. But the same could be said for the Laudian version of the Merry England myth. In Marvell's poetry the freedom to be merry is wrested away from its Laudian implications and reinscribed in a primeval landscape untouched by the barriers of proprietorship.

In "The Mower against Gardens," we encounter a Mower who speaks from a more sophisticated perspective than that articulated in "Damon" and "The Mower's Song" in that he is aware of a mode of existence quite different from his own. He defines the freedom of his own fields through its contrast with the tyranny of enclosed space. As we have seen, one Cavalier remedy against the vulnerability of the meadows was the creation of a sacred enclosure impenetrable to the pitiless "mowing" of war. Damon the Mower had imagined such a protected space. In the heat of summer and of his lovelorn passion, he had searched frantically for the "shade" of some glade or grotto where he could escape the withering rays of the sun. But his efforts had been stymied, either (as Damon himself complained) because the wound inflicted by Juliana was incurable or perhaps, on a deeper level, because the mental disjunction was. The type of enclosure he imagined could not coexist with other elements of his mental universe. His mind was bounded by the meadows and he refused to give up that identification; his fate became the fate of the grass. In the Damon poems, Marvell marks out the pattern of the first half of Lovelace's "The Grasse-hopper" without injecting himself into the situation, as Lovelace did, to offer the consoling remedies of the second. The narrator in "Damon the Mower" stands enigmatically apart, contemplating the image of the "Mower mown" but offering no solution; and in "The Mower's Song" there is no narrator at all.

Nevertheless, Marvell was clearly fascinated by the Cavalier strategy for undoing the cruelty of the meadows, and he subjects it to an analysis from below in "The Mower against Gardens." The Mower in that poem, if he is not to be identified with Damon himself (resurrected from his seemingly terminal "fall" out of the paradise of survivalism), is another May Day leveler like Damon but one whose destructive energies are directed beyond himself and his beloved grass. The poem is Marvell's only epode, adopting the Horatian form used by Jonson to praise country life and associated generally in the Renaissance with the *beatus ille* tradition. But the Mower's invective shatters the measured calm that might be expected to go along with the form. Bruce King has demonstrated important similarities between the Mower's "leveling" opinions and the political doctrines of the group of seventeenth-century radicals also known as Levelers.[29] His attack on the "enclos'd" space of the garden is subtly but pervasively political. By walling off gardens from the fields "Luxurious Man" has created a space for the exercise of autocratic power,

"Lest any Tyrant him out-doe"; he dominates nature by corrupting it. Like many of the poems of country life written by the courtiers themselves, the Mower's diatribe condemns empty artifice. But while the Cavaliers took the court with them to the country, reviving courtly forms through contact with the vital restorative energies of the green world, Marvell's Mower attacks the fusion of court and country—the very basis of court pastoral. Enclosure as he describes it is a form of colonization: the sophisticated garden architects succeed in creating a more static environment than that of the evershifting fields, but it stifles and perverts whatever is shut within its "dead and standing pool of air," a hothouse of fantastic half-forms and perversions whose strange lassitude demonstrates the mastery of those who have enclosed it.

> 'Tis all enforc'd; the Fountain and the Grot;
>   While the sweet Fields do lye forgot:
> Where willing Nature does to all dispence
>   A wild and fragrant Innocence.
>
> (*Marvell*, 44)

If the speaker in "The Mower against Gardens" shows more sophistication than Damon of the other Mower poems in that he has identified a form of social corruption and directed his "leveling" energies against that, he is less knowing than Damon in that he trusts the open fields. The Mower's vision of the meadows heaped with natural blessings, populated by officious *"Fauns"* and *"Faryes,"* fostering a life of sweet freedom, closely resembles Damon's prelapsarian vision and appears vulnerable to the same cycles of change. The Mower who declaims so eloquently against the garden, the "enforc'd" grotto, against all forms of departure from the "plain and pure" innocence of the fields, has no apparent consciousness of the green world's fickleness or of its power against himself.

Taken all together, the Mower poems delineate a broken circle of destructive partial perception: Damon with his desire for protected space, his recognition of his own vulnerability, but no such space available to him; and the Mower "against Gardens" with enclosed space aplenty in the form of the gardens he despises, but no inclination to value their insulating power because he has not discovered his own vulnerability. While the Mower "against Gardens" blasts enclosure, the fallen Damon "depopulates" the countryside, enacting through his vindictive mowing the very abuse of depopulation that contemporary enemies of enclosure were most vehement against. The two half perceptions are not allowed to merge into an enlightened whole but simply exist side by side in separate poems, each viewpoint aired with its own embittered eloquence but undercut by the other, forming an uneasy antithesis with no resolution from within the perceptual system that has generated both of them.

The figure of the Mower appears again in "Upon Appleton House" and in that poem too, holiday leveling marks out a destructive circle. The Mower has no protected refuge against the seasonal violence that he himself enacts. But "Upon Appleton House" is not a portrait of unbridgeable perceptual division: in it the poet offers a program for growth beyond survivalism, a creative way out of the contemporary state of mind—whether in peasant or Cavalier form—that claimed to find its highest fulfillment in the reenactment of some version of the Myth of Merry England.

* iii *

Marvell's "Upon Appleton House, To my Lord Fairfax" is a perilous poem, not only in the playful snares it sets for its hapless readers, but in its preoccupation with images of destruction. It could credibly be described as a series of broken enclosures and pastimes overrun by violence. The mock-heroic assault of the founder of Nun Appleton "levels" the decadent cloister of the nuns; the harvest festival in the meadows turns bloody military triumph; even the garden, traditional *locus* of peace and repose, is modeled after a fortress and subtly invaded by the imagery of war. Nor do the woods offer a satisfactory refuge. Marvell enters Nun Appleton's "sacred grove" to escape the anarchy in the meadows but reads disruption even in the symbolic language of the trees. The noble oak, monarch of the forest, falls to the assault of worms and woodpeckers; the poet, although managing to preserve himself within the woods against the "darts" of passion, must plead for ensnarement by thorns and brambles, a less menacing replication of the assault he has escaped.

As readers have often noted, "Upon Appleton House" is also full of masquing imagery, a language of artistic transformation that jostles uneasily against the rituals of violence.[30] The movement from meadows to woods suggests the transition from antimasque to main masque in Stuart court entertainments: the scenes in the meadows, moving tableaux of disorder, change as though by "Engines strange" controlled by the wondrous machinery of an Inigo Jones. Then in the woods the poet enacts his own Hermetic "mask" in deliberate imitation of the political Hermeticism of masques from the court of Charles. But Marvell's is a masque that undoes masquing. Entertainments at court had created a fusion between Caroline ideals and actual social conditions, a model for social betterment that displayed the transcendent mind of the king as the surest pattern for national renewal. Marvell's masque offers a series of "unmetaphorings" which tease the actual out of the ideal by reversing vehicle and tenor. In Marvell's masque of the meadows and the woods, the realm of high ideals is repeatedly engulfed by history. Like the court masques and Cavalier poems which it imitates, "Upon Appleton House" is deeply immersed in the political climate of its time, a comment upon "present occasions" by its very identification of its own artistic *modus operandi* as akin to the devices of a masque. But if his commendatory poem to Lovelace is any guide, Marvell was less than comfortable with Cavalier strategies for self-insulation. While Lovelace memorialized the forms of court entertainment in his poetry by crystallizing them in a protected space, "Upon Appleton House" violates Royalist images of enclosure. The Cavalier paradise cannot escape the "fallen" world of political conflict but must bow to its reforging energies to emerge something other, quite new.

Of course "Upon Appleton House" is also a country house poem and like other members of the genre in its tendency to impose the imagery of the court upon a rural landscape. But it is a country house poem that, rather than establishing a paradigm for proper "Contentment in the Country," praises rural retreat only in the process of undoing it as an ideal for perpetual imitation. The retirement of Lord Fairfax, commander in chief of the Parliamentary forces, was a profoundly ambiguous act. Through his retreat to the country, he could theoretically be seen as having conformed to time-honored Stuart policy. He "got him to the country" to "till" conscience and renounce the corruption associated with a center of political authority. But as a general, he had struggled against the king; his disavowal of the cause of the regicides did not make him a Cavalier.[31] On his estate, the supposedly antithetical realms of "innocent" country retirement and "corrupt" action at the nation's center keep collapsing into each other. The old Stuart valorization of country life becomes increasingly comic as it is stripped of the ideals of peace and collective social renewal to which it had traditionally been bound. Country pastimes do not fare particularly well at Nun Appleton. They are either assimilated to a troubling vision of mayhem, as in the harvest "festival" of the mowers who have triumphed over grass and nestlings, or they are diminished into triviality, as in the poet's own lolling by the river bank, an image of "Affection for the Country" to be reformed into something tauter and finer by the influence of Fairfax's daughter Maria.

As Raymond Williams has pointed out, many of the estates celebrated in seventeenth-century country house poems, beginning with Jonson's "To Penshurst," were in fact carved out through economic exploitation.[32] Marvell begins his poem by assuring his readers that Fairfax's is none of those. It was built without the mining and deforestation so dear to the hearts of seventeenth-century projectors "That unto Caves the Quarries drew / And Forrests did to Pastures hew" (*Marvell*, 62). Instead, the estate originated in a lawful despoiling of a corrupt enclosure, the medieval convent into which Thwaites had been seduced by the scheming nuns. The image of the ruined cloister is reminiscent of the ruined British sanctuary lamented by Giordano Bruno and depicted in the opening tableau of *Coelum Britannicum*, but in Marvell's poem, there is no nostalgia for the effaced institution. The violation of the convent of *"Suttle Nunns"* is a salutary act of proto-Protestant iconoclasm—a new beginning founded upon the destruction of the old. "'Twas no *Religious House* till now" (*Marvell*, 71). Like the typical seventeenth-century country house, Nun Appleton is commended for its hospitality: its "Stately *Frontispice of Poor*" and "Daily new *Furniture of Friends*" (*Marvell*, 64). But it is significant that the beneficiaries of the estate's generosity are depicted as though detachable from the house itself: a frontispiece and movable furniture rather than some inextricable part of the structure. Nun Appleton is no timeless replication of the feudal order. Its virtues are founded upon a clean break with the past.

Of course most Anglicans would have agreed with Marvell's portrayal of the hidden corruptions of monasticism. The cloister was not a "thing indifferent" to be preserved on account of its "long continuance" but a positive evil prohibited by Scripture. It is questionable, though, whether good Laudian Anglicans would have been comfortable with Marvell's subtle shaping of the rhetoric of the nuns to mimic the politicized Stuart version of the ideal of Christian liberty. The nuns' language of liberty-in-confinement calls to mind the familiar Cavalier praise of enclosure as the only space for freedom. They have their "Liberty" within the walls, hedged about by bars that "inclose" them off from men. It is not the nuns but the rest of the world who live confined, prisoners in the "Den" of the larger world outside:

> 'Within this holy leisure we
> 'Live innocently as you see.
> 'These Walls restrain the World without,
> 'But hedge our Liberty about.
> 'These Bars inclose that wider Den
> 'Of those wild Creatures, called Men.
> 'The Cloyster outward shuts its Gates,
> 'And, from us, locks on them the Grates.
>
> (*Marvell*, 65)

A "suttle" argument indeed that reverses freedom and confinement, but not more subtle, perhaps, than the Royalist mode of argumentation it parodies—a sweetening over of coercion with the claim that real pleasure is to be found only through obedience to the authority of sacred enclosure.

Within the "freedom" of their protected space, the nuns enjoy a paradise of combined ritualism and sensuality—a mingling of the "insense of incessant Pray'r" and the "Holy-water" of pleasant tears shed amidst cushioned opulence. Marvell is of course poking fun at a particularly florid strain of Roman Catholic spirituality. But, again, as in the Mower's attack upon gardens, his verse seems to hit closer to home, to parody that hothouse of combined ritualism and eroticism, the Cavalier libertine enclosure. We are back in the shadows of Comus's palace again, in a ritualized environment where life and art are interwoven to deaden the spirit rather than affording the innocent "Liberty" that is claimed. And, as in earlier versions of the confrontation, the enemy of free mirth is the law. Lord Fairfax's ancestor first checks his instinct to rescue Thwaites by violence because he "reverenceth . . . the Laws" even as he respects "Religion"; he comes himself from a family with eminence in the courts: "For Justice still that Courage led; / First from a Judge, then Souldier bred" (*Marvell*, 69). But law and due "license" are on his side. "The *Court* him grants the lawful Form; Which licens'd either Peace or Force, / To hinder the unjust Divorce." We will recall the juggling with paradoxical notions of "law" and "liberty" in Jonson's *Bartholomew Fair*. At Nun Appleton the other side wins—the law overrides a privileging of ritual space. It would be easy to make too much of Marvell's game with seventeenth-century political commonplace, particularly given the fleeting levity of the narrative in which it is imbedded. But the familiar issues are nevertheless engaged and resurface sporadically for the rest of the poem. Marvell borrowed his nonchalant way with politically charged language from the Cavaliers themselves, taking on their ease of manner, their seeming casualness with matters of great importance, but constructing an alternate vision of the relation of pleasure to virtue.

Having considered the origin and progress of the estate, Marvell appears prepared to abandon history for topography. Like Lovelace's Aramantha he surveys in turn a garden, a meadow, and a wood, finding that events from the nation's recent past keep intruding upon the landscape. He wanders about, reading political lessons in the natural hieroglyphs he encounters. But in each case, the inscribed message is significantly different from that read by Lovelace's heroine. Instead of reimmersing him in a welcome system of continuities, Marvell's reading of the Book of Nature cancels out primordial images of peace, unity, authority. In her garden Aramantha had found vestiges of May Day ritual. There are trace elements of that in Marvell's portrait of Maria: "for She / Seems with the Flow'rs a Flow'r to be," apparently at one, in proper May Day fashion, with the green world about her. But the garden's dominant metaphoric system is military: if Maria is like the flowers, she will turn out to be more warrior than gentle goddess of spring.

Marvell's account of Fairfax's garden wittily parodies the standard elements of maying poetry: the natural worship of the rising sun, the falling of sacramental dew from the heavens, the irenic appeal to an ideal of community. In the garden at Nun Appleton, however, the flowers are exemplars of military preparedness. They awaken not to do obeisance to the sun as some Apollonian source of mirth and holiday fertility but to ready themselves for battle. Their sun is only a standard-bearer; they come to attention out of respect for its morning display of the company "Colours." Their morning music is not the traditional matins sung by choirs of birds, but an insistent reveille hummed out by bees. The flowers, like proper May Day flowers, are adorned with morning dew. But they find the dew corrosive, not sacramental. It inhibits their firepower. They scour it out industriously before filling their flasks with fresh "powder":

> When in the *East* the Morning Ray
> Hangs out the Colours of the Day,
> The Bee through these known Allies hums,
> Beating the *Dian* with its *Drumms*.
> Then Flow'rs their drowsie Eylids raise,
> Their Silken Ensigns each displayes,
> And dries its Pan yet dank with Dew,
> And fills its Flask with Odours new.
>
> (*Marvell*, 71)

Of course all of this bristling militarism is accounted for in terms that seem to cancel out its menace. The garden was laid out by Lord Fairfax himself as a playful reminder of his life before retirement and is only *apparently* a fort; within it, war is not genuine combat but only a metaphor or simile. Yet, in "Upon Appleton House" metaphors have a way of undoing themselves. Before Marvell leaves the garden, its essential nature becomes problematic: is war only gardening or is gardening actually war?

As he strolls about examining the structure of the garden, Marvell begins to read messages there, to meditate on the vaster garden of England "wasted" by a militarism that Fairfax's garden only imitates.

Little by little, as he continues his reflections, war and the garden trade places in the metaphoric scheme of things:

> Unhappy! shall we never more
> That sweet *Militia* restore,
> When Gardens only had their Towrs,
> And all the Garrisons were Flowrs,
> Where Roses only Arms might bear,
> And Men did rosie Garlands wear?
> Tulips, in several Colours barr'd,
> Were then the *Switzers* of our *Guard*.
>
> The *Gardiner* had the *Souldiers* place,
> And his more gentle Forts did trace.
> The Nursery of all things green
> Was then the only *Magazeen*.
> The *Winter Quarters* were the Stoves,
> Where he the tender Plants removes.
> But War all this doth overgrow:
> We Ord'nance Plant and Powder sow.
>
> (*Marvell*, 73)

The very terms of Marvell's comparison suggest that war is intrinsic to the green world rather than antithetical to it. Even the primeval Britain he envisions—the "Garden of the World"—was inscribed with the imagery of battle. What happens in the course of this witty passage is that the imagery engulfs its referents. Once, perhaps, militarism was only a trope. But now, in the present, it has become the reality and gardening its vehicle: "We Ord'nance Plant and Powder sow." War has "overgrown" the garden like some rapid and pernicious weed. Marvell deconstructs the metaphoric system of the garden, and having done so, he can no longer perceive its militarism as purely metaphoric. The poet's expression of regret for Fairfax's retirement is laden with ambiguity in that the general's talents for "cultivation" are inextricable from his militarism. He might have brought renewed fertility to the national garden: "have made our Gardens spring / Fresh as his own and flourishing" (*Marvell*, 73), but he would have done so with the same arts, the same "Pow'r" he had used in his waging of war. And having arrived at that perception, Marvell begins to observe that Fairfax's garden is no absolute retreat from the abandoned national wasteland of the Civil Wars. Instead of basking peaceably within a protected space, the flowers keep up the recent conflict by mimicking the political alignment of Fairfax himself, their "Battery" aimed against Cawood Castle, proud seat of prelacy, as the general had earlier positioned vast armies against

the king and Church hierarchy. By the end of Marvell's seemingly casual
visit, history has invaded the garden.

What happens in the meadows is even more complex, a series of
seriocomic "revolutions" that have teased and maddened readers for over
half a century. There has been considerable resistance lately to political
reading of the "masque of the meadows," and that has had the salutary
effect of broadening our sense of the poem's variety and universality.[33]
But I should like to focus once again on the specific—on the contemporary "lessons" Marvell embedded in his landscape of upheaval. There can
be no question that, for his contemporaries, Marvell's succession of
images would have called to mind the course of the Civil Wars, from an
initial overturn of traditional hierarchy through increasing degrees of
social leveling and disorder. In Interregnum poetry open spaces like the
common fields tended to be associated with imagery of vulnerability and
violence. The meadows at Nun Appleton are similarly open and assail-
able, a place where traditional festival motifs are played out under the
mutable summer sun but also undermined from within by the instability
of their emblematic status. Part of the essence of the Stuart antimasque
had been its containment within a larger vision of order emanating from
the mind of the king. The "pageant" of the fields at Nun Appleton is like
a series of antimasques in that it offers successive tableaux of disorder.
But there is no certainty of containment: the figural representations of
disorder repeatedly overflow the boundaries of the frame in which they
have been placed. Art keeps crashing into life.

Marvell's description of the fields is designed to produce disorientation, or more literally, agoraphobia—an uneasiness with open space
based upon an inability to predict its limits. He makes use of familiar
motifs of festival disorder and inversion but without a clearly implied
social context that would make the inversion comprehensible. In the
usual poetry of mirth, it is possible to distinguish between the festival
and the everyday, between a stable underlying hierarchy and the temporary festival forms that mimic and invert it. In Marvell's antimasque of
the meadows, "normal" hierarchy cannot be distinguished from its
up-ended imitation; holiday topsy-turvydom becomes irreversible in
that it is not followed by a predictable renewal of the everyday but
instead shatters the insulating structure in which it is placed. To observe
this process, let us consider the grasshopper, in Marvell's poem as in
Lucasta, a fragile monarch of the meadows:

> And now to the Abbyss I pass
> Of that unfathomable Grass,
> Where Men like Grashoppers appear,

But Grashoppers are Gyants there:
They, in there squeking Laugh, contemn
Us as we walk more low then them:
And, from the Precipices tall
Of the green spir's, to us do call.

(Marvell, 74)

At first glance, this intriguing passage seems to mark out the traditional holiday motif of *deposuit potentes*: the "Abbyss" of the "unfathomable Grass" is a space marked off from the everyday in which normal hierarchy is inverted. Grasshoppers and men trade places. Given the standard meaning of the grasshopper in Stuart court iconography, however, the passage can be read in just the opposite way. The grasshopper was associated with Stuart "Affection for the Country," as in Lovelace's "The Grasse-hopper." "Upon Appleton House" appears to be drawing upon the same courtly anacreontic tradition of the grasshopper as *basileus*, proprietor of the meadows. But Marvell's image is more radically equivocal: are these squeaking, contemptuous overlords the embodiment of a traditional hierarchy or are they rather "lords of misrule" presiding over its inversion?

Perhaps they are both simultaneously. One way of sorting out the passage would be to read it as social criticism, an indictment of the traditional structure of society as itself a form of misrule in which authority is determined by accidents of social and economic position. It is the temporary luxuriance of the grass that gives the grasshoppers their advantage. They tower over shrinking men despite their ludicrous smallness because they are placed at the top. In Lovelace's "Aramantha" the meadows harbored images of magnanimous self-sacrifice—the "natural" bovine largesse of an aristocratic caste threatened with destruction from outside; but in Marvell, the laws of hospitality are turned topsy-turvy by the "landlords" themselves. The poet places himself among the disadvantaged. He is one of those who "walk more low" than the grasshoppers. The passage is curiously reminiscent of Ben Jonson's earlier complaints against arrogant landlords who withhold hospitality or twist it into a means for asserting their class superiority, except that Marvell offers no immediate counterexample to reaffirm the traditional values. The effect is disorienting. In the abyss of the grass, there is seemingly no place for the old laws of hospitality. The grasshopper is the first of many political hieroglyphs offered for reading in the meadows of Nun Appleton, a sign inscribed in proper Cavalier fashion upon a rural landscape. But in Marvell's poem, reading the hieroglyphs is a very chancy business. They are only partially legible because they have been shaken out of a predictable context.

The grasshopper passage also contains fleeting suggestions of ecclesiastical criticism. The green "spires" that shelter the insects are reminiscent of the heights of Cawood Castle or of a Laudian cathedral; like the Laudian party as seen by its critics, the spires alienate the upper levels of a hierarchy from the lower rather than bringing the two together. Again, Marvell omits the clear context that would allow us to interpret the inversion with confidence. Are the grasshoppers meant to suggest the ecclesiastical authorities themselves or are they rather a tribe of ephemeral holiday substitutes like boy bishops at a Feast of Fools— appearing in the place of authority to squeak out the message of its temporary overthrow? It would be easy to overplay the political specificity of Marvell's imagery (and no doubt, I already have). What is most significant about the passage from our point of view is that it creates a rift between the top of the hierarchy and the bottom. The Stuart appeal to mirth had been intended to renew a sense of community between the highest and lowest elements of society. But in the meadows, what flows down from the top is not benevolence but contempt. Fertility and nurturance do not spread outward from a pinnacle at the center but up from the base of the hierarchy. Men dive through the treacherous meadows, hazard themselves in a "sea" where only the highest seem safe, and miraculously emerge with "Flow'rs" from the bottom.

The second "act" of the meadows, which perhaps we can christen the "Antimasque of Mowers," puts men once again on top. The grass, before a perch for authority, has become its "precipice" and the Mowers, who would earlier have been contemned by the grasshoppers, now become the masters. Like Israelites escaped from an Egyptian bondage, they easily divide the meadow-sea which earlier had seemed to engulf all that was merely human:

> No Scene that turns with Engines strange
> Does oftner then these Meadows change.
> For when the Sun the Grass hath vext,
> The tawny Mowers enter next;
> Who seem like *Israelites* to be,
> Walking on foot through a green Sea.
>
> (*Marvell*, 74)

Suddenly the meadows became amenable to human cultivation, no longer threatening in their vastness. The contemptuous, towering grasshoppers are silent, out of sight. But that does not mean that the landscape is redeemed from its potential for discord. As in the garden at Nun Appleton, so in its fields, cultivation is inseparable from conflict.

Are Marvell's strange mowers, part Hebraic part Virgilian, to be taken as farmers or military conquerers? A more pressing question—how is their victory over the hay related to the earlier militarism of the garden? One vital difference is in the degree of containment. The militarism of the garden was highly disciplined, kept within boundaries determined by the political alignment of General Fairfax himself. In the fields, it is much less discriminating, an efficient engine of destruction that "massacres" all it encounters. The lowly escape no more than the high. When one of the mowers inadvertently kills the fledgling rail, he hates himself for doing so. But in yet another holiday overturn, his compassion is overriden by the rapacity of "bloody *Thestylis*" and the rest of the pillaging women. The harvest turns into a disorderly "rough music" or riot with the traditional "unruly woman" at the top.[34] The mowing episode, like the Mower poems, contains unmistakable echoes from Virgil's Second Eclogue, a lament for something that is lost or unvalued. We will remember the eloquent political use Milton made of a passage from the Eclogue on the title page of *Comus*. But the women have no such sentiment. For Thestylis, the violence of the meadows is to be reveled in as a sign of divine intervention. She proclaims the slaughtered rail a gift from heaven, trusses it up, and prepares to feast upon it:

> But bloody *Thestylis*, that waites
> To bring the mowing Camp their Cates,
> Greedy as Kites has trust it up,
> And forthwith means on it to sup:
> When on another quick She lights,
> And cryes, he call'd us *Israelites*;
> But now, to make his saying true,
> Rails rain for Quails, for Manna Dew.
>
> (*Marvell*, 75)

As several readers have noted, the passage imitates the well-known rhetoric of the Parliamentary forces during the Civil War in that it identifies the reapers with Old Testament models of the righteous warrior. Echoing the annihilating harvest imagery of Isaiah and Jeremiah, Oliver Cromwell had exclaimed after the Royalist debacle at Marston Moor, "God made them as stubble to our swords."[35] In the present instance, however, it is the poet who has likened the mowers to Israelites, and Thestylis overhears and corrects him. She shatters the separateness of the poet's narrative frame and arrests his effort to palliate and distance what he observes by assimilating it to classical or Hebraic analogues. She insists (in accordance with the prevailing pattern of the poem) on the literal truth of his trope. The mowers are indeed Israelites because they are sustained in the wilderness with rails and meadow dew.[36]

Of course, to interpret the mowers as Parliamentary soldiers would reverse the poet's terms. Enlistees in the New Model Army likened themselves to reapers; in the poem reapers are likened to soldiers. But the distinction soon collapses. In the next stanza, as earlier in the garden passage, war and cultivation trade places; vehicle and tenor are reversed. Marvell counsels the hapless rail, emblematic of the innocent victim who falls along with the guilty:

> Or sooner hatch or higher build:
> The Mower now commands the Field;
> In whose new Traverse seemeth wrought
> A Camp of Battail newly fought:
> Where, as the Meads with Hay, the Plain
> Lyes quilted ore with Bodies slain:
> The Women that with forks it fling,
> Do represent the Pillaging.
>
> (*Marvell*, 75)

The word "Traverse" is wonderfully equivocal, suggesting, among other interpretations, the next crossing of the field for the purpose of building the haycocks or, in a usage borrowed from masquing, a "curtain . . . drawn across a . . . theatre" (*Marvell*, 286n). But the iconography of this "new Traverse" is remarkably difficult to read. At the beginning of the stanza, harvesting only seems to be battle: in or upon the traverse "seemeth wrought" a "Camp of Battail." By the end of the passage, however, it is harvesting that only "seems"; harvesting has become a metaphor for war. What the poet invites us to visualize is not a hayfield but a plain of battle, "quilted ore with Bodies slain." The women's flinging of the hay "represents" pillaging and not the other way around. War and harvest are interchanged.

The mowers celebrate the end of their labors with a harvest-home, according to the "good old fashion" of England. Marvell's description of the festival harks back to prewar images of a countryside ringing with the joy of "public mirth." And like the advocates of the *Book of Sports*, he assimilates country folk into landscape: females "fragrant as the Mead" mark out *"Fairy Circles"* as they dance the Hay, an ancient harvest dance; their festivities surround them with an aura of well-being, fertility, renewal:

> And now the careless Victors play,
> Dancing the Triumphs of the Hay;

Where every Mowers wholesome Heat
Smells like an *Alexanders sweat*.
Their Females fragrant as the Mead
Which they in *Fairy Circles* tread:
When at their Dances End they kiss,
Their new-made Hay not sweeter is.

(*Marvell*, 76)

At least some readers of Marvell's poem have found the description innocent and delightful.[37] But after our experience with the treacherousness of meadow rites in the poems of Damon the Mower, and after so much jostling and dislocation of traditional festival motifs in earlier portions of "Upon Appleton House," we are to be forgiven if we approach the passage with wariness. There are some jarring notes. The mowers are not carefree but "careless," which reminds us of their earlier violence against the innocent. The harvest-home of these sweating "*Alexanders*" is also a celebration of martial victory. Marvell's evocation of traditional images of festival peace and prosperity is undermined by the lingering touches of militarism. Much has been sacrificed to allow these simple peasants their holiday dance in the hay. In the Renaissance, war, too, had its traditional language of ritualization: it could be called a "daunce unto the Musicke of the field," but a *danse macabre*, a rite of violence.[38] The dance of the mowers is less a smoothing over of earlier discord than a reveling in its effects. Their holiday sports are severed from the irenic associations with which Stuart policy had invested them, no longer a carefully orchestrated ceremony in which the overturn of hierarchy functions to enhance existing authority but more like a popular festival run rampant and reinvested with the menace that the Stuarts had tried to suppress.

Marvell's interweaving of festivity and military conquest replicates a strain of contemporary rhetoric. Roundheads who opposed the more radical elements in the New Model Army characterized them as lawless Lords of Misrule and some of the radicals saw themselves as restoring a primeval "Merry England" lost as a result of the Norman Conquest and the imposition of an alien hierarchy—a world much like the original Eden of Damon the Mower, in which they controlled their own land and pastimes. They repeated in varying formulas the ancient plaint that "'Twas never merry world since the gentry folk came up."[39] But as usual in "Upon Appleton House," both the degree of historical precision and the poet's attitude toward the doctrine he offers for reading are left suspended in indefiniteness. Like the earlier hegemony of the grasshoppers, the Mowers' triumph is ephemeral, canceled out in the scenes that follow.

As the "Antimasque of the Meadows" proceeds, its "acts" become progressively briefer and more chaotic, less amenable to orderly interpretation. The effect is rather like that of Jonson's *Bartholomew Fair*—a descent into ever deepening anarchy—but an anarchy unlike Jonson's in that it does not generate its own mechanisms for a return to order. The next scene, an "Antimasque of Haycocks," displays a group of treacherous rocks or (Marvell seems to correct his first perception) pyramids like those of the Memphian desert. Again, the vehicle of earlier domination has become a "precipice." The Mowers had proclaimed themselves Israelites in the wilderness, escaped from an Egyptian bondage. But the grass they have mown and triumphed over remains when they have departed, a mocking monument to the authority they had overthrown. By this "act" we can observe that an equalization has taken place in the meadows. Top and bottom are now much closer together than they had been in the antimasque of grasshoppers. The pyramids are "Short" by contrast with the menacing height of the unmown grass. And the leveling proceeds yet further in the following scene, an "Antimasque of the Plain." The haycocks have disappeared, leaving the fields an "equal flat / That *Levellers* take pattern at."

Marvell is quite insistent in his use of the politically charged label. In the early seventeenth century, the term *leveler* had been applied to those who demonstrated their opposition to enclosure by pulling down boundary hedges and fences. But by the Civil War period the leveling of landscape had been assimilated to a vision of political equalization like the "leveled" countryman's paradise we observed in some of Marvell's pastoral poems. That is the social model apparently realized in the empty meadows, where an erasure of monumental landmarks is simultaneously a flattening of social hierarchy. The meadows are returned to the original "commons" which contemporary Levelers and Diggers considered the first condition of humankind, an "ancient community of enjoying the fruits of the earth."[40] Marvell appears initially to countenance the radical vision by portraying the "flat" as a plain of original innocence: "The World when first created sure / Was such a Table rase and pure." But immediately, he undercuts its primal perfection by reinterpreting the "Table" as a site for festive violence: "Or rather such is the *Toril* / Ere the Bulls enter at Madril" (*Marvell*, 76). In the meadows of Nun Appleton, the traditional survivalist pattern of immersion in the seasonal rhythms of growth and harvesting becomes a model for political change. Social systems have their time of flourishing, then fade and perish like all else "under the sun." The Levelers' vision of a peaceful Eden of "equal" unenclosed land survives no longer than the hierarchical structures that had preceded it.

In Lovelace's "Aramantha" the meadows were dominated by a herd of sacred cattle, an intelligible hieroglyph of the feudal aristocracy. At Nun Appleton, the herd appears only after a long series of other "acts" and is described with such a bewildering welter of images that Marvell's purpose seems rather to frustrate than to facilitate reading of the hieroglyph. In his "Antimasque of Cattle," the herd appears first as devourers who are driven onto the common to strip off the remnants of stubble left by the mowers—a fairly negative image of "leveling" as rapacity. Then they are likened to a canvas from the "painted World" of Sir William Davenant, a much more positive depiction of primeval egalitarianism.[41] Marvell's swift and antithetical glimpses of a "leveled" world cancel each other out. And they are followed by other confusing images. The cattle are, in turn, likened to a smaller reflection of the picture as would be seen in a "Looking-Glass," mere "Spots" in the vastness of the pasture like "Spots" on "Faces," fleas magnified through "Multiplying Glasses," and finally *Constellations* in the heavens—the effect being to create a sense of everincreasing smallness or distance. The description of the cattle accelerates a process long at work in the meadow section of the poem: in the course of his "antimasques," Marvell has gradually stepped backwards—from the unnerving immediacy of the initial plunge into the "Abbyss of grass" to a wider and wider "Landskip" that suggests a growing physical and psychological remoteness from the scenes he describes and also a decreasing potential for coherent interpretation.

Then comes the invasion of the tidal flood, the final unmetaphoring that creates the last image of inversion, a return to some primal chaos. The dominant figure of the antimasques had been of the meadows as a sea; now that image spills over into reality, obliterating, at least temporarily, all possibility of metaphor. Imagery and imaged coalesce into paradox, a world intrinsically "upside down," at odds with and "drowning" itself:

> Then, to conclude these pleasant Acts,
> *Denton* sets ope its *Cataracts*;
> And makes the Meadow truly be
> (What it but seem'd before) a Sea.
> For, jealous of its *Lords* long stay,
> It try's t'invite him thus away.
> The River in it self is drown'd,
> And Isl's th' astonisht Cattle round.
>
> Let others tell the *Paradox*,
> How Eels now bellow in the Ox;
> How Horses at their Tails do kick,

Turn'd as they hang to Leeches quick;
How Boats can over Bridges sail;
And Fishes do the Stables scale.
How *Salmons* trespassing are found;
And Pikes are taken in the Pound.

                              (*Marvell*, 77)

Marvell's notion of a world unmetaphored is comical in the extreme, a holiday inversion that cancels out the possibility of its own operation by welding things to their opposites. It is the ultimate "act" of the seemingly endless upheavals. The process has reached a stalemate and can proceed no further. But its new self-devouring stasis is scarcely more comfortable than the transformations that have gone before. Marvell chooses to retreat from his vision of ultimate topsy-turvydom.

In Stuart entertainments the antimasque figures had quite commonly warred against themselves. We may think, for example, of the self-reversing Phantasms from Jonson's *Vision of Delight*. At court, a power associated with kingship had intervened to break the deadlock by banishing, annihilating, or transforming the negative energies of the antimasque. The disorders in the meadows at Nun Appleton are not so easily tidied up. Their slippery reversals operate as though by their own inner logic, impervious to human intervention, and must be allowed to play themselves out. Marvell enjoys the spectacle of it all but also seems to fear its seemingly limitless energy for annihilation. To attempt reform would be futile; instead he retreats into a more ordered realm analogous to that of the Stuart main masque. The transition to the "main masque" of the grove at Nun Appleton is accomplished not by mastery but through an escape. Rather like the war-weary Cavaliers, Marvell fashions for himself a separate realm apart and appears quite willing to give up on a world where change has become so intractable. But the "sacred grove" of Marvell's main masque is provisional rather than eternal, something he unquestionably needs but only for the duration of the chaos outside.

As we have already remarked, Marvell's "sacred grove" at Nun Appleton is very similar to Royalist analogues in the poetry of Lovelace and Vaughan. He calls it a "yet green, yet growing Ark," which suggests the familiar Old Testament type of the church, except that his "Ark" is flourishing at a time when the Anglican Church was not. The grove is dark from without, light within, a sacred space walled off from the world and offering intimations of the political and ecclesiastical institutions that had proved so vulnerable to upheavals like those enacted in the meadows. Marvell begins his account of the grove by noting how it is structured:

Dark all without it knits; within
It opens passable and thin;
And in as loose an order grows,
As the *Corinthean Porticoes.*
The arching Boughs unite between
The Columnes of the Temple green;
And underneath the winged Quires
Echo about their tuned Fires.

(Marvell, 78)

Marvell's natural temple is Roman rather than Gothic, its Corinthian "Columnes" topped with genuine foliage rather than the stylized marble vegetation that adorned its antique counterparts. It closely resembles the Roman Pantheon, which Marvell had seen in his travels (*Marvell,* 289n), and that ancient temple to all the Gods would indeed be a suitable model for the grove in which Marvell learns to read the language of a universal religion. But at least initially, the worship practiced within the grove appears identifiably Christian rather than pagan: its "winged Quires" sing in the antiphonal fashion of Anglican choristers, much as they do in Royalist versions of the sacred grove.

In the grove, unlike the disorienting meadows, natural hieroglyphs are legible, at least to the observing poet. The animals that populate the grove constitute a natural hierarchy of benevolent paternalism. High Oaks and Elders listen like attentive statesmen to the lowly song of the Nightingale; thorns protectively retract their "claws"; a Heron drops one of its young as if in *"Tribute"* to its feudal *"Lord."* Marvell chooses for his special attention—his "Musick"—the mourning song of the Stock-doves, emblems of chaste marriage that suggest the "equal Flames" of Alexis and Lucasta in his poetic model "Aramantha," or perhaps more nearly, their model in the union of Charles I and his queen. There is another analogue in Herrick's poem "To the King and Queene upon their unhappy distances," in which an oracular oak prophesies the reunion of the severed royal pair (*Herrick,* 26). Contemplating the hieroglyph of the doves, Marvell asks, "O why should such a Couple mourn, / That in so equal Flames do burn!"—a riddle which could be answered (if one wished) in terms of the royal pair's sad history, be-moaned as though in advance.

Of course Marvell's "sacred grove" differs from the Cavalier pattern in that he carefully avoids the passion of love himself, even though he admires the chaste amours of the Stockdoves. But a more significant departure is that Marvell's grove proves not to be impervious to change. Its animal and vegetable elements suggest a vision of primeval hierar-chical order, but the hierarchy is undermined from within. Already in

255

the song of the stockdoves, he had read a message of enigmatic sorrow, but his observation of the woodcutter *"Hewel"* brings death into the grove. Like the mowers of the fields triumphing over the grass, the Hewel works doom upon something which had seemed to exceed it by far, the noble Oak:

> The good he numbers up, and hacks;
> As if he mark'd them with the Ax.
> But where he, tinkling with his Beak,
> Does find the hollow Oak to speak,
> That for his building he designs,
> And through the tainted Side he mines.
> Who could have thought the *tallest Oak*
> Should fall by such a *feeble Strok'*!
>
> (*Marvell*, 79)

There has been much discussion of just what this curious allegory might mean. One of the applications it would unquestionably have suggested to Marvell's contemporaries was the recent death of the king. "Royal Oak" imagery was so pervasive in the literature of the period and so consistently linked to the monarchy that the reading would have been inescapable.

Like Charles I as portrayed in the masque, the oak is oracular—it "speaks"—but speaks only the hollow message of its own imperfection. Marvell's oak, unlike most of the trees in the Royal Oak tradition, loses its place of authority in the "palace" of the wood by a measured act of justice. The Hewel is a natural executioner, like the mowers, but unlike them in that he only fells what has already destroyed itself through inner taint. The oak, Marvell observes, had nurtured within itself the *"Traitor-worm"* that had brought on its destruction. The political analogue is almost too obvious to require explication. Charles I, in the eyes of his critics, had countenanced dangerous favorites, "Caterpillars upon the commonwealth," who had with their corrupting influence brought down the towering authority that had sheltered them and therefore destroyed themselves, as the worm is devoured by the offspring of the Hewel that felled the oak. And to carry the reading further, Marvell intimates that even the king himself had finally seen the wisdom of the worm's "execution," content to die, rather like the martyr of *Eikon Basilike*, in order to restore health to the nation:

> And yet that *Worm* triumphs not long,
> But serves to feed the *Hewels young*.
> While the Oake seems to fall content,
> Viewing the Treason's Punishment.
>
> (*Marvell*, 80)

The natural hierarchy of Marvell's grove includes within its mysterious "order" a judicious, controlled mechanism for the overthrow of corrupt authority.

Like the Royalist poets he imitates, Marvell responds to the idea of a monarch destroyed by filling the void himself, becoming a power like the power that was gone. Once he has read the political hieroglyphs of the grove, he terms himself an *"easie Philosopher"* and begins to sense himself at one with it, becoming another bird or tree; he learns their ancient language and they, reciprocally, "divine" his "Signs." Little by little he takes on for himself a role which Charles I had so often played in his masques—the role of divine Magus, ordering his kingdom through the mystical divination of his mind. The Hermeticism of Marvell's natural temple is unmistakable. He reads the future out of the *"Sibyls Leaves"* and the past, *"What Rome, Greece, Palestine,* ere said," in its light *"Mosaick"*—a pattern of legible glints of sun on the leaves. In the *Mosaick* he reads even the wisdom of Moses, who according to Hermetic lore, had brought the Ancient Theology to the Jews from the Egyptians. Finally, all human time becomes "one History." He can claim,

> Thrice happy he who, not mistook,
> Hath read in *Natures mystick Book*.
> (*Marvell*, 80)

He has become a Hermetic Magus—thrice happy as Trismegistus was thrice great—and his reverend status is established in a "Mask" which playfully confers on him the trappings of Anglicanized Druidism. Under his *"antick Cope"* he moves "Like some great *Prelate of the Grove*," a Druid divining in his oak grove, but also the bishop of his sanctuary-church, his elaborate vestments adorned with oakleaves that figure forth the sacred origin of his high "ecclesiastical" authority:

> And see how Chance's better Wit
> Could with a Mask my studies hit!
> The Oak-Leaves me embroyder all,
> Between which Caterpillars crawl:
> And Ivy, with familiar trails,
> Me licks, and clasps, and curles, and hales.
> Under this *antick Cope* I move
> Like some great *Prelate of the Grove*.
> (*Marvell*, 81)

Marvell's "Mask" lacks the high seriousness of Charles I's Hermetic rituals in masques like *Albion's Triumph*, but he has assumed the same posture as high priest of a British Ur-Christianity. What remains to be seen at this point in the poem is whether his Hermetic magic will be as powerful as Charles I's in entertainments at court—whether he envisions its energies as potent enough to heal the chaotic world outside.

The final stage of Marvell's sylvan metamorphosis is the healing of his mind, the shedding of thoughts and mental chaff in a playful ecstasy upon the moss that imitates the Hermetic visionary frenzy and the "sacred rage" of the Cavaliers. He has constructed a model of the vanished order, discovered its participation in an unbroken continuum of sacred mystery from the time of Moses and the Druids through the Civil War period and on into the future. And he has used that perception of continuity in Hermetic fashion to cure his own mind. There are psychological changes in the poet which seem to demonstrate the efficacy of his method. He is altered from a mere witness of the chaos of the meadows into a stronger and more decisive figure who can rise above it, "gaul its Horsemen" instead of being wounded himself.

How seriously are we meant to take Marvell's Hermetic self-transformation? The poet's "mask" in the grove is quite playful, yet Hermeticism was often playful. Indeed, the purging of melancholy humors and restoration of a sanguine temperament was one of its goals, according to Bruno and Ficino.[42] But we may suspect that there is something else happening here as well. Part of Marvell's playfulness was surely defensive, like the Cavalier playfulness it imitates, but for a somewhat different reason. In Lovelace and many of the other Cavaliers, we can sense that the destruction of the idealized institution of sacred absolute monarchy generated real psychic distress in addition to all the external perils. The erosion of a royal power with which the Cavaliers so strongly identified created in some of them a corresponding inner deficit, a self-doubt that had to be countered with various rituals of mastery in which they reestablished their self-worth by adopting the role which the monarch had proved too weak to sustain. There may have been elements of that in Marvell, but for him, the essential issue appears to have been rather the degree of his independence from an order toward which he was profoundly ambivalent. He was attracted to the old ideas, as we can see in his praise for the "Candid age" of Lovelace, yet he was more forcibly aware of their inherent limitations than many who found them appealing. In the magic grove of "Upon Appleton House" he gave them at least provisional credence in order to make his peace with the past, but at the same time he distanced himself from them through his jauntiness of tone. If the Cavaliers crowned themselves monarchs in order to salvage the image of kingship, Marvell adopted the role of king and high prelate to work himself out of the residual power those images continued to exert upon him.

Having played "monarch of the grove" for a space in his own Hermetic masque, Marvell does something utterly characteristic of him and of the topsy-turvy logic of his poem: he departs altogether from the paradigm of Lovelace's "Aramantha" and overturns his own sacred hierarchy by transforming himself from the figure at its pinnacle to one placed at the bottom, the victim of the power that appears so attractive as it was playfully exercised from the top. According to Caesar's *Commentaries*, the Druids of Britain had practiced the amiable custom of staking down human victims within their temples.[43] This is precisely the fate Marvell envisions for himself. If he is to remain within the sacred grove, it will be as Druidic victim rather than Druid Priest. He asks the verdant greenery that had earlier helped fashion his "Cope" of authority to pin him down instead, impale him in thorns and brambles, "That I may never leave this Place." What has happened to the earlier benevolent paternalism of the grove, whereby thorns were retracted lest they injure the lowly? We are suddenly reminded of the Druids' negative side, not unknown in Marvell's day—their reputation for cruel aloofness and for human sacrifice—which tended not to surface in the Hermetic Druidism of the Court. Something approximating that realization appears to strike the poet as well, creating a sudden mental distance from the ceremonial trappings of the grove. He finds himself eager to depart from his place of mental healing, albeit reluctant to allow himself to do so. But the grove opens out as though of its own accord. His poem has said a final farewell to "Aramantha" and its ideal of perpetual retreat.

When Marvell returns to the meadows, he finds them utterly changed. Now they are peaceful, restored to their first greenness, as though his Hermetic magic in the grove has indeed imprinted its order upon the world outside:

> For now the Waves are fal'n and dry'd,
> And now the Meadows fresher dy'd;
> Whose Grass, with moister colour dasht,
> Seems as green Silks but newly washt.
>
> (*Marvell*, 82)

He plays in his new paradise, an image of "Contentment in the Country." Marvell seems to encourage the discovery of likeness between his happy pastoral condition after the "mask" of the grove and the traditional Stuart model of rural bliss. In the 1650s, thanks to the strong influence of Izaak Walton, the literary portrayal of angling tended to carry strong Royalist and Anglican implications. It was an "innocent" pastime that evoked the prewar vision of a countryside at mirth.[44] However, the gleeful extravagance of Marvell's "self-portrait in the throes of lassitude" pokes fun at his slackened condition amidst the twanging lines even while he is enjoying it. It is by no means clear that his comic prelapsarian indolence in a place once so chaotic has been brought about by the Hermetic magic of the grove. Even as he imitates the traditional masquing pattern of drawing peace out of chaos through the application of ancient magic, Marvell suggests another more plausible possibility that subverts it. The rejuvenation may have been brought about instead by the fertile agency of the flood. During the "antimasques of the meadows," the flood had appeared a final act of chaos, the final stage of an escalating series of inversions run out of control. Marvell's language of natural renewal seems to suggest, however, that the seeming catastrophe has worked the survivalist transformation traditionally attributed to holiday inversion—bringing harmony, greenness, renewed fertility, a new beginning of the natural cycle—and all of it quite independent of the poet and his ordering "mask."

Before these half-formed speculations have a chance to coalesce, they are swept aside by the arrival of Maria Fairfax. It is she, Marvell quickly recognizes, and not the poet with his "royal" rites in the grove or the cataclysm of the meadows, that has made them so "whisht and fine." Maria's presence has likewise brought loveliness to Nun Appleton's Gardens, Woods, and River. That does not mean Hermetic magic as a means for renewal is abandoned, at least not yet. The poet has merely mistaken the locus from which it is efficacious, supposing it necessarily tied to traditional images of religious and political authority, as it had been in the Caroline masque, whereas instead it flourishes quietly and free of its Stuart associations on the Fairfax estate. Maria is herself surrounded with the images of Hermeticism. She is conversant in "all the Languages" and seems to practice her own rituals of the grove, charming the elements and inspiring the woods to draw a "Skreen" about her as did the Magus Orpheus of old. Mistletoe was holy to the Druids, reverently cut from the oak tree as a symbol of fertility.[45] So, Maria herself will eventually be "harvested" and given to the world. She,

> like a *sprig of Mistleto*,
> On the *Fairfacian Oak* does grow;
> Whence, for some universal good,
> The *Priest* shall cut the sacred Bud;
>
> (*Marvell*, 85)

Marvell undoubtedly intended a compliment to Lord Fairfax as well as to his daughter since Fairfax took a strong interest in Hermetic ideas during his years of retirement. But, the poet is at pains to suggest, the former general's Hermeticism is not a mere reflection of Platonic magic at court. In the companion poem to "Upon Appleton House," "Upon the Hill and Grove at Bill-borow," Marvell imagines the "sacred Shades" of that oak grove as speaking the *"Oracles"* of the family's renown (*Marvell*, 60–62). But that grove, significantly, is modeled not upon court hierarchy but on a more egalitarian "parliamentary" pattern. There are many oaks, all equal, all prudent and humble despite their eminence. Joseph Summers has wittily termed the passage a "delightfully artificial description of landscape as Republican gentlemen."[46] "Upon Appleton House" is a poem of decentralization, as Milton's *Comus* had been. It "redeems" Royalist motifs by wresting them out of their Caroline context and giving them new and autonomous points of departure.

Unlike *Comus*, however, Marvell's poem allows scant place for the traditional pastimes except in the "antimasques." Maria is severe and reforming by temperament, more like Milton's Lady, who had seemed at least initially to shun all traditional pastimes, than like the Lady's more genial parents, who had assimilated sports into an ethos of reform. In Maria's presence Marvell the poet, even nature, must recollect themselves and give up their foolish levity:

> The *young Maria* walks to night:
> Hide trifling Youth thy Pleasures slight.
> 'Twere shame that such judicious Eyes
> Should with such Toyes a Man surprize.
> (*Marvell*, 83)

The poet has associated Maria with Flora, crowned with the blossoms to which she has given their sweetness. But we will remember the vigilance and preparedness of the Fairfax garden—scarcely the place to encourage an idyll of country indolence. Her moral energy even in retreat is inseparable from the pervasive militarism of the estate. In the "antimasques" of "Upon Appleton House" the old seasonal pastimes with their upending of preexisting order were played over and over again until they were played out and exhausted—they were "rehearsed" in remarkable variety for one last time before being allowed to fall into extinction. The world Maria is about to enter and Marvell about to reenter will demand a new set of equilibrating mechanisms as yet unspecified but based on the recognition that peace is not always the highest good and that moral renewal may require the doing of violence.

In Maria's new world, Marvell implies, the Hermeticism that pervades the Fairfax estates may no longer be important. In "Upon the Hill and Grove at Bill-borow" the oracle of the family grove bespeaks its own undoing in that it confesses its inability to do justice to the *"Garlands"* of civic achievement (*Marvell*, 62). As the estate at Nun Appleton had been founded upon a violation of the past—the storming of the medieval cloister—so Maria's presence erases the magnetism of earlier "sacred groves" and gardens. Marvell offers a list of former beauty spots eclipsed by Nun Appleton and it is perhaps significant that all are either pagan or Roman Catholic: Tempe, *"Aranjuez,"* the *"Bel-Retiro,"* the Idalian Grove, the Elysian Fields (*Marvell*, 86), all of them fading into insignificance before the reforming energy of the Fairfax family estate. It is customary to regard "Upon Appleton House" as Marvell's farewell to his own life of retirement and pleasant immersion in Neoplatonic lore at Nun Appleton, with perhaps an implied message to Lord Fairfax urging him back into the political fray. Through its insistent fusion of traditional Stuart dichotomies, the poem demonstrates that there can be no such thing as permanent peaceful retreat. Even before Maria leaves her parents' house, her influence effaces the Hermetic and Laudian pattern of achieving quietude through the discovery of continuities with pagan and Roman Catholic revelation.

Marvell's long poem closes with one final fillip of playful inversion. The poet imagines the salmon fishermen with their boats as walking images of the antipodes moving tortoiselike homeward and suggests, most preposterously, that the universe at nightfall has assumed a similar aspect. It is almost as though he wanted to indulge himself with one final bout of innocuous perceptual subversion before succumbing to the more severe "law" of Maria. But the effect is rather to suggest the continuing vitality of an "upending," carnivalesque mode of vision.[47] And in fact Marvell never did give up his fascination with the leveling power of popular festival forms. Later on, as a satirist under the Restoration government, he further developed his tendency to explore the spectacles of state from the viewpoint of one at the bottom.

Traditional pastimes returned to England along with the "May Prince" Charles, who was proclaimed king on 8 May 1660, his triumphal entry into London timed to coincide with his birthday, 29 May. His return was celebrated with the erection of a maypole in the Strand and morris dancing "not seen of twenty years before"; he was again heralded as the lord and bringer of May.[48] In many parts of England, May Day festivities were actually shifted to 29 May and celebrated in honor of Charles II's victory over "poor Oliver" Cromwell. And other old festival pastimes were similarly revived. Bartholomew Fair was extended to two weeks and allowed to "license" stage plays. Jonson's *Bartholomew Fair* was more than once performed there—a fair within the fair.[49] Poets also resurrected the earlier court Hermeticism of the masque. We find Edmund Waller, for example, praising Charles II as a Druid Magus restored to the "oraculous shade" of his primeval "palace" of the sacred grove to contemplate the mysteries of government and "reconcile" the "divided world."[50] Marvell remained aloof from all this magic and merriment. Instead, he adopted for himself a mode of popular festivity not inscribed with the power of Stuart kings.

In "The last Instructions to a Painter," Marvell articulates his own poetic role vis-à-vis the renewed "public games" of government as rather like the role played by his railing Mower "against Gardens" but without the Mower's destructive immersion in the survivalist view of life. Marvell envisions himself as keeping up the ancient custom of "rough music" or the Skimmington through his biting satires. He calls attention to his subject like a villager with clattering stick and pan, displaying his caricatures of public figures for criticism as countryfolk might hold up effigies of their wayward neighbors in the "Pastime, Martial and old" of processional public shaming:

> A Punishment invented first to awe
> Masculine Wives, transgressing Natures Law.
> Where when the brawny Female disobeys,
> And beats the Husband till for peace he prays:
> No concern'd *Jury* for him Damage finds,
> Nor partial *Justice* her Behaviour binds;
> But the just Street does the next House invade,
> Mounting the neighbour Couple on lean Jade.
> The Distaff knocks, the Grains from Kettle fly,
> And Boys and Girls in Troops run houting by;
> Prudent Antiquity, that knew by Shame,
> Better than Law, Domestick Crimes to tame
> And taught Youth by Spectacle Innocent!
> So thou and I, dear *Painter*, represent
> In quick *Effigy*, others Faults, and feign
> By making them ridiculous to restrain.
>
> (*Marvell*, 157)

In context, Marvell's Skimmington holds the British nation up to shame. But the "antique" model Marvell adopts is a popular festival form traditionally independent of established authority and unconnected with the holidays of the church. Marvell's role as satirist is like a "Spectacle Innocent" "played" by the villagers themselves for the purpose of moral instruction—merry, celebratory, grotesque, potentially violent, and tending ultimately toward reform.

Notes

Abbreviations

In works cited in the notes, short titles have generally been used. Works cited frequently have been identified in the text, and in some cases in the notes, by the following abbreviations:

Chamberlain	*The Letters of John Chamberlain*, ed. N. E. McClure, *Memoirs of the American Philosophical Society* 12 (Philadelphia: Lancashire Press, 1939).
CSPD Charles I	*Calendar of State Papers, Domestic Series, of the Reign of Charles I* (London: Longman, Brown, Green et al., 1858–97).
CSPD James I	*Calendar of State Papers, Domestic Series, of the Reigns of Edward VI . . . James I* (London: H. M. Stationery Office 1856–72).
Dekker	*The Dramatic Works of Thomas Dekker*, ed. Fredson Bowers, 4 vols. (Cambridge: Cambridge Univ. Press, 1953–61), vol. 3.
Fair	*Ben Jonson: Bartholomew Fair*, ed. Eugene M. Waith (New Haven: Yale Univ. Press, 1963).
Herrick	*The Poetical Works of Robert Herrick*, ed. L. C. Martin (1956; reprint, London: Oxford Univ. Press, 1965).
Inigo	Stephen Orgel and Roy Strong, *Inigo Jones: The Theatre of the Stuart Court*, 2 vols. (Berkeley: Univ. of California Press, 1973).
James	*The Political Works of James I*, ed. C. H. McIlwain (Cambridge, Mass.: Harvard Univ. Press, 1918).
Jonson	*Ben Jonson*, ed. C. H. Herford and Percy and Evelyn Simpson, 11 vols. (Oxford: Clarendon Press, 1925–52).
Lovelace	*The Poems of Richard Lovelace*, ed. C. H. Wilkinson (1930; reprint, Oxford: Clarendon Press, 1963).

Marvell   *The Poems and Letters of Andrew Marvell*, ed. Pierre Legouis, 3d ed. (1927; reprint, Oxford: Clarendon Press, 1971).

Masques   Ben Jonson, *The Complete Masques*, ed. Stephen Orgel (New Haven: Yale Univ. Press, 1969).

Milton   John Milton, *A Maske: The Earlier Versions*, ed. S. E. Sprott (Toronto: Univ. of Toronto Press, 1973).

Chapter I

1. *The Table Talk of John Selden*, ed. Samuel H. Reynolds (Oxford: Clarendon Press, 1892), 31.

2. My thanks to Dorothy Stephens, presently studying at the University of California at Berkeley, for kindly supplying me with the anecdote.

3. *James*, 27. For earlier versions of the same passage, see James Craigie's ed. of James's manuscript version, the 1599 and the 1603 editions, *Scottish Text Society*, 3d ser. 16 (Edinburgh: Blackwood & Sons, 1944) 94–95, and the notes in vol. 18.

4. *The King's Maiesties Declaration to His Subjects, concerning lawfull Sports to be vsed* (London, 1618), 6–7.

5. There is a massive literature on the Sabbatarian controversy under Elizabeth. See (among many others) Elbert N. S. Thompson, *The Controversy between the Puritans and the Stage*, Yale Studies in English, vol. 20 (New York: Holt, 1903); William Pierce, ed., *The Marprelate Tracts, 1588, 1589* (London: James Clarke, 1911), introduction; early portions of Christopher Hill, *Society and Puritanism in Pre-Revolutionary England*, 2d ed. (New York: Schocken, 1967), to which my own work is particularly indebted; and Stuart Burton Babbage, *Puritanism and Richard Bancroft* (London: S·P·C·K, 1962). For Elizabeth's own festival, see Frances Yates, *Astraea: The Imperial Theme in the Sixteenth Century* (London: Routledge & K. Paul, 1975), 100–110; and Paul Johnson, *Elizabeth I* (New York: Holt, Rinehart & Winston, 1974), 111, 194, and 323. There is a list of Elizabethan commands about interdicted pastimes in Frederic A. Youngs, Jr., *The Proclamations of the Tudor Queens* (Cambridge: Cambridge Univ. Press, 1976), 1:270–71. By the criteria of James F. Larkin and Paul L. Hughes, eds., *Stuart Royal Proclamations Vol. I: Royal Proclamations of King James I 1603–1625* (Oxford: Clarendon Press, 1973), the *Book of Sports* was not a proclamation but a declaration. However, it appears to have been publicized as widely as proclamations were and regarded in the same light by contemporaries.

6. See Helena Mennie Shire, *Song, Dance and Poetry of the Court of Scotland under King James VI* (Cambridge: Cambridge Univ. Press, 1969), 7–138 and 194–204. In the manuscript version of *Basilikon Doron*, in connection with the promotion of old pastimes, James had counseled that the king should be as a bard to his people (Craigie ed., 16: 94–95).

7. Christopher Whitfield, ed., *Robert Dover and the Cotswold Games: Annalia Dubrensia* (Evesham, Worcestershire: The Journal Press, 1962), 18–19, 32. We

do not know the precise year in which the clothes were donated; however, King James's support was made clear. I am indebted on this point to Peter Stallybrass, whose study, "Carnival Contained," is forthcoming in *English Literary Renaissance*. See also Dennis Brailsford, *Sport and Society: Elizabeth to Anne* (Toronto: Univ. of Toronto Press, 1969), 103–8.

8. See Max Gluckman, "The License in Ritual," in *Custom and Conflict in Africa* (1955; reprint, New York: Barnes & Noble, 1964), chap. 5, 109–36; Gluckman, "Rituals of Rebellion in South-East Africa," in *Order and Rebellion in Tribal Africa* (New York: Free Press of Glencoe, 1963), chap. 3, 110–36; and Keith Thomas, "Work and Leisure in Pre-Industrial Society," *Past and Present*, no. 29 (1964):53–54. Contemporary evidence will be cited later in the discussion, but see also Edward Muir's *Civic Ritual in Renaissance Venice* (Princeton: Princeton Univ. Press, 1981), 230 where Muir points out that seventeenth-century Englishmen perceived Venetian ritual as contributing to the strength and harmony of the Venetian state.

9. See Lucy Hutchinson, *The Life of Colonel Hutchinson*, ed. James Sutherland (London: Oxford Univ. Press, 1973), 42–44; and the detailed interpretation of the Puritan position in Hill, *Society and Puritanism*.

10. See the discussion of Herrick and Milton in chapters 5 and 6; for survivalism, see Hill, *Society and Puritanism*; Thomas, "Work and Leisure"; John Bossy, "The Character of Elizabethan Catholicism," *Past and Present*, no. 21 (April 1962), 39–59; and Jacques Le Goff, *Time, Work, and Culture in the Middle Ages*, trans. Arthur Goldhammer (1980; reprint, Chicago: Univ. of Chicago Press, 1982), 29–86.

11. Mikhail Bakhtin, *Rabelais and His World*, trans. Helene Iswolsky (Cambridge, Mass.: MIT Press, 1968), 255.

12. For Marx's views and more recent correctives to Bakhtin, see the useful survey in Barbara A. Babcock, ed., *The Reversible World: Symbolic Inversion in Art and Society* (Ithaca: Cornell Univ. Press, 1978), 13–36; and the essay by Natalie Zemon Davis, "Women on Top: Symbolic Sexual Inversion and Political Disorder in Early Modern Europe," reprinted with minor revisions in Babcock, 147–90 from Davis, *Society and Culture in Early Modern France* (Stanford: Stanford Univ. Press, 1975); see also Davis's chapter, "The Reasons of Misrule," 97–123 in *Society and Culture*; and Clifford Geertz, "Ritual and Social Change," in *The Interpretation of Cultures* (New York: Basic Books, 1973), 142–69.

13. The offenders, myself included, are too numerous to mention, but there have been recent correctives by Malcolm Smuts, "The Political Failure of Stuart Cultural Patronage," in *Patronage in the Renaissance*, ed. Guy Fitch Lytle and Stephen Orgel (Princeton: Princeton Univ. Press, 1981), 165–87; Stephen Orgel, "Making Greatness Familiar," 1981, reprinted in David Bergeron, ed., *Pageantry in the Shakespearean Theater* (Athens, Ga.: Univ. of Georgia Press, 1985), 19–25; John M. Wallace, "'Examples are Best Precepts': Readers and Meanings in Seventeenth-Century Poetry," *Critical Inquiry* 1 (1974):273–90; Annabel Patterson, *Censorship and Interpretation: The Conditions of Writing and*

Reading in Early Modern England (Madison: Univ. of Wisconsin Press, 1984); and Richard Helgerson, *Self-Crowned Laureates: Spenser, Jonson, Milton, and the Literary System* (Berkeley: Univ. of California Press, 1983). I am also indebted to Philip J. Finkelpearl's essay "'The Comedians' Liberty': Censorship of the Jacobean Theater Reconsidered," forthcoming in *English Literary Renaissance*, which Mr. Finkelpearl kindly allowed me to read in manuscript.

14. For the precise formulation of "royal misrule" I am indebted to Leonard Tennenhouse, "Strategies of State and Political Plays: *A Midsummer Night's Dream, Henry IV, Henry V, Henry VIII*," in *Political Shakespeare: New Essays in Cultural Materialism*, ed. Jonathan Dollimore and Alan Sinfield (Ithaca: Cornell Univ. Press, 1985), 109–28, esp. p. 119; see also Jonathan Goldberg's brilliant analysis of Jacobean contradictions in *James I and the Politics of Literature* (Baltimore: Johns Hopkins Univ. Press, 1983); and my "Masquing Occasions and Masque Structure," *Research Opportunities in Renaissance Drama* 24 (1981):7–16.

15. *The Letters and Epigrams of Sir John Harington*, ed. N. E. McClure (Philadelphia: Univ. of Pennsylvania Press, 1930), 119–20. See also Graham Parry's discussion in *The Golden Age Restor'd: The Culture of the Stuart Court, 1603–42* (New York: St. Martin's Press, 1981), 58–60.

16. John Nichols, *The Progresses of James I* (1828; reprint, New York: Kraus, n.d.), 2:38n for Weldon's account, and 2:597 for James's reaction to the masque.

17. That is, at least occasionally: see *Jonson*, 1:71.

18. See in particular E. Pearlman, "Ben Jonson: An Anatomy," *English Literary Renaissance* 9 (1979):364–94; and Judith Kegan Gardiner, "'A Wither'd Daffodill': Narcissism and *Cynthia's Revels*," *Literature and Psychology* 30 (1980):26–43.

19. Hutchinson, *Colonel Hutchinson*, 46.

20. Kevin Sharpe, personal communication, the Huntington Library, August 1981. Mr. Sharpe is presently at work on a book-length study of the Personal Rule. See also his contribution "The Personal Rule of Charles I," in *Before the English Civil War*, ed. Howard Tomlinson (London: Macmillan, 1983), 53–78; and Sharpe's review "An Unwanted Civil War," *New York Review of Books* 29, no. 19 (2 December 1982):43–45.

21. See Wallace Notestein et al., eds., *Commons Debates 1621* (New Haven: Yale Univ. Press, 1935), 2:82; 4:52–53; and Robert Zaller, *The Parliament of 1621: A Study in Constitutional Conflict* (Berkeley: Univ. of California Press, 1971), 42–43.

22. The shrovetide structure is discussed briefly in R. Chris Hassel, Jr., *Renaissance Drama and the English Church Year* (Lincoln: Univ. of Nebraska Press, 1979), 130–35. For interpretation of the masque, see *Inigo*, 1:66–70.

23. See, for example, the discussion of *Salmacida Spolia* in chap. 5, and William Drummond of Hawthornden's description of an arch for Charles's 1633 entertainment in Edinburgh: the arch was labeled in "great Characters" "HILARITATI PVBLICÆ" and contained "men, women, and children, dauncing after diverse postures with many Musicall Instruments," *The Poetical*

Works of William Drummond of Hawthornden, ed. L. E. Kostner (1856; reprinted, New York: Haskell House, 1968), 2:121. In the early stages of my research I came across a reproduction of an engraving of this arch, but to my severe frustration, have not been able to find the illustration again.

24. Cited by Amy Charles from B. L. Add MS. 22084 in *A Life of George Herbert* (Ithaca: Cornell Univ. Press, 1977), 228–32. Charles notes that similar charges were leveled against other Wiltshire clergymen. That is not to suggest, of course, that Herbert himself would have gone to such lengths, though his *Country Parson* did suggest that the parson be "a lover of old Customes, if they be good and harmlesse," *Works*, ed. F. E. Hutchinson, rev. ed. (Oxford: Clarendon Press, 1967), 283. Other examples are cited below in chap. 5.

25. *Herrick*, 5.

26. Edmvnd Howes, *Annales or, A Generall Chronicle of England* (London: Richard Meighen, 1631), 997 (from a 1610 sermon by the Bishop of Lincoln); *The Works of . . . William Laud*, Library of Anglo-Catholic Theology, vol. 2 (Oxford: John Henry Parker, 1849), p. xvi; and for another example of Laudian ritual forms as the expression of hierarchy, the Earl of Clarendon's essay "Of Sacrilege," (1641), which argues that removing chalices and candlesticks from churches (the Puritans being implied) was lowering God to a position where none would worship him, *Essays, Divine and Morall* in *A Compleat Collection of Tracts, by . . . Clarendon* (London: for C. Davis, 1747), 213–14.

27. Mark Girouard, *Life in the English Country House: A Social and Architectural History* (New Haven: Yale Univ. Press, 1978), 11–28. The matter will be discussed more fully in chap. 3, but see also Felicity Heal, "The Idea of Hospitality in Early Modern England," *Past and Present*, no. 102 (1984):66–93.

28. James I, *The Poems of James VI of Scotland*, ed. James Craigie, vol. 2 (Edinburgh: Blackwood & Sons, 1958), 179. (Scottish Text Society, 3rd series, vol. 26).

29. Angus Fletcher, *The Transcendental Masque: An Essay on Milton's Comus* (Ithaca: Cornell Univ. Press, 1971), 7.

30. *Masques*, 76. Because of its more accurate dating and commentary, this edition will be used as the standard edition of Jonson's masques for the present study.

31. Quoted from *Racine et Shakespeare*, Letter 5, *Oeuvres complètes*, ed. Pierre Martino (Paris: Librairie Ancienne, Édouard Champion, 1925), vol. 11, pt. 1, p. 107. See also L. C. Knights, *Public Voices: Literature and Politics with Special Reference to the Seventeenth Century* (London: Chatto & Windus, 1971), 14.

Chapter II

1. E. K. Chambers, *The Elizabethan Stage* (Oxford: Clarendon, 1923), 1:129–30; and William Rankins, *A Mirrour of Monsters: Wherein is plainely described the manifold vices . . . caused by the infectious sight of Playes . . .* (London, 1587), fol. 2. The Dryden quotation is from *Absalom and Achitophel*, line 873.

2. Chambers, *Elizabethan Stage*, 2:267–69, from David Calderwood's *Historie of the Kirk of Scotland*. On James's patronage of players in Scotland see also Chambers, 2:205, 209, 265–70.

3. See Virginia Crocheron Gildersleeve, *Government Regulation of the Elizabethan Drama* (1908; reprint, New York: Burt Franklin, 1961), 36–43.

4. Chambers, *Elizabethan Stage*, 1:215.

5. On censorship and its limits see Philip J. Finkelpearl, "'The Comedians' Liberty': Censorship of the Jacobean Theater Reconsidered," forthcoming in *English Literary Renaissance*; Margot Heinemann, *Puritanism and Theatre: Thomas Middleton and Opposition Drama under the Early Stuarts* (Cambridge: Cambridge Univ. Press, 1980), 16–17, 36–47; and Annabel Patterson's reexamination in *Censorship and Interpretation: The Conditions of Writing and Reading in Early Modern England* (Madison: Univ. of Wisconsin Press, 1984).

6. Thomas Heywood, *An Apology for Actors* (London, 1612), sigs. A3^r, B1, and D1^r.

7. William Sanderson, *A Compleat History of the Lives and Reigns of Mary Queen of Scotland and of her Son and Successor, James* (London, 1656), 366.

8. Desiderius Erasmus, "Erasmus' Letter to Martin Dorp (1514)," in *The Praise of Folly*, trans. and ed. Clarence H. Miller (New Haven: Yale Univ. Press, 1979), 146; William Shakespeare, *AYL*, 2.7.47–57.

9. See the commendatory poems to Heywood's *Apology*, especially Richard Perkins', fols. 22^v–23^r; William Prynne, *Histrio-Mastix* (London, 1633), 160; and Ian Donaldson, *The World Upside-Down: Comedy from Jonson to Fielding* (Oxford: Clarendon Press, 1970), 66–69.

10. William Blissett, "Your Majesty is Welcome to a Fair," in *The Elizabethan Theatre IV*, ed. G. R. Hibbard (Hamden, Conn.: Archon Books, 1974), 82.

11. Jonas Barish, *Ben Jonson and the Language of Prose Comedy* (Cambridge, Mass.: Harvard Univ. Press, 1967), 252–56.

12. Stephen Orgel, *The Jonsonian Masque* (Cambridge, Mass.: Harvard Univ. Press, 1965), 73–77. The most detailed study of *Love Restored* in terms of its contemporary background is Jeffrey Fischer, "*Love Restored:* A Defense of Masquing," *Renaissance Drama*, n.s., 8 (1977):231–44, which overlaps with my discussion at several points. *Love Restored* was a smaller, more private production than the usual court masque. Mary Sullivan notes in *The Court Masques of James I* (New York: Putnam, 1913), 69, that the work "seems to have been lacking in diplomatic significance." Foreign ambassadors were almost certainly not present.

13. *CSPD James I*, 8:469 (24 November, 1608); and 8:501 (31 March, 1609).

14. See Samuel R. Gardiner, *History of England from the Accession of James I to the Outbreak of the Civil War*, vol. 2, 3d ed. (London: Longmans, Green, 1889), 105–9.

15. Gardiner, *History*, 2:110–11.

16. As a corrective to this viewpoint, see Robert Ashton's account of the crown's unreliability as a borrower in *The Crown and the Money Market, 1603–1640* (Oxford: Clarendon, 1960).

17. *CSPD James I*, 9:114 (27 January 1612); AND 9:117 ([n.d.], January 1612).

18. *CSPD James I*, 9:102 (25 December 1611).

19. On the connections between Jonson's masque and the Lord Mayor's Show, see my "City Metal and Country Mettle: The Occasion of Ben Jonson's *Golden Age Restored*," in *Pageantry in the Shakespearean Theatre*, ed. David M. Bergeron (Athens, Ga.: Univ. of Georgia Press, 1985), 26–47.

20. *CSPD James I*, 8:508 (1 May 1609).

21. Jonas Barish, "Jonson and the Loathèd Stage," in *A Celebration of Ben Jonson*, ed. William Blissett et al. (Toronto: Univ. of Toronto Press, 1973), 27–53; Barish, *The Antitheatrical Prejudice* (Berkeley: Univ. of California Press, 1981); and Orgel's discussion in *Jonsonian Masque*, 193.

22. See David Norbrook's fine essay "The Reformation of the Masque," in *The Court Masque*, ed. David Lindley (Dover, N.H.: Manchester Univ. Press, 1984), 94–110.

23. From James's 1607 speech before Parliament, reprinted in *James*, 291. See also p. 279, James's apology for his "infirmitie" of not being able to refuse suitors.

24. *The Poems of James VI of Scotland*, ed. James Craigie, vol. 2 (Edinburgh: Blackwood, 1958), 138–40 (Scottish Text Society, 3d ser., vol. 26). As Craigie's introduction demonstrates (pp. xxii–xxiii), a ms. copy of James's masque was circulating widely in court circles in 1616, presumably in connection with the publication of James I's *Works* in 1616; if Jonson did not see this ms., which shows corrections by Prince Charles and James himself, he may well have known an earlier version. James's masque is discussed in Rhodes Dunlap, "King James' Own Masque," *Philological Quarterly* 41 (1962):249–56.

25. I have tried to be exhaustive in my reading of *Bartholomew Fair* criticism and have gleaned some insight from nearly every piece I have read. I cannot hope to be exhaustive here; I mention only those works to which my own discussion is most greatly indebted. These include, among the "fair" critics, Barish, *Language of Prose Comedy*, 230–39; Joel H. Kaplan, "Dramatic and Moral Energy in Ben Jonson's *Bartholomew Fair*," *Renaissance Drama*, n.s. 3 (1970):137–56; Richard Levin, "The Structure of *Bartholomew Fair*," *PMLA* 80 (1965):172–79; Michael McCanles, "Festival in Jonsonian Comedy," *Renaissance Drama*, n.s. 8 (1977):203–19; C. G. Thayer, *Ben Jonson: Studies in the Plays* (Norman, Oklahoma: Univ. of Oklahoma Press, 1963), especially his discussion of Jonson's use of classical motifs; Eugene M. Waith's introduction to *Ben Jonson: Bartholomew Fair* (New Haven: Yale Univ. Press, 1963)1–22; and above all, Ian Donaldson's stimulating discussion in *World Upside-Down*, 46–77 (note 9 above); and Susan Wells, "Jacobean City Comedy and the Ideology of the City," *ELH* 48 (1981):37–60.

Among critics who emphasize the foulness of the fair, I am especially indebted to Jackson Cope, "*Bartholomew Fair* as Blasphemy," *Renaissance Drama* 8 (1965):127–52; and Guy Hamel, "Order and Judgment in *Bartholomew*

Fair," University of Toronto Quarterly 42–43 (Fall 1973):48–67. In "Infantile Sexuality, Adult Critics, and *Bartholomew Fair," Literature and Psychology* 24 (1974):124–32, Judith Kegan Gardiner sorts out various critical responses to the play in terms of its distinctive atmosphere of sexual regression. One of the best studies of the play's historical and economic context is Jonathan Haynes, "Festivity and the Dramatic Economy of Jonson's *Bartholomew Fair," English Literary History* 51 (1984):645–68. L. C. Knights, whose studies of the contemporary context in *Drama and Society in the Age of Jonson* (London: Chatto & Windus, 1937) are otherwise most helpful, does not discuss *Bartholomew Fair* at all. In his essay "Ben Jonson, Dramatist" in Boris Ford, ed., *The New Pelican Guide to Literature 2: The Age of Shakespeare* (1955; reprinted, New York: Penguin, 1982), he claims that the play's "fun is divorced from any rich significance" (p. 416). My thanks also to Michael Shapiro, who generously allowed me to read his manuscript on the play.

26. *Fair*, 23.

27. For the activities of Lord Mayors, see Marchette Chute, *Ben Jonson of Westminster* (New York: Dutton, 1953), 215–16; E. A. Horsman, ed., *Bartholomew Fair* (Cambridge, Mass.: Harvard Univ. Press, 1960), xx–xxi; and David McPherson, "The Origins of Overdo: A Study in Jonsonian Invention," *Modern Language Quarterly* 37 (1976):221–33. The 1613 Lord Mayor's Show had depicted just such activities as Overdo claims to engage in as laudable, so that Jonson's play can be seen on one level as an undoing of the previous year's pageant, just as *Love Restored* "undoes" the pageant for 1611. See David M. Bergeron, "Middleton's Moral Landscape: *A Chaste Maid in Cheapside* and *The Triumphs of Truth*," in *"Accompaninge the Players": Essays Celebrating Thomas Middleton, 1580–1980*, ed. Kenneth Friedenreich (New York: AMS Press, 1983), 133–46. For the Puritans see also the *Dictionary of National Biography* for Whatley; Henry Morley, *Memoirs of Bartholomew Fair*, 4th ed. (London: George Routledge & Sons, 1892), 140–41; the prefatory biography of William Whatley in his *Prototypes, or the Primarie Precedent . . . Practically applied to our Information and Reformation* (London, 1640); and W[illiam] D[urham], *The Life and Death of that Judicious Divine, and Accomplish'd PREACHER, ROBERT HARRIS, DD.* (London, 1660), 25. John Stockwood's *A sermon Preached at Paules Crosse on Barthelmew day, being the 24. of August 1578* (London, 1578) is a splendid example of an attack on the theater made in connection with the fair.

28. Like Overdo, Coke was an "upstart" judge, had a loose and meddling wife, and was "silenced" by being removed from his post of Chief Justice of the Common Pleas to the post of Chief Justice of the King's Bench on 25 October 1613, a year before the premiere of Jonson's play. See Thayer, *Ben Jonson*, 144; and Catherine Drinker Bowen, *The Lion and the Throne: The Life and Times of Sir Edward Coke* (Boston: Little Brown, 1951), 125–26, 313–50.

29. See especially Donaldson, *World Upside-Down*, 50–59; and Wells, "Jacobean City," who has shown the play's engagement with issues relating to royal licensing. I am also indebted to Steven Mullaney's work on the ideology of

theatrical marginality, forthcoming in *The Place of the Stage: License, Play, and Power in Renaissance England*, University of Chicago Press.

30. In the absence of Privy Council records, elements of the conflict must be pieced together from other sources. For the general conflicts between the king and the City or town corporations during these years, see Chambers, *Elizabethan Stage*, 1:337–38 and 4:249; (which describes a inflammatory 1608 sermon by William Crashaw that may have touched off a renewal of the old controversies in London); and Gildersleeve, *Government Regulation*, 44–214. For an account of the controversy as carried out through pamphlet warfare see Thompson, *Controversy*, 134–42; Richard H. Parkinson, ed., *An Apology for Actors (1612) by Thomas Heywood, A Refutation of the Apology for Actors (1615) by I.G.* (New York: Scholars' Facsimiles & Reprints, 1941); and for individual literary works which argue one side or the other, Robert Tailor, *The Hogge Hath Lost His Pearl* (printed in 1614), a play performed illegally by apprentices in 1613 and popularly taken to be about the controversy between the Lord Chamberlain and the Lord Mayor (a proof of the strength of the controversy in the public mind, since the work itself seems to carry only scattered references); *Hogge* is reprinted in Robert Dodsley, *A Select Collection of Old English Plays*, ed. W. Carew Hazlitt, vol. 11, 4th ed. (1875; reprint, New York: B. Blom, 1975), 423–99. See also the dedicatory poems to Heywood's *Apology*; the contemporary sermons and characters cited in Chambers, *Elizabethan Stage*, 4:254–59; and the skirmishes recorded in G. E. Bentley, *The Profession of Dramatist in Shakespeare's Time: 1590–1642* (Princeton: Princeton Univ. Press, 1971), 175–76. Coke himself had argued that local magistrates had the power to suppress the "abuse of *Stage Players*" at least in some cases. See *The Lord Coke His Speech and Charge . . .* (London, 1607), sig. H2ʳ.

31. Morley, *Memoirs*, 80–114.

32. Morley, *Memoirs*, 112; Chambers, *Elizabethan Stage*, 2:480. For an account of some of the limitations of the charter, see also Valerie Pearl, *London and the Outbreak of the Puritan Revolution: City Government and National Politics, 1625–43* (London: Oxford Univ. Press, 1961), 27–33.

33. Morley, *Memoirs*, 114; and for continuing pressure, *Analytical Index to . . . the Remembrancia . . . AD 1579–1664* (London: E. J. Francis, 1878), 471.

34. Morley, *Memoirs*, 172–81.

35. C. W. Hodges, *The Globe Restored: A Study of the Elizabethan Theatre*, 2d ed. (London: Oxford Univ. Press, 1968), 63.

36. Chambers, *Elizabethan Stage*, 2:453–54, 470–71; Gildersleeve, *Government Regulation*, 165.

37. Cope, "*Bartholomew Fair* as Blasphemy," 143–44.

38. See Hamel, "Order and Judgment," 63; William A. Armstrong, "Ben Jonson and Jacobean Stagecraft," in *Stratford-Upon-Avon Studies I, Jacobean Theatre* (London: Arnold, 1960), 54; the discussion of staging in *Fair*, 205–17; and Elliott Averett Dennison's excellent "Jonson's *Bartholomew Fair* and the Jacobean Stage," Ph.D. diss., Univ. of Michigan, 1970, 49.

39. Gildersleeve, *Government Regulation*, 156; and for later recapitulation of the same arguments, the antitheatrical sources cited in note 30 above.

40. Quoted in Gildersleeve, *Government Regulation*, 164 and 156.

41. Gildersleeve, *Government Regulation*, 164; and Morley, *Memoirs*, 1–19.

42. Prynne, *Histrio-Mastix*, 174.

43. The most colorful example I have found is William Rankins' *Mirrour of Monsters* cited in note 1 above. Rankins later fell into the very vice he declaimed against and applied his fertile imagination to the writing of plays. See Elbert N. S. Thompson, *The Controversy between the Puritans and the Stage* (New York: Holt, 1903), 89.

44. Chambers, *Elizabethan Stage*, 1:102–3; and for the early life of Inigo Jones, Peter Cunningham, *Inigo Jones: A Life of the Architect* (London: Shakespeare Society, 1848), 1–4. Cunningham points out that Jones's father was a clothworker who lived in the clothworkers' area and is therefore certain to have had very close connections with the Smithfield cloth fair.

45. See Chambers, *Elizabethan Stage*, 2:119; Heywood, *Apology*, sig. G3^r; and John Stow, *A Survey of London*, ed. C. L. Kingsford (Oxford: Clarendon Press, 1908), 1:16, 104. Morley (*Memoirs*, 65–67) speculates that religious plays may have survived in the Smithfield area even into Ben Jonson's adulthood.

46. On the reputation of the Red Bull, see G. E Bentley *The Jacobean and Caroline Stage* (Oxford: Clarendon, 1968), 6:238–47; on the staging of opposition plays, Heinemann, *Puritanism and Theatre*, 231–32 (n. 5 above); and on the unlicensed theater, Chambers, *Elizabethan Stage*, 4:327. Thomas Dekker's *If This Be Not a Good Play, the Devil Is in It*, a nearly contemporary opposition play to be discussed in the final section of chapter 3, was, according to its 1612 title page, acted at the Red Bull. See also Martin Butler, *Theatre and Crisis 1632–1642* (Cambridge: Cambridge Univ. Press, 1984), 181–250.

47. Jonson may have had in mind works like Thomas Heywood's four plays in badly rhymed couplets on the golden, silver, bronze, and iron ages; they had been acted at the Red Bull and were published in London between 1611 and 1613.

48. Levin, "Structure of *Bartholomew Fair*," 177–78.

49. Barish, *Language of Prose Comedy*, 213.

50. *Chamberlain*, 1:490.

51. Bowen, *Lion and Throne*, 322 (n. 28 above); *Chamberlain*, 1:559 and 601. On the general conflict, see David Little, "Sir Edward Coke and the Conflict in Law and Order," in *Religion, Order and Law: A Study in Pre-Revolutionary England* (New York: Harper & Row, 1969), chap. 6, 167–217; Gardiner, *History*, 2:3–39. Bowen, *Lion and Throne*, chaps. 22 and 24; and Margaret Atwood Judson, *The Crisis of the Constitution* (1949; reprint, New York: Octagon, 1964). Here I have emphasized areas of polarization because those were of primary concern to Jonson. Judson is very good at demonstrating broad areas of consensus which existed alongside them.

52. *James*, 307–8.

53. *James*, 309–10.

54. I quote from the rough contemporary transcript printed in William Cobbett, ed., *Parliamentary History of England* (London: Bagshaw, 1806), vol. 1, cols. 1153–56.

55. Gardiner, *History*, 2:230–48; Bowen, *Lion and Throne*, 349–50; Charles Blitzer, ed., *The Commonwealth of England* (New York: Putnam's Sons, 1963), xiv–xv; and John D. Eusden, *Puritans, Lawyers and Politics in Early Seventeenth-Century England* (1958; reprint, Hamden, Conn.: Archon Books, 1968), 62–63, 83. Thomas L. Moir has revised the standard view and argued that the breakdown of the Addled Parliament was brought about by a failure in leadership on the part of supporters of the crown. See his *The Addled Parliament of 1614* (Oxford: Clarendon Press, 1958), 58–59. However, my emphasis will be on how the Addled Parliament was *perceived* by contemporaries.

56. Cobbett, *Parliamentary History*, vol. 1, col. 1156.

57. *Middlesex County Records Old Series Vol. II 1603–25*, ed. John Cordy Jeaffreson (1887; reprint, Greater London Council, 1974), 64–65, 77, 81, 83, 85.

58. Bowen, *Lion and Throne*, 350; Gardiner, *History*, 2:265–69.

59. Hastings Lyon and Herman Block, *Edward Coke: Oracle of the Law* (New York: Houghton Mifflin, 1929), 177–79.

60. Alfred Beasley, *The History of Banbury* (London: Nichols & Son [1841]), 157–60; and R. Chambers, *The Book of Days* (London: Chambers, 1886), 2:316.

61. See, for example, Stockwood's sermon, n. 27 above; the many examples summarized in the first part of Thompson's *Controversy*; and of course William Prynne's compilation of all earlier arguments in *Histrio-Mastix*. The Puritan "argument from paganism" and Anglican responses will be discussed in more detail in chap. 5. In arguing for the pagan origins of holiday customs, the Puritans were correct in many cases.

62. Thomas Fuller, *The Church History of Britain* (London, 1655), Book X, pp. 76–77.

63. See, in particular, Rankins, *Mirrour of Monsters*, fols. 2–4.

64. For St. Bartholmew, see Jacobus de Voragine, *The Golden Legend*, trans. Granger Ryan and Helmut Ripperger (New York: Longmans, Green, 1941), 479–83; and on the Puritan abolition of history, Boyd M. Berry's fine discussion in *Process of Speech: Puritan Religious Writing and Paradise Lost* (Baltimore: John Hopkins Univ. Press, 1976), 126.

65. Stow, *Survey of London*, 1:74.

66. John Pettingall, *"Of the Courts of* Pypowder," *Archaeologia*, 2d. ed. vol. 1 (London: Society of Antiquaries of London, 1779), 191–204.

67. *Basilikon Doron*, in *James*, 19–21.

68. See Blissett, *A Celebration of Ben Jonson*, 91; Thayer, *Ben Jonson*, 144–45; and for the tobacco project, *CSPD James I*, 9:214 (December? 1613).

69. Barish, *Language of Prose Comedy*, 204–9.

70. Cope, *"Bartholomew Fair* as Blasphemy," 129–30.

71. I[ohn] G[reen], *Refutation of the Apology,* 58.

72. S. Schoenbaum, *William Shakespeare: A Documentary Life* (New York: Oxford Univ. Press, 1975), 195–96.

73. *Book of Common Prayer* (1613–1614), n.p. When the biblical text is given in the prayerbook, I have cited it from that source; if only chapter and verse references are given in the prayerbook, I have cited the passage from the Cambridge Pitt Brevier edition of the King James Bible, since the King James translation was shortly to become the official text for use with the prayer book. There are several other interesting parallels between the liturgy for St. Bartholomew's and Jonson's play; I have mentioned only those most germaine to our discussion here.

74. Sir Roy Strong, *Splendour at Court: Renaissance Spectacle and Illusion* (London: Weidenfeld & Nicholson, 1973), 73–76 and 218.

75. Little, *Religion, Order and Law,* 186–202 (note 51 above). Of course Coke himself had been removed from his post as Chief Justice of Common Pleas in 1613.

76. Schoenbaum, *Shakespeare,* 227; Chambers, *Elizabethan Stage,* 2:423. However, the rumor was almost certainly false.

77. Parkinson, ed., Introduction to I. G.'s *Refutation,* p. iv.

78. H[enry] Ramsay, "Vpon the Death of Beniamin Iohnson" In *Ionsonvs Virbivs: or, The Memorie of Ben: Johnson Revived* (London, 1638), 60–61. The poem is reprinted with minor variations in *Jonson,* 11:471–72. For other examples of contemporary interpretations of the work, see Richard Brome's *The Weeding of the Covent–Garden* in *Five new Playes* (London, 1659) which, as Jackson Cope remarks on p. 128n. of *"Bartholomew Fair* as Blasphemy," refers to *Bartholomew Fair* as a study in arbitrary authority; and Morley, *Memoirs,* 45 and ff., for an account of the political pamphlets.

Chapter III

1. *Jonson,* 7:83. See also Jonathan Goldberg, *James I and the Politics of Literature* (Baltimore: John Hopkins Univ. Press, 1983), 50–54; and Graham Parry's general discussion in *The Golden Age Restor'd: The Culture of the Stuart Court, 1603–42* (New York: St. Martin's Press, 1981), 1–9.

2. Samuel R. Gardiner, *History of England from the Accession of James I to the Outbreak of the Civil War,* vol. 2, 3d ed. (London: Longmans, Green, 1889), 104–11.

3. Enid Welsford, *The Court Masque: A Study in the Relationship between Poetry and the Revels* (Cambridge: Cambridge Univ. Press, 1927), 203.

4. *James,* 326, 331, 333, 337.

5. *James,* 343–44. See also the proclamations for 1603, 1605, 1607, 1611, and 1615 in James F. Larkin and Paul L. Hughes, eds., *Stuart Royal Proclamations Vol. I: Royal Proclamations of King James I 1603–1625* (Oxford: Clarendon Press, 1973), 21–22, 47–48, 171–75, 193–94, 269–71, and 356–58. There had also been proclamations against new building issued at the end of Queen Elizabeth's reign. Contemporaries seem generally not to have perceived Lon-

don's phenomenal population growth as irreversible, a new historical development with which they would have to come to terms. See Robert Ashton, *The City and the Court, 1603–1643* (Cambridge: Cambridge Univ. Press, 1979), 168–71; and for general background, Roger Finlay, *Population and Metropolis: The Demography of London, 1580–1650* (Cambridge: Cambridge Univ. Press, 1981).

6. *James*, 343.

7. *James*, 343-44.

8. Stephen Orgel, *The Illusion of Power* (Berkeley: Univ. of California Press, 1975), 49–50. Orgel dates the shift to 1616, but on the basis of my reading in "City Metal and Country Mettle: The Occasion of Ben Jonson's *Golden Age Restored*," in *Pageantry in the Shakespearean Theatre*, ed. David M. Bergeron (Athens, Ga.: Univ. of Georgia Press, 1985), 26–47, I have suggested that, for Jonson at least, the shift comes about in 1614.

9. Welsford, *The Court Masque*, 199–203.

10. On building and the ostentatious display of wealth see Lawrence Stone, *The Crisis of the Aristocracy 1558–1641* (Oxford: Clarendon, 1965), 184–88, 547–89; and J. Alfred Gotch's survey in *The Growth of the English House: A Short History of Its Architectural Development from 1100 to 1800* (London: Batsford, 1909), 205–20.

11. See *Masques*, 245n, 489–90nn; and John C. Meagher, *Method and Meaning in Jonson's Masques* (Notre Dame: Notre Dame Univ. Press, 1966), 77–79.

12. See Allan H. Gilbert's discussion in *The Symbolic Persons in the Masques of Ben Jonson* (Durham, N.C.: Duke Univ. Press, 1948), 132–43.

13. For responses to the work see G. E. Bentley, *The Jacobean and Caroline Stage*, 7 vols. (Oxford: Clarendon, 1941–68), 4:639; *Jonson*, 7:433; and Gilbert, *Symbolic Persons*, 24.

14. Quoted in Welsford, *The Court Masque*, 38–39 from Harleian Ms. 247; and Mary Sullivan, *The Court Masques of James I* (New York: Putnam, 1913), 7n.

15. On the decline of civic pageantry and its causes, see David M. Bergeron, *English Civic Pageantry 1558–1642* (London: Edward Arnold, 1971), 2–5, 33–105; and for earlier Tudor pageantry, Sydney Anglo, *Spectacle, Pageantry, and Early Tudor Policy* (Oxford: Clarendon, 1969); and Thomas Fiddian Reddaway, "London and the Court in Elizabethan England," *Shakespeare Survey* 17 (1964):3–12.

16. Sullivan, *Court Masques of James I*, 92, 153–54. On strains in the relationship more generally, see Robert Ashton, *The Crown and the Money Market: 1603–1640* (Oxford: Clarendon, 1960); and his *The City and the Court*.

17. *James*, 328.

18. *James*, 27 and 274; See also Appendix C, which catalogues James's stated opinions of the Puritans, pp. xc–xci.

19. See, for example, Nicholas Bownde's discussion in *The True Doctrine of the Sabbath*, 202–72; and for other representative discussions of Christmas and holiday behavior, Barnabe Googe, trans., *The Popish Kingdome* (1570; reprint, London: Chiswick Press, 1880), ed. Robert Charles Hope, fols. 55–58; John

Northbrooke, *A Treatise wherein Dicing, Dauncing, Vaine plaies or Enterludes . . . are reprooved* (London, 1579); and William Prynne's mammoth compilation in *Histrio-Mastix* (London, 1633), 21–24 and 753–83. For discussion of seventeenth-century Puritan opinion see W. B. Whitaker, *Sunday in Tudor and Stuart Times* (London: Houghton, 1933); and Christopher Hill, *Society and Puritanism in Pre-Revolutionary England*, 2d ed. (New York: Schocken, 1967), 124–218.

20. Prynne, *Histrio-Mastix*, 759.

21. *Selected Epistles of Gregory the Great*, trans. James Barmby in *A Select Library of Nicene and Post-Nicene Fathers*, 2d ser. vol. 13, pt. 2 (New York: Scribner, 1905), 84–85. The most available seventeenth-century source for the letter was Bede the Venerable, *The Historie of the Chvrch of England*, trans. Thomas Stapleton (St. Omers, 1622), Bk. I, chap. 30, pp. 144–45. Before that appeared, of course, Gregory could be read in Latin.

22. Prynne, *Histrio-Mastix*, 757. See also Bk. V of Polydore Vergil's *De rerum inventoribus*, a standard Puritan source available in a number of sixteenth- and seventeenth-century editions.

23. See C. R. Baskervill, "The Sources of Jonson's *Masque of Christmas* and *Love's Welcome at Welbeck*," *Modern Philology* 6 (1908):257–69; and R. J. E. Tiddy's background in *The Mummer's Play* (Oxford: Clarendon Press, 1923), 70–131.

24. Baskervill, "Jonson's *Masque of Christmas*," 261.

25. Tiddy, *Mummer's Play*, 71–74.

26. See T. M. Parrott, "Comedy in the Court Masque: A Study of Ben Jonson's Contribution," *Philological Quarterly* 20 (1941):428–41; and *Jonson*, 10:560. Jackson Cope has discussed *The Knight of the Burning Pestle* as a ritual drama structured upon maying festival practices; see his *The Theatre and the Dream: From Metaphor to Form in Renaissance Drama* (Baltimore: Johns Hopkins Univ. Press, 1973), 200–10. *The Vision of Delight* also has several very probable borrowings from Beaumont in Fant'sy's long tirade: "The world it runs on wheels" appears in act 5, scene 3 and a reference to the "pudding" and its two ends in act 1, scene 2.

27. See John Stow's complaints in *A Survey of London*, ed. C. L. Kingsford (Oxford: Clarendon Press, 1908), 1:84–95.

28. Jonas Barish, *Ben Jonson and the Language of Prose Comedy* (Cambridge, Mass: Harvard Univ. Press, 1967), 245.

29. For dating, see *Jonson*, 10:250–51; G. L. Kittredge, "King James I and *The Devil Is an Ass*," *Modern Philology* 9 (1911):195–209.

30. For a defense of the play, see Larry S. Champion, *Ben Jonson's 'Dotages': A Reconsideration of the Late Plays* (Lexington, Ky.: Univ. of Kentucky Press, 1967), 25–32; and for other useful criticism, C. G. Thayer, *Ben Jonson: Studies in the Plays* (Norman, Okla.: Univ. of Oklahoma Press, 1963), 159–73; Brian Gibbons, *Jacobean City Comedy: A Study of Satiric Plays by Jonson, Marston and Middleton* (London: Rupert Hart-Davis, 1968), 89–90 and 189–97; and Alan C. Dessen, *Jonson's Moral Comedy* (Evanston, Ill.: Northwestern Univ. Press, 1971), 221–35. For discussion of the play in its contemporary context, see also

L. C. Knights, *Drama and Society in the Age of Jonson* (London: Chatto & Windus, 1937), 210–18.

31. All subsequent quotations from *The Devil Is an Ass* will be from *Jonson*, vol. 6, still the most readily available edition of the play, and cited by page number in the text. I am also strongly indebted to the copious annotation in W. S. Johnson's edition, *The Devil Is an Ass,* Yale Studies in English, 29 (New York: Henry Holt, 1905); and Maurice Hussey's edition, *The Divell is an Asse* (London: Univ. Tutorial Press, 1967).

32. Quoted in Johnson, *The Devil Is an Ass,* 163 from Samuel Butler's "Character of a Fantastic" and from Thomas Fuller. As Johnson points out, the use of the metaphor was common.

33. Mikhail Bakhtin, *Rabelais and His World,* trans. Helene Iswolsky (Cambridge, Mass.: MIT Press, 1968), 393.

34. Johnson, *The Devil Is an Ass,* p. xix.

35. See Samuel R. Gardiner, *History of England from the Accession of James I to the Outbreak of the Civil War,* vol. 2, 3d ed. (London: Longmans, Green, 1889), 343; T. B. Howell, ed., *A Complete Collection of State Trials, Vol. II: 1603–27* (London: Hansard, 1816), cols. 932–36; and Beatrice White, *Cast of Ravens: The Strange Case of Sir Thomas Overbury* (London: John Murray, 1965). Contemporary accounts of Coke's speech vary somewhat. See *TRUTH Brovght to Light by Time* (London, 1651), 140; and *The Egerton Papers,* ed. J. Payne Collier (London: John Boyer Nichols, for the Camden Society, 1840), 472–73.

36. *Jonson,* 10:224–25; and *CSPD James I,* 9:329 (14 November 1615).

37. *Analytical Index to . . . the Remembrancia . . . A.D. 1579–1664* (London: E. J. Francis, 1878), 269. For the witchcraft law see Edward Coke, *The Third Part of the Institutes,* 6th ed. (London: for Thomas Basset, 1680), chap. 6, pp. 44–47; and for the canon, *Constitvtions and Canons Ecclesiasticall . . .* (London, 1612), Canon 72, sig. I_2.

38. Kittredge, "King James I and *The Devil Is an Ass,*" 196–202.

39. *Chamberlain,* 2:26.

40. Coke's dismissal and James's speech in the Star Chamber grew out of the judicial defiance of James in connection with the Case of Commendams. See Catherine Drinker Bowen, *The Lion and the Throne: The Life and Times of Edward Coke* (Boston: Little Brown, 1957), 358–90. Along with Coke, Winch had been one of the judges who defied the king; however, all but Coke eventually backed down (see Bowen's list, p. 371). Crew had worked closely with Coke in the Overbury trials: see the accounts throughout *TRUTH Brovght to Light*; Kittredge, "King James I and *The Devil Is an Ass,*" 203; and for Crew as a substitute for Coke, the list of itinerant justices in J. S. Cockburn, *A History of English Assizes, 1558–1714* (Cambridge: Cambridge Univ. Press, 1972), 228, 269, and 283n.

41. Coke had helped draft the 1604 statute increasing the penalties for witchcraft and related activities like conjuring. Between that year and 1616 several books purporting to establish reliable criteria for the detection of witches had been dedicated to him. See, for example, William Perkins, *A Discovrse of the*

Damned Art of Witchcraft (Cambridge, 1610), which was dedicated to Coke by Thomas Pickering, who saw it through the press; and John Cotta, *The Triall of Witch-craft* (London, 1616). The quotation about the Assizes is from Thomas Cooper, *The Mystery of Witchcraft* (1617), p. 15, as quoted in Alan Mcfarlane, *Witchcraft in Tudor and Stuart England* (New York: Harper & Row, 1970), 62. On the intensity of convictions see Macfarlane, chap. 3; and C. L'Estrange Ewen, *Witch Hunting and Witch Trials* (London: Kegan Paul, 1929), 100. At least some magistrates became so enamored of their success against the netherworld that they commissioned published accounts of the witch trials over which they had presided. See, for example, Thomas Potts, *The Wonderfvll Discoverie of Witches in the Covntie of Lancaster* (London, 1613), especially Potts' dedicatory epistle which states that the judges celebrated in the work had asked him to write it. At the end of the book, Potts apologizes that he has been at liberty to write only what the judges told him to.

42. Although *Daemonologie* may appear credulous to us, the book was aimed in general against overgullibility and haste in the prosecution of accused witches. Part of James's purpose in publishing the treatise in 1597 had been to impose some order and measure upon the courts and commissions of Scotland, where witch-hunting had become a mania associated with the Presbyterians and carried out in defiance of the authority of the crown. The same year he published *Daemonologie,* James checked prosecutions by revoking all the Scottish commissions for witchcraft. For James's growing skepticism and his activity to stem witchcraft trials, see the highly favorable account in G. L. Kittredge's pamphlet, *English Witchcraft and James the First* (New York: Macmillan, 1912), 5; Thomas Fuller, *The Church History of Britain* (London, 1655), Book 10, p. 74; Francis Osborn, *A Miscellany of Sundry Essayes, Paradoxes, and Problematicall Discourses* (London: John Grismond, 1659), 4–5, 8 (Osborn is quoted in my text); and Harold Spencer Scott, ed., *The Journal of Sir Roger Wilbraham . . . 1593–1616,* The Camden Miscellany (London: Camden Soc., 1902), 10:69–70.

43. Kittredge, "King James," 206–207.

44. Winch owed his eminence to Sir Francis Bacon, whose protégé he had been; he had done the king useful service in subduing the Irish Parliament but had than taken Coke's part against Bacon and the king on the issue of prerogative. See *Acts of the Privy Council of England, 1613–14* (London: His Majesty's Stationery Office, 1921), 174–75, 188–90.

45. *The Merry Devil of Edmonton, 1608* ed. William Amos Abrams, (Durham, N.C.: Duke Univ. Press, 1942), 5. Abrams argues (pp. 22–23 and 72–103) for Dekker's authorship of the play, but Fredson Bowers rejects the work from his edition, *The Dramatic Works of Thomas Dekker,* 4 vols. (Cambridge: Cambridge Univ. Press, 1953–61).

46. *The Merry Devil,* 115.

47. *The Merry Devil,* 126–27.

48. See Frederick O. Waage, *Thomas Dekker's Pamphlets, 1603–1609, and Jacobean Popular Literature,* Salzburg Studies in English Literature: Elizabethan

and Renaissance Studies, no. 53 and 54 (Salzburg: Institut für Englische Sprache und Literatur, 1977).

49. *Dekker,* 113, 119–20.

50. Dekker spent at least some of the period in prison for debt. See G. E. Bentley, *The Jacobean and Caroline Stage,* vol. 3 (Oxford: Clarendon, 1956), 243. It is at least possible, however, that his silence may have been lengthened by government intervention to halt his increasing outspokenness against James I.

51. See Harold G. Fox, *Monopolies and Patents: A Study of the History and Fortune of the Patent Monopoly,* University of Toronto Legal Series, ed. W. P. M. Kennedy, Extra Volume (Toronto: Univ. of Toronto Press, 1947), 57–63, 161–89. Fox defends James's policies in support of monopolies against seventeenth-century and modern criticism on the grounds that the system was crucial in developing English trade and industry. Joan Thirsk takes the same positive position in *Economic Policy and Projects: The Development of a Consumer Society in Early Modern England* (Oxford: Clarendon Press, 1978).

52. *CSPD James I* 9:251 (11 August 1614). I have checked this reference against the Docquet but have not determined whether the monopoly was actually put into effect.

53. For the three Roberts, see *Chamberlain,* 1:510n, 626.

54. See Fox, *Monopolies,* 80–106. I have quoted from the second edition, entitled *A Declaration of His Maiesties Royall pleasure, in what sort He thinketh fit to enlarge, Or reserue Himselfe in matter of bountie* (London, 1619), 21.

55. Fox, *Monopolies,* 184 passim.

56. *Jonson,* 6:215; 10:241–42. For earlier evidence of James's views see Helena Mennie Shire, *Song, Dance and Poetry of the Court of Scotland under King James VI* (Cambridge: Cambridge Univ. Press, 1969), 98.

57. Howell, ed., *State Trials,* cols. 785–862; Wallace Notestein, *A History of Witchcraft in England from 1558 to 1718* (Washington: American Historical Society, 1911), 232–34; Hastings Lyon and Herman Block, *Edward Coke: Oracle of the Law* (New York: Houghton Mifflin, 1929), 233–34; and *Chamberlain,* 2:14 (6 July 1616), and 28–29 (26 October 1616).

58. Johnson, ed., *The Devil Is an Ass,* p. xviii.

59. Bentley, *Jacobean and Caroline Stage,* 6:616. Nearly every commentator on the play has offered some theory about the "accusation": see, for example, Champion, *Dotages,* 25–26 (note 30 above); Johnson, ed., *The Devil Is an Ass,* p. lxii; and *Jonson,* 1:169, 2:151–53.

Chapter IV

1. See Dale B. J. Randall, *Jonson's Gypsies Unmasked: Background and Theme of "The Gypsies Metamorphos'd"* (Durham, N.C.: Duke Univ. Press, 1975).

2. I am omitting consideration of the *Book of Sports* motifs in other late Jonsonian works on the grounds that they have been abundantly noticed, though not from the perspective suggested here. Readers can readily make connections on the basis of the material already offered. Jonson's masques for James during the 1620s centered on foreign policy. See Sara Pearl's interpretive

survey, "Sounding to Present Occasions: Jonson's Masques of 1620–5," in *The Court Masque*, ed. David Lindley (Dover, N.H.: Manchester Univ. Press, 1984), 60–77. Useful material on sports and pastimes in Jonson's later works is to be found in Alice S. Miskimin, "Ben Jonson and Captain Cox: Elizabethan Gothic Reconsidered," *Renaissance Drama*, n. s. 8 (1977):173–202; Anne Barton's invaluable *Ben Jonson, Dramatist* (Cambridge: Cambridge Univ. Press, 1984), 237–371, which incorporates earlier essays on Jonson's late works; Douglas Duncan, "A Guide to 'The New Inn,'" *Essays in Criticism* 20 (1970):311–26; Devra Rowland Kifer, "*The Staple of News:* Jonson's Festive Comedy," *Studies in English Literature, 1500–1900* 12 (1972):329–44; and C. G. Thayer, *Ben Jonson: Studies in the Plays* (Norman, Oklahoma: Univ. of Oklahoma Press, 1963), 203–32.

3. See, for example, Graham Parry, *Golden Age Restor'd: The Culture of the Stuart Court, 1603–42* (New York: St. Martin's Press, 1981), 184–229; Peter Thomas's essay "Charles I of England: The Tragedy of Absolutism," in A. G. Dickens, ed., *The Courts of Europe: Politics, Patronage, and Royalty 1400–1800* (London: Thames and Hudson, 1977), 191–211; Jennifer Chibnall, "'To that Secure Fix'd State': The Function of the Caroline Masque Form"; and Helen Cooper, "Location and Meaning in Masque, Morality, and Royal Entertainment," on the masque and the displacement of landscape in Lindley, *Court Masque*, 78–93 and 135–48.

4. William Sanderson, *A Compleat History of the Lives and Reigns of Mary Queen of Scotland, and of her Son and Successor, James* (London, 1656), 450. See also G. P. V. Akrigg, *Jacobean Pageant or the the Court of King James I* (Cambridge, Mass.: Harvard Univ. Press, 1962), 261; and Menna Prestwich, "English Politics and Administration 1603–1625" in *The Reign of James VI and I*, ed. Alan G. R. Smith (London: Macmillan, 1973), 140–159.

5. See William McElwee, *The Wisest Fool in Christendom* (New York: Faber & Faber, 1958), 238; Akrigg, *Jacobean Pageant*, 261; *Chamberlain*, 2:42; and Sanderson, *Compleat History*, 451.

6. *Chamberlain*, 2:82.

7. See Joseph Hall, *The Collected Poems*, ed. A. Davenport (Liverpool: Liverpool Univ. Press, 1949), xxii–xxiii.

8. Gordon Donaldson, "The Scottish Church, 1567–1625," in Smith, *The Reign of James VI and I*, 40–56.

9. *James*, 18.

10. See Nicholas Bownde, *The True Doctrine of the Sabbath* (London, 1606), 263–68. On Bownde's influence and the Sabbatarian controversy in general, see Christopher Hill, *Society and Puritanism in Pre-Revolutionary England*, 2d ed. (New York: Schocken, 1967), 168–94; J. Sears McGee's very helpful study *The Godly Man in Stuart England: Anglicans, Puritans, and the Two Tables, 1620–1670* (New Haven: Yale Univ. Press, 1976); and for a balanced contemporary view, Thomas Fuller, *The Church History of Britain* (London, 1655), Bk. 10.

11. James F. Larkin and Paul L. Hughes, eds., *Stuart Royal Proclamations Vol. I: Royal Proclamations of King James I 1603–1625* (Oxford: Clarendon Press, 1973), 369–71.

12. Arthur Wilson, *The History of Great Britain, Being the Life and Reign of King Iames the First* (London, 1653), 104; Sanderson, *Compleat History,* 459.

13. L. E. Kostner, ed., *The Poetical Works of William Drummond of Hawthornden* (1856; reprint, New York: Haskell House, 1968), 1:139–53.

14. Quoted in David M. Bergeron, *English Civic Pageantry 1558–1642* (London: Edward Arnold, 1971), 103. As we noted earlier, James himself was not personally fond of participating in civic pageantry but probably still found its omission objectionable.

15. Quoted in Hill, *Society and Puritanism,* 191.

16. Hill, *Society and Puritanism,* 189; John Barwick, *A Summarie Account of the Holy Life and Happy Death of . . . Thomas Late Lord Bishop of Dureseme* (London, 1660), 80. Barwick's account he claims to have taken directly from Morton; it is sufficiently corroborated by other seventeenth-century sources to be basically trustworthy. Morton was also a strong supporter of ecclesiastical ceremony; he had just published, in opposition to Lancashire nonconformists, a defense of the surplice, crossing at baptism, and the use of rings in marriage.

17. Barwick, *Bishop of Dureseme,* 80–81.

18. *The Kings Maiesties Declaration to His Subjects, concerning lawfull Sports to be vsed* (London, 1618), 1–7.

19. Wilson, *History of Great Britain,* 105–6.

20. On James's attitudes and the disastrously polarizing effects of the *Book of Sports,* especially in the next reign, see Hill, *Society and Puritanism,* 194–206; and McGee, *Godly Man,* chaps. 3 and 6, pp. 68–113 and 235–58.

21. Quoted from Alexander Ross, *Mystagogus Poeticus* (London, 1647), in Earl Miner, *The Cavalier Mode from Jonson to Cotton* (Princeton: Princeton Univ. Press, 1971), 29. On Hercules and his iconography see Christopher Whitfield, ed., *Robert Dover and the Cotswold Games: Annalia Dubrensia,* (Eversham, Worcestershire: The Journal Press, 1962), 96, 102 and 103n; Raymond Waddington, *The Mind's Empire: Myth and Form in George Chapman's Narrative Poems* (Baltimore: The Johns Hopkins Univ. Press, 1974), 165–66; Jackson Cope, *The Theatre and the Dream: From Metaphor to Form in Renaissance Drama* (Baltimore: Johns Hopkins Univ. Press, 1973), 37; Jeffrey Shulman, "At the Crossroads of Myth: The Hermeneutics of Hercules from Ovid to Shakespeare," *English Literary History* 50 (1983):83–105; and, for studies of *Pleasure Reconciled to Virtue* in particular, Stephen Orgel, *The Jonsonian Masque* (Cambridge, Mass.: Harvard Univ. Press, 1967), chap. 8; W. Todd Furniss, "Ben Jonson's Masques," in *Three Studies in the Renaissance: Sidney, Jonson, Milton* (1958; reprint, Hamden, Conn.: Archon Books, 1969), 168–76; and Richard S. Peterson, "The Iconography of Jonson's *Pleasure Reconciled to Virtue,*" *The Journal of Medieval and Renaissance Studies* 5 (1975):123–51.

22. "The 1603 Speech before Parliament," *James,* 274; see also Appendix C, pp. xc–xci.

23. See Chamberlain's comments, *Chamberlain,* 2:333; for masque performances and their diplomatic significance, Mary Sullivan, *The Court Masques of James I* (New York: Putnam, 1913), 2–109.

24. See Orgel, *Jonsonian Masque,* 168.

25. *Inigo,* 1:283. Further quotations from Busino will be from *Inigo,* 1:253–54. Orgel assumes that Busino was mistaken and that this transformation came at the end of Mercury's speech, *Jonsonian Masque,* 174; Peterson, "Iconography of *Pleasure Reconciled to Virtue,*" follows Busino, 127. In either case, the transformation would have had the same basic meaning.

26. See Ernst Kantorowicz, *The King's Two Bodies: A Study in Mediaeval Political Theology* (Princeton: Princeton Univ. Press, 1957), chap. 1. Furniss, "Ben Jonson's Masques," 113, has argued that James held three roles in each masque Jonson wrote for presentation before him: a role in the story, as an example of kingship, and as James, King of England. Surely this division between the king as character in a story and the king as exemplar of kingship is based on the Tudor and Stuart commonplace of the king's two bodies.

27. Some of the traditions surrounding Flora and May Day will be discussed in the next chapter.

28. Peterson, "Iconography of *Pleasure Reconciled to Virtue,*" 127–29.

29. "The 1607 Speech before Parliament," *James,* 291.

30. Orgel, *Jonsonian Masque,* 175; see also Furniss, "Ben Jonson's Masques," 107.

31. My evidence, however, dates from later. A ballad purporting to be an "Exact Description" of the opening of Parliament in 1640 notes that the bishops rode in procession "Each one in's Scarlet gowne and hood," *Cavalier and Puritan: Ballads and Broadsides Illustrating the Period of the Great Rebellion 1640–1660,* ed. Hyder E. Rollins (New York: New York Univ. Press, 1923), 80.

32. See *Inigo,* 1:49–75; Willa McClung Evans, *Henry Lawes: Musician and Friend of Poets* (New York: MLA, 1941), 120–137, for a description of "liturgical" masques and plays staged before Charles, some of them arranged by Archbishop Laud himself. See also chap. 7 for a discussion of Anglican Hermeticism in the masque.

33. For Calvin's opinion, see his *Trois traités,* ed. Albert-Marie Schmidt (Paris, 1934), 133. The idea was in fact a Reformation commonplace, to be found even in Luther; see his *Works,* ed. Henry Eyster Jacobs et al. (Philadelphia: A. J. Holman, 1915–32), 4:380–81.

34. See Busino's commentary and Peterson's suggestion, "Iconography of *Pleasure Reconciled to Virtue,*" 132.

35. See, in addition to Busino's observations, other commentary on the masque and atmosphere at court in the introduction to *Masques,* 30–31; *Chamberlain,* 2:121.

36. *Chamberlain,* 2:55–56.

37. Quoted from Francis Osborn in Robert Ashton, *James I by His Contemporaries* (London: Hutchinson, 1969), 232–33.

38. *Chamberlain,* 2:56; Wilson, *History of Great Britain,* 94.

39. *CSPD James I,* 9:494 (7 November 1617); 495–96 (November ? 1617); 501 (6 and 7 December 1617); and 512 (10 January 1618); see also Prestwich in Smith, *The Reign of James VI and I,* 153.

40. *Chamberlain,* 2:127.

41. *James,* 43–44

42. Edward Hyde, Earl of Clarendon, *The History of the Rebellion,* ed. W. Dunn Macray (Oxford: Clarendon Press, 1888), 1:12.

43. Barwick, *Bishop of Dureseme,* 80.

44. Johnson, ed., *The Devil Is an Ass,* Yale Studies in English, 29 (New York: Henry Holt, 1905), p. lxxii.

45. Peterson, "Iconography of *Pleasure Reconciled to Virtue,"* 124, argues that Jonson did have the myths in mind, but he was nevertheless careful to disassociate Hercules from the drunkards in the masque. Jonson creates the possibility of a connection between the well-known weaknesses of Hercules and of James I but leaves the actual drawing of the parallel to the fertile brains of his audience. For the countertradition associating Hercules with foolery and vice, see Shulman, "Crossroads of Myth."

46. For the progress itself and its ecclesiastical implications see Sir Roy Strong, *Splendor at Court: Renaissance Spectacle and Illusion* (London: Weidenfeld & Nicholson, 1973), 233; H. R. Trevor-Roper, *Archbishop Laud 1573–1645,* 2d ed. (London: Macmillan, 1962), 136–42; *CSPD Charles I,* 5:249–50 (3 January 1632); 6:83 (2 June 1633); Samuel R. Gardiner, *History of England from the Accession of James I to the Outbreak of the Civil War,* vol. 7 (London: Longmans, Green, 1886), 274–98; and Conrad Russell, ed., *The Origins of the English Civil War* (New York: Barnes & Noble, 1973), 1–31 and the essays by Hawkins, Tyacke, Clifton, and Thomas.

47. Drummond, *Works,* 2:113–21.

48. *CSPD Charles I,* 6:85 (3 June 1633); and 93 (10 June 1633). In connection with the progress, Charles also revived his father's specialty of inquiring into witchcraft: see Wallace Notestein, "The Lancashire Witches and Charles I," in *A History of Witchcraft in England from 1588–1718* (Washington: American Historical Society, 1911), chap. 7, pp. 146–63.

49. John Nichols, *The Progresses and Public Processions of Queen Elizabeth* (London: John Nichols, 1823), 1:443–48; *Jonson,* 10:706–8. For Newcastle, Jonson, and Elizabethan nostalgia, see in particular Barton, *Ben Jonson,* chap. 14 (note 2 above); and for the Earl (later Duke) of Newcastle's devotion to popular pastimes, David Norbrook, *Poetry and Politics in the English Renaissance* (London: Routledge and K. Paul, 1984), 189; and Peter Stallybrass's "Carnival Contained," forthcoming in *English Literary Renaissance.* I am grateful to Mr. Stallybrass for sending me the essay in manuscript form.

50. *CSPD Charles I,* 6:231 (4 October 1633); 275 (5 November 1633); and, for the king's part in the affair, also, p. 41 (1 May 1633). Some of the documents postdate Jonson's play but are official followups on ordinances and policy measures of the previous year.

51. *CSPD Charles I,* 6:275–76 (5 November 1633). See also the definitive article on the Somerset events, Thomas G. Barnes, "County Politics and a Puritan Cause Célèbre: Somerset ChurchAles, 1633," *Transactions of the Royal Historical Soc.,* 5 ser., 9 (1959):103–22, which argues that the religious question became the focal point for all sorts of other county rivalries; William Holden Hutton, *The English Church from the Accession of Charles I to the Death of*

Anne, 1625–1714 (London: Macmillan, 1903), 107–9: and the "official" Laudian account in Peter Heylyn, *Cyprianus Anglicus* (London: for A. Seile, 1668) 255–58; Richardson's complaint is quoted from p. 257. In *Economic Problems of the Church from Archbishop Whitgift to the Long Parliament,* 2d ed. (Oxford: Clarendon Press, 1963), Christopher Hill discusses some of the reasons why increased church revenues were so important. Among other things, he notes (p. 184) that a major objection to the Laudian innovations was their costliness.

52. See in particular D. J. Gordon's analysis in *The Renaissance Imagination,* ed. Stephen Orgel (1975; reprint, Berkeley: Univ. of California Press, 1980), 77–101.

53. I am grateful to David Riggs for pointing out the association between the play's dialect and Somerset. His forthcoming intellectual biography of Jonson will make some of the same general points about the late entertainments and the *Book of Sports* as I do. It is, by now, pretty well agreed that Jonson's *Tale of a Tub* is indeed a late work, but its imbeddedness in topical issues of 1633 seems to me to offer definitive evidence. My brief discussion is particularly indebted to Barton, *Ben Jonson,* chap. 15; J. A. Bryant, *The Compassionate Satirist: Ben Jonson and His Imperfect World* (Athens, Ga.: Univ. of Georgia Press, 1972), 165–76; and Marchette Chute, *Ben Jonson of Westminster* (New York: E. P. Dutton, 1953), 330–33.

54. This observation has been made many times but most recently and convincingly by Barton, *Ben Jonson,* chap. 1.

55. See, for example, A. D. J. Macfarlane, *Witchcraft in Tudor and Stuart England* (New York: Harper & Row, 1970), 205–7; John Demos, *Entertaining Satan: Witchcraft and the Culture of Early New England* (New York: Oxford Univ. Press, 1982); and Sydney Anglo's critique in *The Damned Art: Essays in the Literature of Witchcraft,* ed. Sydney Anglo (London: Routledge and K. Paul, 1977), 1–31, 246; and Alan Macfarlane's essay "A Tudor Anthropologist: George Gifford's *Discourse and Dialogue,*" in Anglo, *Damned Art,* 140–55. My discussion of *The Sad Shepherd* is too brief to allow proper exploration of these fascinating possibilities. See also the treatment of the play in Barton, *Ben Jonson,* chap. 16; Thayer, *Ben Jonson: Studies in the Plays,* 247–66 (note 2 above); Robert E. Knoll, *Ben Jonson's Plays: An Introduction* (Lincoln: Univ. of Nebraska Press, 1964), 192–94; and Laurence Lerner, "Farewell, Rewards and Fairies: An Essay on *Comus,*" *Journal of English and Germanic Philology* 70 (1971):617–31, which is more enlightening on Jonson than on Milton.

56. See Frances Yates, *Astraea: The Imperial Theme in the Sixteenth Century* (London: Routledge & K. Paul, 1975), 100–109; and Larry S. Champion, *Ben Jonson's 'Dotages': A Reconsideration of the Late Plays* (Lexington, Ky.: Univ. of Kentucky Press, 1967), 137–38.

Chapter V

1. *CSPD Charles I,* 6:350 (undated, 1633); and, for the judicial orders from Devonshire suppressing wakes, ales, and revelry, p. 351.

2. *Herrick,* 5. I must also record a strong debt to the fully annotated edition

of *The Complete Poetry of Robert Herrick*, ed. J. Max Patrick (1963; reprint, New York: Norton & Co., 1968).

The traditional view of Herrick's verse as charmingly naïve has, by now, been challenged from a number of quarters. The best studies to date of Herrick's political rhetoric are Claude J. Summers's "Herrick's Political Poetry: The Strategies of His Art," in *Trust to Good Verses: Herrick Tercentenary Essays*, ed. Roger B. Rollin and J. Max Patrick (Pittsburgh: Univ. of Pittsburgh Press, 1977), 171–83; the same author's "Herrick's Political Counterplots," *Studies in English Literature, 1500–1900*, 25 (1985):165–82; and Peter Stallybrass's "Carnival Contained," forthcoming in *English Literary Renaissance*, which cites my earlier "Herrick's *Hesperides* and the 'Proclamation made for May,'" *Studies in Philology* 76 (1979):49–74, on which the present chapter, though much revised, is based. Other useful and provocative studies to which my own work is indebted include Earl Miner, *The Cavalier Mode from Jonson to Cotton* (Princeton: Princeton Univ. Press, 1971); Roger B. Rollin, *Robert Herrick* (New York: Twayne, 1966); Robert H. Deming, *Ceremony and Art: Robert Herrick's Poetry* (The Hague: Mouton, 1974); A. Leigh DeNeef, *"This Poetic Liturgie": Robert Herrick's Ceremonial Mode* (Durham, N.C.: Duke Univ. Press, 1974); S. Musgrove, *The Universe of Robert Herrick*, Auckland University College Bulletin no. 38, English ser. no. 4 (1950; reprint, Auckland, 1967); A. B. Chambers, "Herrick and the Trans-shifting of Time," *Studies in Philology* 72 (1975):85–114; and Thomas R. Whitaker, "Herrick and the Fruits of the Garden," *ELH* 22 (1955):16–33.

3. See Jonson's *"Epigram on the Princes birth,"* Jonson, 8:237; Thomas Nabbes, "A Presentation Intended for the Prince his Highnesse on his Birtheday the 29 of May, 1638," in *The Springs Glorie* (London, 1638); fol. F1ʳ – G3ʳ and Herrick's own "A Pastorall upon the birth of Prince Charles, Presented to the King," which gracefully supports the theory of divine right by proposing for Charles a ceremony parallel to the Epiphany. Shepherds rejoice in the young prince born "Three days before the shutting in of May" and offer, instead of the Magi's gold, frankincense and myrrh, gifts more appropriate to the maying season—a garland, oaten pipes, and "Leaves dropping downe the honyed dew" (*Herrick*, 86).

4. Patrick, ed., *Complete Poetry*, 9–10; see also Miner, *Cavalier Mode*, 124, 160, passim.

5. This particular example comes from a hostile source, William Prynne's *Histrio-Mastix* (London, 1633), 241, marginal note. However, as we noted above in chap. 1, there are ample records documenting other similar instances. According to Prynne, Widdowes took as his sermon text Psalm 68:25: "The singers went before, the players on instruments followed after; among them were the damsels playing with timbrels."

6. On this point, I am indebted to S. Clark Hulse, "On Herrick's Nose," a paper presented at the Renaissance Society of America Conference in Los Angeles, March 1985, which argues that Herrick presents himself on his frontispiece as Ovid *redivivus*. My thanks for Hulse's kind willingness to let me read his article in manuscript.

7. See A. D. J. Macfarlane, *Witchcraft in Tudor and Stuart England* (New York: Harper & Row, 1970), 205–7; and for the the continuing debate, the sources cited above in n. 55 of chap. 4.

8. One standard way of reading the poem is to take "Incense" as itself a reference to prayer. However, Herrick takes care to separate the two, suggesting that the ritual action symbolizing the ascent of prayer to God is essential to the prayer's success. Laudians may well have used incense in Rogation Day processions, as they sometimes did in ecclesiastical ceremonies.

9. My discussion is strongly indebted to Keith Thomas, *Religion and the Decline of Magic* (1971; reprint, Harmondsworth, Middlesex: Penguin, 1973), chaps. 2, 3, and 19–22.

10. See Christopher Hill, *Society and Puritanism in Pre-Revolutionary England*, 2d ed. (New York: Schocken, 1967), chaps. 4–7, 124–297. Hill's emphasis on socioeconomic changes in their relation to Puritan thinking has been challenged from a number of quarters but has received new confirmation in David Zaret's *The Heavenly Contract: Ideology and Organization in Pre-Revolutionary Puritanism* (Chicago: Univ. of Chicago Press, 1985), which demonstrates convincingly how the "marketplace" language of covenant was spreading into the countryside along with the ideology of competitive commerce. See in particular Zaret's second chap., "Popular Dissent and Its Historical Preconditions," 24–60.

11. Cited from William Perkins in Perry Miller, *The New England Mind: The Seventeenth Century* (Cambridge, Mass.: Harvard Univ. Press, 1954), 86.

12. Richard Baxter, *A Saint or a Brute*, in *The Whole Works* (London, 1838), 2:728. Similar evocations of the insensibility of the "ungodly" recur throughout Baxter: see also *The Divine Appointment of the Lord's Day*, vol. 3; *The Christian Directory*, vol. 1; and *The Poor Man's Family Book*, vol. 4.

13. Raymond Williams, *The Country and the City* (1973; reprint, New York: Oxford Univ. Press, 1975), 33–34. John Bossy, "The Character of Elizabethan Catholicism," *Past and Present* no. 21 (April 1962), 39–57; and, for more extended investigation of this preindustrial "mentality," the other sources cited in chap. 1, n. 10.

14. See the notes to Patrick, ed., *Complete Poetry*, 142; and on Herrick's classicism, DeNeef, *Liturgie*, 51; Deming, *Ceremony and Art*, 48–49, 85–86, 147–57; and Chambers, "Trans-shifting," all cited in full in n. 2 above. The *locus classicus* for Herrick as a neo-pagan remains Cleanth Brooks, *The Well Wrought Urn* (New York: Harcourt, Brace & Co., 1947), chap. 4, pp. 62–73.

15. See Thomas, *Religion and the Decline of Magic*, 383–84; and John Aubrey, *Remaines of Gentilisme and Judaisme*, ed. James Britten (London: W. Satchell, 1881), 36, 83, 131, 142. My discussion of the final portion of the poem is indebted to Stallybrass, "Carnival Contained"; and to James Turner, *The Politics of Landscape* (Cambridge, Mass.: Harvard Univ. Press), 148–51. As Turner has noted, the Earl of Westmorland, to whom Herrick's poem is addressed, wrote a similar poem inviting his laborers to work and festivity.

16. On the problem of church revenue more generally, see Christopher Hill, *Economic Problems of the Church from Archbishop Whitgift to the Long Parlia-*

ment, 2d ed. (Oxford: Clarendon Press, 1963); and the other sources cited above in chap. 4, n. 51.

17. *Chamberlain*, 2:74 (10 May 1617).

18. John Stow, *A Survey of London*, ed. C. L. Kingsford (Oxford: Clarendon Press, 1908), 1:144; Phillip Stubbes, *The Anatomie of Abuses* (London 1583), fol. M3–M4ʳ.

19. Lactantius, *The Works*, trans. William Fletcher (Edinburgh: T. & T. Clark, 1871), 1:53–54; St. Augustine, *The City of God*, ed. Marcus Dods (New York: Hafner, 1948), 1:87. For the history of maygames in standard glossaries, see Hospinian, *De Origine, Progressv, Ceremoniis et Ritibvs . . . Libri Tres* (Tiguri, 1593), fols. 88–90; Rosinus, *Romarnorvm Antiqvitatvm Libri Decem* (Basel, 1583), 86–87, 198–99; and Gyraldi, *Historiae Deorum* in his *Opera Omnia* I (Basel, 1580), 40–41. The argument that English maygames actually stemmed from Roman and indigenous heathen custom usually cited the evidence provided by Pope Gregory the Great; see *Selected Epistles of Gregory the Great*, trans. James Barmby in *A Select Library of Nicene and Post-Nicene Fathers*, 2d ser., vol. 13, pt. 2 (New York: Scribner, 1905), 84–85. A source available in English that recapitulated Gregory was Bede the Venerable, *The Historie of the Chvrch of England*, trans. Thomas Stapleton (St. Omers, 1622), Bk. I, chap. 30, p. 144. On the connections between *pagani* (pagan peasants) and pagan survivals under Christianity see also Jacques Le Goff, *Time, Work, and Culture in the Middle Ages*, trans. Arthur Goldhammer (1980, reprint, Chicago: University of Chicago Press, 1982), 92. For Puritan statements of the "argument from paganism," see Thomas Hall, *Funebria Florae: The Downfall of May-Games* (London, 1660), 7 (cited in my text); and for earlier and fuller statements, Nicholas Bownde, *The True Doctrine of the Sabbath* (London, 1606), 268; Baxter, *Works*, 4:683; and especially Prynne's *Histrio-Mastix*, 233–35, 759–60.

20. For Puritan complaints about the rowdiness and promiscuity of the holiday, see Stubbes, *Anatomie*, fol. M3–M4ʳ; John Northbrooke, *A Treatise wherein Dicing, Daucing, Vaine Plaies or Enterludes . . . are Reprooved* (London, 1579), fol. 68ᵛ; Baxter, *The Divine Appointment of the Lord's Day*, in *Works*, 3:903–4. The same connection recurs in literature. Pearl, in *The Scarlet Letter* is a maychild; so is the bastard fathered by Lucio in Shakespeare's *Measure for Measure*.

21. *Pasquils Palinodia* (London, 1619), sig. B₃.

22. See Thomas Hobbes, *Leviathan Reprinted from the Edition of 1651*, introduction by W. G. Pogson Smith (Oxford: Clarendon Press, 1909), 517–18; *Pasquils Palinodia*, sig. B₂-C; and Hill, *Society and Puritanism*, 184n. As Hill points out (*Economic Problems of the Church*, 174–175), in Beaumont and Fletcher's *The Spanish Curate* (1622) the parson complains that local parishioners aren't marrying and begetting children often enough because they have had "Puritan hearts" and have "spurned at all pastimes."

23. In "Corinna's going a Maying," of course, even the idea that May Day procreation has to take place in the marriage bed is at least indirectly challenged, as will be noted below. On Herrick's intertwining of ritual and

sexuality, see also Peter Schwenger, "Herrick's Fairy State," *English Literary History* 46 (1979):35–55. Herrick's fairies also keep up pagan and Laudian ritual practices. See Daniel H. Woodward, "Herrick's Oberon Poems," *Journal of English and Germanic Philology* 64 (1965):270–84; and Deming, *Ceremony and Art*, 84–86.

24. Since Endymion Porter was a friend and patron of both Herrick and Robert Dover, he could have served as a link between the two men and their common interest. Herrick knew Porter already in the 1620s; indeed, Porter may have been the one responsible for Herrick's appointment as chaplain to the Duke of Buckingham for the Isle of Rhé expedition.

25. On ritualism in general in Herrick, see Deming, *Ceremony and Art;* DeNeef, *Liturgie;* Woodward, "Herrick's Oberon Poems"; and my *Childhood and Cultural Despair: A Theme and Variations in Seventeenth-Century Literature* (Pittsburgh: Univ. of Pittsburgh Press, 1978), 136–37.

26. John Cosin, *A Collection of Private Devotions*, ed. P. G. Stanwood (Oxford, Clarendon Press, 1967), 207–208.

27. For Laudian arguments in defense of the *Book of Sports*, see Peter Heylyn, *The History of the Sabbath* (London: 1636), Bk. 2, pp. 250–71; John Pocklington, *Sunday no Sabbath* (London, 1636), 37–39; and Gilbert Ironside, *Seven Qvestions of the Sabbath* (Oxford, 1637), 272–97. The interpretation of the Psalms is quoted from Thomas Shepherd's speech in defense of the *Book of Sports* before the 1621 Parliament, *Commons Debates 1621*, ed. Wallace Notestein, (New Haven: Yale Univ. Press, 1935), 2:82; the quotation immediately following is from Pocklington. As we will recall, Shepherd was ousted from Parliament for his violent impertinence; see chap. 1 above. An argument paralleling Shepherd's was, according to Heylyn, made in [John] Prideaux's *de Sabbato* (1625), which was republished in Heylyn's English translation as *The Doctrine of the Sabbath*, 2d ed. (London, 1634); see in particular p. 40. Contemporary scholars, sometimes writing under Laudian auspices, also anticipated modern classicists by refuting Lactantius's account of the corrupt origins of maygames. See Vossius, *De origine ac progressv Idololatriae* (Amsterdam, 1642), 91–94; and Henry Spelman, *Glossarium Archaiologicum* (London, 1664), 383–84. See also *BASILIKA: The Works of Charles I* (London, 1662), 1:181–87; and William Prynne's hostile account of the Laudian campaign in *Canterburies Doome* (London, 1646), 128–54, 504–7.

28. See *The Poems of Richard Corbett*, ed. J. A. W. Bennett and H. R. Trevor-Roper (Oxford: Clarendon Press, 1955), 49–52; also his satire against Puritan condemnation of the maypole (pp. 52–56). The editors' introduction presents Corbett as precisely the sort of Laudian who would have made it his business to revive "public mirth" in practice, not only in poetry. See also Richard Mountagu, *Appello Caesarem: A IVST APPEALE from Two Vniust Informers* (London, 1625), 274–75; and his *A Gagg for the new Gospell? NO: A New Gagg for An Old Goose* (London, 1624); Cosin, *Devotions*, 11 (note 26 above), and the editor's introduction, which describes the furor aroused in the 1629 Parliament by the ideas of Cosin and Mountagu. Charles I prorogued Parlia-

ment in 1629 at least in part to save the Arminians from censures being prepared against them. On the role of Arminian churchmen in exalting divine right and thereby helping to create political polarization, see Margaret Atwood Judson, *The Crisis of the Constitution* (1949; reprint, New York: Octagon, 1964), chap. 5, pp. 171–217; and John D. Eusden, *Puritans, Lawyers, and Politics in Early Seventeenth-Century England* (1958; reprint, Hamden, Conn.: Archon Books, 1968), 78–81. See also Hill, *Economic Problems of the Church*, 340–41; J. Sears McGee, *The Godly Man in Stuart England: Anglicans, Puritans, and the Two Tables, 1620–70* (New Haven: Yale Univ. Press, 1976), chaps. 3 and 6; and for Mountagu, Roland G. Usher, *The Reconstruction of the English Church* (New York: Appleton, 1910), 2:48.

29. *The Works of Robert Sanderson*, ed. William Jacobson (Oxford: Oxford Univ. Press, 1854), 1:229. For earlier statements, see Richard Hooker's *Of The Lawes of Ecclesiastical Politie* (London, 1611), Bks. 3–5; and Lancelot Andrewes' 1618 Easter sermon before James I in *XCVI Sermons* (London, 1629), 517–30. Conservatives who made such arguments did not always, however, use them to defend the *Book of Sports*. Andrewes was not at all one of its proponents; Sanderson was but took the moderate position that no one who felt scruples about the sports should feel obliged to participate, *Works*, 5:15–16.

30. On the controversy, see Cosin, *Devotions*, introduction, 76–81; and Peter Smart's attack on Cosin's innovations, *A Sermon Preached in the Cathedrall Chvrch of Durham* Iuly 7: 1628 (n.p., 1628), for which Smart was severely punished. See also Bownde, *True Doctrine of the Sabbath*, 110–17; and for other examples of Anglican defense, Miner, *Cavalier Mode*, 283; and the carol by William Austin (1626) reprinted in Norman Ault, ed., *Seventeenth-Century Lyrics*, 2d ed. (New York: William Sloane Associates, 1950), 31.

31. Baxter, *Works*, 3:904.

32. *Aubrey's Natural History of Wiltshire*, introduction by K. G. Ponting (1847; reprint, Trowbridge, Wiltshire: David & Charles Rpts., 1969), 73n. Maydew appears prominently in Herrick's "Pastorall" for Prince Charles, cited above n. 3.

33. *The Works of the Famous Antiquary, Polidore Virgil*, trans. John Langley (London, 1663), 191–95. See also Pope Gregory, *Selected Epistles*, 84.

34. For seventeenth-century interpretation of these festivals, see Thomas Godwin, *Moses and Aaron: Civil and Ecclesiastical Rites, vsed by the ancient Hebrews* (London, 1626), 144–46; and John Day, *Day's Festivals* (Oxford, 1615), sermon 4.

35. Stubbes, *Anatomie*, fol. M4.

36. I have used the 1632, 1633, and 1634 editions of the *Book of Common Prayer*. Quotations from the liturgies are given from the Cambridge Pitt Brevier edition of the King James Bible; the wording of the passages in the Geneva Bible is similar. May Day carols using motifs from the liturgy are collected in *The Oxford Book of Carols*, ed. Percy Dearmer et al. (London: Oxford Univ. Press, 1928), 98–103, carols no. 47–49. See also "A Huntingdonshire May-Day Song," *Notes and Queries* 3d ser., 9 (1866):388. The May carols have been

collected in many variants from wide areas of England. One of them is referred to in Shakespeare's *As You Like It* 5.3.25–28:

> This carol they began that hour,
>   With a hey, and a ho, and a hey nonino,
> How that a life was but a flower
>   In spring time . . . .

For other literary analogues, see Spenser's May Eclogue in *The Shepheardes Calender; The Knight of the Burning Pestle,* 5.1.175; and Peter Smalle, *Mans May or A Moneths minde* (London, 1615), sig. B₃.

37. See *The Merry Devil of Edmonton, 1608,* ed. W. H. Abrams (Durham, N.C.: Duke Univ. Press, 1942), discussed briefly in chap. 3 above. The play is steeped in May Day customs, including a romp in the forest. There are many other plays with a similar "Maying" structure: among them *As You Like It, A Midsummer Night's Dream,* and *The Knight of the Burning Pestle,* analyzed in Jackson Cope, *The Theatre and the Dream: From Metaphor to Form in Renaissance Drama* (Baltimore: Johns Hopkins Univ. Press, 1973), 204–10. In *Rabelais and His World,* tr. Helene Iswolsky (Cambridge, Mass.: MIT Press, 1968), 257–60, Mikhail Bakhtin notes a medieval analogue, Adam de la Halle's "The Play in the Bower" (*Jeu de la Feuillée*), dating from 1262.

In "Corinna" and these other works, part of the urgency of May Day marriage may relate to ecclesiastical prohibitions. Despite constant Puritan opposition, the Anglican Church still enforced the medieval prohibition of weddings during Lent and between the Sunday before Ascension Day and the Octave of Pentecost; see Thomas, *Religion and the Decline of Magic,* 741. Since Ascension Day varied from April 30 to June 3, falling usually in early or late May, most of that month was in fact unavailable for weddings—hence perhaps, the popularity of the Whitsun Bride-Ale. The last stanza of "Corinna," in addition to its larger meanings, could be interpreted as urging the young couples to "seize" May Day itself or a day immediately after it for marriage, on the grounds that if they delay, they will quite literally be required to "tarry"— not forever, but until the end of the proscribed period.

38. See *Day's Festivals,* 4th Sermon, "The Coming of the Holy Ghost"; Godwin, *Moses and Aaron,* 140, 147–48; the Homily for Whitsunday in *The Second Tome of Homilies* (London, 1623), 206–11; *The Fasti of Ovid,* trans. Henry T. Riley (London: H. G. Bohn, 1851), 165n; and the parallels noted in Aubrey, *Remains,* 16–34. The parallel between Herrick's "Herbe" and the use of herbs in Roman fertility cults was first pointed out to me by Linda Gottlieb in her unpublished master's essay "English Folk Sources for Robert Herrick's May-Poems," May 1973, University of Illinois at Chicago.

39. For the general liturgical and homiletic context, see *The Second Tome of Homilies,* First Homily for Rogation Week, 221–33; and the Lessons and Psalms Proper for Whitsunday and Ascension Day. The same ideas were expounded in sermons; see Andrewes, 11th Whitsunday Sermon, *XCVI Sermons,* 712–14. In some ecclesiastical pronouncements, the creationism of the

spring liturgies was assimilated to the monarch. Margaret Judson quotes John White's *Defence of the Way to the True Church* (London, 1634), 192: "Your Highnesse most happy government is the fountaine of our well-doing: when Princes maintain religion, and execute justice, punishing wicked men, and rewarding the godly, then they *come downe like raine upon the mowen grasse, and as showers that water the earth.*" This is much like Herrick's depiction of the Lord "raining" down blessing in "The Hock-cart."

40. [Henry Burton] *A Divine Tragedie Lately Acted, Or . . . Gods Judgements upon Sabbath-breakers* (n.p., 1636), 6. For earlier examples of May Day piety see Stow, *Survey of London*, 1:98 (note 18 above); and for more recent survivals, Cecil J. Sharp and Herbert C. MacIlwaine, *The Morris Book*, 2d ed. (London: Novello, 1912–24), 23–24. See also Thomas, *Religion and the Decline of Magic*, 83, on the subject of May Day morris dancing: "Between the two world wars an anthropologically-minded German professor asked an elderly member of a party of country mummers who had come to perform at an Oxford garden party whether women were ever allowed to take part. The reply was significant: 'Nay, sir, mumming don't be for the likes of them. There be plenty else for them that be flirty-like, but this here mumming be more like parson's work.'" This accords with the attitude of the elderly gentleman recorded in the Sussex anecdote at the beginning of chap. 1. On Maying as increasing the fertility of the crops, see Thomas, *Religion and the Decline of Magic*, 32–54; Thomas Hall, *Funebria Florae*, 8; and Henry Bourne, *Antiquitates Vulgares* (Newcastle: J. White, 1725), 202 (from which the quotation about "Fruits of the Earth" is taken).

41. Ault, ed., *Seventeenth-Century Lyrics*, 83; see also Nabbes, *The Springs Glorie*, fol. F–G3, in which May's entrance stops time. The same idea is intimated in the main masque of Jonson's *The Vision of Delight*.

42. See Herrick, "TO THE KING, Upon his comming with his Army into the West," 25; "TO THE QUEENE," 107; "The Poets Good Wishes for the Most Hopefull and Handsome Prince, the Duke of Yorke," 108; "A Pastorall sung to the King," 159, in which the failing of crops and feasts is tied to the separation of Charles I and Henrietta Maria; "The Bad Season Makes the Poet Sad," 214; "Farewell Frost, or welcome the Spring," 224; and "To Prince Charles upon his coming to Exeter," 254.

Chapter VI

1. See Bulstrode Whitelock's account of Prynne's entrapment by Laud, conveniently reprinted in *Inigo*, 2:539–45; *CSPD Charles I*, 6:524 (26 March 1634); the *Dictionary of National Biography* under "William Noy." For Prynne's view of dancing, pastorals, and the *Book of Sports*, see *Histrio-Mastix* (London, 1633), 241–54 and the unpaginated "Table" under *Women-Actors*; and *Canterburies Doome* (London, 1644), 128–54, 504–7.

2. Historians have long perceived a tie between the events surrounding Prynne's trial and punishment and Milton's masque. See, for example, Samuel Gardiner, *History of England from the Accession of James I to the Outbreak of the Civil*

War 1603–1642, vol. 7 (1886), 335–37; and H. R. Trevor-Roper, *Archbishop Laud, 1573–1645*, 2d ed. (London: Macmillan, 1962), 164. Trevor-Roper comments that *Comus* was written to dissociate the Puritan Milton from the Puritan Prynne.

For recent studies by literary scholars of Milton's political intent see John D. Cox, "Poetry and History in Milton's Country Masque," *English Literary History* 44 (1977):622–40, which argues that the masque supports what the historian Perez Zagorin has called the "Country Party"; Maryann Cale McGuire's *Milton's Puritan Masque* (Athens, Ga.: Univ. of Georgia Press, 1983), which covers some of the same ground as the present study but without taking Laudian policy into account; David Norbrook's fine article "The Reformation of the Masque," in *The Court Masque*, ed. David Lindley (Dover, N.H.: Manchester Univ. Press, 1984), 94–110, which influenced my own work in an earlier version which Norbrook was kind enough to share with me; and his *Poetry and Politics in the English Renaissance* (London: Routledge & Kegan Paul, 1984), which, like McGuire's book, appeared too late to influence the present discussion. There are, however, a number of ways in which Norbrook's discussion confirms my own analysis. My major point of difference is that while Norbrook shies away from the idea that Milton could have been criticizing contemporary church government, I make a case that he was doing just that. See in particular, Norbrook, *Poetry and Politics*, chaps. 9 and 10. There is also a new essay by John Creaser, " 'The Present Aid of This Occasion': The Setting of *Comus*," also in the Lindley volume, pp. 111–134; Creaser views the masque as much more royalist than I do, but he has made important suggestions that will be cited below. Finally, I must record a debt to Cedric Brown, who was gracious enough to send me proofs of his *John Milton's Aristocratic Entertainments* (Cambridge: Cambridge Univ. Press, 1985) so that I could cite it before my own book went to the press. There is also valuable work in manuscript, especially William S. Miller, Jr., The Mythography of Milton's *Comus*," Ph.D. diss., University of California at Berkeley, 1975, which, although I take issue with many of his conclusions, is a helpful and detailed study. My own study, "The Milieu of Milton's *Comus*: Judicial Reform at Ludlow and the Problem of Sexual Assault," *Criticism* 25 (1983):293–327, examines in detail one aspect of the masque's political occasion which proved too complex in its own right to be included here.

For recent studies of other aspects of the masque's occasion, see Hugh M. Richmond's discussion of *Comus* as a harvest masque in *The Christian Revolutionary: John Milton* (Berkeley: Univ. of California Press, 1974), 70, to which I am considerably indebted; James Taaffe, "Michaelmas, the 'Lawless Hour,' and the Occasion of Milton's *Comus*," *English Language Notes* 6 (1968–69):257–62; and Laurence Lerner, "Farewell, Rewards and Fairies: An Essay on *Comus*," *Journal of English and Germanic Philology* 70 (1971):617–31, which interprets the masque as enacting the death of popular medieval culture under the impact of Puritan ideals. Studies of the meaning of the masque for the Bridgewater family in particular are listed in n. 27 below.

Particularly useful studies of Milton's masque as a defense of the arts include

Franklin R. Baruch, "Milton's *Comus*: Skill, Virtue, and Henry Lawes," *Milton Studies* 5 (1973):289–308; Louis L. Martz, "The Music of *Comus*," in *Illustrious Evidence: Approaches to English Literature of the Early Seventeenth Century*, ed. Earl Miner (Berkeley: Univ. of California Press, 1975), 93–113 and, of course, Angus Fletcher, *The Transcendental Masque: An Essay on Milton's Comus* (Ithaca: Cornell Univ. Press, 1971); and John G. Demaray, *Milton and the Masque Tradition: The Early Poems, "Arcades," & Comus* (Cambridge, Mass.: Harvard Univ. Press, 1968).

Studies of *Comus* as an allegorical treatment of ecclesiastical affairs tend generally to read the Milton of the antiprelatical tracts back into the masque of 1634, which defeats our present endeavor to analyze the work in terms of its immediate political context. Nevertheless, Arthur Barker, *Milton and the Puritan Dilemma, 1641–1660* (1942; reprint, Toronto: Univ. of Toronto Press, 1964); and Alice-Lyle Scoufos, "The Mysteries in Milton's Masque," *Milton Studies*, 6 (1974):113–42, have proved particularly useful to me. More general studies to which I am particularly indebted include Stewart A. Baker, "Eros and the Three Shepherds of *Comus*," *Rice Univ. Studies: Studies in English* 61 (1975):13–26; Gale H. Carrithers, Jr., "Milton's Ludlow *Mask*: From Chaos to Community," *English Literary History* 33 (1966):23–42; John S. Diekhoff, ed., *A Maske at Ludlow: Essays on Milton's Comus* (Cleveland: Case Western Reserve Univ. Press, 1968); Georgia B. Christopher's important article "The Virginity of Faith: *Comus* as a Reformation Conceit," *English Literary History* 43 (1976):479–99; and Stanley Fish, "Problem Solving in *Comus*," in *Illustrious Evidence*, 115–31.

3. See the Yale edition of *The Complete Prose Works of John Milton*, ed. Don M. Wolfe (New Haven, 1953), 1:222, 266, 282, 588–89, 819–20. The "Song" is quoted from Merritt Hughes's edition of the *Complete Poems and Major Prose* (Indianapolis: Bobbs-Merrill, 1957), 41. References to the *Book of Sports* can be found in many of Milton's works. There is a useful survey in McGuire, *Milton's Puritan Masque*, 30 and ff; however, Milton almost always preserved a distinction between the pastimes as promoted in that document and the pastimes in and of themselves.

4. See, among many other discussions, Paul Reyher, *Les Masques anglais: étude sur les ballets et la vie de cour en Angleterre (1512–1640)* (Paris: Hachette, 1909), 205–16; and for Jonson and Ellesmere, *Jonson*, 1:180.

5. Entries for July 1633 in the Trial Books of the Council in the Marches of Wales, HEH EL 7564–74. Although not formally inaugurated as President, the Earl of Bridgewater was in residence at Ludlow that summer. The Trial Books also record numerous prosecutions for "breach of order" and other similar charges; some of these may also have been violations of the *Book of Sports*. For a summary of the Earl's duties as President of Wales, see Caroline A. J. Skeel, *The Council in the Marches of Wales*, Girton College Studies II (London: Hugh Rees, 1904), 272–74.

6. For Bridgewater as a royalist, see Gardiner, *History*, 7:335; and Creaser, "The Setting of *Comus*." For the Earl as a Puritan, see McGuire, *Milton's Puritan*

Masque; Cox, *"Poetry and History"*; and William Riley Parker, *Milton: A Biography* (Oxford: Clarendon, 1968), 2:792n42. By far the most useful account of the Earl's political career is Charles L. Hamilton, "The Earl of Bridgewater and the English Civil War," *Canadian Journal of History* 15 (1980):357–69. There is also a popular history of the family, Bernard Falk, *The Bridgewater Millions: A Candid Family History* (London: Hutchinson, 1942), 49–71, which contains some useful information.

7. Quoted from HEH EL 7770. This and all subsequent quotations from the Bridgewater Collection are made by permission of the Trustees of the Henry E. Huntington Library, San Marino, California. I have kept original spellings but expanded contractions to aid readability. The Bridgewater Collection includes extensive materials on the Earl's impeachment: EL 7621–2, 7628–9, 7697–7710.

On the Earl's questioning of royal absolutism, see HEH EL 2755 and the explanatory note appended to the catalogue description of the document by L. M. Hill. Many of my general observations about Bridgewater are also drawn from my own extensive work with the Bridgewater Collection. For Bridgewater's support of Buckingham, see Conrad Russell, *Parliaments and English Politics 1621–1629* (Oxford: Clarendon Press, 1979), 113, 313, and 317. I should perhaps point out that I have found no evidence that the Earl of Bridgewater was willing to challenge the principle of royal absolutism during his tenure as President of Wales. For the most part, he enforced the orders and proclamations he was expected to enforce.

8. J[ohn] C[ollinges], *Par Nobile* (London, 1669), 30–36.

9. *CSPD Charles I* 1:494–95 (12 December 1626); 2:131 (7 April 1627); 138 (16 April 1627); 232 (28 June 1627). I have drawn a detailed picture of Bridgewater as a legal and administrative reformer in "Milieu," n. 2 above. His scrupulous attempts to get justice for a fourteen-year-old servingmaid who alleged rape by an upper-class neighborhood rake attest to his meticulousness and probity and also to his willingness to act as an agent of the central government in a case of genuine abuse.

10. Valerie Pearl, *London and the Outbreak of the Puritan Revolution* (Oxford: Oxford Univ. Press, 1961), 6. On Bridgewater's father, see W. J. Jones, "Ellesmere and Politics, 1603–1617," in *Early Stuart Studies: Essays in Honor of David Harris Willson*, ed. Howard S. Reinmuth, Jr. (Minneapolis: Univ. of Minnesota Press, 1970), 11–63, especially p. 20.

11. John Malcolm Wallace, "Milton's *Arcades*," *Journal of English and Germanic Philology* 58 (1959):627–36; and for the family and Bishop Williams's opposition to Laud, *Biographia Britannica* (London: for W. Meadows, 1760), 5:2888–91; Collinges, *Par Nobile*, 4; Gardiner, *History*, 2:127–28; J. C. Morrice, *Wales in the Seventeenth Century: Its Literature and Men of Letters and Action* (Bangor: Jarvis & Foster, 1918), 201–2; and Virgil B. Heltzel, "Sir Thomas Egerton as Patron," *Huntington Library Quarterly* 11 (1948):105–27.

12. See Irvonwy Morgan, *Prince Charles's Puritan Chaplain* (London: Allen & Unwin, 1957); James Fulton Maclear, "Puritan Relations with Buckingham,"

Huntington Library Quarterly 21 (1958):111–32; Perez Zagorin, *The Court and the Country: The Beginning of the English Revolution* (London: Routledge & K. Paul, 1969), 58–66; and Gardiner, *History*, vol. 5 (1886), 188–251. There are various indications of Bridgewater's alliance with the Puritan faction surrounding Buckingham. In 1624, for example, when feelings against the Spanish match were running high and Buckingham and Prince Charles aligned themselves with the pro-Puritan and anti-Spanish faction and against James I, Bridgewater entertained Prince Charles and his retinue, perhaps including Buckingham, in ostentatious fashion at his house in London, *Chamberlain*, 2:536–38 (3 January 1624).

13. 1626 was the year in which Buckingham declared his agreement with the Arminian party. See Russell, *Parliaments,* 29–31; Zagorin, *The Court and the Country*, 65–66; and, for Laud's augmentation of the High Commission, Roland G. Usher, *The Rise and Fall of the High Commission* (Oxford: Clarendon Press, 1913), 236–55.

14. Laud reported directly to Charles I on conditions in Wales on 2 January 1635; his report is reprinted in Thomas Rymer, *Foedera*, 2d ed. (London, J. Tonson, 1732), 9:588–91. See also A. H. Dodd, *Studies in Stuart Wales*, 2 ed. (Cardiff: Univ. of Wales Press, 1971), 33–64; A. G. Edwards, *Landmarks in the History of the Welsh Church* (London: J. Murray, 1912), chap. 8; Arthur Ivor Pryce, *The Diocese of Bangor During Three Centuries* (Cardiff: William Lewis, 1929), xxii–xxiii, and for the High Commission generally, Usher, *Rise and Fall*, chap. 11. For Puritan views of Wales and the four English counties under the jurisdiction of the Council of Wales, see Thomas Richards, *A History of the Puritan Movement in Wales from . . . 1639 to . . . 1653* (London: National Eisteddfod Assoc., 1920), 1–30; Thomas Rees, *History of Protestant Nonconformity in Wales from Its Rise to the Present Time*, 2d ed. (London: John Snow, 1883), 34–63; and Richard Baxter, *Reliquiae Baxterianae* (London: For T. Parkhurst *et al*, 1696), Bk. 1, pp. 1–12. For the Council of Wales's jurisdiction over other ecclesiastical matters, see, for example, EL 7230; the subject will receive further discussion below.

My characterization of Bridgewater as working faithfully for Charles but opposed to Laud is implicitly challenged by Kevin Sharpe's "The Personal Rule of Charles I," in *Before the English Civil War*, ed. Howard Tomlinson (London: Macmillan, 1983), 53–78, in that Sharpe argues that Charles I was himself behind Laud's plans for the Church. All the evidence I have read, however, convinces me that Bridgewater was unaware of this, either out of genuine ignorance or out of unwillingness to recognize the full precariousness of his own position.

15. Baxter, *Reliquiae Baxterianae*, Bk. 1, pp. 13–18.

16. Quoted from Lambeth ms. 943, fol. 271, in Pryce, *Diocese of Bangor*, xxii.

17. Skeel, *Council in the Marches*, 157; but see also my qualification of her presentation in n. 55 below. The conflict did not begin only in 1637, nor did it result in any long-term shutdown of the Court of the Marches, as Skeel implies.

It is not clear from the documentary evidence to what extent Council proceedings were halted on the basis of ecclesiastical principle and to what extent Laud's action was a retaliation against the Council's failure to cooperate. However, Laud was known for vindictive maneuvering on other occasions and often tried to get rid of people who disagreed with him. See, for example, G. E. Aylmer, *The King's Servants: The Civil Service of Charles I, 1625–1642* (1961; reprint, London: Routledge & K. Paul, 1974), 374–78; Sir Robert Harley's ouster as Master of the Mint coincided with Laud's appointment as archbishop. Despite the Earl of Bridgewater's reticence on the subject, it is clear that Laud was behind the move against the Council of Wales. A letter from one of the Earl's London associates told him so directly in 1637 (EL 7522), but in the year before he had headed a memorandum to himself dealing with the controversy, among other more minor matters, "Archbishop Cant^e / Counsell Marches" (EL 7495).

18. R. Chris Hassel, Jr., *Renaissance Drama and the English Church Year* (Lincoln: University of Nebraska Press, 1979), 157–61.

19. Christopher Hill, *Milton and the English Revolution* (New York: Viking, 1978), 43–44; Parker, *Biography*, 1:119; 2:779–81. Why the Milton family moved to Horton in particular is not known, but it seems reasonable to suppose that they found the place congenial at least in part because they knew and valued people who lived in the area.

20. See Stephen Orgel, *The Illusion of Power: Political Theater in the English Renaissance* (Berkeley: Univ. of California Press, 1975); and "Platonic Politics," in *Inigo*, 1:49–75.

21. That is, all the children involved in *Comus* had danced in masques at court; as we will note later on, at least one of the Lady's older sisters had refused to do so.

22. On the attendance of Ludlow town officials, see Creaser, "The Setting of *Comus*," 114, 131. See also Charles I's 1633 Instructions to the Earl of Bridgewater, reprinted in Rymer, *Foedera*, 19:455 (note 14 above); Miller, "Mythography of *Comus*," 212–47 (n. 2 above); and my "Milieu," 294–96, in which I worked hard to make a point similar to Creaser's about the public nature of the masque's occasion but without having the new evidence provided by the Ludlow Bailiffs' Accounts.

23. *Milton*, 45. As the ensuing discussion will make clear, I am adopting Sprott's conclusion that the Bridgewater ms. is either the performance version or at least the text closest to the version that was actually performed.

24. See in particular Willa McClung Evans's speculations on the relationship between *Comus* and *Coelum Britannicum* in *Henry Lawes: Musician and Friend of Poets* (New York: MLA, 1941), 79–96.

25. Miller, "Mythography of *Comus*," 234–43; the quotation is from p. 251. Miller sees Milton as frustrating the audience's generic expectations in that there is "no apotheosis of regality by *fiat*," but he nevertheless sees the masque as confirming the power of the central government by confirming the hierarchy of authority. I am heartened to find that Creaser makes the same point about the hierarchy that I do, albeit at the very end of his article (p. 129). He

does not find the "mock" hierarchy as subversive of conventional expectations as I do.

26. For Pembroke and the clandestine opposition, see Margot Heinemann, *Puritanism and Theatre: Thomas Middleton and Opposition Drama under the Early Stuarts* (Cambridge: Cambridge Univ. Press, 1980), 166–69; Aylmer, *The King's Servants*, 61 (note 17 above); and for Lawes, Evans, *Henry Lawes*, 35–40, 74–75, 135, 176–82. In "The Political Failure of Stuart Cultural Patronage," in *Patronage in the Renaissance*, ed. Guy Fitch Lytle and Stephen Orgel (Princeton: Princeton Univ. Press, 1981), 165–87, Malcolm Smuts has pointed out that Charles I was considerably less successful (and perhaps less interested) in controlling the political rhetoric of art outside the court than we might have supposed. See also Martin Butler, *Theatre and Crisis 1632–1642* (Cambridge: Cambridge Univ. Press, 1984), which depicts the Caroline theater in London as more politically probing than we have thought.

27. For the Castlehaven scandal, see Barbara Breasted, "*Comus* and the Castlehaven Scandal," *Milton Studies* 3 (1971):201–24; Rosemary Karmelich Mundhenk's extension of Breasted's contentions in "Dark Scandal and the Sun-Clad Power of Chastity: The Historical Milieu of Milton's *Comus,*" *Studies in English Literature, 1500–1900* 15 (1975):141–52; and William B. Hunter, Jr., *Milton's Comus: Family Piece* (Troy, New York: Whitston Pub., 1983). I have discussed yet another dimension of the masque's treatment of chastity in "Milieu" (see n. 2 above).

28. Stephen Orgel, *The Jonsonian Masque* (Cambridge, Mass.: Harvard Univ. Press, 1967), 153–57. See also Orgel's qualification of his earlier discussion in the revised edition of *The Jonsonian Masque* (New York: Columbia Univ. Press, 1981), ix–x.

29. William G. Madsen, "The Idea of Nature in Milton's Poetry" in *Three Studies in the Renaissance: Sidney, Jonson, Milton* (New Haven: Yale Univ. Press, 1958), 191, and his general discussion, to which I am indebted, pp. 188–92. I am suggesting "Corinna" as an analogue, not a source, although it is conceivable that Milton could have encountered the poem in a manuscript version that has not survived.

30. On the forest courts see Gardiner, *History*, 7:362–66; *CSPD Charles I*, 6:576 (April 1634); 7, preface, xxxiii–xxxvii and 143 (12 July 1634). For Clarendon's comment on the enforcement of forest laws see *The History of the Rebellion*, ed. W. Dunn Macray (Oxford: Clarendon Press, 1888), 1:370–74. For enclosures and rioting see Buchanan Sharp, *In Contempt of All Authority: Rural Artisans and Riot in the West of England, 1586–1660* (Berkeley: Univ. of California Press, 1980); Zagorin, *The Court and the Country*, 113–14; *CSPD Charles I*, 5:90 (24 June 1631); 182 (14 November 1631); 6:151–52 (24 July 1633); for the activities of projectors in the forest see the *Dictionary of National Biography* under Mompesson; *Historical Manuscripts Commission* 23, 12th Report, appendix, part 1, The Manuscript of the Earl of Cowper I (London, 1888), 294, 429–30, 446, and 452; *CSPD Charles I*, 6:380–81 (1633?); and Russell, *Parliaments*, 102 (note 7 above). Privy Council orders in connection with the

rioting are reproduced in *Acts of the Privy Council of England 1630 June–1631 June* (London: Her Majesty's Stationery Office, 1964), 390–91; see also Norbrook, *Poetry and Politics in the English Renaissance*, 257.

31. *The Merry Devil of Edmonton, 1608*, ed. William Amos Abrams (Durham, N.C.: Duke Univ. Press. 1942), 126–27.

32. A. S. P. Woodhouse and Douglas Bush, *A Variorum Commentary on the Poems of John Milton*, vol. 2, part 3 (New York: Columbia Univ. Press, 1972), 955.

33. See, for example, the king's letter to the justices of the Council in the Marches of Wales, *CSPD Charles I*, 7:145 (13 July 1634); and the letter or suggested letter to Bridgewater, p. 420 [1634?]; but also Hamilton, "The Earl of Bridgewater," 364–66 (n. 6 above).

34. See Gardiner, *History*, 7:133–35; and Robert Burton's complaint about the censorship at Oxford in *The Anatomy of Melancholy*, ed. Floyd Dell and Paul Jordan-Smith (New York: Tudor Publishing Co., 1927), p. 964 (part 3, sec. 4, memb. 2, subs. 6).

35. I am indebted to Annabel Patterson's discussion in a paper presented at MLA, New York City, December 1981, "The Queen's Pastoral: or, Whatever Happened to Amaryllis?"; see also her *Censorship and Interpretation: The Conditions of Writing and Reading in Early Modern England* (Madison: Univ. of Wisconsin Press, 1984), 172–74.

36. See *The Works of Francis Beaumont and John Fletcher*, vol. 2, ed. Arnold Glover and A. R. Waller (Cambridge: Cambridge Univ. Press, 1906), 372–448, especially 405.

37. In *Sacred Complex: On the Psychogenesis of "Paradise Lost"* (Cambridge, Mass.: Harvard Univ. Press, 1983), 22–72, William Kerrigan has probed into Milton's identification with the Lady. Roy Flannagan has argued a similar position in his paper " 'The Lady of Christ's' College and the Lady of *Comus*," which he kindly allowed me to read in manuscript. Whether or not Milton's identification was as profound as these readers suggest, it is clear that the problem was no idle issue for Milton.

38. Charlotte Otten, "Milton's Haemony," *English Literary Renaissance* 5 (1975):81–95. I would not, however, want to reduce our understanding of the plant's complex functioning in the masque to its mere biological labeling. In the introduction to a forthcoming volume of essays to be entitled *The Contexts of Comus*, Roy Flannagan, ed., will survey evidence suggesting that Lady Alice herself may have been bewitched in 1633 or 1634. If so, the use of haemony for her liberation in the masque would have been even more appropriate.

39. Of course, Sabrina waits upon Amphitrite, but Amphitrite's court is a "bower" and the pastimes surrounding Sabrina appear not to relate to her duties toward Amphitrite. Sabrina had traditional associations with judgeship: see Jack B. Oruch, "Imitation and Invention in the Sabrina Myths of Drayton and Milton," *Anglia* 90 (1972):60–70; and my "Milieu of *Comus*," which discusses Sabrina as a pattern for judges of the Council of Wales. My account of Sabrina is also greatly indebted to Richmond, *The Christian Revolutionary*, 72–75 (note 2 above).

40. William B. Hunter, Jr., "The Liturgical Context of *Comus*," *English Language Notes* 10 (1972):11–15. Hunter, however, does not discuss the relevance of the festival texts to the masque's political context; see also Hassel, *Renaissance Drama* (n. 18 above); and Miller, "Mythography of *Comus*," 249–55.

41. I have used the 1632, 1633, and 1634 editions of the *Book of Common Prayer*. Biblical quotations are from the Cambridge Pitt Brevier edition of the King James Bible.

42. Hunter, "Context," 13. My interpretation of the Lady as embodying Puritan ideals is quite compatible with Scoufos's account of her as *Ecclesia*—the woman in the wilderness—who, as Scoufos notes, "Mysteries," 135 (n. 2 above), appears in the epistle for the Michaelmas communion service. In terms of Scoufos's argument, Sabrina can be seen as saving the Reformed Church from the stalemate produced by overseverity toward all things ceremonial.

43. Rymer's *Foedera*, 19:455. The original is in the Bridgewater Collection, EL 7571, along with a copy, EL 7397.

44. Rymer's *Foedera*, 19:492–97. For an account of the workings of the ecclesiastical courts under Laud in the area of sexual offenses, see E. R. C. Brinkworth, "The Laudian Church in Buckinghamshire," *University of Birmingham Historical Journal* 5 (1955):31–59.

45. Although most of the dated Bridgewater materials on the conflict go back only to 1636 and 1637, there had been earlier clashes. See, for example, *Calendar of Wynn (of Gwydir) Papers*, ed. John Ballinger (London: Milford, 1926), 68–69 (no. 404). In a 1637 letter to Sir John Bridgeman, the highest official of the Council of Wales under Bridgewater, the Earl notes that he had "long since" discussed the problem with Bridgeman (EL 7521, draft copy). Moreover, the general problem of conflicting court jurisdictions was a particular specialty of the Earl's, and he had served on a royal commission to study the matter before his Ludlow years. Indeed, the two-year gap between his original appointment as President of Wales and his 1633 Instructions may be less attributable to family shame over the Castlehaven scandal than to his maneuvering to get the Council authority over sexual offenses spelled out in terms favorable to the Council. For evidence that Bridgewater was not being informed of important policy matters in connection with the Council of Wales by at least some key figures in Charles's government, see Bridgewater's letter to Sir John Coke, Charles I's Secretary of State, in *Historical Manuscripts Commission*, 23, 12th Report, appendix, part I, The Mss. of Cowper, p. 464 (14 July 1632).

46. EL 7521, draft letter to Bridgeman.

47. EL 7485, undated doc. with corrections in the hand of the Earl of Bridgewater [pp. 1–6]; EL 7509, letter to Bridgewater from Sampson Eure, the Queen's solicitor at the Court of the Marches, 16 July 1636. It should be emphasized that I am not quoting these documents as sources for Milton but as evidence of the general principles involved, principles which the Earl and his associates presented as self-evident, long understood, and long followed.

48. See EL 7509, 7511, 7470 (a more legible copy of 7511), and 7485, [pp. 12, 17–20]. All of the briefs present this "division of labor" between the

two court systems as self-evident and traditional. Milton could not have known the particular briefs, but he is sure to have been acquainted with the traditional arguments.

49. For an exploration of some of the seamy implications of his threat, see John T. Shawcross, "Two Comments," *Milton Quarterly* 7 (1973):97–98, and the sources cited in n. 27 above.

50. Milton, "The Reason of Church Government," in *Complete Prose*, 1:819–20 (note 3 above).

51. See Orgel, *Jonsonian Masque*, 102–3, 151–69; Fletcher, *Transcendental Masque*, 11 and ff.; Miller, "Mythography of *Comus*," 165, 198 passim; Richmond, *The Christian Revolutionary*, 69–70; and above all, Norbrook, "Reformation of the Masque," especially 104–5, which casts the parallel in terms of the first publication and republication of the *Book of Sports* but sees Jonson as much less a reformer than I do.

52. Collinges, *Par Nobile*, 4.

53. Miller, "Mythography of *Comus*," 189–97.

54. EL 7509 (Eure letter, 16 July 1636).

55. See EL 7523, draft letter from Bridgewater to Bridgeman. Despite the conclusions of Skeel and others, the Earl's notes appended to this draft make it clear that he asked the king whether the Council proceedings were to be stayed generally or only in the specific case which had prompted the crisis. Charles I assured him that only the one case had been meant to be stayed and "saide he woulde take order" to redress the misunderstanding. The trial books indicate that the Court of the Marches continued to try cases of incontinence and adultery, though perhaps more sporadically than before.

56. See the epitaph for the First Earl of Bridgewater by his son, quoted in Lady Alix Egerton, ed., *Milton's Comus, Being the Bridgewater Manuscript* (London: Dent & Sons, 1910), 12; and the editor's statement, p. 32. On Bridgewater's alienation from the crown, see Hamilton, "The Earl of Bridgewater" (note 6 above); and EL 7852, 7855, and 7856. Another interesting bit of evidence is provided in the Earl of Bridgewater's funeral sermon. The man who preached it said he could affirm of his own knowledge that the king was satisfied with Bridgewater's service and that his having granted the Earl the governance of such a large province was evidence of his "especiall faire opinion of his Integrity and Abilities," EL 6881, [p. 23]. Such things are not generally pointed out, especially at such a time, unless they have been called into serious question.

57. See Baker, "Eros and the Three Shepherds," 23–25 (note 2 above); and Parker, *Biography* 1:142–43.

Chapter VII

1. My discussion of the situation of Royalists is particularly indebted to Earl Miner, "The Ruins and Remedies of Time," in *The Cavalier Mode from Jonson to Cotton* (Princeton: Princeton Univ. Press, 1971), 100–55 (the Parliamentary ordinance is quoted from p. 113); and to Paul H. Hardacre, *The Royalists during the Puritan Revolution* (The Hague: Martinus Nijhoff, 1956). See also Peter

Thomas's essay "Charles I of England: The Tragedy of Absolutism" in *The Courts of Europe: Politics, Patronage, and Royalty 1400–1800*, ed. A. G. Dickens (London: Thames & Hudson, 1977), 191–211, especially 209. The banned customs did survive sporadically. See Hardacre, *Royalists*, 43–49, 110–112. Martin Butler has recently challenged the idea that the theaters were closed on grounds of their political association with monarchy. See his *Theatre and Crisis 1632–1642* (Cambridge: Cambridge Univ. Press, 1984), 38–39, 246–47. Nevertheless, in terms of public perception, the closing was part of a general pattern of eradication of the signs of monarchy and "public mirth."

2. For historical studies of riot and social inversion during the Civil War years, see Buchanan Sharp, "A Second Western Rising: Riot during the Civil War and Interregnum," in *In Contempt of All Authority: Rural Artisans and Riot in the West of England 1586–1660* (Berkeley: Univ. of California Press, 1980), chap. 9, 220–56; Christopher Hill, *The World Turned Upside-Down: Radical Ideas during the English Revolution* (New York: Viking Press, 1972); Norman Cohn's appendix on the Ranters in *The Pursuit of the Millenium*, rev. ed. (London: Temple Smith, 1970), 287–330; and Michael L. Walzer, *The Revolution of the Saints: A Study in the Origins of Radical Politics* (Cambridge, Mass.: Harvard Univ. Press, 1965). Of course the association between topsy-turvydom and civil war goes back to Horace, *Odes* 1.2; see Rosalie Colie, *"My Ecchoing Song": Andrew Marvell's Poetry of Criticism* (Princeton: Princeton Univ. Press, 1970), 201.

3. See in particular Frank Kermode's essay, "The Argument of Marvell's 'Garden'" (1952; reprinted in William R. Keast, ed., *Seventeenth Century English Poetry: Modern Essays in Criticism* (New York: Oxford Univ. Press, 1962), 290–304; and again in Michael Wilding, ed., *Marvell: Modern Judgements* (London: Macmillan, 1969), 125–40. I attempted to develop some of Kermode's arguments a bit further in chap. 5 of *Childhood and Cultural Despair*; the present chapter will in many ways modify the conclusions drawn in that earlier study.

4. *Marvell*, 2–4. My reading of Marvell's poem on Lovelace is particularly indebted to the suggestions in Annabel M. Patterson, *Marvell and the Civic Crown* (Princeton: Princeton Univ. Press, 1978), 17–20. Although I am arguing for a non-Royalist reading of the poem, I am also indebted to John Dixon Hunt, *Andrew Marvell: His Life and Writings* (Ithaca, New York: Cornell Univ. Press, 1978), 68; and Michael Craze's commentary in *The Life and Lyrics of Andrew Marvell* (London: Barnes & Noble, 1979), 34–36. My reading confirms Barbara Everett's contention that even when Marvell's lyrics appear to resemble those of the Cavaliers, his are characterized by greater openness to the world; see her essay "The Shooting of the Bears: Poetry and Politics in Andrew Marvell" in *Andrew Marvell: Essays on the Tercentenary of His Death*, ed. R. L. Brett (Oxford: Oxford Univ. Press, 1979), 62–103.

5. For details of Lovelace's biography, see Craze, *The Life and Lyrics of Andrew Marvell*, 34–36; *Lovelace*, xlii–xliii; and Manfred Weidhorn, *Richard Lovelace* (New York: Twayne Pub., 1970), pp. 15–30.

6. *Lovelace*, 11.

7. See in particular John Pinchbacke's poem, *Lovelace*, 5, and 10, 12.

8. Steven Mullaney, "Strange Things, Gross Terms, Curious Customs: The Rehearsal of Cultures in the Late Renaissance," *Representations* no. 3 (Summer 1983):40–67.

9. See J[ames] H[owell], "To the Knowing *Reader*," in *Dodona's Grove, or The Vocall Forrest* (London: for H. Mosley, 1640), 5, and the final prayer; and Earl Miner's commentary on Howell, pp. 30–31. In Herrick's "All Things Decay and Die" the oak is, similarly, *"Dictator* of the State-like Wood" and "Soveraigne of all Plants," *Herrick*, 23. There is a detailed account of Charles's exploits in the oak in Hester W. Chapman, *The Tragedy of Charles II in the Years 1630–1660* (London: Jonathan Cape, 1964), 197–98; these events, however, dated after the writing of most or all of *Lucasta*.

10. On dating the poem, see *Lovelace*, 274–75; and H. M. Margoliouth's review in *Review of English Studies* 3 (1927):93–94. My discussion is indebted to Mary Ann C. McGuire, "The Cavalier Country-House Poem: Mutations on a Jonsonian Tradition," *Studies in English Literature, 1500–1900* 19 (1979):93–108. On the subject of pastoralism and enclosure more generally, see the survey in James Turner, *The Politics of Landscape* (Cambridge, Mass: Harvard Univ. Press, 1979), 85–152. I am also indebted to Peter Stallybrass's fine essay "'Drunk with the Cup of Liberty:' Robin Hood, the Carnivalesque and the Rhetoric of Violence in Early Modern England," *Semiotica* 54 (1985):113–45, which he was kind enough to send me in manuscript.

11. The quotation comes from the Cary-Morisson Ode. On the motif in Cavalier poetry, see Miner, "The Good Life," in *Cavalier Mode*, 43–99. There is a more general study of "divine madness" in Edgar Wind, *Pagan Mysteries in the Renaissance*, 2d ed. (London: Faber & Faber, 1958), 162–69. On the courtly Bacchanal, see Willa McClung Evans, *Henry Lawes: Musician and Friend of Poets* (New York: MLA, 1941), 120–32.

12. See Henry Vaughan, *The Works*, ed. L. C. Martin, 2d ed. (Oxford: Clarendon Press, 1957), 39–41, 49; and for a good recent critical treatment of the relevant texts, Jonathan F. S. Post, *Henry Vaughan: The Unfolding Vision* (Princeton: Princeton Univ. Press, 1982), 25–69.

13. See Claude J. Summers and Ted-Larry Pebworth, "Vaughan's Temple in Nature and the Context of 'Regeneration,'" *Journal of English and Germanic Philology* 74 (1975):351–60; and Post, *Henry Vaughan*, 197–98.

14. Some examples are collected in Maren-Sofie Røstvig, *The Happy Man: Studies in the Metamorphoses of a Classical Ideal 1600–1700* (1954; rev. ed. Oslo, Norwegian Univ. Press, 1962), 121–52; and see, for example, [Mildmay Fane], *Otia Sacra* (London: for Richard Cotes, 1648), "My happy Life, to a Friend, 134–40, and E[dward] B[enlowes], *Theophila* (London, 1652), esp. the Latin argument to Canto 12, 218–19. Benlowes clearly wished to hide the significance of his emblem from prying uneducated eyes: the Anglican elements of the grove are much more marked in the Latin argument than in the English verse explication. See also Henry More's mildly satiric treatment of the Laudian "sacred grove" in "Psychozoia," canto 2, stanzas 57 and ff. in Geoffrey Bul-

lough, ed., *Philosophical Poems of Henry More* (Manchester: Manchester Univ. Press, 1931), 51 and ff. The use of the grove and tree emblems for political allegory was, of course, traditional: see Howell, *Grove* (n. 9 above); Henry Peacham, *Minerva Britanna or A Garden of Heroical Deuises* (London, 1612); and Turner, *Politics of Landscape*, 96–97.

15. See *Inigo*, 1:508–9, 584, and for more dubious cases 1:298, 388. In Renaissance drawings, of course, classical ruins always seem to be turning to vegetation. In masques from the Jacobean period for which drawings have not survived, there are also frequent images of Orphic groves, and in those masques, too, as I will hope to argue elsewhere, the image of the magic grove is linked to the ideal of recovering a universal religion. See Thomas Campion, *Lord Hay's Masque, Inigo*, 1:117–119 and *The Lords' Masque, Inigo* 1:244–45. In Peacham, *Minerva Britanna*, 6, an elder tree grown into a high wall and dying as the wall crumbles is offered as an emblem of "Tradition."

16. Quoted from Frances A. Yates's translation in *Giordano Bruno and the Hermetic Tradition* (1964; reprint, Chicago: Univ. of Chicago Press, 1979), 38. See also Walter Scott, ed., *Hermetica* (1924; reprint, London: Dawson's, 1968), 1:340–45; and Giordano Bruno, *The Expulsion of the Triumphant Beast*, trans. Arthur D. Imerti (New Brunswick, N.J.: Rutgers Univ. Press, 1964), 150–51, 241–42. My discussion is strongly indebted to Yates, especially pp. 205–332; and to D. P. Walker, *The Ancient Theology: Studies in Christian Platonism from the Fifteenth to the Eighteenth Century* (Ithaca: Cornell Univ. Press, 1972), 73–131, and pp. 164–93 on Laud and Lord Herbert of Cherbury's Hermetic project for reuniting Christians. On Bruno in England, see also Andrew D. Weiner's interesting suggestions in "Expelling the Beast: Bruno's Adventures in England," *Modern Philology* 78 (1980):1–13.

17. See Rhodes Dunlap, ed., *The Poems of Thomas Carew* (Oxford: Clarendon Press, 1949), 278–82; and *Inigo*, 1:66–67. I am also indebted to Kevin Sharpe, personal communication, The Huntington Library, August 1982.

18. We might note in passing that Milton's masque, which undoes so much of the court-centered imagery of *Coelum Britannicum*, also undoes its exaltation of Hermetic solar magic. Like Carew's masque of the same year, Milton's is steeped in the imagery of ancient Britain; the Attendant Spirit is associated with the priestly functions of the primeval Druids. Haemony is a talisman linked to solar magic, marked with the signature of the sun and hence effective against demons. But it is not all-powerful, like the solar magic of Charles I in *Coelum Britannicum*. Milton's attitudes toward the Druids varied along with his political opinions. Some important passages are collected in A. L. Owen, *The Famous Druids: A Survey of Three Centuries of English Literature on the Druids* (Oxford: Clarendon Press, 1962), 52–58.

19. Yates, *Giordano Bruno*, 62–83 and ff; see also her study *The Art of Memory* (London: Routledge & K. Paul, 1966). The Cavalier endeavor could also be considered a magical memory system in that it uses the device of imagining parts of a building to preserve a clear sense of past institutions. Of course the Royalists were not the only ones who found Hermetic motifs

important; Hugh Ormsby-Lennon is presently at work on a study of Hermeticism and the radical sects during the Interregnum.

20. There are helpful older readings of Vaughan's Hermeticism, in particular, Elizabeth Holmes, *Henry Vaughan and the Hermetic Philosophy* (1932; reprint, New York: Russell & Russell, 1967). But the political dimensions of seventeenth-century Hermeticism are only just emerging, thanks in large part to Stephen Orgel's work on "Platonic Politics" in the masque (*Inigo*, 1:49–75). For some of the relevant passages from Vaughan's prose, see, Martin, ed., *The Works*, 213, 216–17, and on Hermetic physic, pp. 547–92; see also the views of Vaughan's contemporaries on the function of his poetry, as reflected in their commendatory poems, some of them written well before the Restoration, pp. 618–20; and Post's interpretation, *Henry Vaughan*, 124–42. As Alan Rudrum's helpful annotations have reminded us, many of the ideas from "Regeneration," including the image of the sacred grove, parallel the writings of Vaughan's brother Thomas, the Hermetic Anglican priest: see Rudrum's edition *Henry Vaughan: The Complete Poems* (1976; reprint, New Haven: Yale Univ. Press, 1981), 529–32. Henry More's satire on the Anglican grove in "Psychozoia" (n. 14 above) may well have been aimed directly against his archenemy Thomas Vaughan. See also Cedric C. Brown's interesting study of another sacred grove in Vaughan, "The Death of Righteous Men—Prophetic Gesture in Vaughan's 'Daphnis' and Milton's *Lycidas*," *George Herbert Journal* 7 (1984):1–24.

21. In addition to the evidence from the masque, discussed above, see Owen, *Famous Druids*, 62–69, especially the opinions of Laud's spokesman Peter Heylyn cited in Owen, 63–65. Holinshed, on the other hand, had portrayed the bardic ceremonies as corruptions. See Owen, *Famous Druids*, 38–39.

22. See Miner's tactful discussion of "The Ant" in *Cavalier Mode*, 112–15; Elizabeth Skerpan has a more politically sophisticated reading of the poem still in manuscript entitled "Lovelace's Community of Fable: The Significance of the Beast Poems"; she argues that the poem's real target was Royalists who were compounding to save their estates. See also Raymond A. Anselment, "'Griefe Triumphant' and 'Victorious Sorrow': A Reading of Richard Lovelace's 'The Falcon,'" *Journal of English and Germanic Philology* 70 (1971):404–17; and Randolph L. Wadsworth, Jr., "On 'The Snayl' by Richard Lovelace," *Modern Language Review* 65 (1970):750–60.

23. *Inigo*, 2:730. In *The Renaissance Imagination*, ed. Stephen Orgel, p. 10, D. J. Gordon has suggested that the symbol would be obscure to a contemporary audience, but it is common in the poetry of the period, and carries similar connotations. See Miner, *Cavalier Mode*, 286. My discussion of Lovelace's poem is strongly indebted to Miner, 5, 63–65, 286–98; see also Bruce King, "The Grasse-hopper and Allegory," *Ariel* 1 (1970):71–82; and Weidhorn, *Richard Lovelace*, 53–56 (note 5 above).

24. As Kevin Sharpe has recently reemphasized, Charles I and the Cavaliers were not so naïve and self-involved as we tend to think: the business of state did get done and with considerable efficiency. See his essay "The Personal Rule of

Charles I," in Howard Tomlinson, ed. *Before the English Civil War* (London: Macmillan, 1983), 53–78, 63–67.

25. See Miner, *Cavalier Mode*, 282–97; and for other commentary on the poem, Bruce King, "Green Ice and a Breast of Proof," *College English* 26 (1964–65):511–15; Weidhorn, *Richard Lovelace*, 166–67.

26. Miner, *Cavalier Mode*, 291.

27. On the pervasiveness of such attitudes, see Keith Thomas, *Religion and the Decline of Magic* (1971; reprint, Harmondsworth, Middlesex: Penguin, 1973), 189–206.

28. Good studies of the Mower Poems include Ruth Nevo, "Marvell's 'Songs of Innocence and Experience,'" *Studies in English Literature, 1500–1900* 5 (1965):1–21; Elaine Hoffman Baruch, "Theme and Counterthemes in 'Damon the Mower,'" *Comparative Literature* 26 (1974):242–59; David Kalstone's analysis of the Mower poems and Virgil's Second Eclogue in "Marvell and the Fictions of Pastoral," *English Literary Renaissance* 4 (1974):174–88; Ann E. Berthoff, *The Resolved Soul: A Study of Marvell's Major Poems* (Princeton: Princeton Univ. Press, 1970), 132–42; and Donald M. Friedman, *Marvell's Pastoral Art* (Berkeley: Univ. of California Press, 1970), 119–41. Although I approach the Mower from a different perspective, my discussion is developed out of Friedman's observation that the Mower poems "rewrite the story of Eden without a reference to the supernatural" (p. 141). For a general study of some of the garden imagery behind the poems as it appeared in contemporary emblem literature, see Stanley Stewart, *The Enclosed Garden: The Tradition and the Image in Seventeenth Century Poetry* (Madison: Univ. of Wisconsin Press, 1966).

29. See Bruce King, "'The Mower against Gardens' and the Levellers," *Huntington Library Quarterly* 33 (1970):237–42; Turner, *Politics of Landscape*, 116–18; and Christopher Hill, *Puritanism and Revolution* (London: Secker & Warburg, 1958), 50–87, 153–96, and, specifically on Leveling in Marvell, 348–53. Lord Fairfax had had extensive dealing with such groups, both as a general and later on. See Gerrard Winstanley, *The Works*, ed. George H. Sabine (Ithaca: Cornell Univ. Press, 1941), 15–16, 281–292, 343–49. Although Winstanley wrote many harsh words against enclosure, calling it, among other things, "High treason against the King of Righteousnesse" (p. 201), he assured Fairfax that he and his followers would pull down no enclosures. For the form of Marvell's poem, I am indebted to Craze, *The Life and Lyrics of Andrew Marvell*, 130.

30. See in particular Berthoff's discussion, *Resolved Soul*, 163–97; Kitty W. Scoular, *Natural Magic: Studies in the Presentation of Nature in English Poetry from Spenser to Marvell* (Oxford: Clarendon, 1965), 186–90; Frank J. Warnke, "The Meadow-Sequence in *Upon Appleton House:* Questions of Tone and Meaning," in *Approaches to Marvell: The York Tercentenary Lectures*, ed. C. A. Patrides (London: Routledge & K. Paul, 1978), 234–50; Colie, *My Ecchoing Song*, 201–5, 211–18, and 250–63; Turner, *Politics of Landscape*, 33–84; Allan Gray's study "The Surface of Marvell's *Upon Appleton House*," *English Literary Renaissance* 9 (1979):169–82; and Muriel C. Bradbrook, "Marvell and the Masque" in *Tercentenary Essays in Honor of Andrew Marvell*, ed. Kenneth Friedenreich (Ham-

den, Conn.: Archon Books, 1977), 204–23. Unlike most of these critics however, I see no contradiction between the poet's masquing language and his use of topical materials—quite the reverse. To compare his poem to a masque was to invite political "application."

31. Although I take Marvell's playful bout with Hermeticism in the poem more seriously than she does, I am indebted to Patterson's enlightening discussion of Fairfax's interests and contemporary reputation in *Marvell and the Civic Crown*, 95–110 (note 4 above); to Lee Erickson, "Marvell's *Upon Appleton House* and the Fairfax Family," *English Literary Renaissance* 9 (1979): 158–68; and to Turner, *Politics of Landscape*, 70–72.

32. Raymond Williams, *The Country and the City* (1973; reprint, New York: Oxford Univ. Press, 1975), 27–42. I am also indebted to Williams's discussion of Marvell, 55–59. See also Hunt's speculations about the building of Nun Appleton in *Andrew Marvell*, 83 (note 4 above).

33. See, for example, Berthoff, *Resolved Soul*, 171–74; Hunt's interpretation of the poem as attenuating the obvious political implications, *Andrew Marvell*, 109; and on violence and the poem's transformation of the Country House tradition, William A. McClung *The Country House in English Renaissance Poetry* (Berkeley: Univ. of California Press, 1977), 167–69. My own political reading is indebted to Røstvig, *Happy Man*, 174–190; John M. Wallace, *Destiny His Choice: The Loyalism of Andrew Marvell* (London: Cambridge Univ. Press, 1968), 239–57; and Don Cameron Allen, *Image and Meaning*, new edition (Baltimore: Johns Hopkins Univ. Press, 1968), 187–225. The most recent discussion of the poem in its political context is Warren L. Chernaik, *The Poet's Time: Politics and Religion in the Work of Andrew Marvell* (Cambridge: Cambridge Univ. Press, 1983). It seems to me, however, that efforts to fix Marvell's meadow allegory in terms of specific contemporary people and events are unnecessarily limiting; in my discussion I will attempt instead to get at some of the poetic structures that seem to call for political application while at the same time withholding the reader's certainty that the obvious application can be made. I am strongly indebted to John Carey's brilliant essay on frustrating reversals in Marvell's poetry, "Reversals Transposed: An Aspect of Marvell's Imagination" in *Approaches to Marvell*, ed. Patrides, 136–54 (note 30 above); and to Colie, *My Ecchoing Song*, 201–5. At the end of his essay, Carey suggests that the pattern may have been rooted in Marvell's perception of contemporary events.

34. As Buchanan Sharp points out in *Contempt of All Authority*, riots were often led by women or men dressed as women, 104–5. See also Natalie Zemon Davis, "Women on Top: Symbolic Sexual Inversion and Political Disorder in Early Modern Europe," (1975); reprinted with revisions in *The Reversible World*, ed. Barbara B. Babcock (Ithaca: Cornell Univ. Press, 1978), 147–90; and on the temporary prominence of women in the Civil War sects, Keith Thomas, "Women and the Civil War Sects," in *Crisis in Europe 1560–1660*, ed. Trevor Aston (New York: Basic Books, 1965), 317–40. Of course Charivari was not necessarily directed against the social order but could serve any number of

political functions. See E. P. Thompson, "'Rough Music': Le Charivari anglais," *Annales: Économies, Sociétés, Civilisations* 27 (1972):285–312. Winstanley complained that his Diggers had been attacked by men dressed as women, *Works*, 295.

35. Quoted in Hunt, *Andrew Marvell*, 71. Other Biblical analogues are surveyed in King, "Grasse-hopper," 78–80. For the association between harvest and revolution see also Stephen Greenblatt, "Murdering Peasants: Status, Genre, and the Representation of Rebellion," *Representations*, no. 1 (1983):1–29; and Ronald Paulson, *Representations of Revolution (1789–1820)* (New Haven: Yale Univ. Press, 1983), 23.

36. As Wallace has pointed out, *Destiny His Choice*, 247, the scriptural reference rebounds against her in that in the original from Numbers 11, the quails rain down as a punishment.

37. See in particular Warnke's essay in *Approaches to Marvell*, ed. Patrides, 238–43 (note 30 above).

38. See Paul A. Jorgensen's discussion in *Shakespeare's Military World* (1956; reprint, Berkeley: Univ. of California Press, 1973), 4–5.

39. For examples of the formula, see Greenblatt, "Murdering Peasants"; Sharp, *In Contempt of All Authority*, 39; and Christopher Hill, *Puritanism and Revolution*, 50–87. In Shakespeare's *Henry the Sixth, Part 2*, York associates Jack Cade's rebellion with the image of festival disorder; "I have seen / Him caper upright like a wild Morisco, / Shaking the bloody darts as he his bells," 3.1.360–81.

40. Winstanley, *Works*, 15–16. For Leveler doctrine, see J. G. A. Pocock, *The Ancient Constitution and the Feudal Law* (Cambridge: Cambridge Univ. Press, 1957), 126; William Haller and Godfrey Davies, eds., *The Leveller Tracts, 1647–53* (New York: Columbia Univ. Press, 1944), 1–46; and the references in n. 2 above. The notion of a primal egalitarianism was quite common in the period and not peculiar to Levelers. But Marvell's version particularly evokes the Leveler version of the myth by identifying a "leveled" landscape with the name of the political group.

41. David F. Gladish, ed., *Sir William Davenant's Gondibert* (Oxford: Clarendon Press, 1971), 166. Wallace has a very useful reading of Marvell's poem as an answer to *Gondibert*, 239 and ff.

42. Yates, *Giordano Bruno*, 62–63, 278–87, 331; D. P. Walker, *Spiritual and Demonic Magic from Ficino to Campanella* (1958; reprint, Nedeln / Lichtenstein: Kraus Reprints, 1969), 4–5; and Wind, *Pagan Mysteries*, 236.

43. Owen, *Famous Druids*, 20–21. A standard seventeenth-century strategy for justifying Druid sacrifice was to view it as a type of sacrifice of Christ: that idea lurks behind Marvell's playful self-impaling as well.

44. See Miner's discussion, *Cavalier Mode*, 44–45.

45. Owen, *Famous Druids*, 25.

46. Joseph Summers, "Marvell's 'Nature,'" (1953), reprinted in Wilding, *Marvell: Modern Judgments*, 141–54 (note 3 above); the quotation is from p. 143. On Fairfax's Hermeticism see Røstvig, chap. 4, "The Hortulan Saint," in

Happy Man; see also the extensive discussion of documentary evidence as to Fairfax's interests and opinions in R. I. V. Hodge, *Foreshortened Time: Andrew Marvell and Seventeenth Century Revolution* (Cambridge: D. S. Brewer, 1978), 132–58. Hodge concludes that Fairfax was not a Hermeticist in any strict sense because he so consistently bent the texts he worked on in the direction of his own Calvinism; however, such creative use of one's sources was quite standard for the period and cannot be taken as evidence of any lack of interest. Fairfax had family connections with some of the Interregnum poets who wrote in praise of sacred groves. It seems likely that many other temporary Hermeticists of the period, he was immersing himself in arcane texts at least partly out of a desire to undo the shock of the regicide. See Patterson, *Marvell and the Civic Crown*, 95–97 (note 4 above); and Hodge's account, which documents the extent of Fairfax's distress at the execution and his tendency to read that event into unrelated political cataclysms. Although it seems to me that Marvell himself was more than half way interested in the Hermetic ideas, I agree with Patterson's suggestion (p. 108) that the poet's ultimate purpose may have been to wean Fairfax away from Hermeticism and back into active life. I would merely suggest that he was weaning himself back as well.

47. See Colie's analysis, *My Ecchoing Song*, 204.

48. Quoted in Hill, *Society and Puritanism*, 186. For Royalist propaganda linking Charles II with May Day customs, see James Heath, *The Glories and Magnificent Triumphs of The Blessed Restitution of His Sacred Majesty K. Charles II* (London, 1662), 206; and Edward Mathew, *Karolou epiphania: The Most Gloriovs Star* (London, 1661), 68. However, *The Book of Sports* itself was not revived.

49. Robert Gale Noyes, *Ben Jonson on the English Stage, 1660–1776* (1935; reprint, New York: Benjamin Blom, 1966), 223–29. On the fair, see also Henry Morley, *Memoirs of Bartholomew Fair*, 4th ed. (London: George Routledge & Sons, 1892), 186–87. For alterations in maying customs, see W. Carew Hazlitt, *Faiths and Folklore* (1905; reprint, New York: Benjamin Blom, 1965), 1:261; William Hone, *Every Day Book* (London, 1831), vol. 1, cols. 717–18; R. Chambers, *The Book of Days* (London: Chambers, 1886), 1:696–98; and Mrs. Bray, *The Borders of the Tamar and the Tavy: Their Natural History* (London, 1879), 2:121–23.

50. "On St. James's Park, as Lately Improved by His Majesty," Edmund Waller, *The Poems*, ed. G. Thorn Drury (1893; reprint, New York: Greenwood Press, 1968), 170–71, 173.

Index